Design Since 1945

This book has received significant support from the Graham Foundation for Advanced Studies in the Fine Arts.

Major funding has also been provided by COLLAB: The Contemporary Design Group for the Philadelphia Museum of Art; The Pew Memorial Trust; and the Design Arts Program of the National Endowment for the Arts, a Federal agency.

Design Since 1945

Organized by

Kathryn B. Hiesinger

Editors

Kathryn B. Hiesinger

George H. Marcus

Contributing Authors

Max Bill

Achille Castiglioni

Bruno Danese

Niels Diffrient

Herbert J. Gans

Jack Lenor Larsen

Olivier Mourgue

George Nelson

Carl Pott

Jens Quistgaard

Dieter Rams

Paul Reilly

Philip Rosenthal

Timo Sarpaneva

Ettore Sottsass, Jr.

Hans J. Wegner

Marco Zanuso

Philadelphia Museum of Art
Rizzoli, New York

1983

This book accompanies the exhibition "Design Since 1945" at the Philadelphia Museum of Art, October 16, 1983, through January 8, 1984.

The exhibition has been supported by generous grants from Best Products Company, Inc., The Pew Memorial Trust, and the National Endowment for the Humanities, a Federal agency.

Composition by Folio Typographers, Pennsauken, N.J.

Printed in Great Britain by Balding + Mansell, Wisbech, Cambs.

Trade edition published in the United States of America in 1983 by Rizzoli International Publications, Inc., 712 Fifth Avenue, New York
ISBN 0-8478-0519-0

Library of Congress Cataloging in Publication Data

Main entry under title:
Design since 1945.

Catalog of the exhibition held at the Philadelphia Museum of Art, Oct. 16, 1983—Jan. 8, 1984.
Bibliography: p.
Includes index.
1. Design, Industrial—Exhibitions. I. Hiesinger, Kathryn B., 1943—   . II. Marcus, George H. III. Philadelphia Museum of Art.
T180.P47P473 1983   745.2'074'014811   83-17414

Contents

It seems particularly appropriate that the Philadelphia Museum of Art attempt a survey of international design from the vantage point of 1983. The Museum owes its origins not only to the success of the great Exposition of 1876 in Philadelphia, when works of fine and decorative arts from the United States were juxtaposed, without embarrassment, with the latest achievements of England and Europe, but also to the desire of its founders to establish a museum and school "with a special view to the development of the Art Industries of the State.... The institution would be similar in its general features to that of the South Kensington Museum of London."[1] From its inception as the Pennsylvania Museum and School of Industrial Art, the Museum has collected both the decorative arts of its own time and place as well as great examples from the past and from many other cultures, so that furniture of the French Renaissance and the Ming Dynasty shares visitors' attention with eighteenth-century Philadelphia silver, Pennsylvania German pottery, and the simplified forms of Shaker benches and bentwood boxes. Given its broad mandate and varied collections, adherence to a single, even mildly polemical stance was rare in the Museum's program. Its first exhibition devoted to modern design was held within a year of exhibitions surveying rural Pennsylvania crafts and high Victoriana. In early 1932, four years after moving into its vast neoclassical building, this Museum presented an exhibition called "Design for the Machine," whose purpose was set forth succinctly by Joseph Downs in the Museum's *Bulletin*: "To point the way to the logical use of machinery for that large mass of utilitarian and decorative objects embraced in the industrial arts—the utensils and furnishings of our everyday life."[2] Half a century later, the present exhibition seeks to review the wealth of developments in that field during the years following World War II, to discover what has become of that "logical use" of the machine, and to assess the extent to which the machine (and, by extension, myriad new technologies) and the human being (designer and, of course, consumer) have reached that state of harmony anticipated by the prewar generation.

The conception and organization of this exhibition are due to the scholarship and energy of Kathryn B. Hiesinger, the Museum's Curator of European Decorative Arts after 1700, and it was initiated with the encouragement and support of Jean Sutherland Boggs, previous Director of the Museum. Working with a distinguished international group of designers, who both served as consultants for the selection of objects and contributed essays for this publication, Mrs. Hiesinger has assembled over four hundred works to represent four decades of intensely prolific design activity. It should be noted that one important premise of the exhibition is that everything in it was, or continues to be, in production. The temptation to include prototypes, however provocative, has been avoided in favor of objects actually available to the public. Our gratitude to the designers and other specialists listed as the authors of this book is heartfelt, and special thanks are owed to Jack Lenor Larsen and Herbert Gans for their good advice, and to George Nelson, who provided a thoughtful and exciting design for the exhibition installation.

The realization of an exhibition and publication on such a scale, of necessity, draws upon the skills, resources, and hard work of large numbers of the Museum staff. George H. Marcus, Head of Publications, served as co-editor of this volume and author of many biographies included, and is responsible for seeing this complex book through production. The challenge of designing the book as well as coordinating exhibition graphics was handsomely met by Laurence Channing. Donna Corbin, assistant in the Department of European Decorative Arts after 1700, coordinated the myriad arrangements for loans, photography, catalogue captions, and many other details with speed and grace.

To the lenders to the exhibition, many of whom graciously parted with an impressive number of objects, go our warmest thanks. Gifts from many designers and firms have significantly strengthened the Museum's permanent collections, and we are most grateful to those lenders who contributed shipping costs as well. The Sony Corporation kindly provided video equipment for the exhibition installation. The exhibition would not have been possible without generous grants from Best Products Company, Inc., The Pew Memorial Trust, and the National Endowment for the Humanities, a Federal agency. Special and essential funding for this catalogue was provided by the Graham Foundation for Advanced Studies in the Fine Arts as well as the Design Arts Program of the National Endowment for the Arts, a Federal agency, The Pew Memorial Trust, and COLLAB, The Contemporary Design Group for the Philadelphia Museum of Art, whose support for this project has been both generous and enthusiastic, as it has been for every effort in the field of modern design with which this Museum has been involved since the founding of COLLAB in 1970.

Anne d'Harnoncourt
The George D. Widener Director

1. Charter of the Pennsylvania Museum and School of Industrial Art (Feb. 25, 1876).
2. *The Pennsylvania Museum Bulletin,* vol. 27 (Mar. 1932), p. 115.

Introduction: Design Since 1945   Kathryn B. Hiesinger

Kathryn B. Hiesinger is Curator of
European Decorative Arts after 1700
at the Philadelphia Museum of Art,
where in 1974 she organized the
exhibition "British Contemporary
Design" and in 1978 served as co-
organizer of "The Second Empire:
Art in France under Napoleon III."

The triumph of functionalism as the universal modern aesthetic in the 1950s—and the ways in which the vacuum left by its decline and collapse has been filled—is to a large extent the history of design since 1945. Functionalism, the theory that beauty in useful objects is defined by their utility and honesty to materials and structure, was rooted in the mid-nineteenth-century idea of "art in industry," an idea born in the calm and optimistic certainty that aesthetic judgments could be made about objects according to settled and widely held standards, and that the exercise of these standards would improve design while both educating the public and bringing commercial profit to their manufacturers. Progressive Victorians found aesthetic value in utilitarian form and emphasized the relationship of form to function. For Richard Redgrave, editor of Henry Cole's *Journal of Design* and art superintendent in the Department of Practical Art at the museum at South Kensington, London, who reported on the Crystal Palace exhibition of 1851, the critical issue was decoration: "'Design' has reference to the construction of any work both for use and beauty, and therefore includes its ornamentation also. 'Ornament' is merely the decoration of a thing constructed. Ornament is thus necessarily limited, for, so defined, it cannot be other than secondary, and must not usurp a principal place. . . . It is impossible to examine the works of the Great Exhibition, without seeing how often utility and construction are made secondary to decoration. . . . This, on the slightest examination, will be found to be the leading error in the Exhibition . . . which is apt to sicken us of decoration, and leads us to admire those objects of absolute utility (the machines and utensils of various kinds), where use is so paramount that ornament is repudiated, and, fitness of purpose being the end sought, a noble simplicity is the result."[1] Although later critics would scarcely recognize Redgrave's noble simplicity were they actually to see it (his examples generally being more decorated than strictly utilitarian), his standards of what design should be persisted, following the way of Sir Nikolaus Pevsner's *Pioneers of Modern Design* through Adolf Loos ("Ornament and Crime")[2] to Walter Gropius and the Bauhaus and finally to the "good design" aesthetic of the 1940s and 1950s. By 1940 functionalism was widely identified with progressive European architecture and the related style in design that had developed around the Bauhaus. Although Gropius himself had described functionalism as a "catch phrase" and insisted that it wrongly emphasized structural functions and rational, economical solutions at the expense of aesthetic ones,[3] the term had become synonymous with the International Style, Gropius notwithstanding, and with the concept of the basic unity of all design, "combining imaginative design and technical proficiency,"[4] which had inspired Gropius to found the Bauhaus in 1919. For Gropius the style was a synthesis of art and technology, a "bridge uniting opposite poles of thought. . . . The emphasis on its structural functions . . . represent[s] the purely material side. . . . The other, the aesthetic satisfaction of the human soul, is just as important as the material."[5] Despite criticism from within and direct attack from without by apologists of Pop culture and "anti-design," which began in the mid-1950s, functionalism remained the dominant aesthetic standard of the postwar period until the 1960s—the apogee of the progress toward modernism begun a century before.

At the Bauhaus the prevailing form-language of functionalism had been cast in a particular mechanistic idiom, an "engineering" language of regular geometric forms with simple silhouettes and smooth finish that ob-

1. Richard Redgrave, "Supplementary Report on Design," *Exhibition of the Works of Industry of All Nations. 1851* (London, 1852), p. 708.
2. *Pioneers of Modern Design: From William Morris to Walter Gropius* (New York, 1949) [Orig. publ. as *Pioneers of the Modern Movement* (London, 1936)]; and Adolf Loos, in *Trotzdem, 1900–1930* (Innsbruck, 1931), pp. 79ff.
3. Walter Gropius, *The New Architecture and the Bauhaus* (London, 1935), p. 19.
4. *Ibid.*, p. 36.
5. *Ibid.*, pp. 19–20.

literated any sign of manufacture and denied applied ornament. However, by the mid-1940s functional modernism had come to include a number of practical and stylistic transformations that moved away from the pure machine aesthetic, notably Scandinavian designs, which made no significant distinction between craftwork and industrial products, and which, although explicit about their function, honest in material, and spare and neat, deliberately exploited natural, "organic," and historicizing forms, textures, and colors to achieve decorative effects, and often expressed to the point of eccentricity the personalities of their designers. In addition, the free "organic" forms of Charles Eames and Eero Saarinen that emerged from the 1940 competition at the Museum of Modern Art in New York entitled "Organic Design in Home Furnishings" signaled an evolution toward practical engineering technology, which succeeded the abstract formalist exercises that the machine aesthetic inspired. When finally produced in the late 1940s, the Eames chairs, using new molding techniques and new synthetic adhesives, although highly functional and "honest," were hardly meant to be objects of sculptural beauty and bore no resemblance in their distinct, spiky steel-rod frames to the substantive, standardized progressive shapes of the 1920s.

By the mid-1950s the technological revolution in materials and processes, which Eames and Saarinen rode, had begun to alter familiar concepts of materials and the very foundations of an aesthetic insisting that the visible form transparently display the logic of its function. Lightweight nylons and plastics, including resins and acrylics, changed our experience of the relationship between the weight and size of objects; the transistor, a device vastly superior to the vacuum tube in processing electrical signals, invented in 1947, produced such rapid miniaturization in the 1960s and 1970s that it allowed machines to perform functions at a scale impractical for human manipulation, requiring many designers of consumer appliances to provide only suitable containers. The flexibility possible in the molding of the new plastics and their wide range of bright colors allowed new and unconventional colors and shapes in a broad variety of products, sabotaging the more self-effacing, standardized metal finishes and industrial forms of earlier decades. This flexibility lent credence to the postwar critics[6] who argued the inappropriateness of a unified aesthetic standard having eternal validity in an age of accelerating technology and instantly expendable articles, and who found the look of functional efficiency antiseptic and dehumanized for a popular culture that enjoyed the gaudy attractions of Las Vegas.[7] The permanent aesthetic values that functionalism offered in 1945 had been replaced by relativist standards, which accept that a design is valid only in terms of its use to a given group of people in a given set of circumstances, and beyond those limits, may not be valid at all.[8]

The 1940s saw functionalism firmly established in the United States, transplanted with the emigration in the previous decade of the Bauhaus leaders Marcel Breuer, Walter Gropius, and Mies van der Rohe from Germany to the United States. It was championed by the Museum of Modern Art through exhibitions devoted to the European origins of this style[9] as well as through yearly exhibitions of "useful objects,"[10] which were selected by the museum from the commercial marketplace as examples of functional design. In 1940 John McAndrew, who organized the series, proposed "new" standards for industrial design, which he described as "Suitability to purpose . . . form must follow function, . . . Suitability to material,

6. Reyner Banham, "Industrial design e arte populare," *Civiltà delle macchine* (Nov.–Dec. 1955) [Rev. as Reyner Banham, "A Throw-Away Esthetic," *Industrial Design*, vol. 7 (Mar. 1960), pp. 61–65]; and Gillo Dorfles, "The Man-Made Object," in *The Man-Made Object*, ed. Gyorgy Kepes (New York, 1966), pp. 1–2.
7. Tom Wolfe, *The Kandy-Kolored Tangerine-Flake Streamline Baby* (New York, 1965); and Robert Venturi et al., *Learning from Las Vegas* (Cambridge, Mass., 1972).
8. Paul Reilly, "The Challenge of Pop," *Architectural Review*, vol. 142 (Oct. 1967), p. 256.
9. "Modern Architecture: International Exhibition" (Feb. 9–Mar. 23, 1932); "Alvar Aalto: Architecture and Furniture" (Mar. 16–Apr. 18, 1938); and "Bauhaus: 1919–1928" (1939–40).
10. "Useful Objects Under $5.00" (1938–39); "Useful Objects Under $10.00" (1940); etc.

. . . Suitability to process of manufacture and . . . Aesthetic quality."[11] These aesthetic standards were promoted throughout the 1940s and well into the 1950s, when they were applied to a second series of "useful object" shows organized by the museum and known as the "Good Design" exhibitions. "Useful" design became translated into "good" design some time after 1945, when functionalism, described variously in terms of its "honesty," "integrity," "truth" to materials, "decency," and "modesty," came to be regarded as good in a moral as well as an aesthetic sense, particularly in the United States and Britain.

The exigencies of World War II and national shortages of materials and labor confirmed the validity of this vocabulary and of designs that by necessity were intended to be simple in construction and easy to manufacture and maintain. In 1943, illustrating a plastic gun-turret seat (by Bakelite), the nose for a Martin bomber (by Du Pont), and plastic gas mask lenses (by Celanese), *Architectural Forum* starkly characterized "Design for War": "After many decades of functionalist preaching, this century is today producing functionally designed objects for the first time on a tremendous scale. In other words, in an extreme emergency we turn unquestioning to functional design. It is important to note that these products of ingenuity, economy, and utmost exploitation of limited materials have quite unconsciously become the most satisfying designs of our machine civilization."[12]

Acrylic resin plastic Lucite nose by Du Pont for a Martin bomber (1943), one of the largest plastic pieces then manufactured on a mass-production basis, illustrated by *Architectural Forum* to characterize "Design for War"

In the United Kingdom, domestic furniture production was nearly stopped from mid-1940 until 1942, when through the Utility Furniture Advisory Committee the state took total control not only of the supply but also of the design of furniture. The Committee was instituted to provide standardized items at controlled prices, which, it was hoped, would offer the possibility of "influencing popular taste towards good construction in simple, agreeable designs."[13] There, within the trauma and horror of war, flickered brightly that nineteenth-century vision of a sane and prosperous world with dignity and security for the common man, and it was the Arts and Crafts tradition that the Board of Trade pressed into service for its traditional timber forms and unassuming small-patterned textiles. One of the Utility Committee designers, Edwin Clinch, described the results: "All that you see with Utility furniture is pure, it's good."[14]

Members of the Utility Furniture Design Panel and of the faculty of Royal Designers for Industry in 1947: R. Y. Goodden, R.D. Russell, and Gordon Russell (from left to right)

In 1944 the Council of Industrial Design was founded in London to promote these ideas on a national level,[15] and as director of the Council from 1947 until his retirement in 1960, Gordon Russell became Britain's chief spokesman for the philosophy of economical, practical, and utilitarian standards of "good" design. In the immediate postwar years the Council sponsored a series of exhibitions to enlist public support for good design in British industry, including "Britain Can Make It" (1946), "Enterprise Scotland" (1947), and "Design at Work" (1948). In writing the "Design at Work" exhibition catalogue, Russell questioned: "What do we mean by good design? First, does it exist? It is often said that there is no such thing as good design or bad design, that design has no real measurable standards, that it is just a matter of personal taste; that, because an article sells in great quantities, this alone proves it must be well designed . . . [however] the only kind of design which will enable us to make the very most of our scarce labour and raw materials is that of the highest order. . . . What, then, is industrial design? In the first place it is an essential part of a standard of quality. . . . The first design question is 'Does it work?' The second is 'Does it look right?' Good design always takes into account the technique of pro-

11. *Bulletin of the Museum of Modern Art,* vol. 6 (Jan. 1940), pp. 5–6. Descriptions after the fashion of Gropius and Herbert Read, the latter declaring in *Art and Industry: The Principles of Industrial Design* (London, 1934), p. 55: "I have no other desire in this book than to support and propagate the ideals thus expressed by Dr. Gropius."
12. "Design for War," *Architectural Forum,* vol. 79 (Sept. 1943), p. 4.
13. Quoted in London, Geffrye Museum, *CC 41: Utility Furniture and Fashion, 1941–1951* (Sept. 24–Dec. 29, 1974), p. 12.
14. *Ibid.,* p. 13.
15. *Ibid.,* p. 17: "To promote by all practicable means the improvement of design in the products of British Industry."

duction, the material to be used and the purpose for which the object is wanted."[16]

In the United States, Eliot Noyes, as first director of the Museum of Modern Art's department of industrial design (1940), and Edgar Kaufmann, Jr., his successor after the war, also promoted good design, which they turned into a weapon against "styling"—the practice of altering without functional justification the exterior of a product, or introducing a new visual element to make a product appear new. An instrument of commercial competition, as in the annual model change, styling was a practice antithetical to the Bauhaus principle of form determined strictly by use, material, and process of manufacture. Aerodynamic streamlining, originating in shapes designed to move efficiently at high speed, had been the most pervasive system of styling in the United States since the 1930s, and was applied to a fantastic variety of static objects. Partly because the notion of speed which it conveyed was then still closely associated with progressive modern design in the public mind, streamlining came under particular attack.[17] American industry, moreover, identified *new* with *good* and defended planned obsolescence as sound economics: "The American consumer *expects* new and better products every year. He has become accustomed to the yearly automobile show—to national advertising announcing new models. His acceptance of change toward better living is indeed the American's greatest asset. . . . Our custom of trading in our automobiles every year, of having a new refrigerator, vacuum cleaner or electric iron every three or four years is economically sound. Our willingness to part with something *before* it is completely worn out is a phenomenon noticeable in no other society in history. It is truly an American habit, and it is soundly based on our economy of abundance."[18]

Countering commercial claims for novelty with quality as a standard for design to follow, Noyes raised good design to a selective aesthetic preference: "Good design in everyday objects . . . show[s] the taste and good sense of the designers. On none is there arbitrarily applied decoration. . . . These things really look like what they are."[19] For his part Kaufmann minimized the importance of commercial success: "A frequent misconception is that the principal purpose of good modern design is to facilitate trade, and that big sales are a proof of excellence in design. Not so. Sales are episodes in the careers of designed objects. Use is the first consideration."[20]

By far the most important and far-reaching measures taken by Noyes and Kaufmann in their efforts to promote functionalism as *the* modern design aesthetic in the United States were the competitions they organized at the Museum of Modern Art in 1940 and 1948[21] to create new furniture forms based on modern technology, an indigenous modern style that would present an alternative to "vain ornamentation or superfluity" and to "out-of-date and rigidified furniture."[22] Thanks to the chair designs of Charles Eames and Eero Saarinen, the competitions succeeded brilliantly. A British critic remarked that the immediate postwar years in the United States showed "more evidence of a Modern Movement than in the preceding twenty. . . . In 1939, the USA hardly knew that there was a Modern Movement, but today there are signs that . . . their own forms of contemporary design might be evolving. . . . Contemporary designs in all sorts of material and combinations of material have appeared. Solid wood, plywood, laminated wood and fabric, tube and solid steel, aluminum al-

"Organic Design in Home Furnishings" exhibition at the Museum of Modern Art, New York (Sept. 24–Nov. 9, 1941). Selection committee: Frank Parrish, Alfred H. Barr, Jr., Catherine K. Bauer, Edward Stone (seated, from left), Edgar Kaufmann, Jr., Eliot F. Noyes, and Marcel Breuer (standing)

16. London, Royal Academy, *Design at Work* (1948), pp. 7–10, and *passim*. Sponsored by the Royal Society of Arts and the Council of Industrial Design.
17. Edgar Kaufmann, Jr., "Borax, or the Chromium-Plated Calf," *Architectural Review,* vol. 104 (Aug. 1948), pp. 88–93.
18. J. Gordon Lippincott, *Design for Business* (Chicago, 1947), pp. 10, 14.
19. Eliot F. Noyes, "The Shape of Things: Good Design in Everyday Objects," *Consumer Reports* (Jan. 1949), p. 26.
20. Edgar Kaufmann, Jr., "What Is Modern Industrial Design?," *Bulletin of the Museum of Modern Art,* vol. 14 (Fall 1946), p. 3 [Rev. and publ. as *What Is Modern Design?* (New York, 1950)].
21. "Organic Design in Home Furnishings" (1940); "International Competition for Low-cost Furniture Design" (1948).
22. Eliot F. Noyes, *Organic Design in Home Furnishings* (New York, 1941), inside cover, p. 4.

loys, glass, perspex and other plastics have all been used in a variety of ways to produce new forms."[23] For the 1940 competition at the Museum of Modern Art, Noyes awarded first prize to Eames and Saarinen, citing "a manufacturing method never previously applied to furniture . . . employed to make a light structural shell consisting of layers of plastic glue and wood veneer molded in three-dimensional forms;"[24] and for the 1948 competition Kaufmann (with Gordon Russell and Mies van der Rohe as jurors) awarded Eames second prize for his "molded fibre glass chair . . . in many respects an astonishing fulfillment of the ideas developed by . . . Eames . . . and Saarinen in 1940. . . . Now it has been possible to find a plastic substance and a molding process which allow this kind of shape to be produced economically."[25]

The style that emerged from the low-cost furniture design competition and which was to characterize "good" design through the 1950s was adapted to the smaller living spaces of postwar housing, a style of neat, unornamented shapes that could be made or mass-produced at reasonable cost, which were light, portable, and occasionally multipurpose, a style that sometimes combined the smoothness of 1930s streamlined designs with ungainly appendages, a style that exploited new plastic materials and bonding techniques. Among the competitors were the British designers Ernest Race, Robin Day, and Clive Latimer, the Scandinavians Ilmari Tapiovaara, Hans Wegner, and Jørn Utzon, and the Italians Gino Colombini, Marco Zanuso, and Franco Albini, whose designs would in part reflect or parallel the new ideas emanating from the United States and in part reply with ingenuity to the shortages of materials and restrictions on expenditure, which were widespread in Western Europe. In the late 1940s in Sweden, research into the functions of furniture resulted in standardized construction techniques; in Holland, Switzerland, and Denmark progress was made in the design and production of "knock-down" furniture, delivered flat and assembled by the purchaser. In Italy a variety of thin, inexpensive materials were combined with a freedom of form so great as to be dubbed "a design revolution that puts her ahead of almost all others."[26] Everywhere there was interest in the new materials and processes developed during the war, and it was "the spectacular advances of technology,"[27] which the low-cost furniture competition intended to (and did) profit by, that were finally to effect profound changes in postwar living, and ultimately in an aesthetic where value is judged as a fixed relationship between form and function.

The British scientist J. D. Bernal wrote in 1949 that the world was "witnessing . . . a new industrial revolution."[28] In the mid-1940s advances in polymer chemistry and quantum physics gave rise to new families of plastic materials and such inventions as the transistor that made computers possible. After the war, plastic materials, which had had a long if erratic history, began to appear commercially at an increasing rate[29] and these were applied to an enormous variety of functions, from low density polyethylene food and liquid containers (Tupper) to the use of urea as a bonding resin for plywood (the chair designs of Eames and Saarinen). In the textile industry, polymer chemistry resulted in new synthetic fibers.[30] The most spectacular invention of the 1940s, however, was the transistor developed at Bell Laboratories in 1947 and applied to consumer products such as radios and televisions in the 1950s, a device whose success can be indexed by the growth in dollar volume of the semiconductor industry in the United

23. H. McG. Dunnett, "Furniture Since the War," *Architectural Review,* vol. 109 (Mar. 1951), pp. 151, 153.
24. Noyes, *Organic Design,* p. 4.
25. Edgar Kaufmann, Jr., *Prize Designs for Modern Furniture from the International Competition for Low-cost Furniture Design* (New York, 1950), pp. 19–20.
26. Dunnett, "Furniture," p. 153.
27. *Bulletin of the Museum of Modern Art,* vol. 15 (Jan. 1948), p. 13.
28. J. D. Bernal, "After Twenty-Five Years," in Maurice Goldsmith and Alan Mackay, eds., *Society and Science* (New York, 1964), p. 213.
29. *See* Sylvia Katz, *Plastics: Designs and Materials* (London, 1978), p. 11: including polystyrene, GRP, polyurethane, polypropylene, polytetrafluoroethylene, and the polycarbonates.
30. *See* U.S. Department of Commerce, *Patterns and Problems of Technical Innovation in American Industry: Report to National Science Foundation* (Washington, D.C., 1963), pp. 28–34. New fabrics and finishes listed in 1948 included orlon acrylic fiber, Du Pont's second important discovery after nylon in 1939, and, in 1947, cotton drapery and upholstery fabrics first treated with melamine-formaldehyde resins to make them wrinkle-resistant.

States, from fifty thousand dollars in 1948, to twenty million in 1952, to five hundred million in 1960.[31] Most of the technological innovations of succeeding decades would depend on these of the 1940s and the question most often raised in the years to come was whether technology was developing in response to human need.

The 1950s witnessed an unprecedented economic prosperity, first in the United States and subsequently in Western Europe. It was an affluence that engendered a spirit optimistic and self-assured, reflected in what seemed to be permanent aesthetic values, and an unchanging, all-embracing idea of function.

Good design ("a thorough merging of form and function . . . revealing a practical, uncomplicated, sensible beauty"[32]) was promoted by the Museum of Modern Art through a series of biannual "Good Design" exhibitions from 1950 to 1955 under the direction of Edgar Kaufmann, Jr., in collaboration with the Merchandise Mart of Chicago. Objects were selected on the basis of their "eye-appeal, function, construction and price, with emphasis on the first."[33] In June 1953, the exhibition included two hundred items chosen from a record eight thousand entries in the fields of furniture, floor coverings, fabrics, lamps, accessories, tablewares, kitchen and cleaning equipment, and household appliances. Conceived to influence design and public taste in the United States, the "Good Design" exhibitions were an important stimulus to progressive designers, as, on an international scale, were the Triennale exhibitions held in Milan in 1951, 1954, 1957, and thereafter. According to the Finnish designer Saara Hopea, whose products for the Arabia company were shown in the exhibitions, "We had a shortage of almost everything in post-war Finland. . . . We . . . had to design things that were really needed. . . . At the same time, we also designed objects for exhibitions in Finland and abroad. The Milan Triennals were especially important in the '50s. They stimulated Finnish design by placing it in competition with that of other countries. . . . This notice helped Finnish consumers to accept not only these prize winning products, but also other industrial designer products."[34]

Founded as a biennial exhibition in Monza in 1923, the Triennale moved to Milan and a triennial schedule in 1933. A small exhibition was held in 1947, but it was not until the Triennale of 1951 that the exhibition was able to resume its prewar scale. Although the objects included in the "Good Design" and Triennale exhibitions ranged widely in their styles, from simple and unostentatious latter-day 1930s functional designs to handcrafted works that were inherently decorative and expressive, and to technological displays of laminates, alloys, and micromechanics, they were considered exemplars of a single modernist aesthetic as defined by functional efficiency, fitness for purpose, truth to materials, and economy of means, and moreover were distinguished as such with single-minded and certain vision by their respective jurors. At the Museum of Modern Art in 1952 the Olivetti exhibition drew praise for the firm's corporate identity, "the organization of all the visual aspects of an industry, unified under a single high standard of taste . . . [with] presentations unified by one esthetic concept."[35]

Evangelical in this uniform, critical method for passing judgment on individual products, the 1950s witnessed an explosion of juried exhibitions and good design awards. The Festival of Britain of 1951, for which the Council of Industrial Design was given responsibility for selecting the man-

The first transistor was invented at Bell Telephone Laboratories on Dec. 23, 1947, by William Shockley with John Bardeen and Walter H. Brattain.

Primitive by today's standards, this first transistor (1947), a "point-contact" type, amplified electrical signals by passing them through a solid semiconductor material.

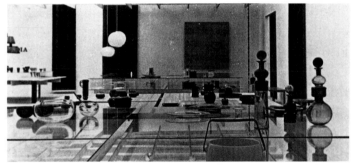

Finnish section of the XI Triennale, Milan, 1957

31. *Ibid.*, p. 140.
32. Edgar Kaufmann, Jr., *What Is Modern Design?* (New York, 1950), p. 9.
33. New York, Museum of Modern Art, *Good Design: An Exhibition of Home Furnishings Selected by the Museum of Modern Art, New York, for the Merchandise Mart, Chicago* (1953), inside cover.
34. *See* Marja Kaipainen, "Generations in Design," *Form Function Finland* (Mar. 1982), p. 12.
35. "Olivetti: Design in Industry," *Bulletin of the Museum of Modern Art,* vol. 20 (Fall 1952), pp. 3, 17.

ufactured objects, celebrated the return of prosperity in Britain and endeavored to set before the British public well-designed, durable consumer goods. If the "Festival style" was not to endure in specific form[36] the concern for standards of design in products ranging from street signs to café chairs, did. In 1953 the Council began to plan for a permanent exhibition in London of well-designed products, and in 1956 the Design Centre opened, supported in part by the government and in part by the manufacturers whose products were selected for exhibition there. From 1957 to the present, the Design Centre (renamed the Council of Industrial Design Awards in 1967) has annually given awards to British products, ranging from silver-plated cutlery to a forklift truck. The Duke of Edinburgh, a sometime juror for the Design Centre, initiated his own Prize for Elegant Design in 1959. Elsewhere throughout Western Europe and Japan, design organizations and awards proliferated, among them the Rat für Formgebung, established in West Germany in 1951, with its Internationales Design Zentrum in Berlin and prizes (Bundespreis "Gute Form"), established in 1969; the Lunning Prize, established by the Danish-American Frederik Lunning in 1951 for Scandinavian design; the Japanese Design Promotion Council, established in 1957 by the Ministry of International Trade and Industry, with its Industrial Design Selection of good designs awarded there from 1958; the Compasso d'Oro awards, sponsored by the Milanese department store La Rinascente from 1954 (from 1959 to 1965 in collaboration with the Associazione per il Disegno Industriale [ADI], and since 1967 entirely by ADI); and finally the Biennial Exhibition of Industrial Design (Bio) in Ljubljana, Yugoslavia, established in 1964. The certainty of aesthetic standards reflected in the selection of designs for exhibition and award is illustrated by the first Compasso d'Oro prizes given in 1954 for "the aesthetics of the product," with the award-winning glass of Flavio Poli, described as "united in form and material," symbolizing the "aesthetic requirements" to which the Compasso d'Oro was dedicated.[37]

Such belief in the primacy of aesthetics was equally present in the opening of a new bastion of functionalism, the Hochschule für Gestaltung in Ulm, West Germany. The most important school of design of the decade, unequalled in significance even since its closing in 1968, the school was founded in 1950 and opened in 1955, designed and first directed by Max Bill, who envisioned Ulm as a successor to the Bauhaus. Bill sought to unify art and industry by training designers in the elements of both form and mechanics: "The founders of the Ulm School believe art to be the highest expression of human life and their aim is therefore to help in turning life itself into a work of art. In the words of that memorable challenge thrown down by Henry van de Velde over 50 years ago, we mean 'to wage war on ugliness'; and ugliness can only be combated with what is intrinsically good—'good' because at once seemly and practical. As the direct heir to van de Velde's own school at Weimar, the Dessau Bauhaus had set itself precisely the same objects. If we intend to go rather further at Ulm than they did at Dessau this is because post-war requirements clearly postulate the necessity for certain additions to the original curriculum. For instance, we mean to give still greater prominence to the design of ordinary things in everyday use."[38] Like the Bauhaus, Ulm was to develop on commission for industry prototypes of products suitable for mass production, and one of the first and most successful programs—a series of combined radio and phonograph sets and their display—was executed for Braun (and with the

David Mellor's "Pride" cutlery (1954), which won a Design Centre Award in 1957

The Hochschule für Gestaltung in Ulm, West Germany

36. See Reyner Banham, "The Style: 'Flimsy . . . Effeminate'?," in Mary Banham and Bevis Hillier, eds., A Tonic to the Nation (London, 1976), pp. 190–98.
37. See Milan, Palazzo delle Stelline, Design & design (May 29–July 31, 1979), pp. 22, 30 (author's translation).
38. Max Bill, "The Bauhaus Idea: From Weimar to Ulm," in The Architects' Year Book, vol. 5 (1953), p. 32.

firm's collaboration) by Ulm faculty members Hans Gugelot and graphic designer Otl Aicher. First shown at the radio exhibition in Düsseldorf in 1955, the series established the formal characteristics of Braun design, which remain to the present—balanced, unified, simple, and undecorated cabinetwork, unequalled as visible demonstrations of functionalist theory.

However, all was not perfect in paradise. Although profiting by commercial association, functional good design, conceived to suit products to needs, found itself running counter to the "economic miracle." Its proponents denounced commercial opportunism and began to substitute technical and sociological values for the aesthetic ones that had hitherto seemed indispensable. Even from the earliest years of the "Good Design" exhibitions their director, Edgar Kaufmann, Jr., found the purism of functional design being compromised by its dependence on success in the marketplace: "Good Design does not represent the best that our designers are capable of; it can show only the best that they have been able to get across in our community—for it is limited to purchasable products."[39] At the 1957 International Design Conference in Aspen, Colorado, the American designer Richard Latham questioned the standards on which "Good Design" judgments had been based: "Can we accept a show of good design without being sure, ourselves, why it's good, and without being sure we can identify bad design as readily? I am prepared to believe that there is good and bad, but I am not prepared to believe that it is a simple matter of a contemporary look, a fad, a style, a matter of good taste."[40] At the same time, at Ulm, a dramatic change took place when Max Bill left the school in 1957 and the curriculum was radically changed, dispensing with the fine arts department and workshop practices that had been inherited from the Bauhaus.[41] Mathematics and mathematical logic were substituted as the conceptual basis of the design method, with secondary emphasis on sociology and cultural history. Otl Aicher, one of the triumvirate of directors of the school replacing Bill, described the change: "the younger lecturers urged evaluating the basic course of study. gugelot and zeischegg developed the program for engineering science, maldonado the instruction plans for information theory and methodical subjects as well as the basic theory. The ulm model was born: a model for design education based on science and technology. the designer was no longer the lofty artist . . . the last remaining relics of the werkbund arts and crafts were abandoned."[42] Tomás Maldonado, chief theorist and architect of the curriculum change and also a member of Ulm's new directing triumvirate, called the primacy of aesthetic standards into question: "The aesthetic factor merely constitutes one factor among others with which the designer can operate, but it is neither the principal nor the predominant one. The productive, constructive, economic factors—perhaps, too, the symbolic factors—also exist. Industrial design is not an art nor is the designer necessarily an artist. The majority of objects exhibited in the museums, and in the exhibitions of 'good design,' are anonymous and often executed in technical offices by subordinate employees who never imagined they were producing art."[43]

Questioned from within Ulm, the functionalist aesthetic as it had developed from the 1920s was also attacked from without by critics such as Reyner Banham who argued that 1950s industrial styling represented a standard more valid than post-Bauhaus formalism for automotive design, and condoned the symbolism that styling sometimes embraced.[44] In legitimizing styling as a kind of popular folk art, Banham argued that "it is

39. Edgar Kaufmann, Jr., "Good Design '51 As Seen by Its Director and by Its Designer," Interiors, vol. 110 (Mar. 1951), p. 100.
40. Richard Latham, "Communication of Values through Design: 1957," in Reyner Banham, ed., The Aspen Papers (New York, 1974), p. 89.
41. See Kenneth Frampton, "Apropos Ulm: Curriculum and Critical Theory," Oppositions, vol. 3 (May 1974), pp. 17–36, esp. p. 21.
42. Otl Aicher, "Hochschule für Gestaltung, the Nine Stages of Its Development," in François Burkhardt and Inez Franksen, eds., Design: Dieter Rams & (Berlin, 1980–81), p. 179.
43. Tomás Maldonado, "Les Nouvelles perspectives industrielles et la formation du designer. Conférence à l'Exposition Universelle, Bruxelles, le 18 septembre 1958," in Jocelyn de Noblet, Design (Paris, 1974), p. 199 [Trans. in Ulm, vol. 2 (Oct. 1958), pp. 29–30].
44. Reyner Banham, "Machine Aesthetic," Architectural Review, vol. 117 (Apr. 1955), pp. 225–28, esp. p. 227: "To manufacturers, utility is a complex affair which, in certain products for certain markets, may require the addition of ornament for ostentation or social prestige."

clearly absurd to demand that objects designed for a short useful life should exhibit qualities signifying eternal validity," and that the Buick V-8 of 1955, with its "glitter, a sense of bulk, a sense of three-dimensionality, [and] deliberate exposure of technical means, all building up to signify power and make an immediate impact on whoever sees it," was a more suitable model for design than the abstract principles of the Bauhaus.[45] According to Banham, accelerated technology demanded a correspondingly transient aesthetic.

The "science and technology" that replaced fine arts in the Ulm curriculum had applications elsewhere in new measurable, quantifiable standards voicing a more conscious regard for the consumer. These included market research studies that established consumer preferences (or, as Vance Packard pointed out in the *Hidden Persuaders* in 1957, inquired into consumer motivation) and ergonomic studies—the engineering of objects and tools for human use by considering all forms of relationships between man and equipment. Following studies of functional anatomy by Scandinavians in the 1940s, ergonomics developed as a separate discipline during the war. Linked to experimental psychology and physiology, it was applied to the design of cockpits in military aircraft, particularly with regard to their visual displays. By the mid-1950s ergonomics had been taken up both by functionalist theorists at Ulm and by America's leading industrial stylists, from Raymond Loewy, who in 1956 redesigned the "DO/MORE" posture chair, to Henry Dreyfuss, whose 1955 pioneering study *Designing for People* did much to make the field popularly known in the United States: "The process is known as human engineering. From the mountainous data we assembled, sifted, and translated, we filled the gaps between human behavior and machine design. We have collected detail measurements of heads and of all the extremities and of thighs and forearms and shoulders and every other conceivable part of the body; we are familiar with the amount of pressure the average foot can comfortably exert on a pedal; we know how hard a hand can effectively squeeze; the reach of an arm—for we must know how far buttons and levers can be placed away from the central controls of a machine; size of earphones; telephone operators' headsets, helmets for the armed services, binoculars—all are determined by our information on head sizes. From these facts we arrived at this maxim—the most efficient machine is the one that is built around a person."[46]

While the visible applications of ergonomics were still few in the 1950s, ergonomics came to have tremendous appeal in the decades to follow as *the* design science, amalgamating as it did several technical fields including psychology, physiology, anthropometry, medicine, biology, and industrial engineering, and claiming humanitarianism as its raison d'être. Aesthetics, it seemed, could scarcely compete. The preoccupation with the appearance of individual forms and the interest in making value judgments about them, so notable in the early 1950s, paled before the scientific study of systems: sociology and technology became the critical determinants. At the Design Centre in London during the 1960s, a new series of selection procedures were introduced to insure that "good design" products accepted for exhibition there satisfied these newly established technical standards, and in 1967 the scope of the Design Centre awards was broadened from household objects to include engineering design in a separate "Capital Goods Section."[47] The nineteenth-century marriage of aesthetics and technology had begun to come apart.

1955 Buick "56R Super" two-door: "A more suitable model"

45. Banham, "A Throw-Away Esthetic," pp. 63–64.
46. Henry Dreyfuss, *Designing for People* (New York, 1955), pp. 27–28.
47. *See* John Blake and Avril Blake, *The Practical Idealists* (London, 1969), p. 49.

The questioning of functionalism, which began in the mid-1950s, only intensified in the 1960s, fed in the United States by economic recession and inflation and by the devastating impact of such political events as the Vietnam War and widespread student protests. There was comfort taken in advances in high technology, although the new processes and endless list of new materials at design's disposal were viewed as challenging in their variety and complexity. From Aspen to Ulm designers voiced the difficulties of defining standards for design in an expanding and changing society and through a variety of economic conditions and forces that seemed to mitigate good design. Eliot Noyes, as program chairman, designated the 1964 International Design Conference at Aspen "Design '64: Directions and Dilemmas," as a means of exploring "the freedoms and restraints within which the designer must work and the ways in which the serious designer may reconcile his standards with the outside forces which affect design today."[48] At the conference "Design in America" held at Princeton in the same spring, Charles Eames announced: "The whole idea of choice in terms of aesthetics or form seems to be really foreign. . . . The fact that, at this point, we have the opportunity to choose puts us in a pretty precarious position, because we are in fact not equipped to choose."[49] In 1967 Abraham Moles, lecturer on information theory at Ulm, formally declared functionalism to be in crisis. "Functionalism in western culture has entered a critical period due to the growth of affluent society. . . . Functionalism necessarily contradicts the doctrine of affluent society which is forced to produce and to sell relentlessly. Finally functionalism tends to reduce the number of objects and to realize an optimal fit between products and needs, whereas the production machinery of an affluent society follows the opposite direction. It creates a system of neokitsch by accumulating objects in the human environment. At this point the crisis of functionalism becomes manifest. It is torn between the neokitsch of the supermarket on the one side and ascetic fulfillment of function on the other side."[50]

Following the lead of Reyner Banham, Gillo Dorfles, Robert Venturi, and others,[51] leaders of good design institutions sought the virtues of a world of disordered complexity, endorsing a relativist aesthetic of transitory, "popular" art. Successor to Gordon Russell as head of the Design Council in 1960, Paul Reilly described "the challenge of Pop" in 1967: "We are shifting perhaps from attachment to permanent, universal values to acceptance that a design may be valid at a given time for a given purpose. . . . All that this means is that a product must be good of its kind for the set of circumstances for which it has been designed. For example, in this age of accelerating technology, to refuse to take notice of the transitory or to reject the ephemeral per se is to ignore a fact of life. . . . For consumer goods, though form may have followed function in the good old days, in this electric age they are neck and neck."[52] Arthur Drexler, succeeding Philip Johnson as director of the Museum of Modern Art's combined department of architecture and design in 1956, rejected any form of utopia in the field of design: "There is no reason why we should want every useful thing to be beautiful. . . . Reality is more complicated than these or any other standards of design would suggest. For us, reality includes the fact that we live in a welter of conflicting attitudes toward what is beautiful and that no one seriously believes in the value of the things we make. . . . Standards of design still current pertain not to the object itself but to the package that most often simply encloses and

48. "Aspen Conference," Industrial Design, vol. 11 (Feb. 1964), p. 14.
49. Quoted in Eric Larrabee, "Summary of the Proceedings," in Laurence B. Holland, ed., Who Designs America? (Garden City, N.Y., 1966), p. 328.
50. Abraham A. Moles, "Functionalism in Crisis," Ulm, vols. 19–20 (Aug. 1967), p. 24.
51. Banham, "A Throw-Away Esthetic," pp. 61–65; Dorfles, "The Man-Made Object," pp. 1–2; and Robert Venturi, Complexity and Contradiction in Architecture (New York, 1966).
52. Reilly, "The Challenge of Pop," pp. 256–57.

protects it. . . . The designer of an appliance may, after all, really be required to provide only an acceptable box. . . . What is inside the box is what is really interesting. . . . It may even be that the proper subject of good design is the machine itself, not the things it can make."[53]

However, while the proponents of good design in the United States and Britain were no longer confident of its aesthetic criteria, at the same time in Italy, a new, positive, language of forms was being created. The 1964 Triennale in Milan seemed to recognize that Italian design had reached a turning point: "Of past Triennales it has been said that they all looked to the future, and that this distinguished them from other exhibitions. . . . The XIII Triennale instead is all in the present . . . This is the first time that the Triennale . . . has been dedicated to a theme, to leisure time . . . a theme extremely current for Italy now increasingly industrialized and witnessing a phenomena of social transformations."[54] At the Triennale's inauguration Carlo Arnaudi, Minister for Scientific Research, linked the economic and social aspects of leisure time to Italy's new technological and scientific capacity.[55]

Using advanced molding techniques and a variety of plastic materials ranging from polyurethane foams for furniture to polyethylene for kitchen storage containers, Italian designers created a viable popular, transient aesthetic, adapted both to limited series and to large-scale mass-production, the latter perhaps best exemplified by the broad range of low-cost, award-winning plastic furniture and consumer objects produced by Kartell from 1954. In their lightness, transparency, and bright color, these objects denied the static, monumental qualities suggested by materials like wood and steel as well as the absolute, permanent values that well-designed forms in these materials seemed to convey.

Joe Colombo's "Closingbed" night environment for Sormani (1971)

The practical concern for lightweight, portable furnishings to suit small spaces that characterized functional good design in the late 1940s and early 1950s had persisted in Italy, and was transmuted during the early 1960s into a wider regard for the total physical environment and lifestyle of the individual consumer, now regarded as freer and more adaptable. From the "Sacco" (beanbag) chair of Gatti, Paolini, Teodoro, which assumes the shape of the user, to the "Additional" seating system of Joe Colombo, which the user arranges as he requires, Italian furniture in the mid-1960s incorporated the ideas of change and interplay with environment as positive elements of their design. A project executed by Joe Colombo for the 1968 Triennale in Milan, and subsequently shown in Paris, was conceived to define such a variable environment: "If it is possible to program as the single criterion of convenience, flexibility, and total articulation, the elements and equipment necessary for man to live, we can design a habitable system adapting itself in the best conditions to any situation in space and time. . . . This research has established the dynamics of a contemporary habitation, punctuating the different moments of the day, defining the use of the furniture and objects, differentiating their static and dynamic aspects."[56]

Joe Colombo's "Rotoliving" day environment for Sormani (1971)

If the concept of furnishing variable, multipurpose living spaces was particularly suitable to Italy, the forms taken there were to be widely imitated throughout Europe and America—with a proliferation from the later 1960s of inflatable, collapsible, stacking, folding, disposable, and semidisposable household objects in bright, emphatic colors. The use of the new plastic materials inspired simultaneous experimentation

53. Arthur Drexler, "The Disappearing Object," *Saturday Review* (May 23, 1964), pp. 12–15.
54. Dino Gentili, "Discorso di inaugurazione," in Milan, Palazzo dell'Arte al Parco, *Tredicesima Triennale di Milano: Tempo libero* (June 12–Sept. 27, 1964), p. 7 (author's translation).
55. Carlo Arnaudi, "Discorso tenuto alla inaugurazione," in *ibid.*, p. 9.
56. Joe Colombo, "Une Architecture différente pour un mode d'habiter différent: 'Le système programmable pour habiter'," in Paris, Centre de Création Industrielle, *Qu'est-ce que le design?* (Oct. 24–Dec. 31, 1969), n.p. (author's translation).

everywhere: with the introduction of high-frequency PVC welding in the mid-1960s, inflatable chairs were designed in PVC plastic by a number of British and French designers,[57] and for the first time commercially produced, by the Italian group of De Pas, D'Urbino, Lomazzi in 1967.

The Italian success in adapting new materials and processes to commercial furniture production in the 1960s was and remains due to the small scale of the industry. As an outgrowth of the traditional family-owned craft shops well endowed with skilled craftsmen and artisans, the industry was able to take risks in developing new products, which were discouraged elsewhere by high engineering costs. The small body of skilled craftsmen permitted furniture manufacturers freedom to experiment and to change models, minimizing investment in research and development through their ability to create not only prototypes, but also molds and tools for manufacture. Among other accomplishments, Italy produced the first structural use of polyethylene in furniture (Marco Zanuso and Richard Sapper's child's chair, 1964) and one of the first all-plastic chairs to be made by injection molding (Joe Colombo's stacking chair, 1965).

The close relationship of the Italian designer to the manufacturer and the artisan in these small shops encouraged the development of personal, expressive styles that ranged from brightly colored but highly rational essays in the new plastic materials, to Pop or otherwise ironically shaped objects rich in symbolic meaning, and hitherto unprecedented multifunctional objects suitable to flexible modes of arrangement. If aestheticism had been called into question in the late 1950s, it returned with a vengeance in Italian design of the mid-1960s, albeit transformed by bright colors and odd shapes and making assertive, dramatic, and sometimes ironic statements.

At the same time that Italy was displaying a rich eclecticism of individual styles, many designers elsewhere were acknowledging the state of "anonymous" design which Kaj Franck, a Finnish designer of ceramics and glass, felt was a more appropriate view of mass-produced objects where forms were often necessarily compromised by marketing and production considerations: "Anonymity belongs only to mass production. . . . It is wrong to make the designer the salesman of the article. This offends against the object, the consumer, and the designer. . . . Instead of resting on the designer's name, the product must stand on its own merits of which the design is an essential part. This is not to belittle the importance of design, merely to restore the perspective of its relationship to the whole."[58] In the Swedish design schools of the 1960s there was new emphasis on teamwork and group production, intended to parallel the present "anonymous" situation in industry and the marketplace.[59]

This anonymity seemed entirely suited to a now fully developed design technocracy that emphasized ergonomics, cybernetics, and scientific concepts and whose membership of designers, engineers, and scientists produced man's first flight to the moon in 1969 as well as a variety of consumer products, from the first portable video tape recorder (Sony, 1964) to electronic calculators. While commercial hi-fi equipment and televisions continued to plagiarize domestic furnishing styles as they had done since the 1940s, and to use furniture materials like wood, engineering products considered examples of good design in the late 1960s and early 1970s were often encased in plastic boxes so anonymous and so minimally detailed that their now increasingly miniaturized function was reduced to near invisibility.

57. Including the British architect Arthur Quarmby in 1965; the British firm of Incadinc in 1966–67; the French group of Jean Aubert, Jean-Paul Jungmann, and Antoine Stinco in 1967; and Quasar Khanh, a Vietnamese working in Paris in 1967.
58. Kaj Franck, "Anonymity," *Craft Horizons*, vol. 27 (Mar. 1967), p. 35.
59. Lennart Lindkvist, ed., *Design in Sweden* (Stockholm, 1972), pp. 7–8.

Polarized between a new "popular" aestheticism and a highly technical "anonymous" rationalism, those concerned with progressive functional design in the late 1960s seemed powerless or unwilling to bridge the gap. In the final issue of the periodical *Ulm* in 1968, Tomás Maldonado described the situation as he saw it, and advocated an increased specialization by designers in the "science" of design: "The view that the problems of design can be solved primarily if not exclusively by designing has been shaken. The relationship between the designer and the sciences must be thought out afresh. . . . This can be achieved if the design schools do not train their students merely to make design objects but also to create design knowledge and design organization. In the last analysis design is more than the creation of three-dimensional forms. The activities of the designer will become differentiated. There will be designers who work on the drawing board; there will be designers who research; and there will be designers who organize and plan."[60]

The 1970s and early 1980s saw Maldonado's prescription for design specialization fulfilled, although not entirely in the ways he intended or for the reasons he foresaw. Functionalism no longer existed as a universal, unified standard for design, its traditional concern for aesthetic value finally discredited by the social and political events of the preceding decade. Beauty, which Edgar Kaufmann, Jr., had considered inherent to good design in 1950, had by 1977, become identified in certain quarters as an "appearance solution."[61] Notwithstanding, Italian design continued in the early years of the 1970s to produce an innovative popular language of forms, which was formally celebrated at the Museum of Modern Art in 1972 with the exhibition, "Italy: The New Domestic Landscape," organized by Emilio Ambasz, the museum's curator of design. The exhibition, however, proved to be a retrospective: with the general energy crisis of 1973, which provoked shortages of all natural resources, followed in 1975 by a worldwide recession, the plastic materials out of which so many of the Italian objects were made were far less economically viable.

The catastrophic economic events of the 1970s reflected in tight money supply, inflation, and energy and materials shortages galvanized attention on the larger social problems many progressive designers in the United States and Britain had long thought their profession should address—seeking, and sometimes finding, enhanced performances in all aspects of consumer design. While at the International Design Conference in Aspen in 1970 student activists polemically "forced the conference to vote on a twelve-point resolution covering every current 'problem' from abortion to Vietnam and the abandonment of design for profit,"[62] the *New York Times* reported from the Southern Furniture Market in High Point, North Carolina, that one American manufacturer had proposed a real, if personal, solution to reducing the pollution caused by waste plastics, by offering the buyers of his designs the opportunity to trade them in for new ones, the returned furniture to be melted down and reused.[63] As *Industrial Design* magazine commended in its annual reviews of American products a radio designed for the blind and an educational ecology kit (1970),[64] and products that were less extravagant in material use and in energy use (1976),[65] and asked whether furniture design was more responsive to human anatomy and to work habits (1977),[66] *Design,* the publication of the Council of Industrial Design, simultaneously reported that Council awards had been made to industrial light fittings for their "economy, safe and easy mount-

Oskar Kogoj's plexiglass baby spoon (1972)

Oskar Kogoj's spoon design responds to a baby's motor ability.

60. [Tomás Maldonado], "Commentary on the Situation of the HfG," *Ulm,* vol. 21 (Apr. 1968), p. 12.
61. *See* Ann Nydele, ed., *Design Review: Industrial Design 23rd Annual* (New York, 1977), p. 102.
62. Reyner Banham, "Polarization," in Banham, ed., *Aspen Papers,* p. 207.
63. Rita Reif, "Thirteen Years after Saarinen," *The New York Times* (Nov. 4, 1970), p. 54C.
64. "Design Review: Consumer Products," *Industrial Design,* vol. 17 (Dec. 1970), p. 53.
65. John Margolies, ed., *Design Review: Industrial Design 22nd Annual* (New York, 1976), p. 11.
66. Nydele, ed., *Design Review,* pp. 60–61.

ing and servicing, and minimal maintenance," and to wall coverings that
exploited "the practical, fire-resistant and acoustic properties of wool."[67]
While in 1964 visitors to the New York World's Fair were presented with an
exhibit of model homes called "The House of Good Taste," the 1982
World's Fair at Knoxville, Tennessee, displayed TVA conservation techniques, a Victorian house remodeled with energy-saving devices and
appliances, and a factory-built home with a solar-heating system,[68] ap-
proaching if not attaining the utopia of Victor Papanek's *Design for the
Real World* (New York, 1972).

Progressive design seemed divided in the 1970s between a variety of
responsibilities—generally described as "humanistic" (which were no
longer perceived as standards or levels of achievement as they had been,
but obligatory conditions)—for product safety, durability, conservation,
ecology, and human engineering. Partly as a result of economic necessity,
designers became specialists in various fields such as engineering, ergonomics (with groups working specifically in the health and medical
fields), corporate management and marketing, and government safety
regulations, and by the same token, many design firms in the United States
felt they had to diversify as well in these same fields. Gui Bonsiepe, a
former Ulm colleague and sometime design partner of Tomás Maldonado,
remarked as early as 1971 on the high degree of flexibility among designers, who with surprising speed had learned to adapt themselves "like
the chameleon."[69]

From the engineers came insistent advances that seemed to equate
technological progress with good design. Increasing miniaturization and
progressively lower prices brought quality consumer electronics to the mass
market and hence could be credited with populism (as well as with profit).
The housing of these products—from calculators to radios and personal
computers (the latter produced first in 1977)—varied in style from a rational
minimalism, which in the case of Sony's "Walkman" (1978), was also physically minimal, to a popular post-Vietnam "commando" style, bristling with
knobs, switches, controls, and indicator dials.[70]

At the other end of the spectrum, from the arena of aesthetic creativity, came in the late 1970s another wave of Italian designs. Made of wood
or chipboard, either painted or faced with patterned laminates, metal,
ceramic and glass, or combinations of unrelated materials, these objects
and furniture were designed first by Alessandro Mendini and Studio Alchymia from 1976, and by an international group of architects and designers led by Ettore Sottsass, Jr., and known from 1981 as Memphis. In their
use of odd, flamboyant shapes and their emotionalism, the Memphis group
recalled the more self-consciously sociopolitical designs of the 1960s as well
as in their interest in establishing a popular "transient" aesthetic: "Memphis does not deny functionality, but looks at it with eyes wide open, more
as an anthropologist than as a marketing man. It sees functionality, therefore, not only as a respect for certain ergonomic rules or for saleability
statistics, but also as a respect for a cultural vision, a public necessity, a historical thrust. The general tiredness and laxity of the international '*bon
goût-bon genre* real design' by now reflects its expressive poverty and in-
capacity to represent the wishes and the nervous energy of a restless, eclectic society which is intolerant of permanent institutions."[71] In spite of the
apparent populism of Memphis—its claim to express the emotional "energy" of society and its use of industrial materials—its objects were and are

67. "1974 Design Council Awards for
Contract & Consumer Goods," *Design*, vol. 304 (Apr. 1974), pp. 35, 37.
68. Kenneth Lelen, "The Once and
Future House," *Metropolis* (Nov.
1982), p. 9.
69. Gui Bonsiepe, "Diseño industrial technologia y ecologia" (1971),
in Gui Bonsiepe, *Diseño industrial*
(Milan, 1975), p. 95.
70. Reyner Banham, "Radio
Machismo," in *Design by Choice*
(New York, 1981), pp. 117–18 [Orig.
publ. in *New Society* (Aug. 22,
1974)].
71. Barbara Radice, ed., *Memphis:
The New International Style* (Milan,
1981), p. 6.

produced in limited quantities at high prices by traditional craft shops. However, in its occasional historicizing parodies of both functional and commercial styles of the 1930s, 1940s, and 1950s, its use of unprecedented, playful shapes, and above all its insistence on pattern and ornament, Memphis deliberately attacks all the criteria of functionalism, conceived from the nineteenth century as rational objective standards, as well as the new government-regulated "humanistic" standards. Although by 1980 functional good design no longer existed on those terms, it is significant that Sottsass, like Mendini in his "Bau Haus" series of 1979 and 1980, chose to design a new environment and also to use a new language based on forms that functionalism traditionally would abhor.

Functionalism led the way of progressive design for over a century and, as formed by the Bauhaus, shaped this century's conception of modernity. Those who found it a criterion too restrictive to address the richness, symbolisms, and accelerating technology of the postwar world have pushed design in a variety of different directions without achieving the influence that functionalism could claim. The loss of a dominant universal concept has left a vacuum, and in 1983 one is left to ponder how the ground between the poles as they now exist will be filled.

Michael Graves's "Plaza" dressing table for Memphis (1981)

**Design and Theory:
Two Points of View**

Max Bill
Ettore Sottsass, Jr.

A sequence of questions on the theory of design was submitted to Max Bill, author of *Form* (1952) and co-founder and rector of the Hochschule für Gestaltung in Ulm, West Germany, the single most influential school of design in this century after the Bauhaus. The same questions were also answered by Ettore Sottsass, Jr., who through the metaphoric and referential components of his work and through his involvement in human and social issues has suggested alternatives to the formal and functional precepts of the school at Ulm. Bill and Sottsass—each a painter and sculptor, as well as a designer, writer, and theorist—have been in the vanguard of what now may be seen as the two most important movements in design in the postwar period.

What are the qualities of good design?
Bill: Good design depends on the harmony established between the form of an object and its use.

How do these qualities endure in the face of changes in technology?
Bill: Technological changes should help to make the object better and more harmonious in form and in function, as well as cheaper.

What is the value of enduring design in a society that plans obsolescence?
Bill: Every object made in an appropriate form retains its value through its inherent quality. It is economical; it is not considered as waste.

How can design be best taught today?
Bill: Design can only be taught by getting to the heart of the problem that is to be solved, by the practical development of a prototype, and/or by the analysis of existing products that have, or have not, solved it. Design education must remain practical; the analysis of realistic problems is the only way to find useful solutions.

Will you comment on the so-called anti-design movements of the last two decades that have been seen as reactions against "formalism" and "functionalism"?
Bill: Functional design considers the visual aspect, that is, the beauty, of an object as a component of its function, but not one that overwhelms its other primary functions. Such other approaches as those we have witnessed in recent years can be amusing and even commercially interesting, but their ethical and aesthetic value is nil.

What do you think is the future of design?
Bill: Design and creation are two different approaches to a problem. Design, as it is understood in Europe, is an aid to commerce, which certainly will have its own future. Since I am not clairvoyant, I am not able to predict if the future will bring what I would like, so-called good or functional design.

What are the qualities of good design?
Sottsass: This is a question that supposes a Platonic view of the situation, that is, it supposes that somewhere, somehow, there is a place where GOOD DESIGN is deposited. The problem then is to come as close as possible to that "good design." My idea instead is that the problem is not to be near "good design" but to design, keeping as near as possible to the anthropological state of things, which, in turn, is to be as near as possible to the need a society has for an image of itself.

How do these qualities endure in the face of changes in technology?
Sottsass: They don't endure at all because in my definition the qualities of good design are exactly the ones that don't endure but follow the changes of history, the changes of the anthropological state of things, and among them, the changes of technology. If you really want to find something that endures, that is the intensity of the research for a relationship between history and a possible image of history. In design what endures is man's curiosity toward existence and the drive to give a metaphoric image to it.

What is the value of enduring design in a society that plans obsolescence?
Sottsass: My answer is always the same. If a society plans obsolescence, the only possible enduring design is one that deals with that obsolescence, a design that comes to terms with it, maybe accelerating it, maybe confronting it, maybe ironizing it, maybe getting along with it. The only design that does not endure is the one that in such a society looks for metaphysics, looks for the absolute, for eternity. And then I don't understand why enduring design is better than disappearing design. I don't understand why stones are better than the feathers of a bird of paradise. I don't understand why pyramids are better than Burmese straw huts. I don't understand why the president's speeches are better than love whispering in a room at night. When I was young I gathered information only from fashion magazines or from very ancient, forgotten, destroyed, dusty civilizations. I gathered information from those areas where life is either just germinating or from the nostalgia of life—never from institutions, never from solidity, never from "reality," never from crystallizations, never from hibernations. So I must admit that obsolescence for me is just the sugar of life.

How can design be best taught today?
Sottsass: To me design, as I said, is a way of discussing life. It is a way of discussing society, politics, eroticism, food, and even design. At the end, it is a way of building up a possible figurative utopia or metaphor about life. Certainly to me design is not restricted to the necessity of giving form to a more or less stupid product for a more or less sophisticated industry. So, if you have to teach something about design, you have to teach, first of all, about life and you have to insist, explaining that technology is one of the metaphors of life.

Will you comment on the so-called anti-design movements of the last two decades that have been seen as reactions against "formalism" and "functionalism"?
Sottsass: I think I was one of the participants in the so-called anti-design movement, which I don't think lasted two decades but only one, from the beginning of the sixties to the beginning of the seventies. This movement, from different angles, through different personalities, and coming from different traditions (Austria, Italy, England), developed the idea that design

should be removed from the acid mechanism of industrial needs and programs to be taken into a wider area of possibilities and necessities. The so-called anti-design movement pushed the idea that design does not end with the product put in production by industry but starts from that moment. It starts when it enters our homes, enters our streets, towns, skies, bodies, and souls. Design starts when it becomes the visual, physical, sensorial representation of the existential metaphor on which we are laying down our lives. This means that design starts when you design the metaphor of life, which also means that so-called anti-design in fact was "anti" nothing at all, it was just all for enlarging and deepening the design event.

What do you think is the future of design?
Sottsass: It is like asking about the future of politics, or the future of poetry, or the future of eroticism, or the future of soccer. It is very, very difficult to answer, but anyway I am working very hard and there are a lot of young people working very hard to carry on the message sent around in the sixties by the small group of the "anti-design" people, trying hard to deliver to design a larger catalogue of communications, more meaning, a wider linguistic flexibility, and a wider awareness of the responsibilities toward private and social life.

The Design Process

George Nelson

In his long career, George Nelson
has considered the process of
design from the viewpoint of
exhibition, product, and interior
designer; teacher; and author of
numerous articles and books on the
subject, including his now-classic
Problems of Design (1957).

The one absolutely irrefutable thing that can be said about design is that it *evolves.* This is something familiar to everyone. We know that a "classic" car does not look like a car of today. We also realize that evolution goes on inside the car as well, and that its mechanical system—brakes, transmission, suspension, and so on—is *different* from the way it used to be.

In a mechanical world, "different" is always supposed to mean "better" in one way or another, so it has become common to equate the idea of evolution with the idea of progress. In reality, there is no particular correlation between the two ideas. One could reasonably assert, for example, that a French cathedral designed six hundred years ago is better architecture than anything being produced today.

What evolution really seems to mean, in this broad sense, is *change,* and change may represent progress, but it may also express retrogression. In the evolution of design, all we can be sure of is that new designs represent the addition of something unfamiliar to something that is already familiar. This simple fact opens up some very interesting questions for us, because we have been rather thoroughly brainwashed through advertising to accept as axiomatic the proposition that "new" always means "better," which is why the word is so prominently displayed on detergents and cold remedies. Now, if we equate evolution with change, this has to mean that some kind of *process* is going on. Things do not change by themselves; there is even a law in physics, one of Sir Isaac Newton's more-inspired insights, to make this point very sharply.

The design process can be described fairly clearly up to a point, but its essence remains elusive. An Olympic champion can describe very generally the correct ways to jump, swim, or throw a discus, but beyond this, if he tries to explain exactly how he wins all those medals against strong competition, he is unable to do so. Some years ago the National Aeronautics and Space Administration (NASA) attempted to build a machine, or robot, which could ride a bicycle, apparently for the purpose of analyzing remote-control systems. Any normal child learns to do this in a very short time, but a machine sensitive to shifts in balance, speed, and direction to the extent necessary to keep the bicycle upright and moving turned out to be a monster so cumbersome that no bicycle could support it. The bicycle-riding machine was never carried through to the stage of building a product, NASA's engineers, we may be sure, being quite as aware as the rest of us that children can do it better, faster, and more cheaply.

The aim of the design process is always to produce an object that *does something:* A scissors has to cut, a shovel has to dig, a raincoat has to repel water, a key has to open locks, a chair has to support a body. So the designer is given a statement of the problem at the outset, and how his work turns out has to do with the way the problem is stated. Stating a problem clearly and completely is not nearly as easy as it may sound, which is apparently what the NASA engineers found out when they tried to learn how a machine might ride a bicycle. This happens to be a problem of enormous complexity, but even simpler problems are difficult to describe.

One of the things the designer learns rather quickly is that in problem solving, the *limitations* are far more important than the freedoms. This seemingly harmless statement goes against almost everything we have learned. Creative people, we are told, need freedom so that they can express themselves without hindrance, but this is not true, assuming that the limitations are real.

Consider one of the minor Old Testament heroes, the young David. His problem was the giant Goliath, who was making life miserable for everyone with his forays and depredations. There was no apparent way to cope since Goliath was bigger and stronger by far than anyone else. David's problem was to find a better design for self-defense. He might have sat down and fantasized a twentieth-century Uzi light machine gun, which would certainly have done the job in short order, but the limitation, of course, was that the technology was lacking. For the same reason, he could not even have imagined the gun. What he did realize, after much thought, was that in combat generally, the greater the striking range, the better the chances of surviving. One possibility he had was to throw rocks at the giant and hope that one would find its mark before he had to run for it. But throwing a stone with lethal force is a solution with inherent limitations as well. The missile may miss, or if it hits, the impact may be insufficient to stop the attacker. We all know the story and its happy ending: Given the strong limitations of technology and available materials, David ended up with a sling. The virtues of this implement are portability, great accuracy once the needed skill is developed, and obedience to another law of physics, which says that available force may be multiplied by using the principle of the lever.

David, we may assume, was a bright boy, but the real point of the story has to do with listing the limitations which always exist, and finding ways to cope with them. In order to ascertain the real limitations of a product, a great deal of information is needed. There is the available range of possible materials, which has grown very large. There is the question of production methods, about which no decision is possible unless one has an idea of how many of the objects are to be made, for the tooling required is costly and can be economical only for long production runs. Furthermore, if one went out to borrow a million dollars to tool up for a product with possible annual sales of only a few hundred items, it is unlikely that a banker could be found who would lend the money.

In fact, the question of markets and marketing can affect the quality of the design in a variety of ways. To understand this, one has only to think back to the ways in which products used to be made and sold. Before furniture factories took over, the customer who needed a set of dining-room furniture went to a cabinetmaker. He could explain what he wanted, show the room in which it was to go, tell the maker how much he could afford. It was a one-to-one relationship, and even if the cabinetmaker did not particularly like his customer, he at least knew whom he was dealing with. In his statement of the design problem, whether he wrote it down or simply tucked it away in his head, he was already familiar with many of the limitations. The customer, on his side, often became a part of the process. Let us say that what he wanted was dining furniture made of rosewood. The cabinetmaker might have to tell him that rosewood was extremely costly, and that it was very hard and difficult to work. This then became a limitation for the buyer, who would have to decide whether to pay the price or to accept something more practical, like mahogany.

The statement of the problem, including limitations, was thus constructed in a give-and-take manner and choices were based on real information. This is not what happens now. The customer today, for all but the simplest handicrafts, is an unknown statistical entity. Surveys have to be made to discover some of the characteristics of the buyer; no one knows the size of his dining room or, more likely, dining area. In this practically universal situation, the designer and the manufacturer work with skimpy and imprecise information and do the best they can. At the same time the buyer has a greatly reduced range of possible products, and he usually ends up settling for something that but approximates what he would really like.

Another problem comes up when marketing takes over. A minority of the possible buyers may be well-educated people; the majority certainly are not. Generally speaking—although this does not hold true for all cases—an educated individual is better equipped to deal with novelty than one who is not. He has been to school longer, is exposed to more influences, probably travels more, certainly reads more, and may know a larger group of people who do interesting work. Confronted with change, say a piece of modern furniture when he was thinking of something reminiscent of nineteenth-century models, he may not like it, but he is much better equipped to understand it and even to accept it. His uneducated counterpart is not likely to be so tolerant. Fearful of change in almost any form, he clings to the comfort of familiar things; his responses tend to be more rigid. In home furniture this comes across very clearly in the stores, where the best-selling merchandise is likely to be classifiable as kitsch.

With regard to the question of limitations and freedoms, David accepted the limitations surrounding his problem of self-defense because they were real. Stones and leather were available to him but not a great deal more. However, the young designer who today finds himself employed by a manufacturer of mass-produced home furniture may find himself intolerably restricted to a series of undesirable options. This is a real lack of freedom, because the designer in such a situation has no way at all of setting up a statement of the problem that will allow him to reach a superior solution. The statement of the problem as given says: "Design some ornate furniture that will suggest furniture of this or that period to the uninformed customer, but don't really try for accurate reproductions because it would cost too much and that isn't what the customers want anyway." His instructions, then, are to design a piece of cheap fakery.

The only creative freedom that is worth anything, in other words, is found in setting up a problem so that it can be solved intelligently. Because consumer-product design is often overly concerned with taste and the market, much of it is mediocre, while survival design, which includes tools, is more basic and can reach high levels of appropriateness. In those art museums that display collections of obsolete military items, such as armor, swords, shields, and crossbows, these can be freely admired as superb solutions to problems of form, materials, and construction. The fact that none of this equipment could stand up for a minute against a .22-caliber rifle has nothing to do with the case. In its time and place it was the best that could be produced and this expression of quality still comes through.

In the course of developing his design, the individual involved generally assumes a fairly experimental attitude. Listen to a group of designers discussing a problem and you hear ideas being tossed around very freely, and accepted or rejected with great equanimity. They all know that there is not likely to be an all-time best answer, and what they are looking for is an answer *that will work.* They also know that the deeper they penetrate into the problem, whatever it is, the greater the chances for a high quality solution.

Protective armor can be appreciated for its superb solutions to the survival design problems of form, material, and construction.

This phase of the process, symbolized by the making of rapid sketches and rough models, is one of indefinite duration. It is close to impossible to predict in advance the length of a search, which is usually established by practical outside factors, like budgetary limitations or pressure of time, such as the client's need to have a product ready for some predetermined date of introduction. Experienced designers and laboratory researchers, who have a similar problem, usually learn how to relate the pace and scope of their efforts to the limitations.

The world of electronics has come up with devices that greatly expand the range of the designer's work and the speed with which he does it. Some computer-aided design (CAD) systems can make drawings of an object, rotate the drawings on a video screen so that the object can be seen from any desired viewpoint, show the inside of the object as well as the outside, and even predict what would happen to it in case of impact.

While such developments will affect designers and draftsmen of all types, but chiefly those at the lower end of the spectrum of skills, the process itself will not change materially from what it was a long time ago. Changing from manual drawing to computerized production will indeed speed things up; it will also expand the range of the designer's search, for the computer can be programmed to develop more views, more alternatives, with great speed. It will even show better responses to the statement of the problem and will quite possibly modify the statement itself in the interest of greater depth and precision. But it will also be used for turning out as many mediocre and unimaginative products as are turned out now.

The design process is a framework within which we can insert a series of components. Computer-aided design can expand and enrich some of these components. However, there are considerations which do not yet comfortably fit within these impressive electronic systems, for example, how does one factor in those elements that make the difference between a routine and creative approach to a problem? At the moment, the machine is unable to do this.

It is a cliché that some occupations are creative, while others are not. Being an artist, for instance, is automatically accepted as a creative occupation, while being a banker, say, is not. There is no demonstrable truth in such judgments. Creativity is a quality possessed by individuals. I doubt if anyone understands completely how this comes to be. Watching small children play, one has the impression that they are all full of imagination, with much talent for free improvisation, although closer observation would probably reveal that some are more lively, in a creative sense, than others.

One of the requirements of the creative act is that something has to be destroyed before something else can be created. To make an omelet, as we often hear, you first have to break the eggs. To become a Cubist painter, it was necessary to destroy an entire way of looking at reality. In order to make his theory of a heliocentric system stick, Copernicus had to attack the prevailing Ptolemaic system. In other words, the creative act requires the courage to fly in the face of accepted wisdom, and it is not surprising that only a limited number of individuals have what it takes to face the risks of creative action. If one digs down to the core of the design process at its best, one is likely to find someone with an ability to identify and to deal with the creation-destruction polarity.

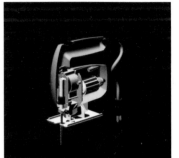
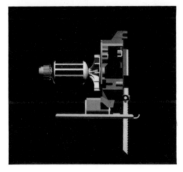

A computer-aided design system can contribute greatly to the design and engineering of a product. The computer can describe the product —here a Black & Decker jigsaw designed on the Computervision CAD/CAM system—from any angle, inside or out; it can rotate the object and show it in cut-away or exploded views.

These are all brave words, no doubt, full of approval for realistic appraisals of limitations and the virtues of creative behavior. At the very end of the line, nonetheless, the social context is going to determine to a very large extent, the ends toward which the means (the design process itself) are directed. An excessively materialistic society like our own will have excessively materialistic ends, and it is not possible for any individual, no matter how talented and courageous, to step very far outside his time. Whenever we hear of some great creative spirit and how far ahead of his time he was said to be, a closer inspection shows that he was only at the most rapidly moving edge of his time, not outside it at all. This appears in small things as well as large. The ill-fated Chrysler "Airflow," one of the re-sounding failures in automotive history, was in reality a design not unlike those we see around us today; it was not out of its time, it was just far enough ahead of the prevailing tastes so that people would not buy it.

The 1934 Chrysler "Airflow" was just a little beyond prevailing taste, making it a failure in the marketplace.

Nobody likes real originality, regardless of what he may say, because it always poses a threat to an entrenched sense of what is safe and suit-able. The degree of resistance always varies with the perception of the magnitude of the threat. For example, the introduction of the quartz watch movement obsoleted a craft that had existed for centuries. The public, however, had no problem in dealing with it because the watches continued to look much as they had; when digital readouts came into the picture, they were a novelty that took on the proportions of a fad, but traditional watches continue to be bought by a large market.

Going through the entire design process, which includes the important collaborations all the way down the line, with materials people, engineers, technicians in specialized areas, and marketing people, the steady movement is in the direction of a solution that is ultimately seen, not as beautiful, but as *appropriate.* The creation of beauty cannot be an aim; beauty is one of the aspects of appropriateness, and it still lies pretty much in the eye of the beholder, which makes it a by-product rather than a goal.

There is very powerful support for this view in nature, which is always the best model to be followed, for God, so to speak, is still the best designer. People who work with natural organisms at any scale, such as biologists, are endlessly confronted with the fact that beauty in nature is invariably the expression of some function or other. The color of flowers is bait for the insects, which do the pollinating; the extraordinary markings on orchids are, for these insects, the clearest directional signs imaginable, showing them the proper route to take; the spectacular displays of peacocks and birds of paradise are functional elements in courtship. Everything in organic nature functions in relation to survival needs; we find these things beautiful, because as creatures of nature we are programmed to respond to evidence of appropriateness as an expression of beauty. For mathematicians, and for scientists generally, words like "elegant," "appropriate," and "beautiful" are synonymous.

Beauty in nature functions according to survival needs: The markings on these orchids are signposts leading insects to pollen.

All of this was common, intuitive knowledge in simpler times. Modern populations, which are largely isolated from the processes of designing and manufacturing by remote, windowless factories girded with chain link fences, have to be taught these things, which formerly came naturally. Once they are learned we can look forward again to livable, appropriate cities and products which are a joy to have and use, and to a life that will be richer. As things are right now, such a happy outcome is not an overnight affair. This is why presentations such as this are indispensable.

Design and Technology   Niels Diffrient

Niels Diffrient is an independent
industrial designer primarily
concerned with the design and
development of innovative
products growing from human-
factors research. He is co-author of
Humanscale, a series of volumes
on human-factors engineering,
and the designer of two ergonomically sound office-seating systems
for Sunar and Knoll.

Design and technology are both synonymous with the activities of human existence. Everyone is to some degree a designer and a technologist. When one plans a meal, for example, the menu is designed by an intuitive and organized choice involving skill and perhaps also artistry. In the preparation of a meal, an ordered and systematic exercise of cooking skills brings it to fruition, while a talented use of design and technology can result in a moment of aesthetic satisfaction. This simple example illustrates to some degree how we are all involved in design and technology, although we do not apply these terms to what we do.

Design in the context of this presentation is clearly understood as product design, an esoteric practice largely centered on the study and application of practical aesthetics. This differs from purely aesthetic endeavors such as painting and sculpture, which have no practical use as an end result: a carved statue is not used for opening beer bottles, nor is a painting rolled down over a window to keep out the afternoon sun. These works exist for their own sake and for the pleasure of the beholder.

Practical aesthetics, according to one personal and very loose definition, which however has a wide acceptancy, says that a useful object has a "natural" form, which when it is in complete harmony with its function is perceived as having a special "rightness" or "fit" that borders on art. Those who devote their time to the subject tacitly claim an unerring sense of judgment in functional aesthetics, to the degree that their selections occupy space in museums of art.

Technology, on the other hand, must currently be perceived as the business of large, bureaucratic organizations with vast power to manufacture millions upon millions of functional, and not so functional, products. Nearly all the day-to-day products that are consumed come from mass-production facilities and have resulted in an elevated way of life for all of us. In the past, only the well-to-do could afford the kinds of products that almost everyone can own today, and indeed, takes for granted.

Ironically, while almost everyone uses and accepts the products of technology, most users disdain interest in the subject and openly confess to ignorance of it. And, while there may be more vitality of expression in reacting to product appearance, informed understanding of it is nonetheless equally low. This is not to say that people are incapable of expressing good taste or of understanding the basics of technology. It is simply that in daily terms design and technology seem as remote as nuclear physics or brain surgery. There is one major difference, however: Most of us will never have to deal in either of these scientific subjects, but we are involved in judgments of aesthetics and technology with every purchase of a mass-produced product.

What becomes very clear from this limited discourse is that the public is largely uninformed about design and technology. Certainly neither subject is taught as part of the general education process and little discussion of it appears in the media or literature destined for broad consumption. What is perhaps even more astounding is that there are virtually no courses in design, and few in technology, taught by schools of business administration even though it is their graduates who most often will be responsible for managing these practices.

The practical result of public ignorance of the finer points of design and technology is that we cannot look to the public for direction based on buying patterns. The purchasing power of an enlightened populace would be one of the most effective ways to assure better products. Admitting the lack of consumer direction, we must look to the other principals in the field—on the design side, to the designers themselves. These practitioners are usually industrial designers, but many architects and some sculptors and craftsmen also engage in this activity and contribute to the aesthetics of mass-produced products. While their skills and talents vary widely, the predominant characteristic of this group is that the locus of their ability is aesthetics.

When most designers voice their aesthetic philosophy today it is generally some version of "form follows function." Yet not being competent in the technology of function, most designers interpret this as aesthetics that *imply* function, not necessarily that which the object in question manifests but the style believed by the designer and others involved to be appropriate to the function, such as redundant and complex controls on appliances to imply advanced technology and service; high-tech facades on electronic equipment (tuners, amplifiers, televisions) to imply advanced performance; cosmetic and personal-care packaging to imply eternal youthfulness; plastic simulated wood to imply friendliness and warmth.

Olof Bäckström's scissors for Fiskars (V-4) is a very successful design in which the form follows the natural forces of manual operations.

Those with true genius in this pursuit sometimes manage to arrive at the magic combination of factors that gives us a living "classic." The more usual result, however, is that much of design is very bad, while a great deal of the remaining good design is found in simple objects that can be readily comprehended by the designer—furniture, tableware, small appliances, lighting, and the like. In these cases, the designer assumes the limited role of a technologist in order to coordinate the function of the object with the desired aesthetic.

In more complex electromechanical products, however, the designer cannot control, even to a small degree, the full spectrum of forces that determines the nature of a modern mass-produced product. As a result, to be effective, he must fall back on a kind of mystique centered on the appropriate relationship (intuitively felt) of applied aesthetics to perceived function. Occasionally this produces star performances by highly gifted and charismatic designers, Raymond Loewy, for example, who can alter product direction by force of personal will. But, mostly, the lesser designer is relegated to being what Ralph Caplan refers to as "an exotic menial."[1] The current complex of products has made the simplistic sweep of a star performance virtually impossible. As a result most designers have drifted into the corporation and team efforts. Under such circumstances it is no wonder that only about fifteen hundred industrial designers are registered with the Industrial Designers Society of America. This is a very meager ratio to the technological side of the equation even though the basic thrust of the design activity is exactly what modern products need to make them better.

It is no secret that the United States has slipped in many respects in the area of product development and production. It was once said that foreign (largely Japanese) products sold only because they could be produced cheaply as a result of cheap labor. The statistics show this is the case only in a small number of instances. It is true that foreign products may often cost less, but the major savings now come not from lower labor costs but from better product development and production practices. The Japanese, and some Europeans, have provided actual examples of how a well-integrated

1. Ralph Caplan, *By Design* (New York, 1982), p. 109.

design function can assist in producing a higher quality product. These products, in addition, come closer to that elusive rightness of the aesthetic and have become the very examples that many American products are now modeled after.

While the design process is not as developed as it could be in America, its broader use in product development would surely improve the quality and the appeal of products. This is not so much because designers are magicians who can mysteriously accomplish this feat; rather, more realistically, it is that the other forces in a corporation must have a wholesome attitude in order to make full use of design. In other words, when design is being fully utilized it suggests that most other aspects of a company are in good balance.

According to Richard Goodwin, "bureaucracy is the logic of technology."[2] This is true in many ways; the by-product of a large and complex technology is bureaucracy. Since design of complex products involves dealing with a bureaucratic institution, design fares poorly because it lacks a compelling economic rationale and is thus virtually powerless within the corporate structure. This is perhaps best summed up in the old saying that nothing ever failed to sell because of bad taste.

As long as design is built on a foundation of applied aesthetics this will be the case. How insubstantial this base of existence is can be illustrated by the fact that many of the most awesome examples of industrial aesthetics are created entirely without the help of a designer: the external form of a jet airplane, the printed electronic circuit board, shop and production tools, ships' propellers, guns, submarines, scientific equipment, and perhaps most impressive of all, the artifacts of space exploration. These are not only impressive visually but they have also inspired styles that designers apply to other products. This may be all right when military uniforms set the style for dress fashion, but it is inappropriate when jets or rockets inspire the shape of an automobile.

As long as designers are disenfranchised from the technological function of mass-produced products, they can only, and very often do, pursue style to excess and merely for fashion. Clearly, they need a more intimate involvement with the determinants of product function and technology. But, having said this, one must reflect on the fact that most manufacturers, in their current state of bureaucratic complexity, really do not have their technology that well in hand either, at least not in the area of consumer-related products, those items that are beyond what is strictly technical.

There is one area of product development with great potential but little understood value where the designer might very well marry his skills with a new understanding of function. Quite simply, he can direct his work toward a better understanding of the interrelationship of the human and the product: how safe, comfortable, convenient, and enjoyable this connection can be.

It is tacitly assumed within the corporate structure that the market is understood through the buying patterns of the public. But sales statistics alone overlook the potential for deeper human satisfaction. Today there are refreshing signs of a new approach to marketing and product development, which has grown out of the field that started in the military during the Second World War called, rather coldly, "human engineering."

In Europe the field is known as "ergonomics" and is so important in

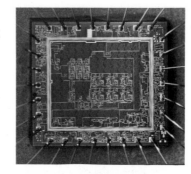

The Ferranti semiconductor chip on a contact panel (greatly enlarged), the Hasselblad 1600E single-lens reflex camera, and the Explorer I satellite were given their "aesthetic" forms without the aid of designers.

The aesthetically impressive forms of the Lockheed SR-71 jet airplane result from adherence to functional principles of design.

The 1959 Cadillac "Coupe de Ville" shows the misapplication of the functional forms of jet planes for aesthetic effect, quite different from the Ford "Sierra XR4," which follows the functional dictates of airflow.

2. Richard N. Goodwin, *The American Condition* (Garden City, N.Y., 1974), p. 353.

Diagram with percentile measurements of United States males and females is one of the many tools of human engineering published in *Humanscale*. This compendium of data, compiled by Henry Dreyfuss Associates for over thirty years, is used by architects, engineers, and designers for designing objects for maximum efficiency, comfort, and safety.

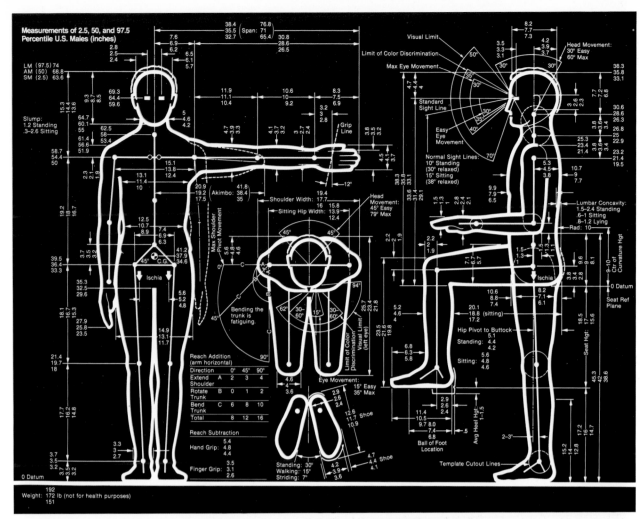

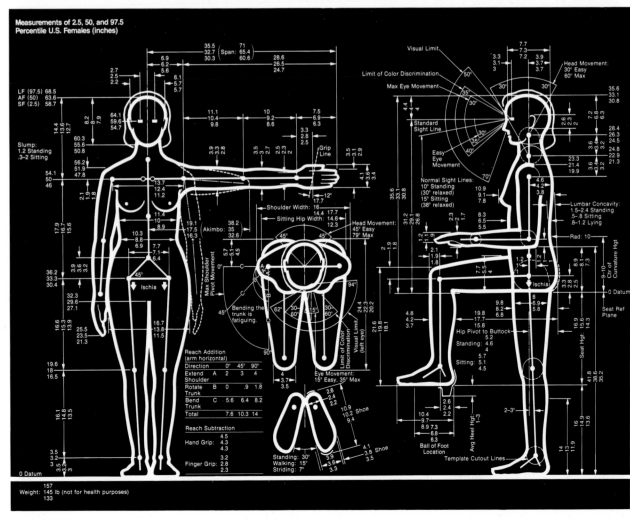

such countries as West Germany and Sweden that product compliance to human needs has been enacted into law. This is not limited to product safety standards but extends much further into the areas of comfort, convenience, and reduction of stress. These standards provide the basis for a new understanding of function. Where function was always taken to mean the inherent mechanical action of the product, it now also means the compatibility of the product with the user. Here certainly is a common ground for the engineer and the designer. There is ample basis for scientific verification of the physiological, psychological, and sociological aspects of a product-to-person relationship.

Ergonomics can also provide, for the designer, a way to achieve the same kind of integrated form and function that the engineer accomplishes naïvely. With increased understanding of the interrelationship of product and person, there grows a product performance program emphasizing human compliance as pervasive as the electromechanical requirements. Aesthetics can find their root in this understanding and be not only appropriate but also innovative.

Perhaps best of all, consideration of human factors makes good business sense. A business manager or marketing person supplied with quantifiable and comparable data of true human attitudes can make better business and product decisions. Finally, there is a strong basis to believe that the integration of human factors into a substantial proportion of a manufacturer's research and development activity will intrinsically evolve a healthy and amendable technology.

Two ergonomically designed chairs by Niels Diffrient, the "Helena" chair for Sunar and the "Advanced Operational" chair for Knoll

Design and Society   Marco Zanuso

Marco Zanuso has considered
design and its role in society from
various vantage points throughout
his career, as designer of appliances, furniture, and lighting using
new methods, materials, and technology; as editor of the design magazines *Domus* and *Casabella;* and as
professor in the faculty of architecture at the Politecnico in Milan.

To understand the relationship between design and society, one must first understand those aspects of today's culture that are structurally related to the role of the designer. To do so, one should begin by examining certain mechanisms set into motion by the industrial revolution; indeed, if design is to be identified with industrial design, it must be considered a phenomenon brought into being not so much by the mere presence of industries as by the advent of industrialized society.

In preindustrial rural and artisan society, technological know-how and formal expression tended to develop in a harmonious relationship as raw material evolved toward a finished product. The outcome was determined by the individual capabilities of the craftsman and by the specific means and methods at his disposal. The actual design of the object was thus wholly encompassed in the act of making/creating in a unity of time and place. This unity implied not only the physical work space, imbued as it was with that special atmosphere of communication and interpretation of diversified meaning systems, but also the single working community on a broader social level, expressed through the artisans' guilds. It was in the artisan's shop, I believe, that the greatest integration of capability, communication, creativity, and production was ever attained.

Among the many and far-reaching effects of the industrial revolution—effects which continue to define our lives today both as individuals and, collectively, as society—is the separation in time and space of the act of design from the act of production. Design thus becomes isolated as an autonomous and distinct activity, while the means of communication and representation, equally isolated, are conditioned by machines and their management. A new engineers' culture is formed around new roles, capabilities, and modes of technical knowledge, thus defining a new intellectual sphere characterized by theoretical and applicative research and calculation.

Although the integration of the processes underlying artisan production is thus destroyed, this new design role broadens the scope of possibilities offered by the industrial revolution, and allows design to take a key position in the rapport between nature and culture; this impetus is a clear expression of a technical will to appropriate the human environment through objects, tools, and structures.

It is possible to identify two specific ways in which the design process is influenced and structured by the mechanisms of industrialized society. The first results from the autonomous definition of design in a theoretical and intellectual sense, namely the close ties the design process necessarily develops with activities related to scientific and technological research.

Interesting examples may be found in a number of early armchairs and sofas that I designed. Immediately after the Second World War, the Pirelli company presented me with some samples of a new material—foam rubber—and asked me to investigate possibilities for its applications. Numerous experiments made it apparent that the implications for the field of upholstered furniture were enormous; it would revolutionize not only padding systems but also structural, manufacturing, and formal possibilities. As prototypes began to take exciting new formal definitions, a company was established to put these models, such as the "Lady" armchair (III-94), into production on an industrial scale never before imagined. That company, Arflex, is still one of the major furniture manufacturers in Italy today.

The outcome of close collaboration between the designer Marco Zanuso and the research department of Pirelli, the "Lady" armchair (III-94) was developed for mass production in a series of specialized operations, with the upholstery and the foam-rubber padding being fully integrated into the structure of the seat, arms, and back.

In the case of the "Lambda" chair (III-95), the research component had its own investigative design structure totally detached from the world of industrial manufacture. The commission for a kitchen chair had originally been resolved in a more conventional manner, but just at this stage in the design process we began to examine the hypothesis of making a chair entirely out of sheet metal, in a continuous system of structural support and seating surfaces. The formal and structural implications of this concept took several years and required more than fifty prototypes to develop it to the point of industrial production, and the end product was manufactured by a company that approached our office only in the final stages of development. But even at this point, research in our office continued. In connection with a commission to design classroom furniture for the city of Milan, we had already been experimenting with a scaled-down stacking version of the "Lambda" for elementary schools. As we were looking for alternatives to sheet metal, a material inappropriate for this particular application, a notable drop in the price of polyethylene on the expiration of international patents, opened up completely new possibilities. This new material, in turn, led to a rethinking of the formal and structural characteristics of the chair and, consequently, to much additional research. The final result, the Kartell child's chair (III-96), surprised even us; because of the various stacking possibilities we had developed as a result of structural requirements imposed by the use of polyethylene, we had created a chair that was also a toy, which would stimulate a child's fantasy in his construction of castles, towers, trains, and slides. At the same time it was indestructible, and soft enough that it could not harm anyone yet too heavy to be thrown.

If these examples illustrate the fundamental relationship between scientific and technological research and the role of the designer, they also reveal much about the second important characteristic of industrialized society and its effect on the design process. With the separation of design from the place and act of production and, consequently, with the increased ties with scientific and technological research, an ever-larger number of specialized working groups contributes to the total definition of a product. The result is that both the industrially produced object and the process leading to its definition and design acquire an ever-greater degree of complexity. This becomes true to the point that, unlike the case of the artisan's workshop, no single person can be said to have complete grasp of every aspect of the design process. This very important phenomenon means that in response to the complex nature of the structure of the object and the various contributions of specialized working groups, the role of the designer becomes increasingly concerned with the integration of these various components and the management and control of the interactions among them.

An example of this can be found in the early sewing machines I designed for Borletti. The starting point was the concept of manufacturing the machine casing in die-cast aluminum rather than in cast iron, as had hitherto been done, so that the resulting pieces could be given a more complex and precise form. This meant joining the entire internal mechanism with the supports that would become an integral part of the interior of the housing. It was thus necessary to redesign the entire machine inside and out; the design process required the coordination of the technicians who had knowledge of the various functional aspects.

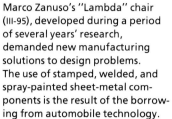

Marco Zanuso's "Lambda" chair (III-95), developed during a period of several years' research, demanded new manufacturing solutions to design problems. The use of stamped, welded, and spray-painted sheet-metal components is the result of the borrowing from automobile technology.

Polyethylene, used for Marco Zanuso and Richard Sapper's child's chair (III-96), had specific structural requirements that opened up new formal possibilities, including the stacking and construction features suited to a chair for children.

In the Borletti sewing machine, designed by Marco Zanuso in conjunction with a group of technicians, the mechanical systems were grouped around the internal support structures.

A similar example can be found in the Brionvega "Doney" television set (I-51). As this was to be the first completely transistorized television designed in Europe, precedents for the circuit layout design were lacking. Again the job had to be done from scratch, and the problem again involved coordination of the various experts involved in tandem with various phases of research and experimentation. The end result, as in the case of the Borletti sewing machine, is distinguished by a total integration of formal, structural, operative, and manufacturing solutions through a procedure comparable to systems engineering. I believe the absolutely innovative characteristics of the design of these products are largely due to the level of integration achieved in response to the complexity of the factors originally generated by scientific and technological research.

The "Doney" portable television (I-51), designed by Marco Zanuso and Richard Sapper for Brionvega, was the first fully transistorized television designed in Europe (1962). Achieving a total integration of formal and functional elements, its components are grouped in four parts according to function—power, reception, emission, screen—while the overall form is governed by the size and shape of the picture screen.

A significant result of these factors can be seen in the modified nature of the object of the design process. In this context, the design moment is aimed not uniquely toward the formal definition of a single object but rather toward the configuration of a systemic process in which the original object is "open" to programmed modifications. These can thus grow naturally out of the original physical configuration, not in a casual and contradictory manner but as an extension of the evolutionary possibilities explicitly inherent in the overall governing concept and concretely embodied in the original realization. It is evident that in this conception of the design process, the formulation of the systemic structure that governs these transformations assumes primary importance for the role of the designer.

A final factor introduced in the design process by the nature of industrialized society deserves mention, for it is emerging today with increasing importance. The growing complexity of the service economy and the ever-greater part public structures are called upon to play in the management of the social environment pose an ever-greater problem in the definition of the "client" in relation to public administrative and political structures. This is again a case in which the role of the designer is a necessary moment in the continuity of the process through which our culture inhabits the public domain. A reevaluation of this role in relation to the dynamic interaction between the end user, the manufacturing apparatus, and the nature of the commission under which the designer professionally operates is required. More and more the designer's job becomes one of the integration of complex systems. The feeble success rate of recent efforts in such areas as street furniture and pedestrian spaces underlines the lack of awareness of the nature of this problem. This can be seen in the difficulty of defining specific roles for the various groups who must necessarily converge in order to confront the design process at this level, and provides continued evidence that the role of the designer in relation to society cannot be defined in static terms.

It should by now be evident that these and other conditions that the increasingly industrialized productive structure imposes on the design process require a more rigorous technical-scientific approach as the necessary and indispensable means of operation and communication. This approach must be far more exacting than that implied by those who, on the one hand, flee to more- or less-inspired reminiscent dreams and those who, on the other, entrench themselves in sterile positions of technological determinism and are incapable of responding to the growing complexity of the design process.

The problem is not whether consciously or agnostically to refute scientific and technological research (to which there do not seem to be any viable alternatives), but in both the cultural and social sense, to reappropriate control over science and technology. Only by displacing the notion of a technocratic society with that of acculturized technology is it possible to configure a design culture in a dimension of greater responsibility where values take the place of gratification. In the same sense, real creativity can emerge from the boundaries of subliminal consciousness only through the awareness and knowledge by which it can manifest itself in concrete reality.

Recent discussions on the nature of the "new professionalism" are aimed at a better understanding of the professional role of the designer, the meaning of the design process, and the responsibilities involved in it. One aspect of this debate centers on participatory design methods as a means of making a conscious commitment toward further understanding of public needs and a consequent redefinition of roles. In this context, an awareness of the various components that contribute to the complexity of the design process is ever-more important.

Understandably, the democratic nature of design depends on adherence to a careful interpretation of need expressed through broadened participation. But it is also a question of the management of the converging forces involved in the creative process and the appropriation of the technological and scientific tools and resources available. It is this fundamental aspect of acculturized participation that is able to guarantee fully a renewed creativity in response to social needs in a coherent, expressive context.

In this manner, design culture, rather than expressing itself through isolated moments of intuition and numeric calculation, can once again communicate through the multiplicity of functions and complex interdisciplinary interactions on a unified cybernetic level. In saying "once again," I am referring to the model of the artisan in preindustrial society discussed above, where the integration of function and meaning grew spontaneously out of the unity of design, creativity, craft, and production. Reestablishing a design culture in cybernetic union with, and not enslaved by, awareness means recovering a quality of communication and language capable of a reciprocal dialogue with creative design. This underlines the necessity of a continued openness toward innovative and alternative directions in research whose implications and interpretations lead to new, more authentic, and less conformist cultural possibilities.

The design process, then, must be identified with the entire range of programmed decision-making activities. The design of the actual manufactured object may be the most important phase of the process, but without a precise reference to the entire system of which it is a part, it loses meaning and the capacity to respond to the needs that generated its original definition. The goal, then, is to be found in the structure of the design process, where an operative praxis clearly identifies the role of the designer in a context that is in line with technical-scientific evolution and thus with modern culture.

It is necessary to go beyond the dualism of a design activity vacillating between art and technology, culture and practice, and experiential expression and operative realities without favoring one extreme at the expense of the other. Design activity, in order to fulfill its role in an industrialized society, needs the support of the vast and diversified technical, scientific, and humanistic resources from that society.

In addition to creative capabilities, then, the designer must have the specific capacity to coordinate and integrate these diverse activities and knowledge structures. The role of the designer in society is not to translate the accumulation of specialized research or to optimize the economic and manufacturing functions into concrete reality, but rather to convey, through the creative process, a suggestion, an idea capable of synthesizing those elements and judging and expressing the present historical and social context, which has always led design to be considered the meaningful embodiment of the society that generates it.

Design, Invention, and Fantasy

Olivier Mourgue

During the 1960s Olivier Mourgue was the most celebrated industrial designer in France, creating much publicized series of furniture and environments, as well as the interiors of the French government pavilions at Montreal (1967) and Osaka (1970). Today, from the vantage point of his life in a small village in Brittany where he both designs simple objects and paints watercolors, he views design as a broader involvement in life, as changing not objects and environments but human attitudes.

Beginning in the 1960s, I sought through successive constructions—toy seats, sitting rugs, canvas wall organizers, animated canvases—to separate myself from the great family of designers. I have never felt at ease among them. Functionalism and rationalism cannot be the goal of design, an end in themselves; they are simply part of the honesty required for the construction of an object. I have the feeling that one must pursue other paths, and the condition of visual poetry interests me. I also find it more appropriate to call myself a *constructeur,* a builder.

Reality seems to me to lie more in the streets, shops, and large department stores, in the everyday object, in working tools. One must pay attention and observe. It seems to me in 1983 that it would be important to take stock of all the objects on earth, a great classification operation and a lesson in humility. There are many ways of speaking about objects; personally, I would be happy to address the subject "Hardware and Its Environment." I spend hours in hardware stores on all my trips, looking and observing with childish pleasure. One could proceed with the methodology of an ethnologist and assemble in one place hardware from all over Europe, Scandinavia, Asia, the United States, the Soviet Union, and South America, using films to show the object in its use and development.

Environmental habitat created by Olivier Mourgue for "Visiona 3" in 1971

Charles Eames has shown us that well-constructed objects are so in the invention of details, or transitions, or connections between different materials; in some way, there is harmony in the ensemble.

The object lives its life, which can be long. Its environment is multiple, and intelligible objects may exist side by side even when they come from different periods. In the harmony of which I speak, there is the weight of objects. This harmony means perfect precision in the use of the material. There is no perfect environment, incoherence is part of life, and people's houses are often incoherent. Fantasy and memories can exist side by side with the object of high technology, and this is a good thing. Life is like that, full of chance, encounters, contradictions.

The good object is very movable and displaceable; inventions and creations are light. It was in this spirit that I constructed my "Djinn" seats (III-54). In these models, simple in their construction—a curved metal tube and some foam rubber—I was looking for several things: the use of new covering materials (jersey, a stretch fabric), but also lightness, so that one could carry it under one's arm. The models were round and in bright colors.

Sitting rug by Olivier Mourgue (1966)

At the same time, I was concerned with something else: the floor seat, or seating surfaces. How uncomfortable it was for three people to talk to each other while sitting on a sofa. In 1966 I designed and executed my first sitting rug. It was a woolen carpet that folded back to form a seat; four or five persons could sit on it.

There was an overall aspect that I had a lot of trouble getting people to understand. Creation means danger, raising problems and taking risks. One cannot expect immediate marketability, nor make it a firm's banner. A strategy is needed, a total commitment by the factory to invest in the tools, to have patience, and above all to stand fast in a choice, an industrial decision. To stand fast—that already eliminates a lot of people.

The year 1968 was a very important one for me. During that month of May, I certainly heard the demonstrations from my studio in Montparnasse. I watched and walked for hours in the midst of all those people in the street. For the first time everybody spoke to each other; there was a sense of regained solidarity, a postwar feeling.

Soon afterward, with a photographer friend whom I made sit in plywood cutouts, I constructed a person seat (III-55). It was called "Bouloum," the childhood nickname of this friend. It made people smile, but it was very comfortable. It used to scare me when I came home at night. I took it everywhere, in order to photograph it in different situations. I recall having made a number of photos in New York, in the neighborhood of Broome Street, in the midst of its black cast-iron architecture. It traveled as baggage on airplanes, and people truly laughed, which touched me very much. I wrote stories about "Bouloum." I would have liked to make a film about it.

Olivier Mourgue's "Bouloum" (III-55)

Creation is sometimes a cry, a reaction against something. Why go on designing objects that claim to be perfect but are already so numerous?

One cannot speak of objects without imagining other forms of instruction and new schools. Instruction at present concerns the measurable, the logical, the marketable. Instruction in the schools seems to ignore imagination, the staging of objects, pantomime, knowing how to place oneself in a space or before an exercise. For the coming years it will be necessary to take a different view. We must go back to the gaze of the child, be eight or ten years old again, and seek to marvel. Invention ought to preserve the dreamlike and poetic aspect, but at the same time have the precision of an engineer. I have the feeling that in the coming years our tools will change, their purpose will be different, and there will be other forms of expression of visual poetry.

In architecture and in objects there is a mystical or spiritual aspect, or one of fantasy. It seems to me very important to take a close look at traditional Japanese and Finnish and certain agricultural communities, for example, the Shakers. One should reread the sayings and rules of the Shakers: functionalism, beauty, order, and so forth.

It is also possible to imagine the "object" and the "marvelous" as something ephemeral, an accessory, a scene, a film, and to attain by its construction and presence a situation of fantasy.

One ought to conceive large carpentry workshops, with simple, essential tools—hammer, wood chisel, plane, saw—to carry out an entire operation of a basic nature. It is important that one's approach preserve touch, odors, sounds, silences, and the relations among the various materials.

There are some objects that attract the sympathy of adults and children; they are eternal in their proper visibility: a jeep, a tent, a glider, a chair, a bicycle, tools, and so on. Will they change? I think so, with materials and technological discoveries, but one can imagine their development and foresee it. At the same time, however, there will be situations, places, and objects that are completely invented, for example, the English collapsible stroller for transporting a child. In these areas, there is an enormous amount of work for which we must be prepared, but the working teams will be different. More and more there will be a flexible and high-technology "industrial craftsmanship," capable of responding to particular needs. New operations will be carried out in cities to construct particular places, small squares filled with fantasy, a restful visual poetry.

A habitat changes completely after new thought is given to the use of passive energies and their immediate application. Light can be diffused or focused, shadows studied as in traditional Japanese architecture, and mirrors used in architecture very scientifically.

It is necessary to set up or build neighborhood laboratories or workshops, or country workshops. For man should construct objects himself so as to understand them better. In this spirit I built a mobile studio in a truck for my own work, and I am still using it.

The progress of my work with toy seats, begun in 1968 with "Bouloum," was continued later with other seats. These toy seats have become a large family. There was, of course, the grandfather, "Bouloum," a person seat, but then all his offspring came along: leaf seat, butterfly seat, serpent seat, airplane seat, doll seats, kite seat, and recently bird seats. The materials, somewhat as in the theater, are deliberately simple: wood, canvas, and paint. I was looking for a language in the pieces, interchangeable elements, an object that could often be folded or dismantled.

Bird, butterfly, and doll seats by Olivier Mourgue (1974 and 1981)

Man has always invented while playing. I often look at the first flying machines built by man to study the principle of flight. Weight was the sworn enemy, as in that last solar airplane. I like to seek connections with flying objects from the beginning of the century. I am engrossed by the inventor aspect.

A whole form of design seems to me to have died since the seventies. I travel, I attend exhibitions, and the showrooms are very boring. Young people are not interested in them; they are in search of the "marvelous."

In the coming years, objects will be different. I remember a wonderful airplane that I had as a child. Pilotless, with tarlatan wings and a rubber band, it flew so well and soared endlessly; its very obvious construction was remarkably intelligent.

Gaiety in objects, enjoyment in their construction, in making them work—this to me seems very important, unlike repetitive objects or systems in which I don't have much interest. There are objects of the "popular" and "traditional" kind; they are separate, unique, ageless. In their life and humor they touch people endlessly, not just a tiny group, but the man in the street and the child.

Design for Market   Philip Rosenthal

Philip Rosenthal, chairman of the
Supervisory Board of Rosenthal AG,
served as president of the company
from 1958 to 1981. In 1954 he created
the Rosenthal Studio Line, a range
of consumer products designed by
artists and independent designers
in collaboration with staff
technicians.

What is a market? People, of course. People who produce, people who sell, and people who buy. This hasn't changed from the marketplace in ancient Greece to that on Fifth Avenue. Whether it's meat, motorcars, or Moore (Henry), it's still people who produce, people who sell, and people who buy. The only difference today is that there are no longer individuals but groups of people who make and sell, and even buy, because the power of makers and sellers tends to meld buyers into groups.

The motives, however, remain the same. The maker wants to get something for what he produces, the seller, for what he sells, the buyer, for what he buys. Get what? A profit, an increase in his material standard of living? Certainly! But again, he wants something more: an increase in his *mental* and *emotional* standard of living. This is something that has been underestimated in our industrial civilization: the satisfaction and pride the producer gets in making and selling a better product.

The Austrian artist Hundertwasser said: "A human being has three skins. First, the real skin; second, the clothes he or she wears; and third, his personal environment, i.e., his house, his room, his table." This first proposition—and it is not new, but we often tend to forget the obvious— stood behind the creation of the Rosenthal Studio Line in the 1950s: What could we make and sell in porcelain—and later, in ceramics, glass, and furniture—that would increase the mental prosperity of the makers, sellers, and buyers of these parts of the third skin?

This brought me to the second proposition (I should add that like the first and third propositions, which together form the ideology of the Studio Line, it was not the result of my own thinking but of contact with greater thinkers and greater designers: Walter Gropius, Richard Latham, Wilhelm Wagenfeld, Christian Wolters, and many others). History has shown that nothing that was an imitation and not a genuine expression by artists and designers of its time—from Greek vases to Meissen porcelain, from a Jacobean chair to one by Marcel Breuer—has ever maintained cultural or material value. Thus, we realized we had to find, motivate, and work with the genuine designers of our time.

But, the third proposition—in which direction? I remember the Deutscher Werkbund people telling me: The practical function of a cup or a glass is everything; shapes or reliefs or, above all, decorations that have no practical function are almost a crime. Now, pure functionalism was a necessary reaction to all the limitations and kitsch that eclecticism— perhaps with the exception of Art Nouveau—produced after the Rococo period. But like all necessary reaction, whether in politics or porcelain, it went too far; it destroyed the flowers with the weeds. The purely aesthetic function is genuine and important too, whether it be on a Greek column or a woman's dress. Once I arrived at this conclusion, it was a question of analyzing the necessary and acceptable part of the practical and aesthetic function of each article. The porcelain, glass, or furniture we make lies somewhere in between, because the things on a dinner table are there not only to refresh our stomachs but also to refresh our eyes. Even here there are differences. For a fork, more important than its appearance is that it fit our hands and can be used to spear a piece of meat or shovel peas to our mouths. For a coffeepot the aesthetic function is more permissible, as for instance, in Tapio Wirkkala's "Variation": The unequal and lively relief reveals the qualities of the porcelain, and the black saucer heightens the whiteness of the cup. Again with glass. One of my favorite

Tapio Wirkkala's "Variation" porcelain dinnerware

Kaj Franck's "Prisma" glass for Arabia, accepted for the Rosenthal Studio Line

glasses for water or fruit juice is Arabia's "Prisma": The only deliberately aesthetic touch is the slight angle of the rim, but this makes the glass come to life. Very different is the "Maître" series of crystal stemware by Michael Boehm, with thirteen different glasses for sixty-six different beverages. Certainly, any goblet must be functional—wide to let the champagne bubble, enclosed to keep the bouquet of burgundy. Even the thickening of the stem has a function, because it allows the glass to be held more easily with thumb and fingers, but the glass bubble in the "Maître" stem is there purely for aesthetic reasons.

Michael Boehm's "Maître" crystal stemware

Bjørn Wiinblad's "Tulipa" candlesticks: Candlelight is not necessary for eating; it is an aesthetic means to make people look more enchanting. The different heights of the "Tulipa" series make the light of one candlestick reflect on the bubbles of the taller ones.

Bjørn Wiinblad's "Tulipa" crystal candleholders

Flower vases: Flowers on the table are aesthetic, not functional, and you could put them in simpler vases than those of Johan Van Loon. But his method of rolling porcelain very thin and letting it swell in waves not only brings out a special quality of the material but also makes it one with the flowers, which also are not symmetrical.

Victor Vasarely: To me Vasarely is a great artist because he enlivens surfaces without destroying them. His vase has the function of holding flowers but, with or without them, it is a work of art. Or the tea set by Ernst Fuchs: You can certainly drink tea from it but its fantastic art content is greater. Paul Wunderlich's "Anubis" is a box, but mainly it is a work of art. Or the "Hombre" chair by Burkhard Vogtherr: Yes, it is comfortable. You can sit up straight for eating at the table, or you can lean back and your hand feels comfortable gripping the armrest. Continuing the rounded edge of the armrest down to the floor, however, is purely aesthetic, but it makes the chair.

Above: Johan Van Loon's "Parchment Porcelain" vases; Victor Vasarely's decoration on a porcelain vase; and Ernst Fuchs's "Magic Lake" porcelain tea service

Right: Paul Wunderlich's "Anubis" porcelain box

The question does not seem to me to be whether art or aesthetic content is permissible in an object as well as on the table and in the room. I believe there must be a balance of liveliness and calm, of the practical and the aesthetic. Two strong aesthetics destroy each other: If you use a coffee service designed by HAP Grieshaber or Eduardo Paolozzi, then the rest of the table must be monochromatic and quiet.

Even the division of fine art and design is not an historical one. From the temples of Greece to Rococo churches, from the thrones of the pharaohs to those of the lords and bishops of the Renaissance and Baroque eras, fine artists and designers (architects) worked together. There is no reason why art should be confined to the wall. For example, the bronze columns of Arnoldo Pomodoro's table are pure art, but they do not disturb the function; they support the table very well.

Burkhard Vogtherr's "Hombre" chairs and table

And which direction of art or design is the right one? There, we must remain modest. No plate or limited edition in the Rosenthal Studio Line is allowed to be produced under the trademark Rosenthal unless the majority of an independent jury agrees that it represents original art and design of our time. The same jury also selects objects from competitors that meet similar standards for about thirty Rosenthal Studio Houses throughout Europe—because in the struggle for genuine design, progressive firms must be allies as well as competitors. The Studio Houses are not allowed to display or sell any article made by Rosenthal or our competitors that has not been selected by these independent jurors. But even the jurors may be wrong. Whether someday a fantastic Bjørn Wiinblad will be considered

Arnoldo Pomodoro's glass and bronze table

more or less valuable than a restrained Herbert Bayer, only the future can tell. All we can do is to try to be producers—makers and promoters of what is genuine, and therefore may last.

Hans Theo Baumann, Tapio Wirkkala, Wilhelm Wagenfeld, Timo Sarpaneva, and Wiinblad have all worked for the Studio Line. The stylistic diversity among contemporary artists and designers results in no single approach in the Studio Line; instead it incorporates very different but genuine expressions of our time. This allows it to cushion stylistic changes and, culturally and economically, to reach not just one group but a wide range of buyers.

We have learned from the Bauhaus what many architects and artists of our time seem to have forgotten: the importance of the partnership of creative people, technicians, and the sensitive marketing man—he who knows not what the retailers or the public want now but what they may accept. In our experience this collaboration has not spoiled things but, on the contrary, has improved them. I have often found the great artists and designers —for instance, Henry Moore and Tapio Wirkkala—more open to creative cooperation than the average ones. The factory Walter Gropius designed for the Thomas glassworks seems to me another example of how the needs of production, the needs of better working conditions, the technical possibilities, and architectural creativity together have achieved much more than if either the architect or the technician had been dominant.

But what can realistic idealists in industry achieve? Art, architecture, and design have always been connected with power, whether it was the power of kings, of bishops, or of industry. The question is only what comes out: Is it good or bad?

Not too much will come out and succeed unless we alter our system of education, where we now learn more and more about being specialists in production and less and less about becoming satisfied human beings. This applies not only to physical health and to becoming members of a community but also to what we do not learn in our schools about our third skin. Only if through education we give children the chance to understand and love design and art in their personal surroundings, will they, as grown-ups, not be manipulated, but have the chance and the joy to choose their own pieces of their own third skins.

Walter Gropius's factory at Amberg, West Germany, for Thomas

**Design and the Consumer:
A View of the Sociology and
Culture of "Good Design"**

Herbert J. Gans

Herbert Gans, a sociologist, has
viewed the tastes and cultural
preferences of Americans in all
strata of society in his numerous
articles and books, including *The
Levittowners* (1967) and *Popular
Culture and High Culture* (1974).

We all choose consumer goods, entertainment, and art by applying taste, and taste is both personal and shared. In fact, a well-known popular analysis divides American society into three sets of shared tastes, or taste-cultures: highbrow, middlebrow, and lowbrow.[1] Although these terms are often used invidiously, one can also think of them as descriptive —and then argue that in a pluralist America, all cultures, whether of taste or ethnicity, are equally valid and contribute to the diversity of the American scene.

The trio of taste-cultures roughly parallels three social classes, upper, middle, and lower, for people's tastes are affected by their incomes. Still, taste is most shaped by schooling. A good liberal arts education may be necessary to understand the works of T.S. Eliot, but the same kind of schooling is typically found among people who enjoy gourmet cooking, attend the ballet—and like what is thought of as "good design."

A subtler division of the taste-cultures would place "good design" into upper-middle culture. The people who "belong" to this culture are not quite highbrow and not quite middlebrow. For example, they tend to read more books than the average American, mostly nonfiction but not scholarly titles, yet they are unlikely to buy best-selling paperback novels. They read the *New Yorker,* but stay away both from the *Partisan Review* and the *Reader's Digest.* If they watch television, their fare includes a high proportion of public television documentaries, dramas, and British comedies. They go to the theater and concerts, but prefer opera and symphony to chamber music, and they shun blockbuster films. They are more apt to buy quiches than TV dinners and wine rather than beer; they play tennis but do not bowl; and they spend their vacations in European cities rather than at the beach.

When it comes to artistic and design preferences, however, upper-middle culture can be divided further, into progressive and traditional wings, on the assumption that a liking for contemporary art, architecture, and furniture go together, as does a liking for traditional versions of each. Of course, some people like both; others swear by contemporary art but like traditional furniture, or vice versa; and yet others select combinations of each, for example, "good design" enthusiasts may also collect Shaker furniture.

In terms of social class, the people who prefer "good design" and other aspects of progressive upper-middle culture are mostly upper-middle class. Many work as professionals and are probably found especially in the symbolic professions: in design, of course, the arts and communications (broadly defined), and in academia. Some are doctors, lawyers, or housewives-mothers; others, male and female, hold managerial and technical positions, especially in the so-called knowledge and service sectors of postindustrial society. Many, perhaps most, are economically comfortable, if not rich, and they hold degrees from the better private and public universities. They live in Main Line-type suburbs (but not the exclusive ones, and they do not inhabit mansions) or in fashionable outer- or inner-city neighborhoods. The younger generation includes gentrifiers or tenants of recently gentrified buildings.

"Design Since 1945" is, for this sociologist, a treasure trove of progressive upper-middle culture and a collection of its more typical artifacts. The practitioners of that culture would be likely to relax in Eero Saarinen's "Womb" chair (III-78), and the head of the household in

1. Russell Lynes, *The Tastemakers* (New York, 1980), chap. 13. The book was first published by Harper and Brothers in 1954; that chapter had originally appeared in the February 1949 issue of *Harper's Magazine.*

Charles Eames's lounge chair (III-26), or copies thereof. Upper-middlebrow living rooms might be lighted with Isamu Noguchi's "Akari" hanging lamps (IV-30) and Kurt Versen's floor lamps (IV-36), and *rya* rugs might be found on the floors. Dinner parties might use Nick Roericht's white stacking dishes (II-53) or Heinrich Löffelhardt's "Arzberg 2000" porcelain (II-34), Carl Pott's flatware (V-31,32), and Marimekko tablecloths. Innumerable other items illustrated here are equally part of the domestic landscape of progressive upper-middle culture, so much so that it could be called the "culture of good design."

(Originally, of course, "good design" was conceived at the Museum of Modern Art in New York in the early 1950s to present manufactured objects selected on the basis of "eye appeal, function, construction and price." Indeed, some of the pieces chosen by the Museum of Modern Art and also illustrated here are now "classics," which are beginning to appear in antique stores, for example, Russel Wright's ceramics [II-76]. Others became popular upper-middle- *and* lower-middlebrow objects, notably Freda Diamond's "Classic" tumblers [II-15] and Paul McCobb's "Planner" furniture [III-51]. The selection of objects pictured here also includes items currently being purchased for lower-middle culture homes, for example, Giancarlo Piretti's "Plia" folding chair [III-66] and Eureka's "Mighty Mite" vacuum cleaner [I-12]. Other items are preferred by the avant-garde, while still others are very expensive and can be afforded only by the very rich.)

Of course, being upper-middle class and upper-middlebrow does not, by itself, explain the liking for "good design." Moreover, no one knows why people choose the design they do, for the necessary studies remain undone or unpublished. All one can do, therefore, is to speculate. Obviously, people who choose "good design" select, like everyone else, what they find attractive, but that begs the question of why they think "good design" is attractive. Designers may find the explanation in the talent that goes into "good design," but that explanation is self-serving, for "good design" refers to a specific style and philosophy, not to a particular talent. Equally important, designers of similar talent can be found who consider "good design" unattractive, or drab, or uncomfortable. People from other taste-cultures may agree; high culture's avant-garde sees "good design" as conventional and old-fashioned.

I would guess that the people who choose "good design" do so for a variety of reasons. For one thing, the conscious pursuit of aesthetics is significant in upper-middle culture generally, and even utilitarian goods are expected to serve artistic functions. Tablecloths and rugs should bear some resemblance to paintings, while chairs, glassware, and even toasters should remind people of sculpture. To be sure, everyone wants attractive furniture and appliances, but I suspect that in other taste-cultures, attractiveness is less influenced by museum and gallery art. Perhaps upper-middlebrows buy their housewares together with, or instead of, art; equally important, the buyers of "good design" share the aesthetic tradition that led Mies van der Rohe, one of the founders of International Style architecture, to emphasize the kinship of architecture with sculpture.

But why that particular aesthetic tradition? I think that some professional and educational values of progressive upper-middle culture play a role. The workers in the symbolic professions—and the knowledge and service sectors—are a new class, which sees itself as forward-looking, enlightened and enlightening, contemporary and reformist, out to vanquish the obsolescent, the unnecessarily complicated, and the dishonest in American culture and everyday life. They may not all be aware of the cultural and political struggles of the Bauhaus and other European and American design pioneers of a half-century ago, but they want artifacts that they perceive as simple, honest, and serious, with forms that follow or at least do not interfere with function.

Simplicity has, of course, long been a sign of high status in America; the furniture of the upper class, antique or new, is, like its clothing, often expensively simple. Ornament seems unnecessary at the higher levels of society, but is desirable to the less affluent, to whom the starkness of "good design" is often dehumanizing, even though superficial decoration is often used also to hide construction shortcuts and cheap materials. Likewise, massiveness may suggest solidity for people whose economic and social position is not secure.

Professional values are significant in another way, for I would imagine that as professionals, progressive upper-middlebrow people prefer goods that are *designed*—and by other, equally forward-looking professionals. Correlatively, they want design that has been judged *good* by the critics, magazines, and stores that they and their friends respect. This is another reason why progressive upper-middle culture could be labeled the "culture of good design." In addition, these professionals respect the well-known expert, and will therefore prefer goods that bear the names of their designers, just as they go to films that are known by the names of their directors. Also, upper-middle culture is, like high culture, respectful of Europe and Europeans; as a result, "good design" purchasers continue to be impressed by European designers and artists. Indeed, in the 1950s and 1960s, the Americans who first furnished their homes with the work of Scandinavian and Italian designers were also going to films made by Bergman, Rossellini, and Fellini.

The "overstuffed" couch is a symbol of a parental taste-culture given up by purchasers of "good design."

Last but not least, the purchasers of "good design" include people who come from lower-middle or working-class homes and parental taste-cultures, which they dropped when they went to college. What they gave up, culturally, is nicely symbolized—or stereotyped—by the "overstuffed" armchairs and couches still available in most department stores, covered with flowery fabric—and on which a plastic slipcover may be placed later. "Good design" does not reject comfort, but it taboos the overstuffed look. It also rejects "realistic" flowery prints, although live plants, Ficus, for example, may be part of the living-room layout. Man-made materials are in fact eschewed when possible; plastic, even expensive varieties, never became truly acceptable for furniture, and is permissible only in kitchen and bathroom goods, or for offices.

I do not mean to suggest that the preference for "good design" is mainly an effect of status seeking, for surely other "good design" enthusiasts have turned their backs on very different parental tastes, including English or early American styles popular with the upper class. Nor is the choice of "good design" an expression of youthful rebellion, because young people often develop their own tastes without in any way rejecting their parents. Rather, new lifestyles and new occupational, educational, and other values alter people's perception of what is attractive.

While many of the best-known artifacts seen here have now been available on a mass-produced basis for over a generation and have become "classics" of upper-middle culture, only some have been taken up by the rest of America, by purchasers from lower-middle taste-cultures. (People with low incomes can rarely afford new furnishings and must choose from the secondhand goods of other cultures.) To some extent, the lack of popularity of good design is a result of price, although if it were more popular, it could and would be copied at lower cost, much as other styles are so copied. I saw cheaper, somewhat more massive, and slightly overstuffed versions of Scandinavian "Modern" in working-class furniture stores in Copenhagen and Stockholm twenty-five years ago, but these have never crossed the Atlantic. True, "good design" has had some influence on American consumer goods. Popularly priced furniture and housewares have become "cleaner" in line and lighter in mass in the last decades, and department store living-room and bedroom furniture labeled "contemporary" shows that its designers are not unfamiliar with "good design," but have married some of its principles to styles popular in lower-middle culture. Likewise, a number of moderately priced plastic dinette chairs and even some living-room chairs show their indebtedness to Saarinen or Eames, while the "Sacco" chair (III-27) was translated into the beanbag chair sold at Woolworth's and other stores for children's rooms.

Nonetheless, the major impact of "good design" outside upper-middle culture seems to have been felt in office and related commercial furnishing, although more in professional than industrial environments. The Eames armchair (III-25), Saarinen's pedestal furniture (III-79, 80), and, of course, Eliot Noyes's IBM "Selectric" typewriter (I-30) are good examples of this. Airplane cutlery has also been affected by "good design," for example, by Sigurd Persson's "Jet Line" flatware (V-29). Conversely, I can think of only a few items of residential "good design" that have become widely available without significant stylistic change, and one I see most often, the Breuer dining chair, was designed in 1928. (Its popularity cannot be explained by its venerable age, however.) Probably the best indication of the smallness of the "good design" constituency is the absence of "good design" refrigerators, dishwashers, and other "big-ticket" appliance versions of the small appliances issued by Braun—and also of automobiles, although the 1949 Studebaker, designed by Raymond Loewy, has become a "good design" antique and museum piece.

Marcel Breuer's dining chair (1928) is one of the few "good design" objects that have become widely imitated and accepted in other taste-cultures.

To be sure, the kin of "good design," International Style architecture and abstract advertising art, are now virtually conventional, although that does not necessarily mean that they are popular among the general public. Certainly, the International Style has not found favor with builders of suburban subdivisions, who tend to reflect middle-culture preferences for vernacular neo-Colonial, Spanish, and ranch-house designs. And periodically, citizens object vocally to International Style public buildings and abstract public sculpture, most recently after the unveiling of the Vietnam War memorial in Washington, D.C.

Furthermore, abstract art is rapidly disappearing from the galleries and architects are embracing Post-Modernism, complete with a strong penchant for ornamentation. As a result, the constituency for what is traditionally thought of as "good design" may also be disappearing—and then "good design" may come to mean something new. Perhaps we will soon be reading and talking about Post-Modern "good design," although what shapes and styles it will take remains to be seen. Among other things, we must wait to see exactly how the designers of tomorrow's consumer goods will react to architectural Post-Modernism, and what the young gentrifiers of today purchase when they choose the furnishings with which they will settle down. One prediction is safe, however. As long as the professional upper-middle class continues to grow in size and affluence, it will indulge and develop its taste for consumer goods, and that taste will diverge from the lower-middlebrow culture popular with the majority of Americans.

Design and Government

Paul Reilly

Paul Reilly served as director of the British Design Council from 1960 to 1977 and is currently chairman of the Conran Foundation's Boiler-house Project at the Victoria and Albert Museum, London.

In democratic societies, the origins of many state-supported activities are to be found in small private beginnings often sponsored by personal voluntary effort. As the value of the work is demonstrated, so official recognition is gained, as has occurred in the fields of education, medicine, transportation, and communications, to name a few. In Britain, industrial design is no exception, for the present position whereby industrial design is an officially recognized and government-sponsored endeavor has been reached through a long history of unofficial, private effort and propaganda.

It was, of course, not surprising that the country with the earliest record of industrial production should have been the first to try to ward off industry's worst social and cultural consequences. It is, though, often forgotten with what early warning prescience our mid-eighteenth-century ancestors foresaw the cultural dangers of the incipient industrial revolution. The Society (now the Royal Society) of Arts, established in 1754 for "the Encouragement of Arts, Manufactures and Commerce," was founded as a sort of watchdog over the standards of design for contemporary artifacts, whether made by machine or by hand, and it was thus by a clear margin the forerunner of a long line of similar bodies both in Britain and abroad.

Had it not been for the pioneer work of the Royal Society of Arts and of another voluntary organization called the Design and Industries Association, which was founded in 1915, Winston Churchill's wartime coalition government might not have been persuaded in 1944 to set up the Design Council, or Council of Industrial Design as it was originally called. To be strictly accurate, the Council owes its existence directly to two coincidental wartime reports, one by the then-Federation of British Industries and the other by the then-Board of Trade, both of which advocated in almost the same words the setting up of some government-sponsored agency to promote improvements in design.

The Design Council is, I think, one of those typically English devices that are a frequent source of wonder to the foreigner: an official organization with almost complete independence of action; a publicly financed body with a substantial earned income; a government-sponsored agency with no controls or sanctions in its armory; an educational establishment set up, in a sense, to tilt against the Establishment or at least against many sacred cows and conventions and thus either a stimulant or an irritant, according to one's point of view. Perhaps the overworked word "catalyst" is the most appropriate one to describe the Council's role, since its original terms of reference were so widely drawn that they could be carried out only by persuading others to do most of the work.

The Council was charged "to promote by all practicable means the improvement of design in the products of British industry," but no indication was given of the industries to be tackled nor any limits, other than financial, placed on the means of persuasion or promotion to be adopted. It was thus clear from the start that the Council could operate only through the goodwill and good offices of other bodies with wider contacts in industry and commerce and among the general public. Equally, it was obvious in the early postwar years, when any manufacturer could sell anything he was making, however horrible, that exhortation would not be likely to have much effect. A manufacturer would reasonably expect evidence of a demand for higher standards of design before raising his sights. This pointed to a natural division of the Council's activities—on the one hand, an approach to the maker to persuade him to offer higher standards through employing qualified designers, and, on the other, simultaneous propaganda to the consumer to encourage a demand for better things.

Thus the Council developed its two-pronged pattern of activity, which is still reflected in its two main staff divisions—the industrial and the information—with its exhibitions staff serving both as occasion demands, which it has indeed been continuously ever since the Council's first popular display called "Britain Can Make It" in 1946, through the Festival of Britain in 1951, to the opening of its permanent, but constantly changing, Design Centre in 1956. Exhibitions and illustrated publications are the most obvious and effective tools for any organization that sets out to encourage people to use their eyes, and the Council has taken full advantage of both. Its Design Centre has been copied in many countries, while its monthly magazine, *Design,* has almost as many readers abroad as it has at home.

There is still an immense educational job to be done before industrial design is generally accepted in Britain as a proper responsibility of industrial management, but in an increasingly competitive world, in which every industrialized country has access to almost identical raw materials and almost identical means of production, design is bound to become a deciding factor, and the imaginative, creative, inventive designer, the most valuable of assets. The Council's aim has therefore all along been so to change the climate in British industry and commerce that whenever a British businessman is faced with a design problem he will not only recognize it as such, but will also automatically reach for a qualified designer, while the pleasure of working for such a body lies in the range and multiplicity of situations open to it. The problem for a design council is therefore not *what* to do, but what *not* to do, for there are all too many tempting battles to be fought.

I have personally often felt that we could do most good simply by acting as a public watchdog over public expenditure, for there is no excuse whatsoever in an educated society for public money to be spent on any but the highest standards of design. To stimulate the design conscience and the design intelligence of public purchasing authorities might in itself be a worthwhile full-time occupation for a design council, since the resulting upgrading of orders placed with all manner of suppliers could change the whole industrial, social picture out of all recognition. Or one could argue that the most certain way to attain our objectives would be to put all our eggs into the educational basket in order to win over the schoolteachers, thereby ensuring future generations of discriminating patrons and consumers. Or, together with a myriad of other ax-grinders, one could concentrate all the blame and all one's hopes on that much-abused abstraction "top management." In real life, of course, one follows middle courses, distributing one's eggs among different baskets as occasion offers, for an educational, propagandist body like a design council must remain keenly opportunist, without falling into the trap of mistaking improvisations for priorities.

One basket into which the Design Council has placed relatively few eggs has been the commissioning of new products, such commissioning as has transpired having been largely confined to exhibition and graphic design. But, indirectly, through the Council's efforts, the government has

Bed-sitting room designed by T.A.L. Belton for the "Britain Can Make It" exhibition, 1946

The Regatta restaurant (Misha Black and Alexander Gibson, architects) at London's South Bank exhibition for the Festival of Britain, 1951

The Design Centre at Haymarket in London presents changing exhibitions of British industrial design and dispenses product information to design professionals and to consumers.

An early issue of *Design* magazine (no. 6, June 1949)

itself performed the function of patron. For instance, the Supplies Division of the then-Ministry of Works commissioned excellent china, glass, and silver for use in modern embassy buildings, the china from Richard Guyatt, the glass from Robert Goodden (both on the staff of the Royal College of Art), and the silver from David Mellor (a former student at the Royal College of Art). Mellor was later commissioned to design a range of stainless-steel cutlery for the public service, which was called "Thrift" (V-27) since one of its features was to dispense with two sizes of knives and forks. In the field of furniture and soft furnishings, the same ministry commissioned from its in-house designers some modern furniture and from Bernat Klein several ranges of upholstery textiles, but, good as these were, they did not have the influence of the embassy commissions, some of which gained Design Centre Awards. It has always seemed, however, to the Council that the purchasing of consumer goods from the private sector is a better row for government to hoe than commissioning new products.

Being a great believer in education by emulation, the Design Council had, from the inception of its Design Centre, organized an annual award scheme. All Britons are more or less attached to their school days and most have nostalgic memories of prizegivings, so it was natural for the Council to take the fullest advantage of Prince Philip's goodwill toward design by having our royal headmaster present each year not only our Design Council Awards, but also his own Duke of Edinburgh's Prize for Elegant Design. There has been no doubt in my mind that however critical journalists may be when the juries' choices do not coincide with their own, these annual prizegivings have had an immensely beneficial influence on the whole design scene in Britain. They have certainly performed wonders of bridge building between the Council and the successful manufacturers, and, more importantly, once a year they produce a great reverberation in the media, which reaches back to government.

The present government in Britain, under Mrs. Thatcher's leadership, has not been slow to take up the challenge of design, for as the Prime Minister affirmed at a seminar at Number 10 Downing Street in January of 1982, the whole weight of her government is behind the importance of design, now and in the future. Her Secretary of State for Industry proceeded shortly afterward to illustrate the government's readiness to put its money where its mouth is by announcing a substantial increase in the Design Council's funding. He added: "The entire manufacturing process should come under the designer's purview. The materials from which a product is made, the method of manufacture, even the layout of the production machinery on the factory floor, should be subject to the designer's influence. And in the board room he should be a key figure in matters of investment in new products, product development and marketing strategy. We must all, not just the government, be prepared to convert others to this wider understanding of the meaning of design." He ended that speech at the Design Council's annual dinner with the words: "There can be no doubt that the Design Council, throughout its life, has been one of the most significant and beneficial influences on the attitude in this country to design. And not just in this country. Its international reputation is enormous; and, if imitation is the sincerest form of flattery, then the national design bodies established in many foreign countries in the image of the Council provide the Council with just cause to be proud."

Teapot, sugar bowl, and creamer from David Mellor's "Embassy" silver table service, 1963, commissioned along with china (from Richard Guyatt) and glass (from Robert Goodden) for use in British embassies

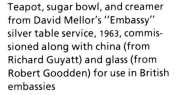

Robin Day's convertible sofa for Hille was selected in 1957 as recipient of one of the first Design Centre Awards.

The Design Council recognizes meritorious achievements broadly throughout the industry: Awards went to Brian Asquith's hoe and rake (for Spear and Jackson) in 1962, to Alex Moulton's bicycle in 1964, and to Dunlop's injection-molded tennis racket in 1981.

Of course, other countries had revealed an interest in design long before the Design Council had been established. In the United States, for instance, the first professional designers—men like Raymond Loewy, Norman Bel Geddes, Walter Dorwin Teague, and Henry Dreyfuss—had got their practices under way at the time of the first great slump, while in Europe people like Walter Gropius and Peter Behrens had started fifteen or twenty years earlier, but all these were free-lance individuals. They were not in receipt of any public funds. It was in Scandinavia that public funding began with the institution of the Swedish Society of Arts and Crafts (Svenska Slöjdföreningen) in the nineteenth century, but they were concerned more with craftsmanship than with design. So perhaps the British Secretary of State for Industry was right in suggesting that Britain had been the first country to set up a council to promote an interest in industrial design. At least it was in London in 1957 that the first international body concerned with design was assembled, following two earlier conferences—the first in London in 1951 and the second in Paris in 1953—at which airings had been given to the thought that some longer-term organization should be created. Thus in 1959 the first convention of the International Council of Societies of Industrial Design (ICSID) was held in Stockholm under the presidency of Count Sigvard Bernadotte. That body now comprises some fifty countries. Its head office is in Brussels and its constitution is still roughly the same, with a general assembly plus a congress, held every two years at a different venue.

One of the turning points that brought ICSID into line with UNESCO was the arrival of the Soviet Union into membership, for once that superpower had joined there was little to prevent its satellites from following suit. The Soviets, though, had first to form a design council, an activity that grew out of a visit to Moscow by the director of London's Design Centre, followed two years later by a visit to London of Yuri Soloviev, now not only director of the largest design council in the world but also a past president of ICSID.

The international council stands not only for the emergence of inter-national design activities, such as Interdesigns—conferences at which a dozen or more designers meet for a couple of weeks to study a particular problem—but also for the adherence of new countries from the Third World; for just as it is the duty of developed countries to stimulate interest in design by the undeveloped and the less-well-developed ones, so it is the obligation of all design councils, particularly those that are looked after by governments, to spare time and thought for the problems of the underprivileged.

The Duke of Edinburgh's Prize for Elegant Design was awarded to Kenneth Grange's "Courier" electric shaver (for Milward) in 1963 and to Rediffusion Simulation's advanced technology flight sim-ulator (shown here installed at Lufthansa's flight training center in Frankfort) in 1982.

A Survey of Design Since 1945

The quotations that appear in the captions to the Plates are the words of the designers. The appended dates refer not to the years in which the texts were written but to the years of publication of the sources from which they were quoted. These citations may be found following each designer's biography at the back of this book. Where no date follows a quotation, the text has been taken from unpublished material in the files of the Philadelphia Museum of Art.

The dates that are cited in the listing of objects are the dates of design. Production dates, when known, are listed in parentheses afterward.

Plate 1
**Raymond Loewy Associates,
Mini Push-Button Television,
1948 (I-21)**

With the end of fighting in sight, American manufacturers looked to the development of goods for the home market, anticipating a frenzied demand for the consumer products that had been scantily produced during the war. Known since the 1930s for their high-quality audio equipment used by professionals and ham operators, the Hallicrafters company approached the Chicago office of America's best-known industrial designer, Raymond Loewy, to restyle their line of radios to appeal to the domestic buyer. Headed by Richard Latham, the Loewy design team simplified the controls of the earlier models and created a cabinet more compatible with the home environment. The team went on to develop this fledgling push-button television in 1948, a more fully realized version of their radio design, with a strict organization of knobs, legible graphics, and rigid, formal division of cabinet elements.

Plate 2
**Isamu Noguchi, Table Lamp,
1948 (IV-29)**

Light and economical in form, this simple plastic cylinder lamp was highly successful for use in the smaller living spaces of postwar housing and was widely imitated after it appeared on the American market in 1948. The first lamp designed by the sculptor Isamu Noguchi, it expressed his preoccupation with the quality and sensibility of light, which was to lead in the 1950s to the creation of his well-known paper "Akari" lamps.

Plate 3
Hans Wegner, Chair, 1949
(III-90)

Almost entirely dependent on wood in the early postwar years, the Danish furniture industry followed the traditional pattern of manufacture by trained craftsmen in small workshops. Meticulously produced, and respecting its natural materials, this armchair by Hans Wegner symbolizes the high standards of Danish design as it became known abroad in the 1950s. The powerfully curved, vigorously modeled top rail is fashioned from three pieces of teak, which require almost two years to cure; the pieces are carefully cut, joined, shaped, and finished to insure that the rail is strong and the edges and surfaces are well rounded for daily use.

Plate 4
Børge Mogensen, Sofa, 1945 (III-52); Lis Ahlmann and Børge Mogensen, Fabric, 1963 (VII-1)

The honest execution and regular silhouette of this sofa demonstrate features considered requisite for progressive design during this period. Nevertheless, its turned spindles, use of stretchers, and precise detailing owe much to the vocabulary of traditional furniture forms—especially American Shaker and English Windsor—which Børge Mogensen called upon repeatedly in his work. Shown in a mahogany prototype at the Copenhagen Cabinetmakers' Guild furniture exhibition in 1945, this sofa was marketed successfully only in the early 1960s, when reissued in beechwood with this trim, woven fabric, which Mogensen designed with Lis Ahlmann.

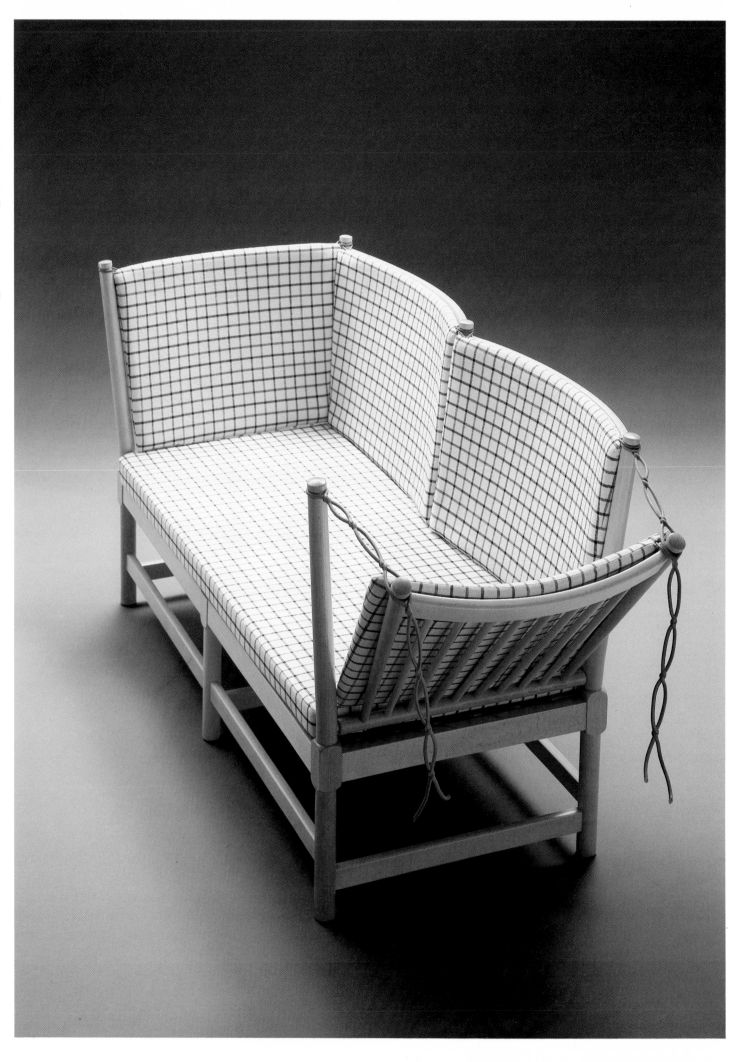

Plate 5
Paolo Venini, "Fazzoletto" Bowl, 1951 (II-67)

Reviving traditional Venetian glass-making techniques, Paolo Venini brought effects of handmade irregularity, color, and texture to the simple shapes he often adopted in his glasswares, and in so doing, introduced ornamental and expressive qualities to the modernism of the 1950s. Decorated with waved edges and internally laced with twisted threads of opaque-white and pink glass, the bowl is formed from a square of glass which is loosely "folded" into its characteristic *fazzoletto* ("handkerchief") shape.

Plate 6
Charles Eames, Chair, 1945 (III-24)

Exhibited in 1946 at the Museum of Modern Art in New York, this molded-plywood and steel-rod chair by Charles Eames became a pattern for designers in many countries, and drew attention to innovative American design in the late 1940s. Its small, light, and nearly indestructible form derives from prewar experiments by Eames and Eero Saarinen with the lamination of wood veneers into compound curves and from molded-plywood splints and glider shells that Eames had developed during the war years. The molded seat and back, formed in a hydraulic press, are attached to the thin metal frame with flexible rubber shock mounts, which yield with body pressures. The result of years of experimentation, this chair fulfills Eames's overriding concern for human scale and function.

Plate 7
**Dorothy Liebes, Blinds, c. 1950
(VII-39)**

Combining traditional yarns with
new synthetic fibers and other
materials—here, rayon and metallics with cotton and bamboo—and
introducing unexpected combinations of colors, Dorothy Liebes
brought opulent effects to interior
furnishings in America. The style
she created in her handwoven work
became highly influential through
her production fabrics, and many of
today's textile designers owe their
daring use of color and texture to
her example.

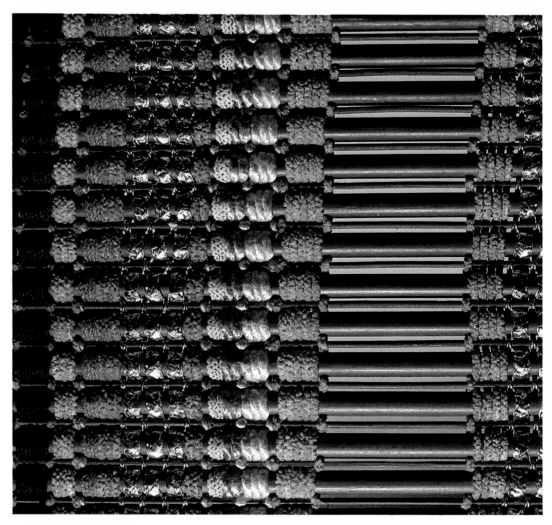

Plate 8
**Ernest Race, "Antelope" Chair,
1951 (III-71)**

Introduced at the Festival of Britain
in 1951, which signaled the country's return to prosperity after the
bleak war years, Ernest Race's "Antelope" chair was noted for the
whimsical style of its spidery frame
and ball feet. The use of shaped
steel rods was an innovation in
British furniture production, although the molded-plastic seat
owes much to Charles Eames's
plywood chair then in production in
the United States.

**Plate 9
Lucienne Day, "Calyx" Fabric,
1951 (VII-10)**

First shown at the Festival of Britain, Lucienne Day's printed "Calyx" fabric departed from the small-scale geometric patterns of wartime utility textiles and restrained British floral designs to introduce abstracted images of plant motifs in large areas of bright color. Well received at home, "Calyx" was also recognized abroad, where it was awarded a gold medal at the Triennale in Milan in 1951 and judged the best textile on the American market in 1952.

Plate 10
Greta von Nessen, "Anywhere"
Lamp, 1952 (IV-28)

The use of industrial materials and undisguised construction in Greta von Nessen's "Anywhere" lamp followed Bauhaus aesthetic principles, which she and her husband, the architect Walter von Nessen, brought with them to the United States from Germany. Like many other postwar products, the lamp was designed for adaptability: it can be suspended, mounted on a wall, or placed on a table.

Plate 11
Sigvard Bernadotte and Acton Bjørn, "Margrethe" Bowls, 1950 (VI-2)

As Denmark's economy became increasingly industrialized after the war, Danish designers looked beyond natural materials to plastics and other man-made substances. This set of mixing bowls was created specifically to expand a line of products in melamine, a hard, mar-resistant plastic. Designed by the founders of Bernadotte & Bjørn, Denmark's first industrial design firm, the bowls were thoroughly researched and consciously engineered to meet all the basic functional needs of the product, surpassing any set then on the market. They have a skid-proof base and a rim to steady them for mixing, as well as a lip for pouring.

Plate 12
The Sony Corporation, Portable Transistor Television, 1959 (I-43)

Sony's introduction of the world's first fully transistorized television in 1959 challenged the international television and radio industry to compete in the areas of miniaturization and technology, in addition to cabinet design and marketing. Its immediate popularity drew attention to the standards of quality and technological achievement of Japanese industry. Reduced to essentials of tube and battery pack tightly sheathed in a metal cabinet, and with handle, knobs, antenna, and stand arranged as function dictated, this boldly reduced eight-inch-screen model was at the time considered amazingly light, weighing only 13¼ pounds.

Plate 13
Dieter Rams, Combination Phonograph and Pocket Radio, 1959 (I-36)

Plate 14
Carl Pott, Cutlery, 1952 (V-31)

Deliberately economical in form and material, these objects exemplify the functional style that was so strongly identified with modernism in the 1950s. Inspired by progressive movements in Germany in the 1920s, the firms of Braun and Pott radically altered their traditional products to pursue a policy of uncompromising modern design, a policy that has set enduring standards of technology and form in their fields. Dieter Rams, Braun's chief designer since 1955, standardized his radios and phonographs into component elements, here joining a radio and a phonograph into a portable, separable, combination. Carl Pott, eliminating ornament and, in this cutlery series, standardizing the size of the handles, succeeded in creating simple, unified designs that were readily adapted to mass production.

Plate 15
Gio Ponti, Toilet, 1953 (I-33)

Gio Ponti reinterpreted the design of sanitary fittings with his series for Ideal Standard in Italy, for which he developed "not new forms (which would only have become one more variant), but the true forms, the forms that in their essence, approach those archetypes that definitively identify an object.... I took myself back to the form that these objects would have had if they had not existed in the minds of those who concern themselves with appearances—a stylistic superstructure with regard to form. It is for this reason that as an analogy a natural form, a leaf, has often been placed next to illustrations of these fittings, the most successful of which has emerged as a sculpture . . . and has formal values in itself" (1959).

Plate 16
Sori Yanagi, "Butterfly" Stool, 1956 (III-93)

Caught up in Western modernism but rooted still in tradition and craftsmanship, Sori Yanagi synthesized his diverse sources in this sculptural, molded-plywood "Butterfly" stool. Although the stool form has no precedent in Japanese domestic design, its curving seat echoes the elegant shapes of traditional architecture, and its focus on the wood grain reemphasizes the beauty of natural materials found in Japanese everyday objects.

Plate 17
Eero Saarinen, Chair, 1956 (III-79)

From his earliest experiments with Charles Eames for the 1940 Organic Furniture competition at the Museum of Modern Art in New York, Eero Saarinen pursued solutions to the problem of molding a multicurved chair in one piece—first, in the "Womb" chair of 1946, supported on a wire frame, and then, elegantly, in this chair of 1956. Although it gives the impression of having been formed as a single unit, its sculptural shell is supported by a separate pedestal, painted like the shell to create visual unity. "We have a design of a chair which elim-inates the legs going off in different directions. When one sees all the chairs together, they bring a much more quiet and serene feeling into the room. The lower part is cast aluminum and the upper part plastic. Purists can argue with me that one should not mix two materials like that, but technology has not quite caught up with the problem of making the base from a strong enough plastic. Eventually these chairs will be made of all plastic, but one has to wait sometimes" (1957).

Plate 18
Peter Schlumbohm, "Filterjet" Fan, 1951 (I-39)

Inventor and entrepreneur, Peter Schlumbohm capitalized on the success of his hourglass-shaped Chemex coffeemaker (1941) to market, through his own manufacturing firm, many of his other inventions designed as improvements and timesaving devices for modern living. Utilizing the virtues of filter paper, which had proved so important in establishing the reputation of his familiar glass coffeemaker, he designed this "Filterjet" fan to clean the air with five discs of porous paper revolving in a colorful housing.

Plate 19
Timo Sarpaneva, "The Sun in the Forest" Plate, 1957 (Variant of II-56)

A craftsman as well as an inventor of techniques for production, Timo Sarpaneva devised the process by which a glassblower can float color in isolated areas of a single object, alternating it with areas or bands of clear or colored glass. "In 1956 I developed I-glass, which emphasized colors. The color scheme was subdued, grayish green, blue, and lilac. This created an intense effect, the colors glowing as if diffused by a cloud of mist. I aimed at a union of materials and colors, and these large objects were, in fact, watercolors in glass" (see p. 100).

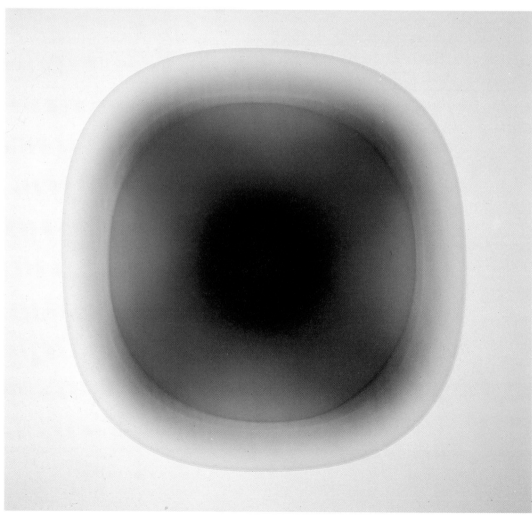

Plate 20
Earl Tupper, "Handolier"
Container, c. 1956 (VI-20)

Employing two of Earl Tupper's inventions, a method for molding polyethylene and a seal that made his plastic containers airtight, Tupperware presented a clever solution to the common problems of the serving and storage of food. Conceived in cool, pastel colors, Tupperware products were praised for fine design as early as 1947, when in an article in *House Beautiful* their forms were compared to "art objects" and their material, to alabaster and jade.

Plate 21
Charles Eames, Lounge Chair and Ottoman, 1956 (III-26)

In contrast to his inexpensive and lightweight metal-frame chairs of the 1940s, Charles Eames's lounge chair of the following decade was designed for maximum comfort and luxurious appearance, with its laminated rosewood shells joined by aluminum connectors and upholstered with soft, leather-covered cushions. Eames envisioned his chair as a twentieth-century successor to the old-fashioned club armchair and footstool—a modern incarnation of the Morris chair, and like it, fabricated principally by hand.

Plate 22
Marcello Nizzoli, "Mirella" Sewing Machine, 1957 (I-29)

Sleek, elegant, and stylish, the "Mirella" revolutionized the domestic sewing machine in Italy and enhanced the self-image of the modern housewife, suggesting as it did creativity and individuality in home sewing. The "Mirella" represented a high point in Marcello Nizzoli's personal style in which the form he gave to an object, albeit dependent on function, materials, and methods of production, might still allow what he referred to as the "freedom of fantasy."

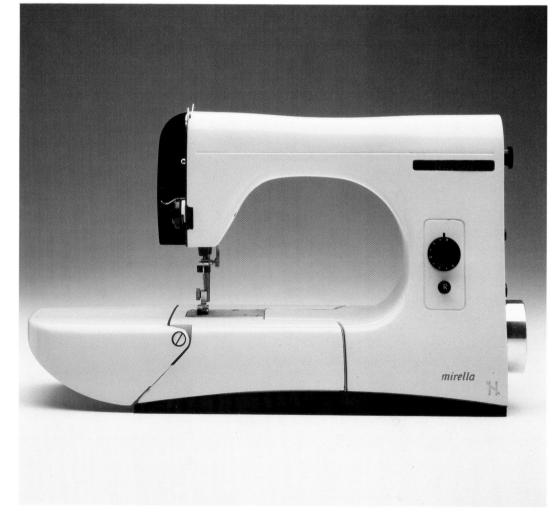

Plate 23
Arne Jacobsen, "Egg" Chair, 1957 (III-35)

Affectionately known as the "Egg" from its simple oval profile, this chair was designed by the Danish architect Arne Jacobsen for the broad interior spaces of his Royal Hotel in Copenhagen (1959). Jacobsen's vision of the total integration of architecture and furnishings achieved its most complete expression in the hotel, where, according to the press, he designed everything "down to the ashtrays." Dramatic as a sculptural form, the "Egg" is nonetheless exceedingly comfortable and flexible as it swivels and tilts on its base. The chair is also a tour de force of Danish craftsmanship in modern materials, with the construction of its molded fiberglass-and-foam-rubber shell and the precision required to fit its luxurious upholstery tightly to the rounded shape.

Plate 24
Max Bill, Wall Clock, 1957 (I-5)

Reduced to the utmost simplicity in its shape and numberless, clean-lined graphic display, Max Bill's clock epitomizes the functional style based on mathematical logic that the Swiss designer promoted through his teaching at the Hochschule für Gestaltung in Ulm, West Germany. "The mainspring of all visual art is Geometry, the correlation of elements on a surface or in space. Thus, even as mathematics is one of the essential forms of primary thought . . . it is also intrinsically a science of the relationship of object to object, group to group, and movement to movement" (1949). Hence, all the dimensions of the clock, including those of its indicators and hour and minute hands, are mathematically determined and proportionately related, with the hour hand, for example, being equal in length to the radius of the face.

Plate 25
Marco Zanuso and Richard Sapper, Child's Chair, 1964 (III-96)

The sudden availability of poly-ethylene at economical prices when international patents expired gave great impetus to its wide application in the mid-1960s, particularly by Italian designers. Marco Zanuso and Richard Sapper, searching for a suitable material for elementary-school furniture, explored the possibilities of this rigid plastic, and produced the first injection-molded chair in this material. The innate requirements of plastics manufacturing provided structural elements that facilitated stacking and building, enabling them to create a chair that was also a toy, an added advantage in furniture meant for children.

Plate 26
George Nelson, "Sling" Sofa, 1964 (III-58)

A pioneer of modular storage systems in the 1950s, George Nelson reinterpreted the functionalist tradition of bent, tubular-metal seating by modern means in this impressive sofa. Designed for ease of assembly without costly, high-speed production machinery, the sofa incorporates such innovations as the use of an epoxy glue to join the steel hoop to the legs, and a reinforced rubber platform slung inside the frame, which supports the leather seat cushions without any internal substructure.

Plate 27
Marco Zanuso and Richard Sapper, "Grillo" Telephone, 1965 (I-53)

Giving form to the technology of miniaturization, Marco Zanuso and Richard Sapper endowed this small, hinged-unit "cricket" (*grillo*) telephone with a particular tactile friendliness. In 1967 the Compasso d'Oro judges praised the designers for their technological innovations and sensitivity toward the user, for reducing the mass of the object without sacrificing any functional requirements or elements of the traditional telephone.

Plate 28
Robert Welch, "Alveston" Teapot, 1962 (V-50)

Bridging the gap between craft and industry, Robert Welch applied the techniques of the silverwork made in his Cotswold studio to his designs for industry. Production of his squat "Alveston" teapot utilizes the lost-wax process, an age-old metal-casting technique newly adapted for stainless-steel products. The process is "particularly advantageous where great accuracy and good surface finish are required, and by using a casting for this spout it has been possible to blend a complex shape into the body of the pot" (1973).

Plate 29
Achille and Piergiacomo
Castiglioni, ''Arco'' Floor Lamp,
1962 (IV-9)

Pulled taut like a great fishing pole
as it arches broadly into an environment, the Castiglioni brothers'
''Arco'' lamp displays all of the
self-conscious theatricality of the
stage sets and exhibition installations they designed in the 1940s and
1950s. One of a series of extraordinary domestic objects that they
created in rapid succession, the
lamp is produced with simple
materials—a block of marble, a
stainless-steel rod, and an aluminum reflector.

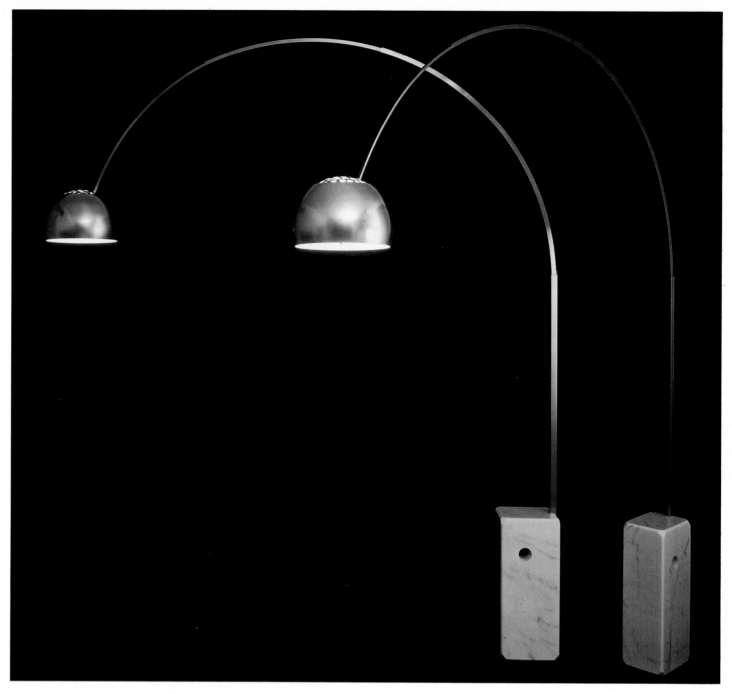

The graduated sizes of Joe Colombo's polyurethane-foam cushions, covered with jersey and set into metal bases, allow a small range of standard components to be combined into a wide variety of seating forms. Typical of the 1960s' concern for flexibility and variability within an open plan, the grouping and function of the system depend entirely on the user. "The problem today is to offer furnishings that are basically autonomous, that is independent of their architectonic housing and so interchangeable and programmable that they can be adapted to every present and future spatial situation" (1972).

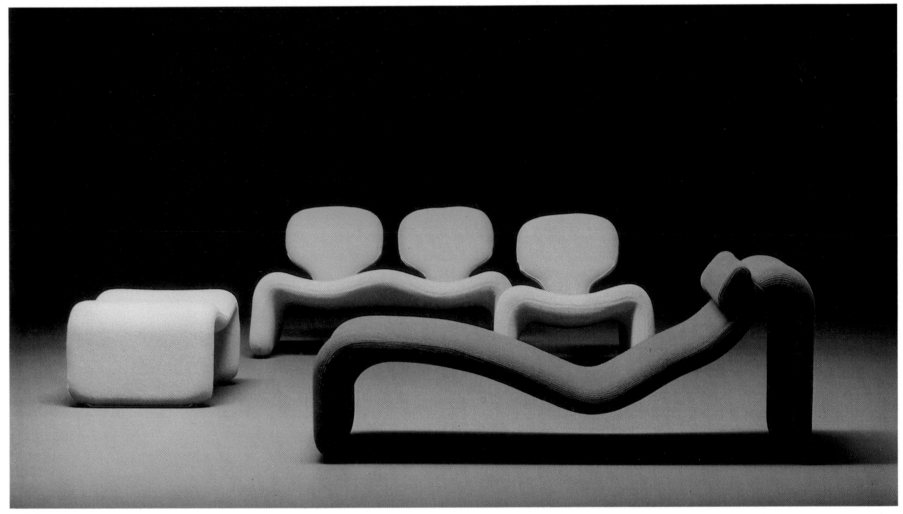

Invading domestic living spaces with bold sculptural forms, Olivier Mourgue's "Djinn" series stands at the very center of this period in its style and fabrication. Constructed of a conventional tubular-steel frame and with recognizable elements of seat, back, and legs, the forms are wrapped in urethane foam and upholstered in nylon stretch jersey. Within a few years, such expensive metal skeletons would be replaced entirely by plastic foams, and the free-flowing forms pioneered by Mourgue would become exaggerated as they reflected the fluidity of the plastic materials out of which they were made.

Plate 32
Arne Jacobsen, "Cylinda Line" Tableware, 1967 (V-18)

The "Cylinda Line," Arne Jacobsen's stainless-steel cookware and tableware in cylindrical and circular shapes, was designed for the rigorous precision of machine tooling, through which the sleek surfaces and crisp outlines of its pure geometric forms could be achieved. The line was also conceived for the marketplace, with the wide range of utensils—from water jug to saucepan and tea strainer—stylishly packaged in cylindrical cartons with circular imprints. Jacobsen gave careful consideration to the unity of the large line of utensils and to its formal relationships, vividly illustrated by the way the nylon handles accent and balance the proportions of the cylinders.

Plate 33
Tapio Wirkkala, "Composition" Cutlery, 1963 (V-52)

The "Composition" cutlery series demonstrates Tapio Wirkkala's sculptural approach to industrial production. Developed and tested in wooden prototypes and then in stainless-steel models, the final designs were worked out in close collaboration with the technicians of the Rosenthal factory. Knife, fork, and spoon are each forged from a single piece of steel, and the knife drawn and abruptly turned—not unlike one of Wirkkala's own plywood sculptures—to provide an angled cutting edge.

Plate 34
Maija Isola, "Melooni" Fabric, 1963 (VII-26)

Using traditional hand-printing techniques and ordinary cotton fabrics, Maija Isola dramatically altered the Finnish textile industry with her brightly colored geometric patterns. Her fabric designs acquired a new boldness of scale in the 1960s, and paralleled directions in painting with their simplicity of form and saturated, basic colors, achieving international success in both the furnishing fabrics and clothing that Marimekko produced from them.

Plate 35
Jens Quistgaard, Ice Bucket, 1960 (VIII-8)

Drawing on his experience as a sculptor and craftsman, Jens Quistgaard created lines of cookware and tableware that were marketed by Dansk, the company he co-founded in 1954. Reflecting the new informal lifestyle of the period, his products were designed both for food preparation and for serving. He brought to dining, materials previously restricted to the kitchen—cast iron, earthenware, and wood. As his most flamboyant product, this teak ice bucket helped promote the company's popular image as a craft-oriented manufacturer favoring natural materials and careful workmanship.

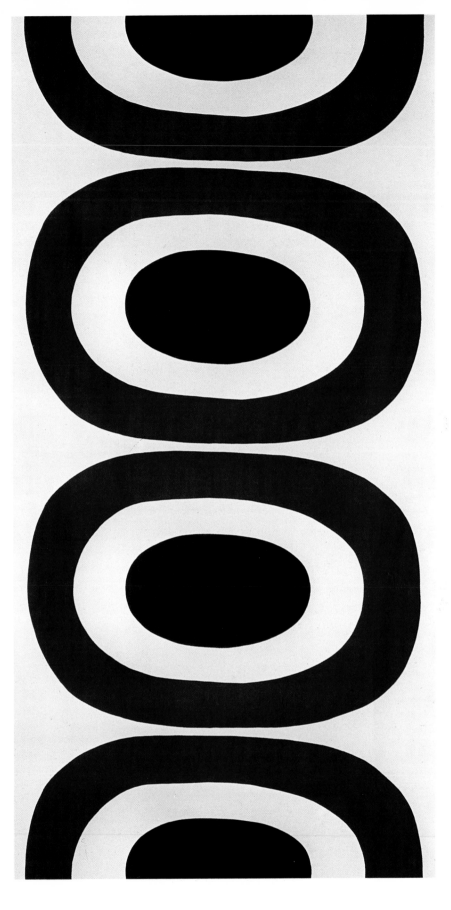

Plate 36
Verner Panton, Stacking Chair, 1960 (III-61)

If the perfect chair—however elusive—was the aesthetic goal of virtually every furniture designer of this period, single-piece continuous construction was their technological goal, one that was first achieved by Verner Panton in rigid polyurethane in 1960, but not produced widely until 1967, when Herman Miller issued it in molded fiberglass and polyester. Following the example of Bauhaus cantilevered furniture (for example, Marcel Breuer's familiar dining chair), and the experiments of Charles Eames and Eero Saarinen with molded plywood and fiberglass seating in the 1940s, Panton used the cantilever principle in molded plastic to produce the flowing lines of this chair, whose success was rooted in the application of its technology.

Plate 37
Ettore Sottsass, Jr., and Perry King, "Valentine" Portable Typewriter, 1969 (I-47)

"Aware of all the commitment of open-minded but rigorous design, which starts from a secure knowledge of good technology," Ettore Sottsass, Jr., and Perry King invented the "Valentine" typewriter and transformed it for use "any place except in an office, so as not to remind anyone of monotonous working hours, but rather to keep amateur poets company on quiet Sundays in the country or to provide a highly colored object on a table in a studio apartment. An anti-machine machine, built around the commonest mass-produced mechanism, the works inside any typewriter, it may also seem to be an unpretentious toy.... The two elements of the machine itself, which is all one with the handle and cover, and its container with the two black rubber hooks, are made of orange-red injection molded ABS. Yellow, and also in ABS, are the two buttons of the ribbon spools, like the two eyes of a robot" (Sottsass, 1979).

Plate 38
Roberto Sambonet, "Center Line" Cooking Set, 1964 (V-38)

A series of eight concentric, stainless-steel containers for cooking, serving, and storing food, Roberto Sambonet's "Center Line" has four graduated pots and four shallow pans of corresponding diameters, which can be used as lids or trays for bringing the pots to the table. Planned according to a geometrical progression, the containers nest one within the other to form a single unit for economical storage. This abstract, geometrical organization represents Italian functionalist design at its most severely logical, but at the same time, the exaggeration and repetition of the circular shape, enlarged and echoed in the flaring, segmental handles, create a rich and complex aesthetic fantasy.

Plate 39
Frank O. Gehry, "Easy Edges"
Rocking Chair, 1972 (III-28)

Noting that no other material at a
comparable price had the strength
and the adaptability of corrugated
cardboard, Frank O. Gehry used this
material transversely to create a
soft, suedelike surface on a range
of furniture that he called "Easy
Edges." Unlike the simply constructed paper furniture of the
1960s, which was considered semi-
disposable, his line was offered as a
serious alternative to furniture in
traditional materials. The ease of
manufacturing with cardboard
gave Gehry the freedom to vary his
forms from crisp rectangles to the
elegant arabesques of this rocking
chair.

Plate 40
Jack Lenor Larsen, "Magnum"
Fabric, 1970 (VII-34)

Distinguished by the richness and
variety of their colors and textures,
Jack Lenor Larsen's textiles demonstrate both his technological re-
sourcefulness and his fascination
with traditional styles and processes. In his "Magnum" fabric, he
applied the technique of embroi-
dery, machine-stitching several
combinations of colored yarns.
Using mirrored, Mylar polyester
film as a ground, Larsen created an
extravagant and distinctly modern
fabric.

Plate 41
Enzo Mari, "Pago-Pago" Vases, 1969 (VI-12)

Enzo Mari has designed his modest table objects with very much the same methodology (although on a smaller scale) as that of a designer or design team confronting a new appliance or automobile. In creating these elegant vases for Danese, Mari examined consumer preferences (for decorative, unique vases or for anonymous containers), considered the functional problem of adapting to large and small bouquets of flowers, and explored plastics technology for efficiency of molding and economy and appropriateness of material. His solution was a multi-use vase with a small container on one end and a larger one on the other, the two sharing common walls, stamped economically out of colored ABS plastic.

Plate 42
Jean-Pierre Vitrac, Floor Lamp, 1970 (IV-38)

With development of new lighting technology, designers directed their attention to the quality and effects of illumination as much as to the formal elements of the fixture. Jean-Pierre Vitrac acknowledged both aspects in this floor lamp, which he initially conceived as a participatory sculpture-lamp. It offers seemingly infinite possibilities for the arrangement of its polished segments, which can be raised on telescoping antennas and adjusted at different angles, giving great variety both of form and of lighting effects.

Plate 43
**De Pas, D'Urbino, Lomazzi,
"Joe" Chair, 1970 (III-21)**

Pop art has found expression in design through out-of-scale and out-of-context objects, such as De Pas, D'Urbino, Lomazzi's chair in the form of a baseball glove. Considered an expensive joke by some critics, the chair may as well be a witty comment on the equally expensive Bauhaus furniture then being reissued in glove leather and reproduced widely in architectural magazines. The Italian designers gave the glove a heroic association by naming it "Joe," a reference to New York Yankee centerfielder Joe DiMaggio, who had become well known abroad after his marriage to the actress Marilyn Monroe.

Plate 44
Livio Castiglioni and Gianfranco Frattini, "Boalum" Table Lamp, 1971 (IV-14)

Among the most poetic applications of undisguised industrial materials, Livio Castiglioni and Gianfranco Frattini's "Boalum" lamp looks like a luminescent sculpture, attracting attention to its snakelike form with a soft, ambient glow. The six-feet-long flexible plastic tubes, reinforced with coiled springs and housing only wiring and small bulbs, can be variably arranged for specific illumination or decoration.

Plate 45
Clive Sinclair (with Iain Sinclair), "Executive" Pocket Calculator, 1972 (I-40)

As familiar as microelectronics became in the 1980s, enabling appliances to be condensed to any size practical for use, only a decade earlier engineers were still battling to reduce common products to miniature sizes. Clive Sinclair's sleek and trim electronic calculator was the first to be manufactured in pocket size: only ⅜-inch thick and 5½-inches long, one-tenth the size of its nearest competitor, it included a seven-thousand-transistor integrated circuit—the most complex then available for commercial application—and was the first to be powered by a wafer-thin battery.

Plate 46
Kaj Franck, Goblets, c. 1974 (II-19)

Densely saturated with rich color and fused-in metal particles, these goblets show a lesser-known aspect of the work of Kaj Franck, Finland's most important designer of every-day ceramics and glass. Here, embellishing a functional shape with bravura effects of material and decoration, Franck seems to emphasize the Scandinavian tradition that makes little distinction between craftwork and the products of industry.

Plate 47
František Vízner, "Blue" Vase, 1978 (II-69)

With his series of angular vases, František Vízner introduced new formal possibilities for glass objects, contradicting the fluidity of the medium through the exaggerated precision of its hard edges. The mimicry of machine-achieved refinements by hand-cutting methods, as well as the floating color within, succeeds in infusing the rigid form with an ambiguous and poetic quality.

Plate 48
Inger Persson, "Pop" Service,
1972 (II-47)

Updated with bright enamel colors,
"Pop" reinterpreted the concept of
combining different forms and colors within a single service, which
Kaj Franck had introduced in his
ceramic "Kilta" tableware in the
early 1950s. Boldly differentiating
each piece, Inger Persson created a
strikingly assertive design, which in
its gleam, sense of solidity, and bold
outlines, discards the simple and
reticent style of its predecessors for
an image designed to appeal to the
"popular" culture of the period.

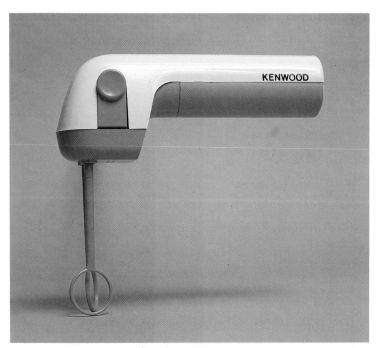

Plate 49
Kenneth Grange, Battery Whisk, 1971 (I-14)

Kenneth Grange's battery whisk responded to an increasing fashion during the 1970s for the mechanization of simple kitchen tools. Lightweight, portable, and easily gripped, the whisk is distinguished by color into its basic elements: case, power source, and operational parts. For Grange, the function of such a product is defined not only by its use but also by its interaction with the consumer: "There is a lot of nonsense talked about fitness for purpose which implies that products should be stripped of everything superfluous to their function. I submit that this is not enough. Part of the purpose of every product is to give pleasure, and that . . . is one of the designer's key contributions" (1983).

Plate 51
Sergio Asti, "Boca" Cutlery, 1976 (V-2)

Turning away from the elaborate research into balance, weight, form of grips, and cutting angles that occupied cutlery designers in the 1950s and 1960s, Sergio Asti implied that the way a service looks may ultimately be a more important consideration for human fulfillment. For "Boca" he chose to combine basic geometric forms—circles and rectangles—whose bold simplicity suggests a fresh outlook, an antidote to the overconsidered designs of this period. Asti strives "to give a product its full expression . . . to invest with meaning that which we create, a meaning beyond that of the object's function and beyond its role as an item in a production/consumer-oriented economy" (*Interiors*, 1970).

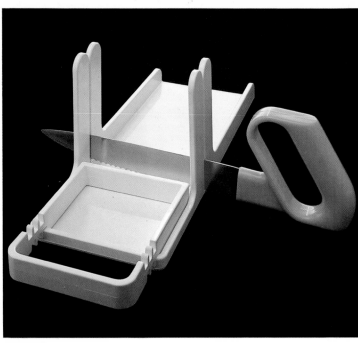

Plate 50
Maria Benktzon and Sven-Eric Juhlin, Knife and Cutting Board, 1974 (VI-1)

Consideration for individual needs—of the left-handed person, for example, or the disabled—became a strong motivating factor in certain design quarters by the 1970s, spurred by group activism and government regulation. Much innovative work in ergonomics has occurred in Scandinavia, led by such collaboratives as Sweden's Ergonomi Design Gruppen. For more than a decade Maria Benktzon and Sven-Eric Juhlin, two members of this recently formed group, have been studying the special problems of the handicapped. Their aim has been to design products, such as this weight-adjusted knife and cutting board, that are not limited by particular adaptions for use by special individuals but are thoughtfully conceived so that they may be used by the entire population.

Plate 52
California Drop Cloth,
"Celebration" Fabric, 1979 (VII-7)

Through the curious reversals of
California's informal culture, which
during the 1960s and 1970s firmly established the validity of its design
independence, a painter's drop
cloth is translated into a custom
upholstery fabric, prized for the
beauty of its color combinations.
Alluding to the spontaneous ges-
tures of Abstract Expressionism, the
paint-splattered effect of California
Drop Cloth's "Celebration" fabric is
punctuated by splashes of dripped
or thrown paint, in a design created
to order by each artist-craftsman
within the limits of loosely structured patterns.

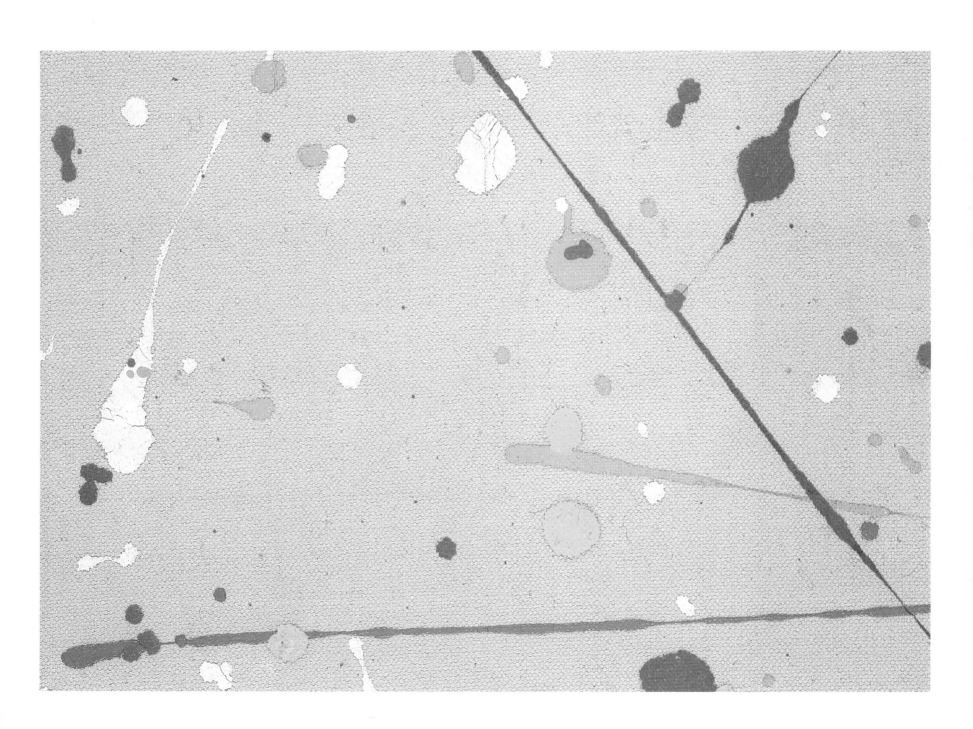

Plate 53
Timo Sarpaneva, "Suomi"
Service, 1974 (II-58)

Bringing a craftsman's sense of
form and material to utility
ceramics, Timo Sarpaneva endowed
the "Suomi" service with a dramatic
sculptural presence. At the same
time he conceived his smooth
shapes with broad surfaces suitable
for painted decoration, which was
to be added in several variants of
the service. Designed by a number
of independent artists whose collaboration is considered essential to
the concept of the Rosenthal Studio
Line, the "Suomi" decorations
range from a dense, geometric pattern by the British artist Eduardo
Paolozzi to Surrealist designs by the
Spaniard Salvador Dali.

Plate 54
Aldo van den Nieuwelaar,
Cupboard, 1979 (III-59)

The qualities of simplicity, anonymity of design, and functionality promoted by the Dutch de Stijl group in the early years of this century have had a continuing influence on architects and designers in the Netherlands, as Aldo van den Nieuwelaar's conception of his work demonstrates: "I try to capture the essence of a utility product with a minimum of material and means. Industrial design is a visual realization of that process. I prefer introverted forms, since they have less influence on their surroundings" (1981). This component unit, designed to function independently as well as in conjunction with other storage pieces in the series, makes a boldly mannered aesthetic statement through its exaggerated, narrow proportions.

Plate 55
Vico Magistretti, "Atollo" Table
Lamp, 1977 (IV-25)

In its regular geometric forms of cone, cylinder, and hemisphere, smooth finish, and suppression of all details, Vico Magistretti's "Atollo" lamp extolls the engineering virtues of functional design. However, in contriving to balance the hemispherical shade on an apex in apparent defiance of gravity, Magistretti contradicts the mathematical rationalism that the aesthetic otherwise expresses.

Plate 56
Achille Castiglioni, ''Gibigiana''
Table Lamp, 1981 (IV-13)

Achille Castiglioni conceived this lamp above all as a machine for lighting, impeccably engineered with controls that can be manipulated to vary the intensity of the light and the angle at which it is reflected by the mirror housed in the disk at top. But in its monumental, conelike conception, the lamp strongly calls attention to itself as it takes on an eccentric form, animated in its configuration.

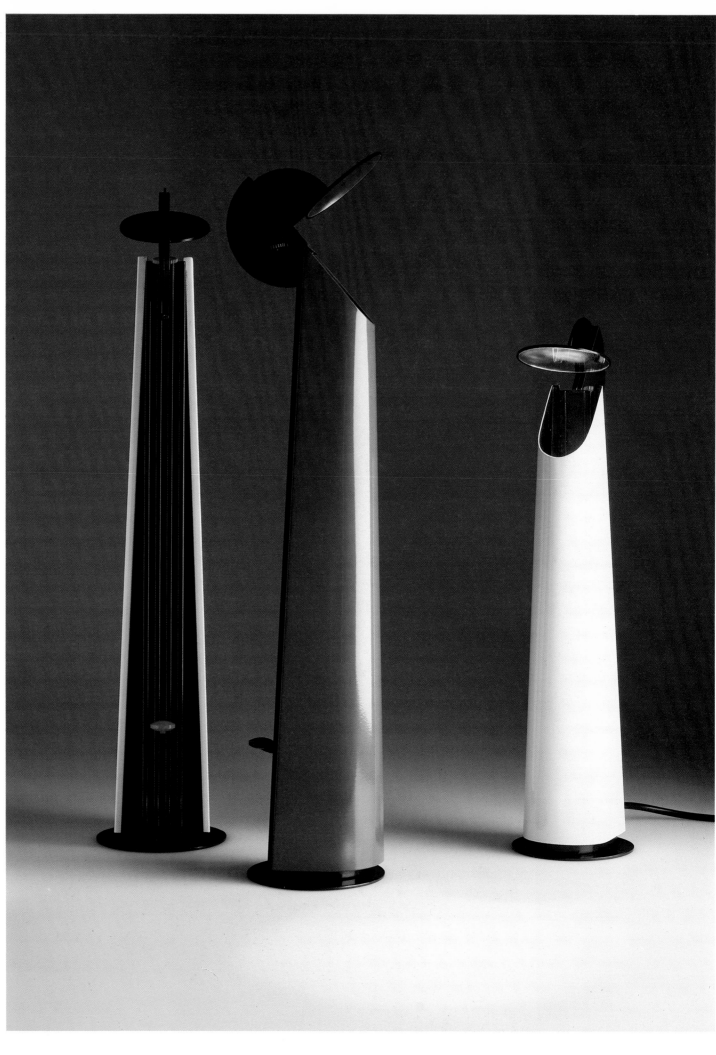

Plate 57
Ettore Sottsass, Jr.,
"Casablanca" Sideboard,
1981 (III-84)

With its shelves angled obliquely
and its entire surface veneered in
vibrant printed plastic laminates,
Ettore Sottsass's "Casablanca" self-
consciously avoids allusion to historical styles and demands isolation
from its interior surroundings.
Functional—it is conceived to store
dishes and glassware and to hold
bottles in its arms—as well as decorative, the sideboard uses common industrial materials although
its costly and time-consuming manufacture is principally by hand.
Offered by Sottsass's Memphis
group in Milan as a provocative alternative to what they considered
the vacuity of design in the 1970s,
"Casablanca" and other Memphis
pieces have become an assertive
force, challenging other designers to rethink today's furnishing
vocabulary and to offer counter-
suggestions for directions in the
1980s.

Plate 58
David Rowland, "Sof-Tech"
Stacking Chair, 1979 (III-77)

A sophisticated manifestation of the "high-tech" furnishings of the 1970s, David Rowland's chair not only borrows ordinary industrial materials, it transforms them. Constructed of a tubular-steel frame with seat and back of steel-wire furniture springs, the chair was first conceived by Rowland when he was a student in the 1950s. Unable to make the hard, metal wires comfortable for seating, he did not succeed with his design until two decades later, when he coated the springs with PVC elastomer. The coating, which fattened the wires, held them in alignment without making them rigid and allowed them to stretch slightly when subjected to weight or pressure, and thus a new flexible, resilient system was created.

Plate 59
I. D. Two, "Compass"
Computer, 1982 (I-16)

Combining technologies new since the first personal computer was introduced in 1977, the "Compass" computer is small and light, designed to take into account the consumer's need for a compact, portable machine that is easy to operate. Used in an increasing number of households in the 1980s for budgeting, text editing, and communications, as well as in offices, computers have been designed in recent years to humanize technology, to be "user-friendly." In the first stages of the design process, Bill Moggridge of I. D. Two outlined the requirements of the "Compass" computer in terms of its application as a personal product: "In the portable state, it should be simple, hard, severe, technical and extremely robust. When opened, it should reveal a visually exciting and friendly interior. The excitement would be based on the display and the visual details to go with it, so that the most interesting appearance would be achieved when the product was actually being used" (1983).

Plate 60
Verner Panton, "Mira Columba" Fabric, 1983 (VII-49)

Highly complex and logical both in its geometrical system of squares and progressive alternation of colors, Verner Panton's "Mira Columba" fabric recalls electronic displays made familiar in the 1980s. The double-square design in a multiplicity of color combinations may be read in horizontal, vertical, or diagonal configurations. Lavishly enriched by glossy enamel colors as well as gold and silver, "Mira Columba" demonstrates the preoccupation with color that has been one of the most significant aspects of

Panton's work. "I generally work with parallel colors whose hues follow one another in the spectrum. This permits me to control the character of coolness or warmth and to create a deliberate atmosphere. It is also possible to work with complementary colors, notably in using groups of dominant colors punctuated by other shades. One must equally recall that color and light are intimately bound and . . . that the structures of materials influence the sensation of color" (1969).

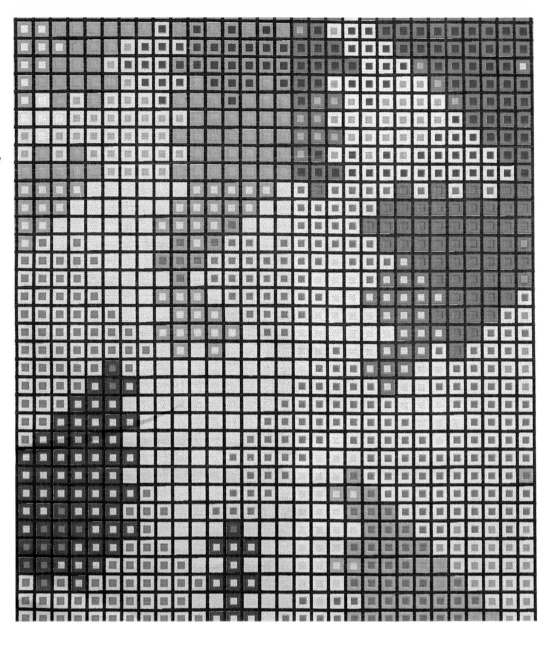

Plate 61
Giorgetto Giugiaro, "Logica" Electronic Sewing Machine, 1981 (I-13)

Controlled by three electronic circuits, which replace most of the mechanical parts of the traditional sewing machine, Giorgetto Giugiaro's "Logica" brings electronics to domestic sewing. In contrast to earlier models, which had concentrated on the style of the machine, this design is intended to expand the possibilities of use. Through its extensive programming, a complicated succession of operations may be preselected and executed with great rapidity.

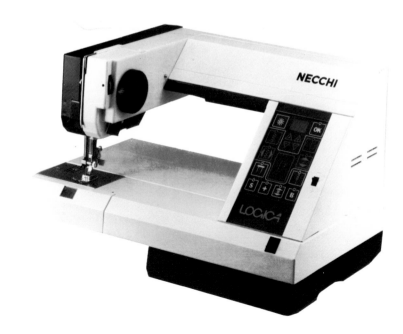

Plate 62
Paolo Deganello, "Torso"
Lounge Chair, 1982 (III-19)

Design in the 1980s has been distinguished by a high degree of specialization, and Paolo Deganello's "Torso" series represents a deliberately individualistic aesthetic, combining stylistic features of the 1950s (such as the splayed metal legs) with concern for human comfort and use. "The theme of this project is the dialogue between an animate body, and that of the inanimate body, produced industrially, upon which it is seated. By virtue of its movement, the one dominates the other, bending it into shape. It is not just one single plastic body, but a whole made up of two soft forms, clothed, warm and well wrapped, capable of any number of possible variations. . . . One needs a landscape not of aseptic forms, white, geometric, or objective, acceptable to a multiple of consumers, but one of strongly characterized forms, which in the choice on the part of the consumer is one of a strong declaration of identity; sensual forms, warm, differing in color and decoration, where the body wants to move and search for its right position and nestle up into it feeling protected."

Appliances

Introduction by Dieter Rams

As head of the product design department of Braun AG since 1962, Dieter Rams has defined the product image that has built the firm's reputation on an international scale.

Technology permeates the world in which we live. Over the last four decades, technology has also won general acceptance as an essential component of human culture. Such acceptance clearly could never have been achieved had it depended on the efforts of designers and architects themselves, and of those few industrialists who have come under their influence. Major credit for the popular acceptance of technology as culture must rather be given to the trade associations and professional journals, to the media, and in no small measure also to the various exhibitions that have been made widely available through museums. These alone could create within society generally, and the business community in particular, an enhanced appreciation of the philosophy that underlies today's well-designed domestic appliances.

Design is an important theme—of that I have no doubt. We are all strongly influenced by the design of the things we constantly see about us. The objects we use every day unquestionably have an effect on how we feel about life, about ourselves, and about our world. Indeed, they affect the whole climate of our society, the ways in which we relate to ourselves and to one another. Design can be a most revealing measure of change as well as a catalyst for effecting change.

For this reason it is not only wise but also absolutely necessary that careful consideration be given to the whole question of industrial design. We designers and the firms that take design seriously stand in need of just such deliberations. We welcome feedback. When I say that, I am not thinking about enhancing our public image; what I prefer is, through critical reflection and in dialogue with others, to arrive at a clearer and more adequate understanding of what I as a designer am about—what truly falls within the scope of my competence and responsibility, what I can and should in fact be doing.

The very attempt to gather together the best-designed works, prime examples of the designer's art, brings into question the very criteria by which design is to be judged. In recent decades we have witnessed a growing appreciation of just how complex a thing "design" really is. At the same time we have become aware of an ever-mounting uneasiness on the part of many designers, an uneasiness that is still increasing today. We designers are uneasy, for example, about having to put a fixed label on something that is continually in flux. We are uneasy about having to dissect, as it were, something whose very essence is rooted not in any of its distinct parts but in its very totality. We are uneasy about having to attempt objective evaluation of something that does not simply lend itself to objective analysis, given the complex way in which its otherwise precisely measurable components are intricately intertwined, not to speak of its more elusive and unmeasurable symbolic and spiritual significance.

I for one am certainly not able to look at and evaluate recent developments in industrial design in an objective way, as a disinterested observer. I can look at the period only as one who has been both involved in and affected by these very developments, as one who has himself helped to shape them.

If I were to look only at the appliances assembled here, and do so as through the eyes of an art historian, what would interest me most would be the various modulations in style that have occurred over the last several decades. Indeed, one can hardly deny that in comparison with the appliances of the seventies, in outward appearance those of the fifties have a charm all their own. The whole area of style itself merits a great deal of serious attention, but for the designer it is clearly not the central concern.

The underlying concern, for me at any rate, is rather the question of how a designer accomplishes what specifically is the designer's task, namely, to shape an appliance in such a way that it will fulfill its purpose. After all, radios and toasters, lamps and razors, television sets and ballpoint pens are meant to be used. They are instruments, not works of art. They fulfill a function, and design must serve that function. Indeed, this requirement is so fundamental and so crucial that it is sometimes overlooked. When this happens, design is treated as if it were simply a matter of imparting to an appliance some kind of aesthetic quality—a quality so pretentious that the device would be set apart as almost a work of art or so trivial as to accommodate it to the lowest levels of mass taste.

Developments in design over the last forty years have convinced me that designers and industrialists have increasingly come to see and respect this functional requirement. Over these decades design has really come into its own; it has become more professional, more sensitive, and more self-conscious. There has been less and less emphasis on artistic flair and more and more attention given to the values of experience and technical know-how. Design and designers have come to play a more significant role in the whole complicated and time-consuming business of product development. While this is not true in every instance, it is increasingly true in so many firms that it seems to me to constitute a trend.

In the fifties, well-designed appliances were few and far between, the creations of individual designers and pioneering companies. Often such products were unique, lonely portents of some distant future; indeed, they attracted attention precisely because they stood out from all the rest. Today well-executed design is more common and less spectacular, less apt to attract special notice. With many of the appliances on the market, the designer's individual contribution is no longer apparent. This is because, from the very outset, design is worked into the total concept of the product, into its very constitution and construction, even into the way it is produced. It is not readily apparent on simple examination, but is recognized only after actual experience with the appliance over an extended period of use.

For my team and me what is important is not just coming up with an overall concept of the product—which is what people generally take to be the chief objective of a designer. We are as intent on achieving a meaningful and functional shaping of all its details as well, of everything that pertains to the usefulness of the product. We go into such questions as the most up-to-date technologies, the best materials, the most efficient approaches to production. We seek to become as knowledgeable as possible about the actual uses to which the appliance will be put. Together with a whole team of specialists, we address the task of creating a good, durable product, and one that can be offered for sale at a reasonable price.

Naturally, this does not mean that we are indifferent to matters of visual appeal, but we do not regard the appearance of a product as an end in itself; style and appearance are rather part and parcel of its function as a whole. An appliance that is meant to be used should of course manifest some external appeal; it should also hold a certain charm and fascination, and it should be able to communicate its nature and purpose quickly and unambiguously.

Some of today's newer technologies—those in the field of micro-electronics, for example—probably seem strange to many people, who may even perceive them somehow as threatening. In such instances, design has both the chance and the challenge to communicate the technology to the user. The designer can give such appliances a form that will let the user feel more at ease with them, more familiar and accepting, more willing to use them.

In recent years the entrepreneurial firm has become increasingly significant in the field of design. A designer is very much dependent on the prerequisites and conditions that are established by the firm for which he is working. Good design presupposes a corresponding readiness and desire on the part of the firm actually to develop new, improved, and usable products, and to that end, to provide the means required to do so.

It is not sufficient, for instance, for the firm simply to grant the designer a free hand. When it comes to industrial design, nothing is accomplished merely by an unstinting generosity on the part of management—the kind of profligate benevolence often practiced by American firms. Rather than providing a blank check, a firm needs capable workers in its various departments, dedicated people with competence and experience, and it needs resources of many kinds—if good design is to be achieved and actually implemented. Today there are still far too few businesses that demonstrate both the will and means to achieve quality in their appliance design, but there have been a number of positive signs of promising developments.

Can it be said, then, that appliance design in the eighties is superior to what it was in the fifties? A wholesale affirmation—or for that matter, denial—of such a proposition would probably be inappropriate. The prerequisites for design have changed so greatly over the years—as have human needs and social realities in general—that a direct comparison of this kind would be of little meaning. What might be fairer would be an assessment based solely on my own work. From that perspective, it can be said that in the fifties my appliances were designed as well as the technical possibilities and my own skills and experience then permitted. Today, other solutions are possible—solutions that in many instances are better than before. I am convinced that designers must in every age pursue better design solutions. Indeed, without that conviction, it would be meaningless, for me at least, to go on working.

For design, so far as I am concerned, is not—like fashion—a value-free undertaking. It is not just a matter—and this bears constant repeating—of forever coming up with some new style that can help people satisfy their needs, but in ways that are now more pleasurable, now more attractive. No, what we designers are after is, to put it bluntly, progress.

By this I do not mean the sort of naïve faith in progress that impelled so many designers of the previous generation. We are beyond that. Experience has taught us in no uncertain terms how difficult and demanding a task it is just to grasp the real needs of human beings, and on the basis of such understanding, to design products that will actually meet those needs.

For me, however, the difficulty of the task does not offer grounds for despair. True, we are only on the threshold of performing the task. We have a long way to go yet—but there is a way! I firmly believe that it is indeed possible to learn about human beings, to learn more than we presently know, to learn what people really need and what can truly serve and benefit them. Many designers today, for instance, are zealously seeking to keep abreast of the latest developments in the human sciences, where specialized studies of our ways of living, thinking, reacting, socializing, and working provide insights on which designers can responsibly build.

The experience of recent years has given us a clear picture of the direction in which design must go. My hope is simply that my own work might help to move things along in the proper direction. The goal, it seems to me, is to help limit and reduce the chaos of the world about us. Accordingly, the best design for me is the least design. I am encouraged by the mounting dissatisfaction being voiced today over our common penchant for growth at any price, over the ravaging of nature, and over the unmerciful bombarding of the human nervous system with an endless barrage of stimuli and sensations. I also find encouragement in the fact that the exhibits now being offered as models of good design are almost without exception models of a kind of design that is reserved and chaste, modest and unimposing, neutral and balanced.

Mario Bellini Italian, born 1935
**I-1 "Totem" radio and record
player, 1971**
Lacquered-wood housing, height
20¹/₁₆" (51 cm)
Manufacturer: Brionvega
Prizes: Honorable mention, Ljubljana,
Bio, 1973; Compasso d'Oro, 1979
Brionvega S.p.A., Milan

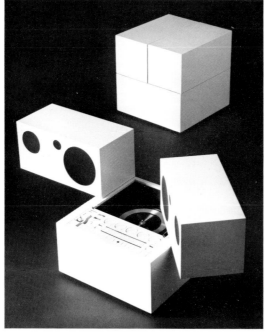

Mario Bellini Italian, born 1935
I-2 "Divisumma 18" calculator, 1973
ABS thermoplastic housing, length
10¹/₁₆" (25.5 cm)
Manufacturer: Olivetti
ING. C. Olivetti C.S.p.A., Milan

Mario Bellini Italian, born 1935
I-3 Cassette deck, 1975 (1976–78)
ABS plastic housing, width 12" (30.5 cm)
Manufacturer: Yamaha
Collection of J. Randolph Hawkins,
Blackwood, New Jersey

Mario Bellini Italian, born 1935
**I-4 "Praxis 35" portable electric
typewriter, 1981**
Metal housing, width 16½" (41.9 cm)
Manufacturer: Olivetti
ING. C. Olivetti C.S.p.A., Milan

Max Bill Swiss, born 1908
I-5 Wall clock, 1957
Stainless-steel and aluminum housing,
diameter 11⅞" (30.2 cm)
Manufacturer: Junghans
The Museum of Modern Art,
New York. Philip C. Johnson Fund.
347.61
Plate 24

Artur Braun German, born 1925
Fritz Eichler German, born 1911
I-6 Radio, 1955
Plastic housing, length 9¼" (23.4 cm)
Manufacturer: Braun
Braun AG, Taunus, West Germany

Achille Castiglioni Italian, born 1918
Piergiacomo Castiglioni Italian,
1913–1968
I-7 Vacuum cleaner, 1956
Plastic housing, height 15¼" (38.7 cm)
Manufacturer: R.E.M. di Rossetti Enrico
Prizes: Silver medal, Milan, Triennale,
1957; Compasso d'Oro, 1957
The Museum of Modern Art,
New York. Gift of the manufacturer.
6.SC.58

Wells Coates British, born Japan,
1895–1958
I-8 "Princess" radio, 1947 (1948–49)
Plastic housing, width 8" (20.3 cm)
Manufacturer: E. K. Cole
Collection of Gordon Bussey, England

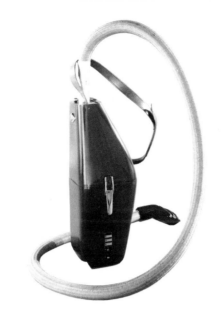

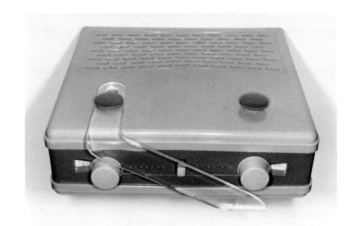

Joe Colombo Italian, 1930–1971
I-9 Mini kitchen on casters, 1963
Wood and stainless steel, height 37⅜"
(94.9 cm)
Manufacturer: Boffi
Prize: Silver medal, Milan, Triennale,
1964
The Museum of Modern Art, New
York. Gift of the manufacturer

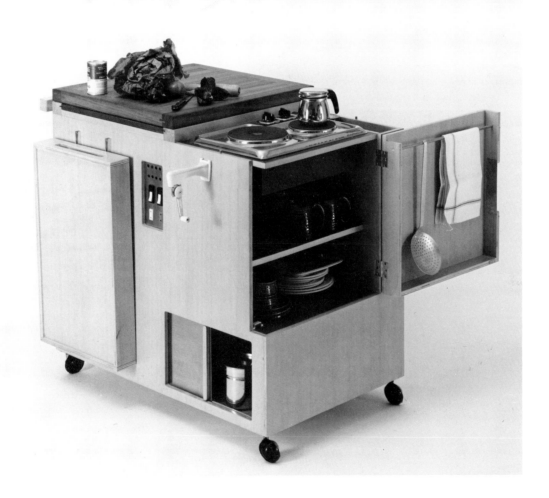

Henry Dreyfuss (Henry Dreyfuss Associates, in collaboration with Bell Telephone Laboratories) American, 1904–1972
I-10 "Trimline" telephone, 1965 (from 1965)
Plastic housing, length 8⁷/₁₆" (21.5 cm)
Manufacturer: Western Electric
Philadelphia Museum of Art. Gift of American Bell. 1983-2-1

L M Ericsson Company Swedish, established Stockholm, 1876
I-11 "Ericofon" telephone, 1954 (1955–82)
SAN plastic housing, height 8³/₈" (21.4 cm)
Manufacturer: Ericsson
Philadelphia Museum of Art. Gift of Ericsson Information Systems

The Eureka Company American, established Detroit, 1909
I-12 "Mighty Mite" vacuum cleaner, 1982 (from 1982)
ABS plastic housing, length 11¹/₂" (29.2 cm)
Manufacturer: Eureka
The Eureka Company, Bloomington, Illinois

Giorgetto Giugiaro Italian, born 1938
I-13 "Logica" electronic sewing machine, 1981 (from 1982)
Plastic and die-cast aluminum housing, width 16¹/₂" (42 cm)
Manufacturer: Necchi
Necchi S.p.A., Pavia, Italy
Plate 61

Kenneth Grange British, born 1929
I-14 Battery whisk, 1971 (from 1972)
ABS plastic housing, length 7¹/₄" (18.5 cm)
Manufacturer: Kenwood
Philadelphia Museum of Art. Gift of THORN EMI (Kenwood)
Plate 49

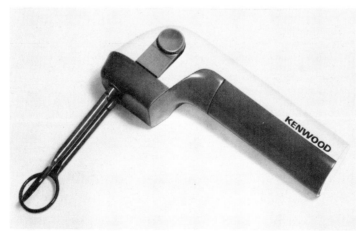

Marc Harrison (Marc Harrison Associates) American, born 1936
I-15 "Cuisinart DLC-X" food processor, 1981 (from 1982)
Polycarbonate plastic and nylon housing, height 17¹/₄" (43.8 cm)
Manufacturer: Cuisinarts
Cuisinarts, Inc., Greenwich, Connecticut

I. D. Two American, established
Palo Alto, 1979
**I-16 "Compass" computer, 1982
(from 1982)**
Magnesium housing, width 11½"
(29 cm)
Manufacturer: Grid Systems
Grid Systems Corporation, Mountain
View, California
Plate 59

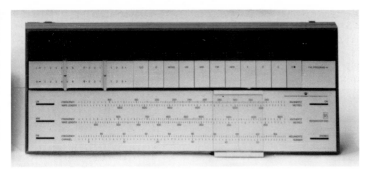

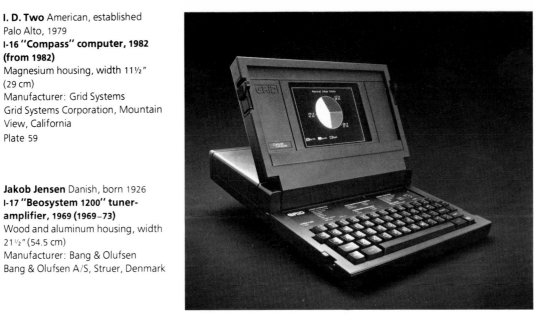

Jakob Jensen Danish, born 1926
**I-17 "Beosystem 1200" tuner-
amplifier, 1969 (1969–73)**
Wood and aluminum housing, width
21½" (54.5 cm)
Manufacturer: Bang & Olufsen
Bang & Olufsen A/S, Struer, Denmark

Jakob Jensen Danish, born 1926
**I-18 "Beogram 4000" turntable, 1972
(1972–74)**
Wood, aluminum, and stainless-steel
housing, width 18⅞" (48 cm)
Manufacturer: Bang & Olufsen
Bang & Olufsen A/S, Struer, Denmark

Fabio Lenci Italian, born 1935
**I-19 "Aquarius" bath and shower
unit, 1974 (from 1975)**
Glass-resin reinforced methacrylate,
height 82½" (209.5 cm)
Manufacturer: Teuco-Guzzini
Hastings Tile & Il Bagno Collection,
New York

Raymond Loewy (Raymond Loewy
Associates) American, born France,
1893
I-20 Radio, 1945
Metal and plastic housing, width
18½" (47 cm)
Manufacturer: Hallicrafters
Division of Electricity and Nuclear
Energy, National Museum of American
History, Smithsonian Institution,
Washington, D.C.

Raymond Loewy (Raymond Loewy
Associates) American, born France, 1893
**I-21 Mini push-button television,
1948**
Metal, plastic, and wood housing,
width 21" (53.3 cm)
Manufacturer: Hallicrafters
Division of Electricity and Nuclear
Energy, National Museum of American
History, Smithsonian Institution,
Washington, D.C.
Plate 1

I Appliances

Angelo Mangiarotti Italian,
born 1921
**I-22 "Secticon" table clock, 1962
(1962–68)**
Phenol-melamine and brass housing,
height 6⅛" (15.5 cm)
Manufacturer: Portescap
Portescap, La Chaux-de-Fonds,
Switzerland

Manfred Meinzer (with Guido
Besimo) German, born 1943
**I-23 Stereo tape recorder, 1967
(1967–80)**
Stainless-steel, aluminum, plastic, and
copper housing, width 16¼" (41.3 cm)
Manufacturer: Revox
Studer Revox America, Inc., Nashville

Gerd Alfred Müller German, born
1932
I-24 Kitchen machine, 1957
Polystyrol housing, height 15" (38 cm)
Manufacturer: Braun
Braun AG, Taunus, West Germany

George Nelson American, born 1908
I-25 Wall clock, 1949 (1949–69)
Brass and birch housing, diameter
13⅜" (34 cm)
Manufacturer: Howard Miller
Philadelphia Museum of Art. Purchased
with funds contributed by COLLAB: The
Contemporary Design Group for the
Philadelphia Museum of Art

Marcello Nizzoli Italian, 1887–1969
**I-26 "Elettrosumma 14" adding
machine, 1946 (1946–56)**
Enameled-metal housing, width 5½"
(14 cm)
Manufacturer: Olivetti
ING. C. Olivetti C.S.p.A., Milan

Marcello Nizzoli Italian, 1887–1969
I-27 "Lexicon 80" typewriter, 1948
Enameled-metal housing, width 17½"
(44.5 cm)
Manufacturer: Olivetti
ING. C. Olivetti C.S.p.A., Milan

Marcello Nizzoli Italian, 1887–1969
I-28 "Lettera 22" portable typewriter, 1950
Enameled-metal housing, width 11⅜"
(28.9 cm)
Manufacturer: Olivetti
Prize: Compasso d'Oro, 1954
ING. C. Olivetti C.S.p.A., Milan

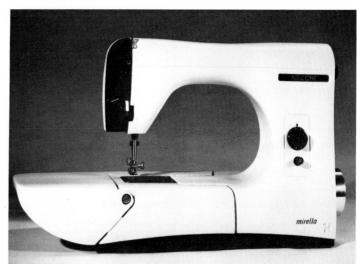

Marcello Nizzoli Italian, 1887–1969
**I-29 "Mirella" sewing machine, 1957
(1958–61)**
Enameled-aluminum housing, length
19¹/₁₆" (48.5 cm)
Manufacturer: Necchi
Prizes: Grand prize, Milan, Triennale,
1957; Compasso d'Oro, 1957
Necchi S.p.A., Milan
Plate 22

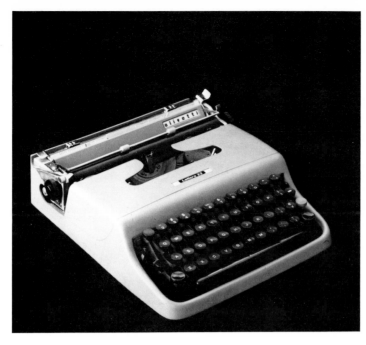

Eliot Noyes American, 1910–1977
**I-30 "Selectric" typewriter, 1961
(from 1961)**
Die-cast aluminum housing, length
15¼" (38.7 cm)
Manufacturer: IBM
The IBM Corporation, Armonk,
New York

Philco American, established
Philadelphia, 1892
**I-31 "Predicta" television, 1958
(1959)**
Metal housing, height 24" (61 cm)
Manufacturer: Philco
Collection of Arnold Chase, Hartford

Ezio Pirali Italian, born 1921
I-32 Table fan, 1954 (1954–60)
Metal and rubber housing, height 7⅞"
(20 cm)
Manufacturer: Zerowatt
Prizes: Compasso d'Oro, 1954; Silver
medal, Milan, Triennale, 1954
Zerowatt S.p.A., Bergamo, Italy

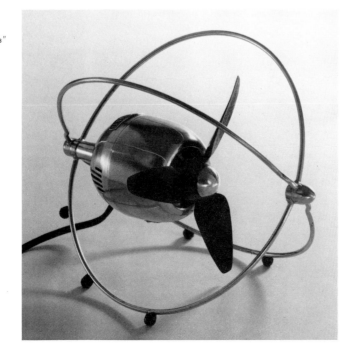

Gio Ponti Italian, 1891–1979
**I-33 Sink and toilet, 1953 (sink
1954–71; toilet from 1954)**
Porcelain, height of sink 31½″
(80 cm); height of toilet 15″ (38.1 cm)
Manufacturer: Ideal Standard
Prize: Gold medal, Milan,
Triennale, 1954
Philadelphia Museum of Art. Gift of
Ideal Standard. 1983-52-1,2
Plate 15

Dieter Rams German, born 1932
I-34 Portable transistor radio, 1956
Metal housing, length 11¼″ (28.5 cm)
Manufacturer: Braun
Braun AG, Taunus, West Germany

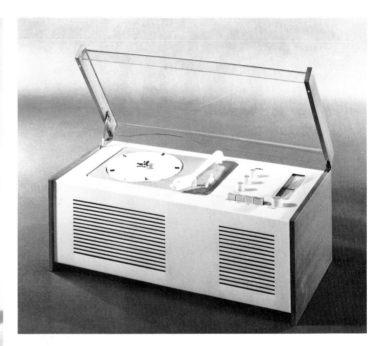

Dieter Rams German, born 1932
Hans Gugelot Swiss, born Indonesia,
1920–1965
**I-35 "Phonosuper" phonograph and
radio, 1956 (1956–60)**
Metal and wood housing, length 22⅞″
(58 cm)
Manufacturer: Braun
Braun AG, Taunus, West Germany

Dieter Rams German, born 1932
**I-36 Combination phonograph and
pocket radio, 1959 (1959–62)**
Plastic and metal housing, length 9½″
(23.5 cm)
Manufacturer: Braun
Braun AG, Taunus, West Germany
Plate 13

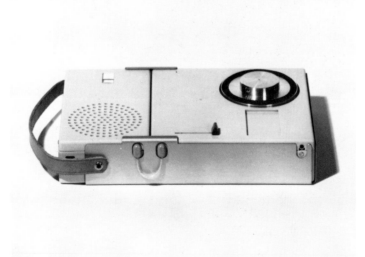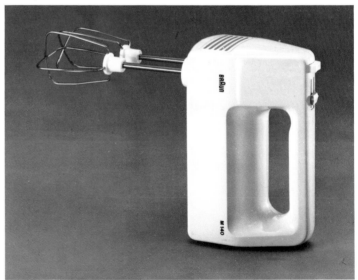

Dieter Rams German, born 1932
I-37 Mixer, 1968
Plastic housing, length 6⅞″ (17.5 cm)
Manufacturer: Braun
Prize: Bundespreis "Gute Form," 1970
Braun AG, Taunus, West Germany

Richard Sapper Italian, born
Germany, 1932
**I-38 "Static" table clock, 1959
(from 1960)**
Stainless-steel housing, height 3¼"
(8 cm)
Manufacturer: Lorenz
Prize: Compasso d'Oro, 1960
Philadelphia Museum of Art. Gift of
Lorenz S.p.A.

Peter Schlumbohm American, born
Germany, 1896–1962
I-39 "Filterjet" fan, 1951
Plastic and rubber composite housing,
diameter 22" (55.9 cm)
Manufacturer: Chemex
Chemex International Housewares
Corporation, Pittsfield, Massachusetts
Plate 18

Clive Sinclair (with Iain Sinclair)
British, born 1940
**I-40 "Executive" pocket calculator,
1972 (1972–75)**
Plastic housing, length 5½" (14 cm)
Manufacturer: Sinclair Radionics
Prize: Design Council Award, 1973
Sinclair Research Ltd., Boston
Plate 45

Clive Sinclair British, born 1940
**I-41 "Microvision" pocket tele-
vision, 1976 (1977–78)**
Metal housing, height 1½" (3.8 cm)
Manufacturer: Sinclair Radionics
Prize: Design Council Award, 1978
Sinclair Research Ltd., Boston

Hans Erich Slany German, born 1926
I-42 Knife sharpener, 1974
ABS plastic housing, length 6" (15.2 cm)
Manufacturer: Leifheit
Philadelphia Museum of Art. Gift of
Leifheit International GmbH

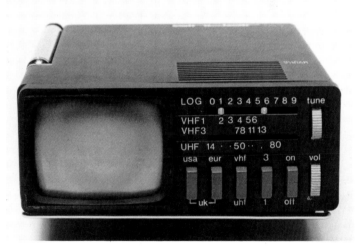
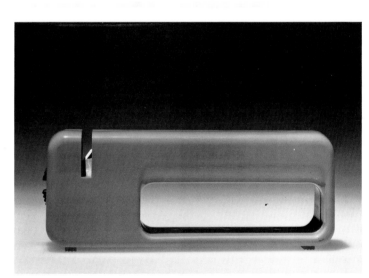

The Sony Corporation Japanese,
established Tokyo, 1945
**I-43 Portable transistor television,
1959 (1960– 62)**
Metal housing, width 8¼" (21 cm)
Manufacturer: Sony
Prize: Gold medal, Milan, Triennale,
1960
The Sony Corporation, Park Ridge,
New Jersey
Plate 12

The Sony Corporation Japanese,
established Tokyo, 1945
**I-44 "Walkman" portable radio,
1978 (1979– 80)**
Anodized-aluminum housing, height
5¼" (13.3 cm)
Manufacturer: Sony
The Sony Corporation, Park Ridge,
New Jersey

The Sony Corporation Japanese,
established Tokyo, 1945
**I-45 "Profeel" component television
system, 1979 (from 1980)**
ABS plastic housing, width 19¹³/₁₆"
(50.4 cm)
Manufacturer: Sony
The Sony Corporation, Park Ridge,
New Jersey

The Sony Corporation Japanese,
established Tokyo, 1945
I-46 Clock radio, 1981 (from 1982)
Polystyrene housing, height 4⅝"
(11.8 cm)
Manufacturer: Sony
The Sony Corporation, Park Ridge,
New Jersey

Ettore Sottsass, Jr. Italian, born
Austria, 1917
Perry King British, born 1938
**I-47 "Valentine" portable
typewriter, 1969**
ABS plastic housing, width 17⅛"
(43.5 cm)
Manufacturer: Olivetti
Prize: Honorable mention, Ljubljana,
Bio, 1973
ING. C. Olivetti C.S.p.A., Milan
Plate 37

Gino Valle Italian, born 1923
I-48 "Cifra 3" table clock, 1966
Plastic housing, length 7¹/₁₆" (18 cm)
Manufacturer: Solari
Collection of the designer, Udine, Italy

Daniel Weil Argentine, lives in
England, born 1953
I-49 "Bag" radio, 1981 (from 1981)
Flexible PVC housing, length 11¹¹/₁₆"
(29.7 cm)
Manufacturer: Parenthesis
Philadelphia Museum of Art. Gift of
the designer

Reinhold Weiss German, lives in the
United States, born 1934
I-50 Desk fan, 1961 (1961–70)
Plastic housing, height 5½" (14 cm)
Manufacturer: Braun
Prize: Bundespreis "Gute Form," 1970
Braun AG, Taunus, West Germany

Marco Zanuso Italian, born 1916
Richard Sapper Italian, born
Germany, 1932
I-51 "Doney 14" television, 1962
ABS plastic housing, width 14³/₁₆"
(36 cm)
Manufacturer: Brionvega
Prize: Compasso d'Oro, 1962
Brionvega S.p.A., Milan

Marco Zanuso Italian, born 1916
Richard Sapper Italian, born
Germany, 1932
I-52 Radio, 1965 (1965–78)
ABS plastic housing, width 8⅝" (22 cm)
Manufacturer: Brionvega
Prizes: Gold medal, Ljubljana, Bio,
1966; Bundespreis "Gute Form," 1969
Brionvega S.p.A., Milan

Marco Zanuso Italian, born 1916
Richard Sapper Italian, born
Germany, 1932
I-53 "Grillo" telephone, 1965
ABS plastic housing, length 6⁵/₁₆"
(16 cm)
Manufacturer: Italtel
Prizes: Compasso d'Oro, 1967; Gold
medal, Ljubljana, Bio, 1968
Philadelphia Museum of Art. Gift of
Italtel. 1982-54-1
Plate 27

Marco Zanuso Italian, born 1916
Richard Sapper Italian, born
Germany, 1932
I-54 "Black 12" television, 1969
Methacrylate housing, width 12⅜"
(31.5 cm)
Manufacturer: Brionvega
Prize: Honorable mention, Ljubljana,
Bio, 1973
Brionvega S.p.A., Milan

Marco Zanuso Italian, born 1916
I-55 Kitchen scale, 1970 (from 1971)
ABS plastic housing, width 6½"
(16.5 cm)
Manufacturer: Terraillon
Terraillon, Annemasse Cedex, France

Marco Zanuso Italian, born 1916
I-56 "Ariante" fan, 1973 (from 1974)
ABS plastic housing, height 7³/₁₆"
(18.3 cm)
Manufacturer: Vortice
Prizes: Compasso d'Oro, 1979;
Honorable mention, Ljubljana,
Bio, 1981
Philadelphia Museum of Art. Gift of
Vortice Elettrosociali. 1983-13-1

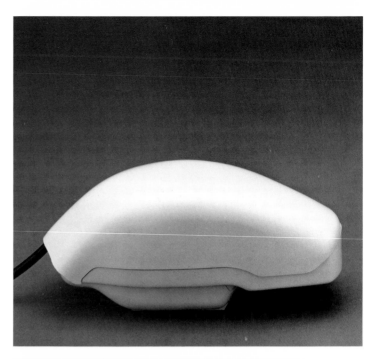

Ceramics and Glass

Introduction by Timo Sarpaneva

A Finnish industrial designer and
artist in glass, Timo Sarpaneva
surveys the recent history of
ceramics and glass from the
viewpoint of a craftsman who has
also conceived works for mass
production.

The Second World War had a far greater effect on the arts than the First World War had. No wonder: thirty-five million people died, and countless numbers were wounded, physically and mentally. Ten million people lived in a nightmare existence in concentration camps. The chaos of war paralyzed the minds of artists, especially in Europe, for a long time. Creativity seemed to have died in the war, and if it existed at all on a broader scale, it was diabolical, governed by the forces of destruction. When atom bombs were dropped on Hiroshima and Nagasaki in 1945, creativity directed toward the destruction of mankind reached its apex.

The end of the war signaled the dawning of a new age; it was a fresh start. The aim was to create a different framework for a new age, which everybody hoped would be better than the preceding one. It was a time of rapid progress and innovation. Generally speaking, one could say that the period between the war and the mid-1960s was one of growing optimism, while from the mid-1960s to the 1970s, inflation and global ecological problems gave their own tone to the arts. Today we are evidently undergoing another period of change, both social and artistic.

It is said that history repeats itself. This is true of ideas, too. An examination of Suprematism in Russia during the early decades of this century shows that the Pop style and Post-Modernism in the spirit of the collection of works issued by the Memphis group in Milan are like phenomena that existed a long time ago in design. Examples are the porcelain teapot designed by Kasimir Malevich in 1923, an excellent example of three-dimensional graphics and eye-pleasing object architecture; his porcelain cups of the same year; and his graphic art and that of El Lissitzky and Nikolia Suetini. The new wave is, in fact, the post-post-wave.

Mattheo Thun's "Lagoda" vase for Memphis (1982)

Postwar architecture, strange as it may sound, had a profound influence on pottery and glass design. The architecture of Charles Eames and Eero Saarinen during the 1940s has sometimes been called Organic Modernism. The union of free forms and abstract masses is excellently demonstrated in Frank Lloyd Wright's Guggenheim Museum in New York. The organic vocabulary is visible in earlier works, too, for instance, in Salvador Dali's fluid objects, Joan Miró's flowing rhythms, and Barbara Hepworth's spatially innovative wood sculptures. Jackson Pollock's spontaneous paintings of massed, densely colored lines should not be excluded from this language of forms. His rhythmic lines unite to build comprehensive organic shapes by means of optical confusion; lines create masses.

Bernard Leach's bottle (1972)

The effect of the organic was felt immediately in glass design, and specifically in Scandinavia. Simplicity, abstraction, and asymmetry were clearly evident in the shapes of studio glass. Their profiles were even representational at times.

Two important pioneers in the art of modern pottery were Bernard Leach in Great Britain and Shoji Hamada, Leach's student, who revived the Japanese pottery tradition. His influence was of great significance, Japan being a prime source of inspiration for a novice potter. Leach's other well-known students include Michael Cardew and Katherine Pleydell-Bouverie. Another prominent potter was William Staite Murray, an artist who emphasized the aesthetic function of the objects he designed, which he consciously created as *objets d'art*. Lucie Rie, who founded her work-shop in 1939, is among the more modern potters. Hans Coper has been

Shoji Hamada's dish (c. 1950)

working with Rie since 1946, after he moved to London from Germany. The results of their combined work have served as an inspiration to many younger potters. The London Central School of Art also played an important role in the development of the art of pottery, especially in the 1950s.

In Scandinavia, industry has actively supported the art of pottery. In Finland, for example, the Arabia porcelain factory founded a special art department as early as 1932. Among the very talented Finnish potters were Friedl Kjellberg, who was engaged in developing porcelain manufacturing techniques and who, in 1942, was the first European to succeed in making rice porcelain; Aune Siimes, whose specialties included translucent, thin-walled porcelain objects; Toini Muona, who also created some extremely beautiful porcelains; and Kyllikki Salmenhaara, who worked systematically on ceramic material and examined glazes with an almost scientific accuracy, achieving results that earlier were thought impossible. Birger Kaipiainen, an original artist whose work maintains high production standards, draws his subjects from the world of fantasy and music; his work reveals a strong Byzantine influence, richness of color, and a certain mysticism. The Danish potter Axel Salto deserves mention, and among the Swedes, Carl-Harry Stålhane and Wilhelm Kåge, whose wealth of ideas are reflected in his broad production (II-29).

Finnish designers of the 1950s include Kaj Franck, whose "Kilta" dinner service (II-17), which came on the market in 1952, was playfully said to have caused a revolution in the kitchen. Another skillful designer at the Arabia factory was Ulla Procopé, who created beautiful and practical table services (II-50). In Norway, Tias Eckhoff designed simple and aesthetically pleasing everyday kitchenware for industrial production.

In the United States studio pottery was greatly influenced by two émigrés from Vienna, Otto and Gertrud Natzler, and by Karen Barnes and her husband David Weinrib. The work of the American Peter Voulkos is a prime example of the importance of Picasso's art to potters; he handles his material with strength, in the spirit of Abstract Expressionism. Of the Americans of the 1960s Robert Arneson took a new approach to his material, in the direction of Pop art. The use of graphic ornamental subjects, from neo-primitive themes to the style of Picasso, was typical of the postwar Italian potters, for example, Guido Gambone.

The Rosenthal factory's Studio Line production and display ceramics play an important part in the history of modern pottery and porcelain. Philip Rosenthal deserves special acknowledgment for his courage in backing artists in their efforts to design independently, combining the pictorial arts with porcelain, which has had an enormous effect on the field. Designers who have worked for Rosenthal include Walter Gropius, whose teapot "TAC 1" from 1959 deserves mention; Lucio Fontana, whose porcelain sculpture "Oval Spatial Concept" was designed in 1968; and Henry Moore, whose "Moonhead" is of the same year. The "Suomi" dinner service (II-58), designed by this writer, represents Rosenthal's production in 1976.

France lost its preeminence in glass design after the war; from the mid-1940s onward, Finland generally took the lead over Italy (Venice at its center) and Sweden. The death of Paolo Venini in 1959 was a serious blow to Italian glass design. Venini had adopted old glassmaking techniques, including *latticino, vetro tessuto, vetro pezzato,* and *vetro murrina.* Many other skilled designers reflect the power, tenacity, and uncompromising

Lucie Rie's bottle (1974)

Peter Voulkos's plate (1973)

Robert Arneson's "David" (1977)

Walter Gropius's "TAC 1" tea service (1959)

Henry Moore's "Moonhead" (1968)

nature of Venini; his influence on European glassmaking began with a series of important exhibitions in the early 1950s as a result of which many museums purchased Venini's works. Artists who worked under Venini include Franco Albini, whose lamps drew much attention in 1954; Gio Ponti; and Fulvio Bianconi, whose decorative bottles were much admired. During the "Italia 61" exhibition in Turin, Carlo Scarpa displayed his chandelier sculpture, which became a symbol of new Italian glass design. Flavio Poli worked for Seguso Vetri d'Arte in Murano; his production abounds with the spirit of organic sculpture, particularly his vases from around 1958 (II-48).

In the history of Scandinavian glass, there is a special ring to the names of Orrefors, Kosta, Nuutajärvi, Riihimäki, and Iittala. The successes of the Orrefors factory were largely due to Simon Gate and Edward Hald. Although Gate died in 1945, Hald continued designing into the 1950s; techniques such as *graal* and *ariel* are associated with Hald's name. Other influential artists with Orrefors include Sven Palmquist, whose many innovations include his famous "Ravenna" glass (II-45); Nils Landberg (II-30); Edvin Öhrström; and Ingeborg Lundin. Since 1950 the leading artist at the Kosta factory has been Vicke Lindstrand, who had earlier worked with both Gate and Hald at Orrefors, and who has continued to develop the *graal* and *ariel* techniques. The heavy-sided glass objects created by Lindstrand had links with the works of Henry Moore and Barbara Hepworth, and should be regarded as truly innovative.

The most important names in modern Finnish studio glass are Henry Ericsson, Göran Hongell, Arttu Brummer, and Gunnel Nyman. Nyman, in particular, worked for all the leading glass manufacturers in Finland and designed a number of purely sculptural objects in glass. In the late 1940s and early 1950s, Tapio Wirkkala designed a number of excellent glass pieces (II-72), many of which won immediate recognition abroad.

I undertook to design glass for the first time in 1950 for the Iittala glass factory. These objects, called "Hiidenkirnut" ("Devil's Churns"), were round walled as if worn by water. The method, developed in 1951, required great accuracy, with the glass itself having to be heated and cut several times. Sand blowing (for an opaque effect) and acid (for sheen) were used in the final treatment.

In the "Sydan" ("Heart") objects that I designed in 1953, I created an air bubble within the glass by the traditional method of using a damp wooden stick to produce steam in the glass; two types of wood, apple and haw-thorn, were used for this purpose at the Iittala glass factory. I also used the same method in 1954 for a sculpture that *House Beautiful* called the "most beautiful object of the year."

In 1956 I developed I-glass, which emphasized colors (II-56). The color scheme was subdued, grayish green, blue, and lilac. This created an intense effect, the colors glowing as if diffused by a cloud of mist. I aimed at a union of materials and colors, and these large objects were, in fact, watercolors in glass.

The Leerdam factory and the free style of Andries Copier may be cited as fine examples of Dutch glass design. The French Daum factory has been manufacturing fine crystal since the mid-1940s. In the United States the Steuben glassworks with Arthur Houghton and Sidney Waugh also had a strong influence; the factory provided well-known artists with a place to work. Glass design in England in the 1940s and 1950s can be described as

Simon Gate's glass vase (c. 1926)

Edward Hald's glass vase (c. 1935)

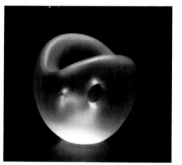

Timo Sarpaneva's "Devil's Churn" (1951)

Timo Sarpaneva's glass sculpture (1954), called the "most beautiful object of the year"

Timo Sarpaneva's "Tear" (1953)

Timo Sarpaneva's "Finlandia" glass bowl (1964)

conservative in style; John Hutton and Laurence Whistler deserve mention as skillful engravers.

The development of new studio glass is mostly due to the American Dominick Labino and to Harvey Littleton, who continued his work. As a result of experiments carried out by Labino in 1962, artists could start working with small glass-melting furnaces. The first course specializing in studio glass was organized at the University of Wisconsin. Marvin Lipofsky and Samuel Herman are the two most important of Littleton's students. Their work combines French Art Nouveau glass design and the ingredients of Pop art in a union which dissolves the form to a rich experience. The 1960s showed a general interest in Art Nouveau techniques; one of the most commonly used was *pâte de verre.*

The glass objects by the Finnish artist Oiva Toikka in the 1960s clearly display the influence of Art Nouveau and Pop art. Of my own 1960s production I would like to mention my "Finlandia" series. In the manufacturing technique I combined spontaneous and material-oriented work with strict discipline. The subject matter of these sculptures in a way chose its own form, though under careful supervision.

And the future? What can I say about it? Where should I look for it? In my own fantasy or in the fast-fleeting present? Personally I believe that the importance of space will become more pronounced. One example is my own Colin King Grand Prix sculpture, which I think extends beyond its outer form and shapes the space around it.

The great review of modern glass, the "New Glass" exhibition arranged by the Corning Museum of Glass in 1979, reveals the interest of its participants in time, the environment, and outer space. Many of the most beautiful exhibition objects were like altars dedicated to unknown gods. Heavy glass materials dominated and seemed to incorporate new extensions within the transparency of the glass. I do not think I am mistaken in saying that the "New Glass" exhibition contained much in new aesthetic material, mysticism, and meditation. The exhibition will undoubtedly continue as a source of inspiration into the 1980s.

Our technological world sets its own requirements on design. One cannot overemphasize the importance of handicrafts and artisans. The original ideas born in the studio should be combined with the technical, machine-implemented manufacturing process. Handicrafts and industrial production go hand in hand. One would like to see the number of workshops and studios increase rapidly everywhere, for they foster new ideas for the industry, and to see the original ideas of the artisans being used in industrial production. It is difficult for small workshops to survive if industry makes no effort to guard their budding, aesthetically rich ideas. We need human design, sensitivity, and the power of machines. Perhaps we will see this come true in the future. Perhaps in this lies the legacy we can leave our children and grandchildren.

Dominick Labino's "Emergence VI" (1971)

Timo Sarpaneva's "Gateway to Dreams" (1981), Colin King Grand Prix winner in 1981

Yūsuke Aida Japanese, born 1931
**II-1 "Classic" service, 1961
(from 1961)**
Stoneware, height of casserole 6³/₁₆"
(15.7 cm)
Manufacturer: Bennington Potters
Bennington Potters, Inc., Bennington,
Vermont

Winslow Anderson American, born
1917
II-2 Decanter, c. 1951
Blown glass, height 12⅞" (32.7 cm)
Manufacturer: Blenko
The Corning Museum of Glass,
Corning, New York. 51.4.570

John Andersson Swedish, born 1900
II-3 "Old Höganäs" service, 1955
Earthenware, height of teapot 5¾"
(14.6 cm)
Manufacturer: Andersson & Johansson
Höganäs Museum, Höganäs, Sweden

Sergio Asti Italian, born 1926
II-4 "Marco" vase, 1961 (from 1962)
Blown glass, height 11¹³/₁₆" (30 cm)
Manufacturer: Salviati
Prize: Compasso d'Oro, 1962
Salviati & C., Venice

Masakichi Awashima Japanese,
1914–1979
II-5 Goblet, 1955
Blown and cast *shizuku* glass, height
3⁷/₁₆″ (8.7 cm)
Manufacturer: Awashima
Philadelphia Museum of Art. Gift of
Mrs. Masakichi Awashima

Monica Backström Swedish, born
1939
II-6 Bowl, 1978
Blown glass, height 8⁹/₁₆″ (21.8 cm)
Manufacturer: Boda
The Corning Museum of Glass,
Corning, New York. 79.3.38B

Jacob Bang Danish, 1889–1965
II-7 Decanter, 1957
Blown glass, height 8½″ (21.6 cm)
Manufacturer: Kastrup
The Corning Museum of Glass,
Corning, New York. 61.3.203

Hans Theo Baumann German, born
Switzerland, 1924
**II-8 "Brasilia" coffee and tea
service, 1975 (from 1975)**
Porcelain, height of coffeepot 7¾″
(19.7 cm)
Manufacturer: Arzberg
Philadelphia Museum of Art. Gift of
Porzellanfabrik Arzberg. 1982-57-1–6

Michael Boehm German, born 1944
**II-9 "Papyrus" stemware, 1976
(from 1976)**
Blown glass, height of flute 9½″
(24.2 cm)
Manufacturer: Rosenthal
Rosenthal Studio Line

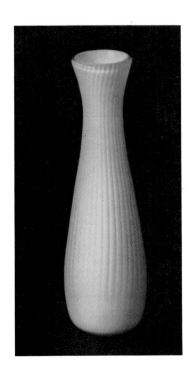

Hermann Bongard Norwegian, born
1921
II-10 Vase, 1954 (1954–58)
Blown glass, height 7¹³/₁₆″ (19.8 cm)
Manufacturer: Hadelands
A/S Christiania Glasmagasin, Oslo

Axel Brüel Danish, 1900–1977
II-11 "Thermodan" coffee service, 1957
Porcelain, height of coffeepot 10⅝"
(27 cm)
Manufacturer: Danmark
Prize: Silver medal, Milan, Triennale, 1957
The Metropolitan Museum of Art, New York. Purchase, Edward C. Moore, Jr., Gift, 1961. 61.7.36–40

Luigi Colani German, born 1928
II-12 "Drop" tea service, 1970 (from 1971)
Porcelain, height of teapot 4³/₁₆"
(10.7 cm)
Manufacturer: Rosenthal
Prize: Hanover, Gute Industrieform, 1972
Rosenthal Studio Line

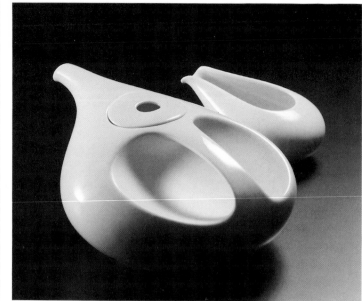

Andries Copier Dutch, born 1901
II-13 "Primula" service, 1947 (1947–c. 1960)
Pressed glass, diameter of saucer 5¾"
(14.7 cm)
Manufacturer: Leerdam
National Glasmuseum, Leerdam, The Netherlands

Gunnar Cyrén Swedish, born 1931
II-14 "Pop" goblets, 1967
Blown glass, height 6¾" (17.1 cm)
Manufacturer: Orrefors
AB Orrefors Glasbruk, Orrefors, Sweden

Freda Diamond American, born 1905
II-15 "Classic Crystal" glasses, 1949 (from 1950)
Glass, height of tallest glass 6" (15.2 cm)
Manufacturer: Libbey
Philadelphia Museum of Art. Gift of Libbey Glass. 1982-151-1–5

Elsa Fischer-Treyden German, born Russia, 1901
II-16 "Fuga" stemware, 1965 (from 1965)
Blown glass, height of flute 8¾"
(22.2 cm)
Manufacturer: Rosenthal
Prize: Bundespreis "Gute Form," 1969
Rosenthal Studio Line

Kaj Franck Finnish, born 1911
II-17 "Kilta" service, 1952 (1952–74)
Earthenware, height of cup 2⅜"
(6 cm)
Manufacturer: Arabia
Prize: Grand prize, Milan, Triennale,
1957
Oy Wärtsilä Ab Arabia, Helsinki

Kaj Franck Finnish, born 1911
II-18 "Kremlin Bells" decanter, 1957
Blown glass, height 13¾" (35 cm)
Manufacturer: Nuutajärvi
Philadelphia Museum of Art. Purchased
with funds contributed by COLLAB: The
Contemporary Design Group for the
Philadelphia Museum of Art. 1982-33-1

Kaj Franck Finnish, born 1911
II-19 Goblets, c. 1974
Blown glass, height 6⅛" (15.6 cm)
Manufacturer: Nuutajärvi
The Corning Museum of Glass,
Corning, New York. 74.3.86,88
Plate 46

Saburō Funakoshi Japanese, born
1931
II-20 Condiment set, 1969 (from 1969)
Blown glass, height of soy sauce bottle
4¾" (12.1 cm)
Manufacturer: Hoya
Hoya Corporation, Tokyo

Saburō Funakoshi Japanese, born 1931
II-21 Soy sauce bottle, 1978 (from 1978)
Blown glass, height 4⁵/₁₆″ (11 cm)
Manufacturer: Hoya
Hoya Corporation, Tokyo

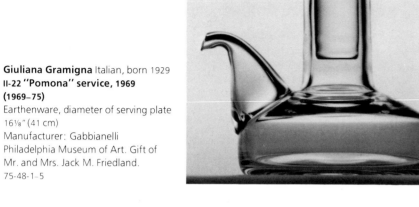

Giuliana Gramigna Italian, born 1929
II-22 "Pomona" service, 1969 (1969–75)
Earthenware, diameter of serving plate 16⅛″ (41 cm)
Manufacturer: Gabbianelli
Philadelphia Museum of Art. Gift of Mr. and Mrs. Jack M. Friedland. 75-48-1–5

Edith Heath American, born 1911
II-23 "Coupe" casseroles, 1947 (from 1949)
Stoneware, diameter of largest casserole 11″ (28 cm)
Manufacturer: Heath Ceramics
Philadelphia Museum of Art. Gift of the designer. 1983-49-1–3

David Hills American, born 1923
II-24 Vase, 1949 (from 1949)
Blown glass, height 7⅞″ (20 cm)
Manufacturer: Steuben
Philadelphia Museum of Art. Gift of Steuben Glass

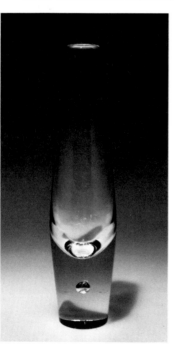
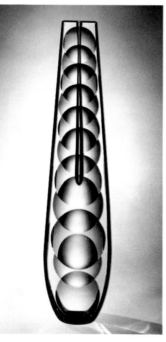

Pavel Hlava Czechoslovakian, born 1924
II-25 Vase, c. 1959
Blown and cut glass, height 15¼″ (38.7 cm)
Manufacturer: Art Center for Glass Industry
The Corning Museum of Glass, Corning, New York. 62.3.128

Saara Hopea Finnish, born 1925
II-26 Nesting glasses, 1951
Blown glass, height 3⁵/₁₆″ (8.5 cm)
Manufacturer: Nuutajärvi
Taideteollisuusmuseo, Helsinki

Willy Johansson Norwegian, born 1921
II-27 Vase, 1954 (1954–58)
Blown and cut glass, height 4⅞"
(12.4 cm)
Manufacturer: Hadelands
A/S Christiania Glasmagasin, Oslo

Arne Jon Jutrem Norwegian, born 1929
II-28 Vase, 1959
Blown glass, height 10⅞" (27.6 cm)
Manufacturer: Hadelands
The Corning Museum of Glass,
Corning, New York. 61.3.276A,B

Wilhelm Kåge Swedish, 1889–1960
**II-29 "Farsta" vases, 1952 and 1957;
bowl, 1953**
Stoneware, height of larger vase 6⅛"
(15.5 cm)
Manufacturer: Gustavsberg
Philadelphia Museum of Art. Gift of AB
Gustavsberg

Nils Landberg Swedish, born 1907
**II-30 "Tulip" wineglass, 1956
(1956–81)**
Blown glass, height 16" (40.6 cm)
Manufacturer: Orrefors
Philadelphia Museum of Art. Purchased
with funds contributed by COLLAB: The
Contemporary Design Group for the
Philadelphia Museum of Art. 1983-5-1

Richard Latham American, born 1920
Raymond Loewy American, born
France, 1893
**II-31 "Coffee Service 2000," 1954
(1954–78)**
Porcelain, height of coffeepot 9³/₁₆"
(23.3 cm)
Manufacturer: Rosenthal
Rosenthal Studio Line

Stig Lindberg Swedish, 1916–1982
II-32 "Spisa-Ribb" service, 1955 (1955–79)
Stoneware, diameter of plate 9⅞"
(25 cm)
Manufacturer: Gustavsberg
AB Gustavsberg, Gustavsberg, Sweden

Stig Lindberg Swedish, 1916–1982
II-33 "Terma" service, 1955 (1955–79)
Stoneware, height of coffeepot 7¹¹⁄₁₆"
(19.5 cm)
Manufacturer: Gustavsberg
Prizes: Gold medal, Milan, Triennale, 1957; Gold medal, Ljubljana, Bio, 1964
AB Gustavsberg, Gustavsberg, Sweden

Heinrich Löffelhardt German, 1901–1979
II-34 "Arzberg 2000" service, 1954 (1954–77)
Porcelain, height of teapot 5⅜"
(13.7 cm)
Manufacturer: Arzberg
Prize: Gold medal, Milan, Triennale, 1954
Philadelphia Museum of Art. Gift of Porzellanfabrik Arzberg. 1982-57-12a,b, 13a,b

Heinrich Löffelhardt German, 1901–1979
II-35 Covered dish, 1956
Pressed glass, length 11¹¹⁄₁₆" (29.7 cm)
Manufacturer: Schott
Prize: Grand prize, Milan, Triennale, 1960
The Corning Museum of Glass, Corning, New York. 61.3.349

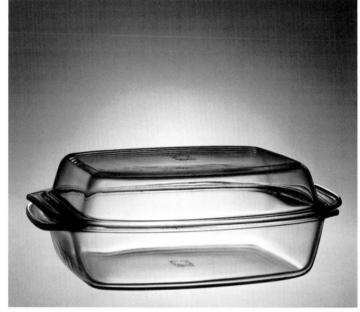

Heinrich Löffelhardt German, 1901–1979
II-36 "Arzberg 2050" service, 1959 (1959–80)
Porcelain, height of teapot 6⁷⁄₁₆"
(16.3 cm)
Manufacturer: Arzberg
Prize: Grand prize, Milan, Triennale, 1960
Philadelphia Museum of Art. Gift of Porzellanfabrik Arzberg. 1982-57-7a,b, 10a,b

Ennio Lucini Italian, born 1934
II-37 "Ponte di Brera" glasses, 1964 (from 1965 by Ponte di Brera; 1968–75 by Gabbianelli)
Blown glass, height 5½" (14 cm)
Manufacturer: Gabbianelli
Philadelphia Museum of Art. Gift of Mr. and Mrs. Jack M. Friedland. 75-48-6,7

Per Lütken Danish, born 1916
II-38 Bowl, 1958
Blown glass, diameter 10⁹/₁₆" (26.8 cm)
Manufacturer: Holmegaard
The Corning Museum of Glass,
Corning, New York. 61.3.262C

Erik Magnussen Danish, born 1940
II-39 "Termo" service, 1965 (from 1965)
Porcelain, height of creamer 2³/₁₆"
(5.6 cm)
Manufacturer: Bing & Grøndahl
Philadelphia Museum of Art. Gift of
Bing & Grøndahl

Floris Meydam Dutch, born 1919
II-40 "Granada" liquor set, 1954 (1954– c. 1965)
Blown glass, height of decanter 8¼"
(21 cm)
Manufacturer: Leerdam
National Glasmuseum, Leerdam,
The Netherlands

Grethe Meyer Danish, born 1918
Ibi Trier Mørch Danish, born 1910
II-41 "Stub" stacking wineglasses, 1958 (from 1958)
Blown glass, height of shortest
wineglass 2⅛" (5.5 cm)
Manufacturer: Kastrup
Philadelphia Museum of Art. Gift
of Holmegaards Glasvaerker.
1982-147-1–9

Grethe Meyer Danish, born 1918
II-42 "Blue Line" service, 1962 (from 1962)
Faience, height of teapot 5½" (14 cm)
Manufacturer: Royal Copenhagen
Prize: ID Prize, Danish Society of
Industrial Design, 1965
Royal Copenhagen Porcelain, New
York

Elmer Miller American, 1901–1960
II-43 Pitcher, 1957 (1957–63)
Blown glass, height 13½″ (34.3 cm)
Manufacturer: Viking
The Corning Museum of Glass,
Corning, New York. 61.4.162

Nason & Moretti Italian, established
Venice, 1923
**II-44 Cocktail pitcher and glasses,
1954**
Blown glass, height of pitcher 8¼″
(21 cm)
Manufacturer: Nason & Moretti
Prize: Compasso d'Oro, 1955
The Museum of Modern Art, New
York. Phyllis B. Lambert Fund.
256.58.1–3

Sven Palmquist Swedish, born 1906
II-45 "Ravenna" bowl, 1950 (1950–81)
Blown glass, height 3¹¹/₁₆″ (9.4 cm)
Manufacturer: Orrefors
Philadelphia Museum of Art. Gift of
Mr. and Mrs. Louis Sherman.
1982-141-5

Sven Palmquist Swedish, born 1906
II-46 "Fuga" bowls, 1950 (from 1950)
Centrifugally cast glass, diameter of
largest bowl 8⅜″ (21.3 cm)
Manufacturer: Orrefors
Prizes: Grand prize, Milan, Triennale,
1957; Gold medal, Ljubljana, Bio, 1964
AB Orrefors Glasbruk, Orrefors,
Sweden

Inger Persson Swedish, born 1936
II-47 "Pop" service, 1972 (from 1972)
Porcelain, height of teapot 5½″ (14 cm)
Manufacturer: Rörstrand
Philadelphia Museum of Art. Gift of
Rörstrand AB
Plate 48

Flavio Poli Italian, born 1900
II-48 Vase, c. 1958
Blown glass, height 10⅝″ (27 cm)
Manufacturer: Seguso
The Corning Museum of Glass,
Corning, New York. 63.3.28

Ambrogio Pozzi Italian, born 1931
II-49 "Duo" service, 1968
Porcelain, height of coffeepot 2¾" (7 cm)
Manufacturer: Rosenthal
Prize: Gold medal of the president of
Italy, Faenza, International Porcelain
and Ceramics Competition, 1968
Rosenthal Studio Line

Ulla Procopé Finnish, 1921–1968
**II-50 "Ruska" service, 1960 (from
1960)**
Stoneware, height of teapot 4⁵/₁₆"
(11 cm)
Manufacturer: Arabia
Oy Wärtsilä Ab Arabia, Helsinki

Hans Rath Austrian, 1904–1968
**II-51 "Alpha" service, 1952 (from
1952)**
Blown glass, height of pitcher 8"
(20.3 cm)
Manufacturer: Lobmeyr
Prize: Bundespreis "Gute Form," 1969
J & L Lobmeyr, Vienna

Claus Josef Riedel Austrian, born
1925
**II-52 "Exquisit" stemware, 1958
(from 1958)**
Blown glass, height of tallest wineglass
8⅞" (22.5 cm)
Manufacturer: Tiroler
Philadelphia Museum of Art. Gift of
Tiroler Glashütte KG–Riedel Crystal of
America

Nick Roericht German, born 1932
**II-53 Stacking service, 1959 (from
1961)**
Porcelain, height of cup 2¾" (7 cm)
Manufacturer: Thomas
Thomas China and Crystal U.S.A., Ltd.,
Des Plaines, Illinois

Roberto Sambonet Italian, born 1924
II-54 "Angle" vases, 1977 (from 1977)
Glass, height of tallest vase 11¹³/₁₆"
(30 cm)
Manufacturer: Baccarat
Baccarat, Inc., New York

Ludovico de Santillana Italian, born
1931
Tobia Scarpa Italian, born 1935
II-55 "Battuto" bowl, 1960
Blown glass, height 6" (15.2 cm)
Manufacturer: Venini
Venini S.p.A., Murano, Italy

Timo Sarpaneva Finnish, born 1926
**II-56 "Shadow of the Water" plate,
1956**
Blown glass, width 11¹³/₁₆" (30 cm)
Manufacturer: littala
Prize: Grand prize, Milan, Triennale,
1957
littala Glass Museum, littala, Finland
Plate 19 (variant)

Timo Sarpaneva Finnish, born 1926
II-57 Bowl, 1957
Blown glass, diameter 8¼" (21 cm)
Manufacturer: littala
The Corning Museum of Glass,
Corning, New York. 61.3.286

Timo Sarpaneva Finnish, born 1926
**II-58 "Suomi" service, 1974 (from
1976)**
Porcelain and stainless steel, height of
teapot 6⁹/₁₆" (16.7 cm)
Manufacturer: Rosenthal
Prize: Gold medal of the president of
Italy, Faenza, International Porcelain
and Ceramics Competition, 1976
Philadelphia Museum of Art. Gift of
Rosenthal AG. 1982-154-7–11
Plate 53

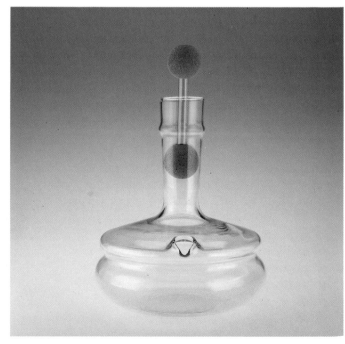

Peter Schlumbohm, American, born
Germany, 1896–1962
II-59 Water kettle, 1949 (from 1949)
Blown glass, height 12⁵/₁₆" (31.3 cm)
Manufacturer: Chemex
Philadelphia Museum of Art. Gift of
Chemex. 1983-4-2a,b

Harold Sitterle American, born 1910s
Trudi Sitterle American, born 1920s
II-60 Pepper mill, 1949 (1949–67); salt dish with spoon, 1950 (1950–67)
Porcelain and steel, height of pepper mill 4½" (11.4 cm)
Manufacturer: Sitterle Ceramics
Collection of Trudi and Harold Sitterle, Croton Falls, New York

Harold Sitterle (with Keith Hovis) American, born 1910s
II-61 Salad servers and ladle, 1951 (1951–62)
Porcelain and rosewood, length of ladle 16¼" (41.3 cm)
Manufacturer: Sitterle Ceramics
Salad servers: Collection of Trudi and Harold Sitterle, Croton Falls, New York
Ladle: Collection of Muriel Brooks, Croton Falls, New York

Magnus Stephensen Danish, born 1903
II-62 "Patella" covered bowl, 1957
Porcelain, height 5⅞" (15 cm)
Manufacturer: Royal Copenhagen
Prize: Gold medal, Milan, Triennale, 1957
The Metropolitan Museum of Art, New York. Purchase, Edward C. Moore, Jr., Gift, 1961. 61.7.50a,b

Nanny Still McKinney Finnish, lives in Belgium, born 1925
II-63 "Flindari" decanter, 1964 (1964–72)
Blown glass, height 13" (33 cm)
Manufacturer: Riihimäen Lasi
Prize: A.I.D. International Design Award, 1965
Finnish Glassmuseum, Riihimäki, Finland. B271

Richard Süssmuth German, born 1900
II-64 "Capitol" glasses, 1948 (from 1948)
Blown glass, height of tallest glass 5¹/₁₆" (12.8 cm)
Manufacturer: Süssmuth
Philadelphia Museum of Art. Gift of Glashütte Süssmuth

La Gardo Tackett American, born 1911
II-65 Planters, 1959 (from 1959)
Stoneware, height of taller planter 14¼" (36.2 cm)
Manufacturer: Architectural Pottery
Architectural Pottery, Los Angeles

Gertrud Vasegaard Danish, born 1913
II-66 Tea service, 1957 (from 1957)
Porcelain, height of teapot 5½" (14 cm)
Manufacturer: Bing & Grøndahl
Prize: Gold medal, Milan, Triennale, 1957
Philadelphia Museum of Art. Gift of Bing & Grøndahl

Paolo Venini Italian, 1895–1959
II-67 "Fazzoletto" bowl, 1951
Blown glass, diameter 10⅝" (27 cm)
Manufacturer: Venini
Venini S.p.A., Murano, Italy
Plate 5

Paolo Venini Italian, 1895–1959
II-68 "Morandiane" bottle, 1956
Blown glass, height 19¹¹/₁₆" (50 cm)
Manufacturer: Venini
Venini S.p.A., Murano, Italy

František Vízner Czechoslovakian, born 1936
II-69 "Blue" vase, 1978
Blown and cut glass, height 6⅞" (17.5 cm)
Manufacturer: Škrdlovice
The Corning Museum of Glass, Corning, New York. 79.3.9
Plate 47

Wilhelm Wagenfeld German, born 1900
II-70 Vase, 1950
Blown glass, height 12³/₁₆" (31 cm)
Manufacturer: WMF
Württembergische Metallwarenfabrik AG, Geislingen, West Germany—WMF of America

Wilhelm Wagenfeld German, born 1900
II-71 Salt and pepper shakers, 1953 (from 1953)
Blown glass and stainless steel, height 2¹/₁₆" (5.3 cm)
Manufacturer: WMF
Philadelphia Museum of Art. Gift of Württembergische Metallwarenfabrik AG—WMF of America. 1983-59-1,2

Tapio Wirkkala Finnish, born 1915
II-72 "Kanttarelli" vase, 1947 (1947–60)
Blown glass, height 8¹³/₁₆" (22.4 cm)
Manufacturer: littala
The Metropolitan Museum of Art, New York. Gift of Aarne Simonen, Minister of Commerce and Industry of Finland, 1956. 56.31.1

Tapio Wirkkala Finnish, born 1915
II-73 "Coreano" dish, 1970
Blown glass, diameter 15¾" (40 cm)
Manufacturer: Venini
Venini S.p.A., Murano, Italy

Tapio Wirkkala Finnish, born 1915
II-74 "Bolla" vase, 1970
Blown glass, height 13⅜" (34 cm)
Manufacturer: Venini
Venini S.p.A., Murano, Italy

Russel Wright American, 1904–1976
II-75 "Casual China" covered casserole, 1946 (1946–59)
Porcelain, height 5¼" (13.4 cm)
Manufacturer: Iroquois
Philadelphia Museum of Art. Gift of
Mr. and Mrs. Benjamin Bloom.
1983-45-1

Russel Wright American, 1904–1976
II-76 "Flair" tumblers, 1949
Blown glass, height 4⁷/₁₆" (11.2 cm)
Manufacturer: Imperial
Philadelphia Museum of Art. Gift of
Mrs. Phyllis E. Sunstein. 73-220-1,2

Marco Zanini Italian, born 1954
II-77 "Alpha Centauri" vase, 1982 (from 1982)
Blown glass, height 15⅝" (39.7 cm)
Manufacturer: Toso
Philadelphia Museum of Art. Gift of
Furniture of the Twentieth Century,
Inc.

Eva Zeisel American, born Hungary, 1906
II-78 "Museum" service, 1946
Porcelain, diameter of plate 8¹/₁₆"
(20.5 cm)
Manufacturer: Castleton
Collection of the designer, New City,
New York

Furniture

Introduction by Hans J. Wegner

Hans Wegner has designed a
number of the classic chairs of the
postwar period using materials and
methods traditional to Danish
craftsmanship.

The first important event in furniture design after the war occurred in 1948, when the Museum of Modern Art in New York arranged the International Competition for Low-cost Furniture Design. I myself participated and had the pleasure of seeing my entry reproduced in a book showing the results of the competition that was published later by the Museum.[1]

Apart from Charles Eames's chairs, few other award-winning projects were ever mass-produced, but in a way, that was not so important. What was essential in my opinion was that the competition got a lot of people going. We felt as if a window had been opened and we were given a chance to show what we could do. It gave us confidence that one day our efforts would be considered worthwhile.

What had been happening in the United States and in most European countries was much the same as what had occurred in Denmark, that is, that large-scale furniture production at the major factories had degenerated from a functional point of view and lacked architectural purpose. Furniture was enormous and clumsy, merely distorted versions of earlier styles (in Denmark called butcher furniture), out of proportion to the apartments where ordinary people lived.

In the past a craftsman came into direct contact with his customer and could draw inspiration from him, whereas now this very basic matter had been taken over by furniture dealers and department stores. Unfortunately, the latter did not have the craftsman's feeling for quality nor his ability to guide customers and thus to assure that production would follow in a contemporary style. It was not quality but financial considerations that increasingly determined production. New ideas were not being accepted. A "revolution" was needed!

The Danish "revolution" started about 1925–30. A group of the younger master cabinetmakers felt that if their workshops were to survive, something serious had to be done. So each spring they invited the younger, as well as some older, idealistically disposed architects to take part in a competition for designs for modern furniture. The prize-winning entries were then executed in the following summer and exhibited in the autumn.

Gradually these exhibitions became successful in the sense that a considerable group of people looked forward to them every year. The exhibitions were discussed in the newspapers and talented young people had the opportunity to present their ideas. The furniture was of excellent craftsmanship, and thorough investigations concerning the function of the various pieces were undertaken by the furniture school of the Royal Danish Academy of Fine Arts under the supervision of the eminent architect Professor Kaare Klint. He was a true functionalist (before this designation was even invented), but he felt that what was functionally right did not necessarily have to find expression in an extreme design.

From an artistic point of view the architects built on and were inspired by the experiences and traditions of the past; they did not want to copy specific styles, but on the other hand, they thought it would be absurd not to learn from what had existed for generations. Many younger architects were especially attracted to the simple rusticity of Danish furniture, to the structural elegance of Windsor chairs, to the honest and restrained expression of Shaker chairs, and to the brilliance of Thonet's bentwood chairs from the middle of the last century. The great historical styles were of interest only when sound structural details could be found, for example, in English eighteenth-century furniture.

Winning entries in the International Competition for Low-cost Furniture Design were shown at the Museum of Modern Art in New York in 1950.

1. In Edgar Kaufmann, Jr., *Prize Designs for Modern Furniture from the International Competition for Low-cost Furniture Design* (New York, 1950), p. 71.

We admired good tools, which had developed their present forms over a number of generations. We dreamed of being able to make furniture as plain and natural as they were. Our material was wood, and in the mid-forties there were still a number of good craftsmen left; we found it natural to use their know-how and competence to help us build the new things we wanted to create. In fact, we had no alternative, since it was the cabinetmakers themselves who every year invited us to work with them.

This collaborative effort culminated in 1949–51 after twenty-five years of development. It could well be said that the second generation was behind the achievements that attracted attention abroad, and in the long run formed the basis of what later came to be known as Danish design. To people like me the activity of this period was only a natural development, a continuation of what had earlier been done by way of experimentation, and appreciation for us within our own land did not come until people in foreign countries, especially in the United States, developed a sympathetic attitude to our work.

Paradoxically, one could venture to say that the basic reason for our success was that Denmark was lagging behind in industrial development. Technically there was nothing new in our work, and there was certainly no money to carry out major technical experiments. The philosophy behind it was not to make the process of work more complicated than necessary, but to show what we were able to do with our hands: to try to make the material come alive, to give it a sense of spirit, to make our works look so natural that one could conceive of them in that form only and in no other.

I believe that everyone who is engaged in art or design dreams of creating a perfect object: The Chair. This is only a dream, a goal that will never be achieved. It becomes, on the contrary, more and more unattainable with each new attempt, with each new experience. I often feel that I am at the end of a long tradition, and that I stand with one foot in the past, several thousand years ago, at a time when man produced his own tools and thus had a close relationship to them.

A good friend of mine, the Danish silversmith and designer Kay Bojesen, said to me around 1955: "Things should not be designed, but made." What he meant, I think (and I have also experienced it myself), was that when you stand with the material in your hands, everything becomes form and construction, and in fact the whole process of work becomes obvious.

Time has passed. The machine has taken over the harder parts of manual labor, and the designer has taken over the creative aspects of the craftsman's work and has thereby become an indispensible link in industrial routine. We have systematized the equipment and furniture of our houses, their storage units and kitchens. We have systematized the furnishings of airports, airplanes, ships, movie theaters, offices, and so forth. We have studied human anatomy in cooperation with doctors to find the ideal posture for sitting, to figure out where the vertebral column of the sedentary computer operator ought to be supported so that his or her back is not strained, and we have realized that, nevertheless, this happens all the time. Man was not created to sit in the same position for six to eight hours straight every day; what is actually most important is that one should be able to move in a chair, to shift one's position.

But what about man's new materials: steel, glass, fiberglass, plastic, acrylic, and the like? Practically anything is technically possible today. We are able to design these things with precisely this or that bend or with any of the three-dimensional curves we may want. Many outstanding chairs have been developed over the past fifty or sixty years in Europe and in the United States, and if we look upon this selection, it is interesting to see how many of them found their enduring form the very first time they were produced. In most cases, brilliant designers have succeeded in giving these chairs an artistic, aesthetic expression, which is emphasized by the characteristics of the materials used.

I am thinking especially of Charles Eames's dining chairs with steel legs from 1945 (III-24), his larger lounge chair from 1956 (III-26), and his and Eero Saarinen's fiberglass chairs (III-25, 79). I am also thinking of Harry Bertoia's "Diamond" chair from 1952 (III-9) and of every young designer's dream of creating a chair in one single production process, for instance, Verner Panton's fiberglass chair from 1960 (III-61). Naturally enough, great progress in design seems to take place each time new materials or methods of production are developed.

One may ask then, What is good design? I do not think it could be put more appropriately than in the words of the Danish author and poet Piet Hein:

TWO VERSES ON
FORM AND CONTENT

I.
Most design
is sheer disaster:
hiding what one
doesn't master.

II.
True design
asks one thing of us:
to uncover
what it covers.[2]

TO VERS OM
FORM OG INDHOLD

I.
Den meste form
er tomme fagter,
som skjuler det
man ikke magter.

II.
Hvor skønt, naar form
og indhold følges,
saa dét som dækkes
ikke dølges.

2. Translation, copyright 1983 by Piet Hein.

Alvar Aalto Finnish, 1898–1976
III-1 Stool, 1954 (from 1954)
Birch plywood, height 17¹¹/₁₆"
(45 cm)
Manufacturer: Huonekalutehdas
Korhonen for Artek
International Contract Furnishings Inc.,
New York

Eero Aarnio Finnish, born 1932
III-2 "Ball" chair, 1965 (from 1965)
Fiberglass, metal, and upholstery,
height 49" (124.5 cm)
Manufacturer: Asko
Finnair—National Airline of Finland,
New York

Eero Aarnio Finnish, born 1932
III-3 "Gyro" chair, 1968 (from 1968)
Fiberglass, height 21" (53.3 cm)
Manufacturer: Asko
Prize: A.I.D. International Design
Award, 1968
Stendig Inc., New York

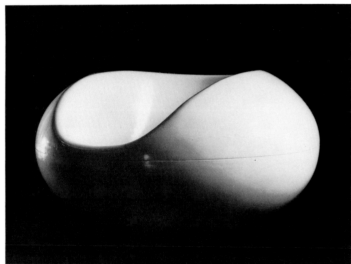

Franco Albini Italian, 1905–1977
III-4 Desk, c. 1945 (c. 1945–67)
Glass, birch, and enameled steel, width
48" (121.9 cm)
Manufacturer: Knoll
Knoll International, New York

Franco Albini Italian, 1905–1977
**III-5 "Margherita" chair, 1950 (from
1951)**
Rattan and upholstery, height 39⅜"
(100 cm)
Manufacturer: Bonacina
Philadelphia Museum of Art. Gift of
Vittorio Bonacina

Archizoom Associati Italian,
established Florence, 1966–1974
III-6 "Mies" chairs, 1970 (1970–76)
Chromed metal, rubber, and
upholstered Dacron, height 29⅛"
(74 cm)
Manufacturer: Poltronova
Private collection

III Furniture

Alessandro Becchi Italian, born 1946
III-7 "Anfibio" convertible sofa, 1970 (from 1970)
Vinyl-upholstered polyurethane and steel, length 94½" (240 cm)
Manufacturer: Giovannetti
Prize: Compasso d'Oro, 1979
Philadelphia Museum of Art. Gift of Giovannetti/Italia

Mario Bellini Italian, born 1935
III-8 "Cab" chair, 1977 (from 1977)
Steel and leather, height 32¼" (82 cm)
Manufacturer: Cassina
Atelier International, Ltd., New York

Harry Bertoia American, born Italy, 1915–1978
III-9 "Diamond" chair, 1952 (from 1952)
Steel and upholstery, height 30½" (77.5 cm)
Manufacturer: Knoll
Knoll International, New York

Rodolfo Bonetto Italian, born 1929
III-10 "Quattroquarti" table, 1969 (1970–78)
ABS plastic, height 11¹³/₁₆" (30 cm)
Manufacturer: Bernini
Philadelphia Museum of Art. Gift of G. B. Bernini

Anna Castelli Ferrieri Italian, born 1920
III-11 "Round-up" system, 1969 (from 1969)
ABS plastic, diameter 16½" (42 cm)
Manufacturer: Kartell
Kartell USA, Easley, South Carolina

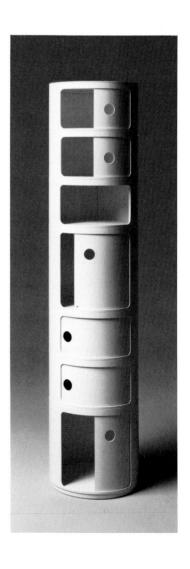

Anna Castelli Ferrieri Italian, born 1920
III-12 "Outline" system, 1977 (from 1977)
Polystyrene, length of strip section 35⅜" (89.9 cm)
Manufacturer: Kartell
Prize: Compasso d'Oro, 1979
Kartell USA, Easley, South Carolina

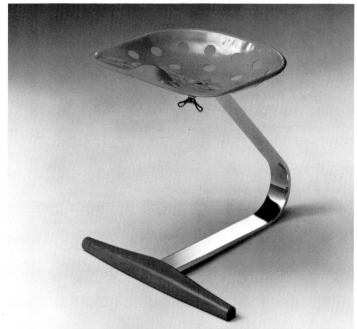

Achille Castiglioni Italian, born 1918
Piergiacomo Castiglioni Italian, 1913–1968
III-13 "Mezzadro" chair, 1957 (from 1957)
Chromed steel, enameled metal, and wood, height 20¹/₁₆" (51 cm)
Manufacturer: Zanotta
International Contract Furnishings Inc., New York

Achille Castiglioni Italian, born 1918
III-14 "Primate" kneeling stool, 1970 (from 1970)
Stainless steel and vinyl-upholstered polystyrene, height 18½" (47 cm)
Manufacturer: Zanotta
International Contract Furnishings Inc., New York

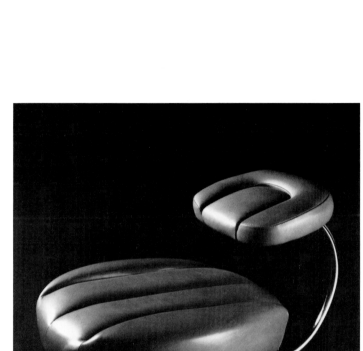

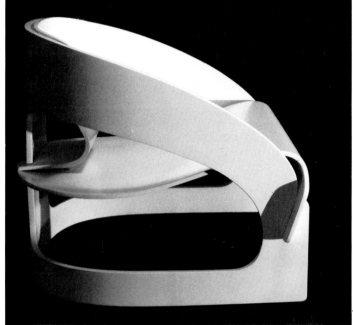

Joe Colombo Italian, 1930–1971
III-15 Chair, 1965 (1965–75)
Plywood, height 23¼" (59 cm)
Manufacturer: Kartell
Kartell USA, Easley, South Carolina

Joe Colombo Italian, 1930–1971
III-16 Stacking chair, 1965 (from 1968)
Nylon and polypropylene, height 28" (71.1 cm)
Manufacturer: Kartell
Kartell USA, Easley, South Carolina

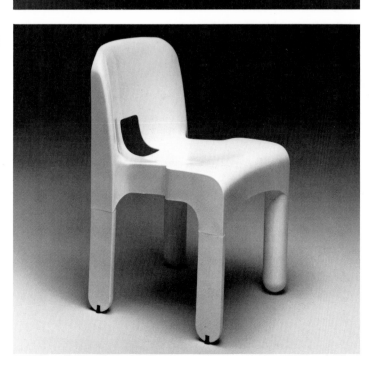

Joe Colombo Italian, 1930–1971
III-17 "Additional" system, 1968
Upholstered polyurethane foam
and metal, height of tallest section
26⅜" (67 cm)
Manufacturer: Sormani
Studio Joe Colombo, Milan
Plate 30

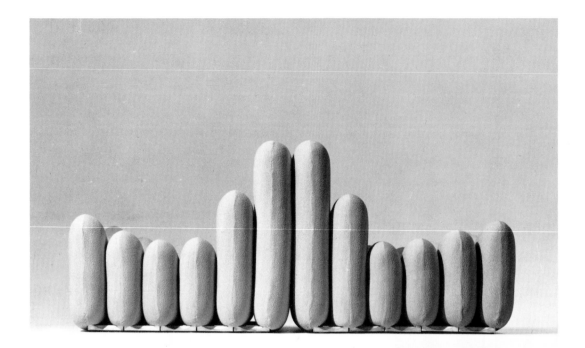

Robin Day British, born 1915
**III-18 "Polyprop" stacking chairs,
1963 (from 1964)**
Polypropylene and steel, height 29"
(73.7 cm)
Manufacturer: Hille
Prize: Design Centre Award, 1965
Philadelphia Museum of Art. Gift of
John Stuart International. 74-150-1–4

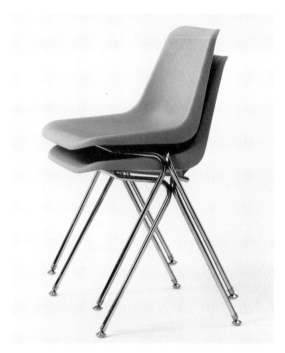

Paolo Deganello Italian, born 1940
**III-19 "Torso" lounge chair, 1982
(from 1982)**
Steel, upholstered foam and polyester,
and wood, height 45¹¹/₁₆" (116 cm)
Manufacturer: Cassina
Atelier International, Ltd., New York
Plate 62

De Pas, D'Urbino, Lomazzi Italian,
established Milan, 1966
III-20 "Blow" chair, 1967
PVC plastic, height 23⅝" (60 cm)
Manufacturer: Zanotta
The Museum of Modern Art, New
York. Gift of the manufacturer. 3.SC.72

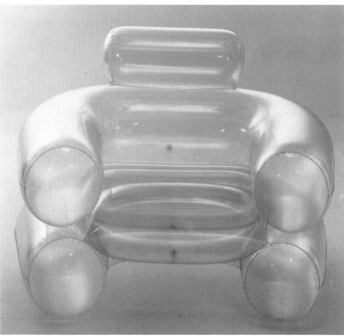

De Pas, D'Urbino, Lomazzi Italian,
established Milan, 1966
III-21 "Joe" chair, 1970 (from 1971)
Leather-upholstered polyurethane,
width 65¾" (167 cm)
Manufacturer: Poltronova
Stendig Inc., New York
Plate 43

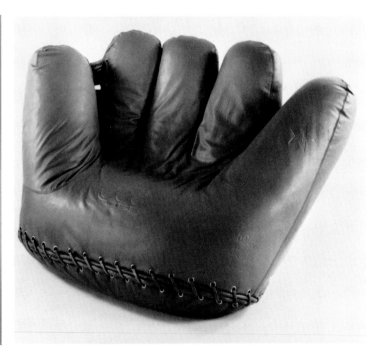

De Pas, D'Urbino, Lomazzi Italian, established Milan, 1966
III-22 "Sciangai" folding clothes stand, 1974 (from 1974)
Ash, height (open) 57^{1}/$_{16}$" (145 cm)
Manufacturer: Zanotta
Prizes: Compasso d'Oro, 1979; Honorable mention, Ljubljana, Bio, 1981
International Contract Furnishings Inc., New York

Nanna Ditzel Danish, lives in England, born 1923
III-23 Chair and stool, 1961 (1961–68 by Wengler; 1968–73 by Fennkong)
Cane, height of chair 19^{11}/$_{16}$" (50 cm)
Manufacturer: Wengler
Collection of the designer, London

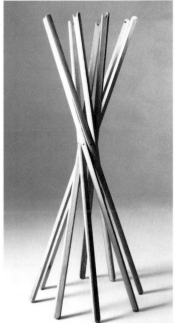

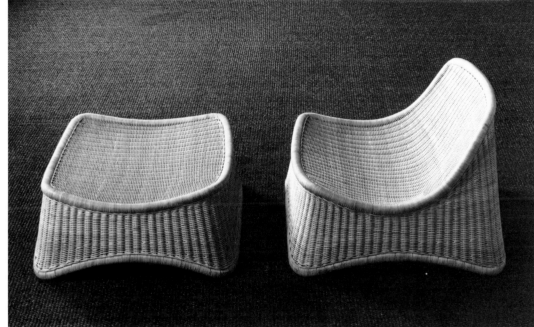

Charles Eames American, 1907–1978
III-24 Chair, 1945 (1945–49 by Evans; 1949–67 by Herman Miller)
Plywood and chromed steel, height 29^{1}/$_{4}$" (74.3 cm)
Manufacturer: Herman Miller
Herman Miller, Inc., Zeeland, Michigan
Plate 6

Charles Eames American, 1907–1978
III-25 Chair, 1948 (1950–67)
Fiberglass and steel, height 25^{5}/$_{8}$" (65.1 cm)
Manufacturer: Herman Miller
Prize: Co-winner, second prize, seating units, New York, The Museum of Modern Art, International Competition for Low-cost Furniture Design, 1948
Philadelphia Museum of Art. Gift of Mrs. L. Talbot Adamson. 72-37-1

Charles Eames American, 1907–1978
III-26 Lounge chair and ottoman, 1956
Laminated rosewood, aluminum, and leather upholstery, height of chair 33^{1}/$_{4}$" (84.5 cm)
Manufacturer: Herman Miller
Philadelphia Museum of Art. Purchased with funds contributed by Mr. and Mrs. Adolph G. Rosengarten in memory of Calvin S. Hathaway. 1976-133-1
Plate 21

Gatti, Paolini, Teodoro Italian, established Turin, 1965
III-27 "Sacco" chair, 1969 (from 1969)
Leather and polystyrene pellets, width 31^{1}/$_{2}$" (80 cm)
Manufacturer: Zanotta
Prize: Honorable mention, Ljubljana, Bio, 1973
International Contract Furnishings Inc., New York

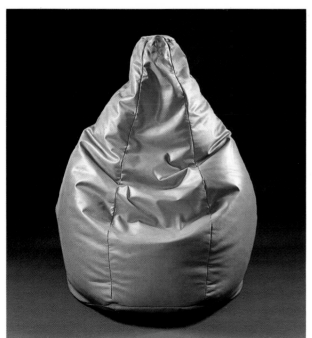

Frank O. Gehry American, born Canada, 1929
III-28 "Easy Edges" rocking chair, 1972 (1972 by Jack Brogan; from 1982 by Chiru)
Cardboard, length 42" (106.6 cm)
Manufacturer: Chiru
Philadelphia Museum of Art. Gift of the designer. 1983-7-1
Plate 39

Michael Graves American, born 1934
III-29 Chair, 1981 (from 1981)
Bird's-eye maple veneer, ebony, and upholstery, height 32¾" (83.2 cm)
Manufacturer: Sunar
Collection of the designer, Princeton, New Jersey

Hans Gugelot Swiss, born Indonesia, 1920–1965
III-30 Cabinet system, 1954 (from 1956)
PVC-plastic-foil-covered chipboard and metal, height 64" (162.5 cm)
Manufacturer: Bofinger
Prize: Bundespreis "Gute Form," 1973
Wilhelm Bofinger GmbH & Co KG, Stuttgart

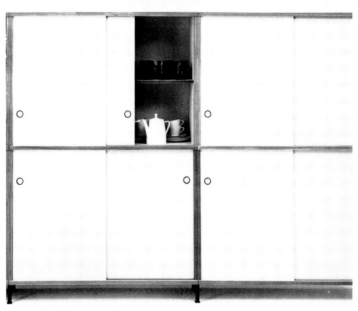

Peter Hvidt Danish, born 1916
Orla Mølgaard-Nielsen Danish, born 1907
III-31 "Ax" chair, 1950
Beech and plywood, height 29¼" (75.5 cm)
Manufacturer: Fritz Hansen
Prize: Diploma of honor, Milan, Triennale, 1954
The Danish Museum of Decorative Art, Copenhagen. 159/1950

Vittorio Introini Italian, born 1935
III-32 Library system, 1969 (from 1969)
Steel, height 91⁵⁄₁₆" (232 cm)
Manufacturer: Saporiti
Philadelphia Museum of Art. Gift of the American Institute of Interior Designers, Pennsylvania Eastern District. 71-32-1a–e

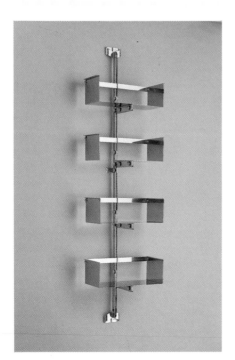

Arne Jacobsen Danish, 1902–1971
III-33 Stacking chair, 1951
Plywood and chromed steel, height 30⅝" (77.7 cm)
Manufacturer: Fritz Hansen
Philadelphia Museum of Art. Gift of Fritz Hansen Inc., New York. 73-104-1

Arne Jacobsen Danish, 1902–1971
III-34 "Swan" chair, 1957
Fiberglass, upholstered foam rubber, and chromed steel, height 29½"
(75 cm)
Manufacturer: Fritz Hansen
Philadelphia Museum of Art.
Purchased: Marie Josephine Rozet
Fund. 74-61-2

Arne Jacobsen Danish, 1902–1971
III-35 "Egg" chair and ottoman, 1957
Fiberglass, leather-upholstered foam rubber, and chromed steel, height of chair 41⅞" (106.4 cm)
Manufacturer: Fritz Hansen
Philadelphia Museum of Art. Gift of the National Society of Interior Designers, Pennsylvania Chapter. 71-30-1,2
Plate 23

Finn Juhl Danish, born 1912
III-36 Table, 1950
Teak and maple, length 63¼"
(160.6 cm)
Manufacturer: Vodder
Philadelphia College of Art Collection.
PC7

Finn Juhl Danish, born 1912
III-37 Chair, 1951 (1952–60)
Teak and leather upholstery, height 32"
(81.3 cm)
Manufacturer: Baker
Philadelphia Museum of Art. Gift of
Mr. and Mrs. N. Richard Miller.
1980-138-1

Katavolos-Littell-Kelley American,
established New York, 1949–1955
III-38 "T" chair, 1952 (from 1952)
Chromed steel and leather, height
27¼" (69.2 cm)
Manufacturer: Laverne
Prize: First A.I.D. International Design
Award, 1952
Philadelphia Museum of Art. Gift of
Carl L. Steele. 72-5-1

Toshiyuki Kita Japanese, born 1942
III-39 "Wink" chair, 1980 (from 1980)
Upholstered polyurethane foam and
Dacron, and steel, length (extended)
78¾" (200 cm)
Manufacturer: Cassina
Atelier International, Ltd., New York

Poul Kjaerholm Danish, 1929–1980
III-40 Chair, 1956 (from 1956)
Chromed steel and leather, height 28"
(71.1 cm)
Manufacturer: Fritz Hansen
Prize: Grand prize, Milan, Triennale,
1957
Design Selections International, Inc.,
New York

Florence Schust Knoll American,
born 1917
III-41 Coffee table, c. 1953
Walnut and chromed steel, height
15" (38.1 cm)
Manufacturer: Knoll
Knoll International, New York

Ray Komai American, born 1918
III-42 Chair, 1949
Plywood and chromed steel, height
29½" (74.9 cm)
Manufacturer: J. G. Furniture
The Museum of Modern Art, New
York. Gift of the manufacturer. 467.51

Gerd Lange German, born 1931
III-43 "Flex" chair, 1974 (from 1976)
Polypropylene, beech, and nylon,
height 31" (78.7 cm)
Manufacturer: Beylerian
Philadelphia Museum of Art. Gift of
Beylerian Limited

Erwine Laverne American, born 1909
Estelle Laverne American, born 1915
**III-44 "Champagne" chair, 1957
(from 1957)**
Plexiglass, aluminum, and upholstery,
height 31⅝" (80.3 cm)
Manufacturer: Laverne
Philadelphia Museum of Art. Gift of
Laverne International Ltd. 71-1-1

Cesare Leonardi-Franca Stagi Italian, established Modena, 1962
III-45 Rocking chair, 1967 (1967–70)
Fiberglass, length 68⅞" (174.9 cm)
Manufacturer: Elco
The Museum of Modern Art, New York. Gift of Stendig Inc. 460.70

Vico Magistretti Italian, born 1920
III-46 "Maralunga" chair, 1973
Upholstered polyurethane foam and Dacron, and steel, height 28½" (72.4 cm)
Manufacturer: Cassina
Prize: Compasso d'Oro, 1979
Philadelphia Museum of Art. Gift of Atelier International, Ltd. 1978-21-6

Javier Mariscal Spanish, born 1950
III-47 "Hilton" trolley, 1981
Enameled metal and glass, height 33½" (85 cm)
Manufacturer: Abet
Philadelphia Museum of Art. Gift of Abet Laminati S.p.A.

Bruno Mathsson Swedish, born 1907
Piet Hein Danish, born 1905
III-48 Table, 1964 (from 1964)
Birch and chromed steel, diameter 35⁷⁄₁₆" (90 cm)
Manufacturer: Mathsson
Mathsson International AB, Värnamo, Sweden

Roberto Sebastian Matta French, born Chile, 1911
III-49 "Malitte" cushion system, 1966 (1966–74)
Upholstered polyurethane foam, height (stacked) 63" (160 cm)
Manufacturer: Gavina
Knoll International, New York

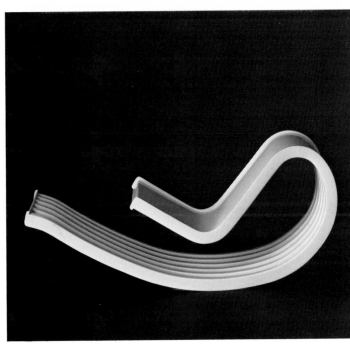

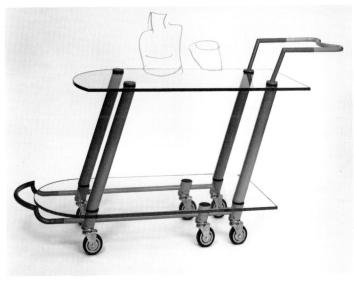

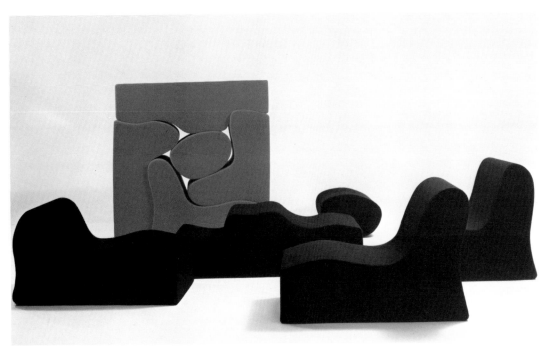

Sergio Mazza Italian, born 1931
III-50 "Bacco" mobile bar, 1969 (from 1969)
ABS plastic, height 16½" (42 cm)
Manufacturer: Artemide
Philadelphia Museum of Art. Gift of
Artemide Inc.

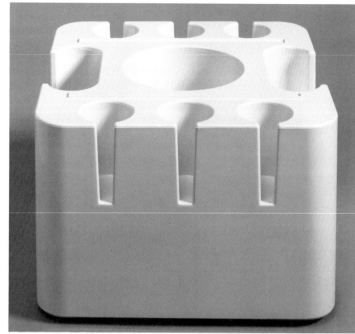

Paul McCobb American, 1917–1969
III-51 "Planner Group" components, 1949
Maple, length 48" (122 cm)
Manufacturer: Winchendon
Philadelphia Museum of Art. Purchased
with funds contributed by COLLAB: The
Contemporary Design Group for the
Philadelphia Museum of Art. 1983-5-2,3

Børge Mogensen Danish, 1914–1972
III-52 Sofa, 1945 (from 1962)
Beech and upholstery, length 63"
(160 cm)
Manufacturer: Fritz Hansen
Fritz Hansens Eft. A/S, Allerød,
Denmark
Plate 4

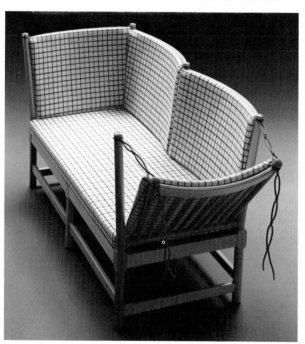

Carlo Mollino Italian, 1905–1973
III-53 Chair, 1950
Brass and vinyl upholstery, height 37"
(94 cm)
Manufacturer: Carlo Mollino
Collection of Barbara Jakobson,
New York

Olivier Mourgue French, born 1939
**III-54 "Djinn" chaise longue, 1965
(1965–76)**
Steel and upholstered urethane foam,
length 66" (167.6 cm)
Manufacturer: Airborne
The Museum of Modern Art, New York.
Gift of George Tanier, Inc. 347.66
Plate 31

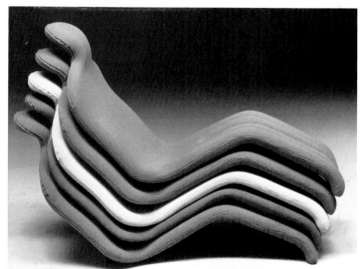

Olivier Mourgue French, born 1939
**III-55 "Bouloum" lounge chairs, 1968
(from 1973)**
Upholstered fiberglass, length 57"
(144.8 cm)
Manufacturer: Airborne
Philadelphia Museum of Art. Gift of
Arconas Corporation

Peter Murdoch British, born 1940
III-56 "Spotty" child's chair, 1963 (1964–65)
Polyethylene-coated fiberboard, height 20¼" (51.4 cm)
Manufacturer: International Paper
Victoria and Albert Museum, London. circ. 17-1970

George Nakashima American, born 1905
III-57 "Conoid" chair, 1962 (from 1962)
Walnut, height 35" (88.9 cm)
Manufacturer: George Nakashima
Collection of the designer, New Hope, Pennsylvania

George Nelson American, born 1908
III-58 "Sling" sofa, 1964 (from 1964)
Chromed steel, leather-upholstered urethane foam, and neoprene, width 87" (221 cm)
Manufacturer: Herman Miller
Herman Miller, Inc., Zeeland, Michigan
Plate 26

Aldo van den Nieuwelaar Dutch, born 1944
III-59 Cupboard, 1979 (from 1979)
Fiberboard and polystyrene, height 87" (221 cm)
Manufacturer: Ums-Pastoe
Beylerian Limited, New York
Plate 54

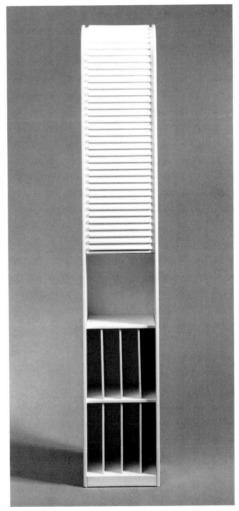

Antti Nurmesniemi Finnish, born 1927
III-60 Sauna stool, 1952 (from 1952)
Laminated birch and teak, height 19⅝" (49.8 cm)
Manufacturer: Söderström
Prize: Silver medal, Milan, Triennale, 1964
Scandinavian Design, Inc., New York

Verner Panton Danish, lives in Switzerland, born 1926
III-61 Stacking chair, 1960 (1967–75)
Polyester and fiberglass, height 32½"
(82.5 cm)
Manufacturer: Herman Miller
Prize: A.I.D. International Design Award, 1967
Philadelphia Museum of Art. Purchased with funds contributed by Mr. and Mrs. John W. Drayton. 73-95-1
Plate 36

Pierre Paulin French, born 1927
III-62 "Ribbon" chair, 1966 (from 1966)
Metal, upholstered rubber, and wood, height 27⅜" (69.5 cm)
Manufacturer: Artifort
Prize: A.I.D. International Design Award, 1969
Artifort, Annalaan, The Netherlands

Pierre Paulin French, born 1927
III-63 Stacking chair, 1967 (from 1967
Metal and upholstered foam rubber, length 35⁷⁄₁₆" (90 cm)
Manufacturer: Artifort
Artifort, Annalaan, The Netherlands

Gaetano Pesce Italian, born 1939
III-64 "Up-1" chair, 1969
Fabric and polyurethane, height 26¾" (67.9 cm)
Manufacturer: C & B Italia
The Museum of Modern Art, New York. Gift of Atelier International. 1113.69

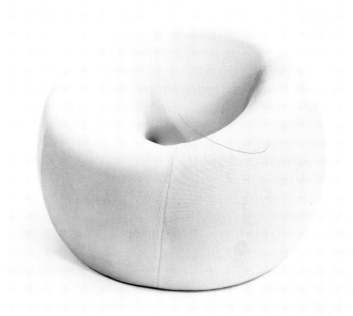

Gaetano Pesce Italian, born 1939
III-65 "Sit Down" chair, 1975 (from 1976)
Dacron-filled upholstery over polyurethane foam, width 34½" (87.6 cm)
Manufacturer: Cassina
Atelier International, Ltd., New York

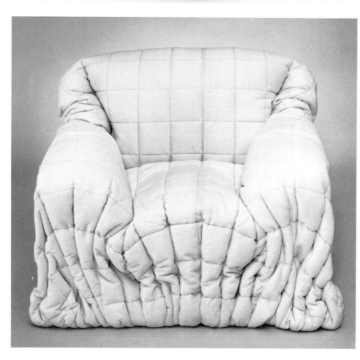

Giancarlo Piretti Italian, born 1940
III-66 "Plia" folding chairs, 1969 (from 1969)
Aluminum and plastic, height 30⅛" (76.5 cm)
Manufacturer: Castelli
Prizes: Bundespreis "Gute Form," 1973; Gold medal, Ljubljana, Bio, 1973
Philadelphia Museum of Art. Gift of Mrs. Marilyn Druckman. 71-31-1–4

Warren Platner American, born 1919
III-67 Chair and ottoman, 1966 (from 1966)
Nickeled steel and upholstery, height of chair 39½" (100.3 cm)
Manufacturer: Knoll
Prize: A.I.D. International Design Award, 1966
Philadelphia Museum of Art. Gift of Peter L. Buttenwieser. 1983-46-2,3

Gio Ponti Italian, 1891–1979
III-68 "Superleggera" chair, 1957 (from 1957)
Ash and cane, height 32¾" (83.2 cm)
Manufacturer: Cassina
Atelier International, Ltd., New York

Peter Raacke German, born 1928
III-69 "Papp" chair, 1967
Cardboard, height 26⅜" (67 cm)
Manufacturer: Faltmöbel Ellen Raacke
Musée des Arts Décoratifs, Paris. 41949

Ernest Race British, 1913–1963
III-70 "BA" chair, 1945 (1945–69)
Aluminum and upholstery, height 32" (81.3 cm)
Manufacturer: Race
Prize: Gold medal, Milan, Triennale, 1954
Victoria and Albert Museum, London. circ. 766-1969

Ernest Race British, 1913–1963
III-71 "Antelope" chair, 1951 (1951–65)
Enameled steel and plywood, height 31⅛" (79 cm)
Manufacturer: Race
Prize: Silver medal, Milan, Triennale, 1954
Collection of Betty Elzea, Wilmington, Delaware
Plate 8

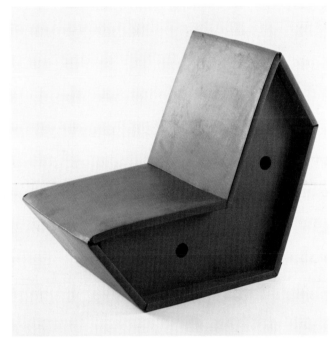

Dieter Rams German, born 1932
III-72 Chair, 1962 (from 1964)
Wood, fiberglass, and leather
upholstery, height 27⁹/₁₆" (70 cm)
Manufacturer: Vitsoe
Vitsoe, Frankfort, West Germany

Carlos Riart Spanish, born 1944
III-73 "Desnuda" chair, 1973 (from 1979)
Enameled iron, brass, and upholstery,
height 39⅜" (100 cm)
Manufacturer: Tecmo
Philadelphia Museum of Art. Gift of
the designer

Gastone Rinaldi Italian, born 1920
III-74 "Dafne" folding chairs, 1979 (from 1979)
Lacquered steel and plywood, height
31½" (80 cm)
Manufacturer: Thema
Prize: Compasso d'Oro, 1981
Thema S.p.A., Limena, Italy

Alberto Rosselli Italian, 1921–1976
III-75 "Jumbo" chair, 1970 (1970–78)
Fiberglass, height 18½" (47 cm)
Manufacturer: Saporiti
Philadelphia Museum of Art. Gift of
Campaniello Imports, Ltd. 1983-47-1

David Rowland American, born 1924
III-76 "40-in-4" stacking chairs, 1964 (from 1964)
Chromed steel and upholstery, height
30" (76.2 cm)
Manufacturer: General Fireproofing
Prizes: Grand prize, Milan, Triennale,
1964; A.I.D. International Design
Award, 1965
Philadelphia Museum of Art. Gift of
the designer. 72-226-1

David Rowland American, born 1924
III-77 "Sof-Tech" stacking chair, 1979 (from 1980)
Steel and vinyl-covered metal, height
29¾" (75.5 cm)
Manufacturer: Thonet
Thonet, York, Pennsylvania
Plate 58

Eero Saarinen American, born
Finland, 1910–1961
**III-78 "Womb" chair, 1946 (from
1948)**
Plastic, chromed steel, and upholstered
latex foam, height 35½" (90.1 cm)
Manufacturer: Knoll
Knoll International, New York

Eero Saarinen American, born
Finland, 1910–1961
III-79 Chair, 1956 (from 1956)
Fiberglass, aluminum, and upholstery,
height 32" (81.3 cm)
Manufacturer: Knoll
Philadelphia Museum of Art. Gift of
Gregory M. Harvey. 73-96-1
Plate 17

Eero Saarinen American, born
Finland, 1910–1961
III-80 Table, 1956 (from 1956)
Metal and plastic laminate, diameter
16" (40.6 cm)
Manufacturer: Knoll
Knoll International, New York

Tobia Scarpa Italian, born 1935
Afra Scarpa Italian, born 1937
**III-81 "Soriana" lounge chair and
ottoman, 1970**
Leather-upholstered polyurethane and
Dacron, and chromed metal, height of
chair 28" (71.1 cm)
Manufacturer: Cassina
Prize: Compasso d'Oro, 1970
Philadelphia Museum of Art. Gift of
Atelier International, Ltd. 1978-21-1a,b

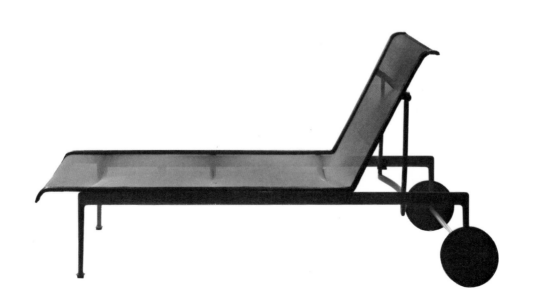

Richard Schultz American, born 1926
III-82 Chaise longue, 1966 (from 1966)
Aluminum, vinyl, and Dacron webbing,
length 76" (193 cm)
Manufacturer: Knoll
Prize: A.I.D. International Design
Award, 1967
Knoll International, New York

Ettore Sottsass, Jr. Italian, born
Austria, 1917
**III-83 "Nefertiti" desk, 1969 (from
1969)**
Plywood and plastic laminate, width
51¼" (130.2 cm)
Manufacturer: Abet
Philadelphia Museum of Art. Gift of
Abet Laminati S.p.A. 1983-40-1

Ettore Sottsass, Jr. Italian, born
Austria, 1917
III-84 "Casablanca" sideboard, 1981
Wood and plastic laminate, height
90⁹/₁₆" (230 cm)
Manufacturer: Abet
Philadelphia Museum of Art. Gift of
Abet Laminati S.p.A.
Plate 57

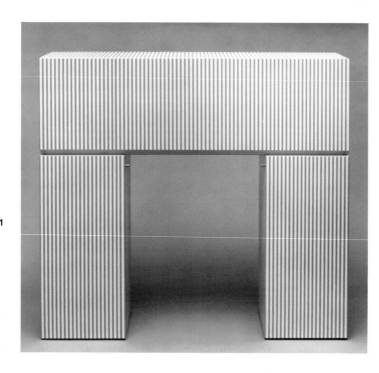

Roger Tallon French, born 1929
III-85 Stool, 1965
Aluminum and polyester foam, height
16½" (42 cm)
Manufacturer: Lacloche
Collection of Francis Lacloche, Paris

Utility Furniture Design Panel
British, 1943–1952
III-86 "Cotswold" table, 1946
Mahogany, height 30" (76.2 cm)
Manufacturer: Utility
Geffrye Museum, London

Van Keppel-Green American,
established Los Angeles, 1938–1972
**III-87 Lounge chair and ottoman,
1947 (1947–70)**
Enameled steel and cotton cord, length
of chair 36" (91.4 cm)
Manufacturer: Van Keppel-Green
Collection of Taylor Green, Huntington
Beach, California

Kristian Vedel Danish, born 1923
III-88 Child's chair, 1957
Beech plywood, height 16" (40.6 cm)
Manufacturer: Torben Ørskov
Prize: Silver medal, Milan, Triennale,
1957
The Alderman Company, High Point,
North Carolina

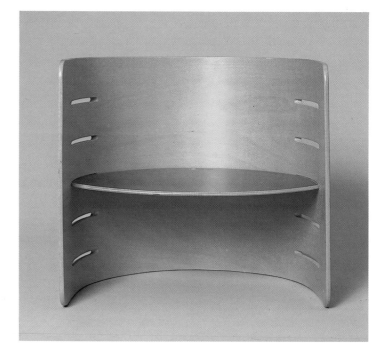

Hans Wegner Danish, born 1914
III-89 "Peacock" chair, 1947 (from 1947)
Ash, teak, and cord, height 40½"
(102.9 cm)
Manufacturer: Johannes Hansen
Design Selections International, Inc.,
New York

Hans Wegner Danish, born 1914
III-90 Chair, 1949 (from 1949)
Beech and cane, height 30" (76.2 cm)
Manufacturer: Johannes Hansen
Philadelphia Museum of Art. Gift of
Carl L. Steele. 72-5-2
Plate 3

Hans Wegner Danish, born 1914
III-91 Folding chair, 1949 (from 1949)
Oak and cane, height 30" (76.2 cm)
Manufacturer: Johannes Hansen
Design Selections International, Inc.,
New York

Edward Wormley American, born 1907
III-92 Chaise longue, 1947 (1947–55)
Maple, cherry, metal, and upholstery,
length 75" (190.5 cm)
Manufacturer: Dunbar
Le Château Du Fresne, Musée des Arts
Décoratifs, Montreal. The Liliane
Stewart Collection

Sori Yanagi Japanese, born 1915
III-93 "Butterfly" stool, 1956
Plywood and metal, height 15¹¹/₁₆"
(39.9 cm)
Manufacturer: Tendo
Philadelphia Museum of Art. Gift of
Tendo Co., Ltd. 1983-11-1
Plate 16

Marco Zanuso Italian, born 1916
III-94 "Lady" chair, 1951
Metal and upholstered foam rubber,
height 32¼" (82 cm)
Manufacturer: Arflex
Prize: Gold medal, Milan, Triennale,
1951
Beylerian Limited, New York

Marco Zanuso Italian, born 1916
III-95 "Lambda" chair, 1962
Enameled steel, height 30¹¹/₁₆" (78 cm)
Manufacturer: Gavina
Collection of the designer, Milan

Marco Zanuso Italian, born 1916
Richard Sapper Italian, born Germany,
1932
III-96 Child's chair, 1964
Polyethylene, height 19½" (49.5 cm)
Manufacturer: Kartell
Prize: Compasso d'Oro, 1964
Kartell USA, Easley, South Carolina
Plate 25

Marco Zanuso Italian, born 1916
**III-97 "Marcuso" table, 1971 (from
1971)**
Stainless steel and glass, length 59"
(149.9 cm)
Manufacturer: Zanotta
Prizes: Compasso d'Oro, 1979;
Honorable mention, Ljubljana, Bio,
1980
International Contract Furnishings Inc.,
New York

Lighting

Introduction by Achille Castiglioni

From 1945 to the present, Achille Castiglioni's inventive fixtures and innovative illumination methods set standards that have spurred developments in the field of lighting design both in Italy and abroad. His views on lighting are presented in an interview with Raffaella Crespi, his colleague in the faculty of architecture at the university of Milan.

Will you describe how your approach to the design of lighting developed since your professional activity began immediately after the war?

Castiglioni: We always considered this area of industrial design in a very special way. (I say "we" because from 1945 to 1968 all my work was carried out with the closest collaboration of my brother Piergiacomo, who died in 1968.) My approach to design, and every step from planning through production, is still characterized by the same method, the same purpose, and especially the same desire to create something innovative, be it in function or form.

If one maintains that design consists primarily of inventing a function and then giving form to that function, which of your creations could be interpreted in this way?

Castiglioni: Much of the lighting we designed could be interpreted using this concept, to cite two examples, the "Taccia" of 1962 (IV-10) and the "Gibigiana" of 1981 (IV-13); in both the technical innovations lay in directing a path of light beams, with the method of projecting the light being solved very differently in each case.

Among the lamps you have designed there seems to be a tendency to minimize the importance of the fixture in favor of the light itself. What are the reasons for this?

Castiglioni: Any device made for lighting can be considered a proper exercise of industrial design only if the fixture-object is subordinated to the effects of light it produces. Only when the function actually calls for an autonomous object, indifferent to the purpose of lighting, can the design be allowed to de-emphasize the production of artificial light.

A lighting fixture is itself an "unnatural" object. Can, or should, artificial light compete with natural light? What is the correlation, if any, between natural and artificial light?

Castiglioni: Lighting engineers try to devise light sources that come closer and closer to natural daylight. But apart from the fact that natural light varies geographically and seasonally, so-called natural light is virtually impossible to simulate. Consequently, the very choice of a light source, as well as the color of the light, becomes part of the task of designing for either indoor or outdoor use. For this reason I would say that natural and artificial lighting are completely separate from each other.

During the last forty years a number of technological innovations have occurred in the field of lighting. In what way are they—as well as technology in general—factors in the design of lighting devices?

Castiglioni: It goes without saying that whenever a new light source is introduced onto the market—this being one of the main concerns of the lighting field—it often becomes the dominant feature of a design.

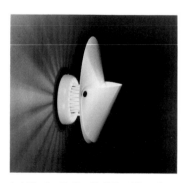

Achille Castiglioni's "Giovi" wall lamp (1982)

Lighting devices can also serve a decorative function. In your designs you seem to entrust this function to the light itself rather than to the fixture. Is this an accurate statement?

Castiglioni: That is a fair appraisal, and I would add that lighting devices serve a decorative function not so much through the formal characteristics of the light generated as through the varied lighting effects that can be achieved with it. One recent example of mine that demonstrates this well is the "Giovi" wall lamp.

In recent years, objects have been produced which emphasize their technology (hi-fi systems, for example). Do you think that the indication of and emphasis upon technological features represent a true expression of our age, or is this simply a degenerate element of formalism? Can this phenomenon also be found in the field of lighting?

Castiglioni: Unfortunately this has been true of many recent products, and it has occurred because certain manufacturers have forced the design process into formal compromises that are falsely technological.

Do you think that lighting devices in recent years have come up with new formal solutions for illumination, or are they only part of a continuing reinterpretation of the forms of the fixtures?

Castiglioni: Unfortunately, many companies that engage in the production of light fixtures, in Italy and abroad, have paid more attention in their designs to updating new forms in an imitative way rather than to searching for higher quality of illumination.

In creating forms, you seem to give an importance to the role of memory, to the quotation of "things already seen," to the paradoxical or ironic rendering of certain elements, and to the unconventional use of materials. Do you think that this particular approach to form is typical of Italian design?

Castiglioni: This approach to the problem of form is widely seen in Italian design, but it is most particularly apparent in the Castiglioni designs.

Is creativity an individual or a collective phenomenon? Is there a creative element in the collaboration between designers and technicians, or between designers and manufacturers? Does Italian industry favor such collaboration even during the earliest stages of design?

Castiglioni: As you know, I define the enterprise of industrial design as the result of a creativity that is truly collective, in which the most important activities usually take place in realizing the prototype, activities that require the collaboration of specialized workers that even in this day I would call artisans.

In the history of design one can perceive two opposing forces at work simultaneously: One tends to stabilize the market by keeping goods in production for as long as possible, that is, until they are totally consumed, functionally, aesthetically, and technologically; the second tends to activate the market by constantly introducing new models of the same product, thus stimulating consumption and hastening the process by which the product itself becomes obsolete. This second tendency predominates today even in the field of lighting. Flos, the company that produces your designs, seems, however, to adhere to the first, even keeping in production models you designed more than twenty years ago. What is the reason for this policy of stability in production? In designing do you consider the question of how long your works will last?

Castiglioni: Obviously I favor the first tendency, and my designs—including those outside the field of lighting—have always been created for long-term use. I do this also out of respect for the buyer, who has to be able to count on a quality that will last.

Which Italian manufacturers and designers have made especially interesting contributions to the recent history of lighting?

Castiglioni: During the 1950s and 1960s a number of interesting encounters took place between designers and manufacturers—Luigi Caccia Dominioni with Azucena; Vittoriano Viganó, BBPR, and Franco Albini with Arteluce; Joe Colombo with O-Luce; Vico Magistretti with Artemide; and the Castiglionis with Kartell and Flos. These brought about an important change of direction in the field of lighting, operating at that time with perhaps more empiricism and with lower production costs.

What do you find significant in the lighting designs of the 1970s and early 1980s?
Castiglioni: The designs of the 1970s and 1980s have demanded a kind of research that is much more involved and costly, requiring increasing collaboration between the forces of culture, those of management and those of distribution. In some of the most recent designs one finds that the interest is centered not so much on solving the problems of lighting in its fullest sense as on emphasizing the decorative quality of fixtures when they are without light. This tendency can be harmful, especially when certain formal solutions encourage a facile imitation devoid of any concrete meaning.

In the past, Italian design has experienced great international success, as it still does today. How has this been possible in the absence of schools of design and an institutionalized profession?
Castiglioni: I think that the success of so-called Italian design is due to the fact that design, in my opinion, is not a discipline but an attitude growing out of one's humanistic, technological, economic, and political beliefs. In our society the function of productivity is entrusted to industry. To ensure that the bonds between teaching and production have positive results, future designers must become involved during their education in developing their own personalities as part of the continuous inquiry into products and methods of production. In this way future practitioners will participate more knowledgeably in bringing about the products that enter society and contribute more and more to shaping them.

Alvar Aalto Finnish, 1898–1976
IV-1 Floor lamp, 1954 (from 1954)
Iron, leather, and brass, height 69"
(175.3 cm)
Manufacturer: Artek
Scandinavian Design, Inc., New York

Gerald Abramovitz British, born
South Africa, 1928
IV-2 "Cantilever" desk lamp, 1961
Aluminum and steel, height 20"
(50.8 cm)
Manufacturer: Best & Lloyd
Prize: Design Centre Award, 1966
Philadelphia Museum of Art. Gift of
Duncan and Huggins Ltd. 74-58-1

Gae Aulenti (with Piero Castiglioni)
Italian, born 1927
**IV-3 "Mini-Box" table lamp, 1981
(from 1981)**
Lacquered metal, height 6⁵/₁₆" (16 cm)
Manufacturer: Stilnovo
Thunder and Light, Ltd., I/M, New York

Mario Bellini Italian, born 1935
**IV-4 "Area 50" table lamps, 1975
(from 1975)**
Porcelain and plastic, height of larger
lamp 19⁵/₈" (49.8 cm)
Manufacturer: Artemide
Prize: Compasso d'Oro, 1979
Philadelphia Museum of Art. Gift of
Artemide Inc.

Max Bill Swiss, born 1908
IV-5 Sun lamp, 1950
Enameled metal, height (extended)
22½" (57.1 cm)
Manufacturer: Novelectric
The Museum of Modern Art, New
York. Gift of the manufacturer. 455.56

Cini Boeri Italian, born 1924
IV-6 Table lamp, 1968
PVC plastic, height (extended) 47¼"
(120 cm)
Manufacturer: Arteluce
Flos S.p.A., Brescia, Italy, through
Atelier International, Ltd., New York

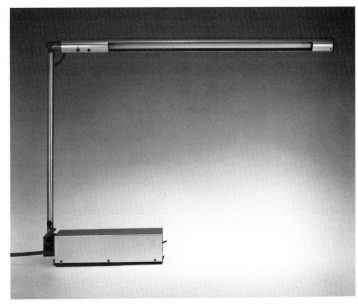

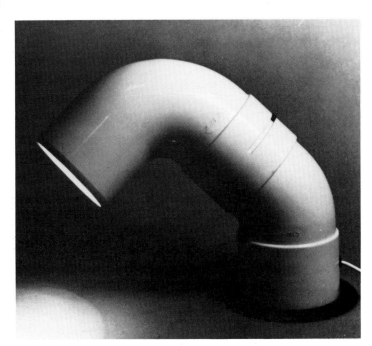

Achille Castiglioni Italian, born 1918
Piergiacomo Castiglioni Italian,
1913–1968
**IV-7 "Tubino" desk lamp, 1949 (from
1949 by Arredoluce; 1971–75 by Flos)**
Enameled metal and aluminum, height
11⁷/₁₆" (29 cm)
Manufacturer: Flos
Flos S.p.A., Brescia, Italy, through
Atelier International, Ltd., New York

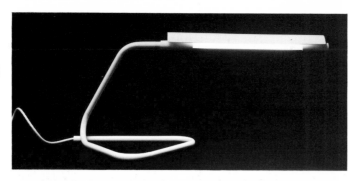

Achille Castiglioni Italian, born 1918
Piergiacomo Castiglioni Italian,
1913–1968
**IV-8 "Taraxacum" hanging lamps,
1950 (from 1950)**
Spun fiberglass, height of larger lamp
25³/₁₆" (64 cm)
Manufacturer: Flos
Atelier International, Ltd., New York

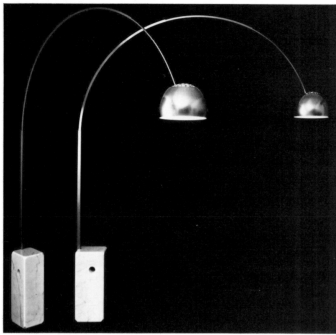

Achille Castiglioni Italian, born 1918
Piergiacomo Castiglioni Italian,
1913–1968
**IV-9 "Arco" floor lamp, 1962
(from 1962)**
Marble, stainless steel, and aluminum,
height 95" (241.3 cm)
Manufacturer: Flos
Atelier International, Ltd., New York
Plate 29

Achille Castiglioni Italian, born 1918
Piergiacomo Castiglioni Italian,
1913–1968
**IV-10 "Taccia" table lamp, 1962
(from 1962)**
Aluminum and glass, height 21"
(53.3 cm)
Manufacturer: Flos
Philadelphia Museum of Art. Gift of
Atelier International, Ltd. 1977-199-1

Achille Castiglioni Italian, born 1918
Piergiacomo Castiglioni Italian,
1913–1968
**IV-11 "Toio" floor lamp, 1965
(from 1965)**
Enameled steel and brass, height
(extended) 78¹³/₁₆" (200.2 cm)
Manufacturer: Flos
Atelier International, Ltd., New York

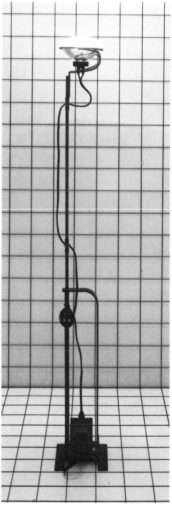

Achille Castiglioni Italian, born 1918
Pio Manzù Italian, 1939–1969
**IV-12 "Parentesi" floor lamp, 1972
(from 1972)**
Stainless steel and rubber, height
(extended) 157½" (400 cm)
Manufacturer: Flos
Prizes: Honorable mention, Ljubljana,
Bio, 1973; Compasso d'Oro, 1979
Atelier International, Ltd., New York

Achille Castiglioni Italian, born 1918
**IV-13 "Gibigiana" table lamp, 1981
(from 1981)**
Enameled steel, height 16½" (41.9 cm)
Manufacturer: Flos
Atelier International, Ltd., New York
Plate 56

Livio Castiglioni Italian, 1911–1979
Gianfranco Frattini Italian, born 1926
**IV-14 "Boalum" table lamp, 1971
(from 1971)**
Plastic and metal, length 78¾" (200 cm)
Manufacturer: Artemide
Prize: Honorable mention, Ljubljana,
Bio, 1973
Philadelphia Museum of Art. Gift of
Artemide Inc.
Plate 44

Joe Colombo Italian, 1930–1971
**IV-15 "Colombo" table lamp, 1962
(from 1963)**
Brass and Perspex, height 9⁷/₁₆" (24 cm)
Manufacturer: O-Luce
Philadelphia Museum of Art. Gift of
O-Luce Italia S.p.A.

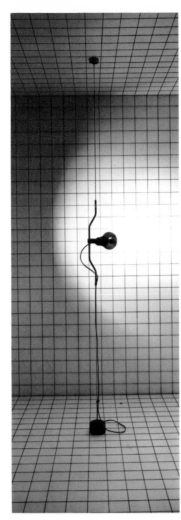

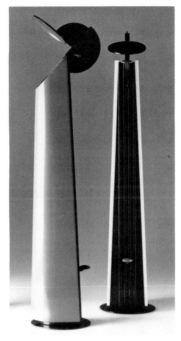

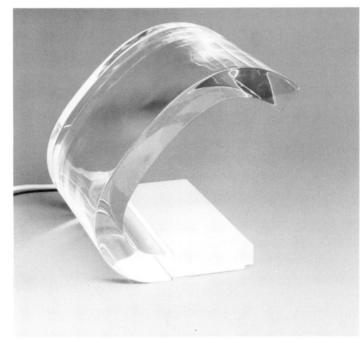

Joe Colombo Italian, 1930–1971
**IV-16 "Spider" table lamp, 1966
(from 1967)**
Lacquered aluminum, height 15¾"
(40 cm)
Manufacturer: O-Luce
Prizes: A.I.D. International Design
Award, 1967; Compasso d'Oro, 1967
Philadelphia Museum of Art. Gift of
O-Luce Italia S.p.A.

Cedric Hartman American, born 1929
IV-17 Floor lamp, 1966 (from 1967)
Nickel, height 37" (93.9 cm)
Manufacturer: Hartman
Philadelphia Museum of Art. Gift of
Cedric Hartman Inc.

Poul Henningsen Danish, 1894–1967
**IV-18 "PH Artichoke" hanging lamp,
1958 (from 1958)**
Stainless steel, diameter 23⅝" (60 cm)
Manufacturer: Poulsen
Philadelphia Museum of Art. Gift of
Louis Poulsen & Co. A/S

Poul Henningsen Danish, 1894–1967
**IV-19 "PH-5" hanging lamp, 1958
(from 1958)**
Metal, diameter 19¹¹/₁₆" (50 cm)
Manufacturer: Poulsen
Philadelphia Museum of Art. Gift of
Louis Poulsen & Co. A/S

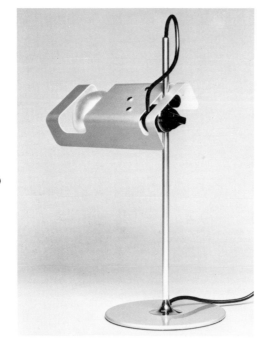

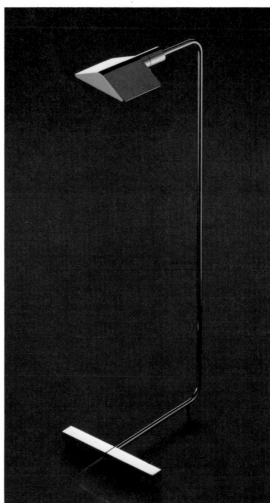

Robert Heritage British, born 1927
IV-20 "Pan Parabolic" track lamp, 1973
Enameled metal, height 9" (22.9 cm)
Manufacturer: Concord
Prize: Design Council Award, 1973
Philadelphia Museum of Art. Gift of
Lightolier, Inc. 74-197-1

Arne Jacobsen Danish, 1902–1971
**IV-21 "AJ" hanging lamp, 1956
(from 1956)**
Enameled metal, diameter 19¹¹/₁₆"
(50 cm)
Manufacturer: Poulsen
Prize: Bundespreis "Gute Form," 1972
Philadelphia Museum of Art. Gift of
Louis Poulsen & Co. A/S

Lisa Johansson-Pape Finnish, born
1907
IV-22 Hanging lamp, c. 1955
Enameled metal, height 9⁷/₁₆" (24 cm)
Manufacturer: Stockmann
Taideteollisuusmuseo, Helsinki

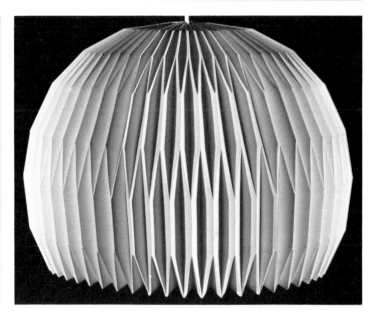

Esben Klint Danish, 1915–1969
**IV-23 Hanging lamp, 1947
(from 1947)**
Plastic-coated paper, height 11" (28 cm)
Manufacturer: Le Klint
Philadelphia Museum of Art. Gift of Le
Klint A/S

Michael Lax American, born 1929
**IV-24 "Lytegem" table lamp, 1965
(1966–72)**
Zinc, brass, and aluminum, height
(extended) 15" (38.1 cm)
Manufacturer: Lightolier
Collection of William Blitzer, Claremont,
New Jersey

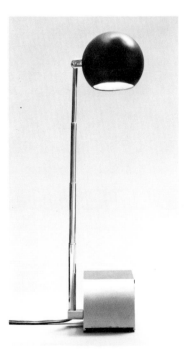

Vico Magistretti Italian, born 1920
**IV-25 "Atollo" table lamp, 1977
(from 1977)**
Enameled aluminum, height 27⁹/₁₆"
(70 cm)
Manufacturer: O-Luce
Prize: Compasso d'Oro, 1979
Philadelphia Museum of Art. Gift of
O-Luce Italia S.p.A.
Plate 55

Bruno Munari Italian, born 1907
**IV-26 "Falkland" hanging lamp, 1964
(from 1964)**
Elasticized fabric and metal, height
64¹⁵/₁₆" (165 cm)
Manufacturer: Danese
Philadelphia Museum of Art. Gift of
Jacqueline and Bruno Danese

George Nelson American, born 1908
**IV-27 "Bubble" hanging lamps, 1952
(from 1952)**
Plastic and steel wire, height of largest
lamp 33" (83.8 cm)
Manufacturer: Howard Miller
Philadelphia Museum of Art. Gift of
Howard Miller Clock Company

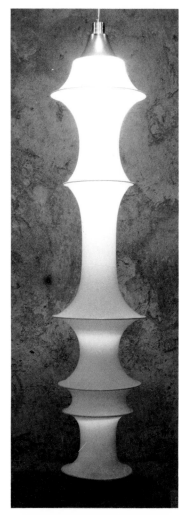

Greta von Nessen American, born
Germany, c. 1900–c. 1978
IV-28 "Anywhere" lamp, 1952
Aluminum and enameled metal, height
14" (35.5 cm)
Manufacturer: Nessen
Philadelphia Museum of Art. Gift of
Nessen Lamps Inc. 74-57-1
Plate 10

Isamu Noguchi American, born 1904
IV-29 Table lamp, 1948
Plastic and wood, height 15¾" (40 cm)
Manufacturer: Knoll
Philadelphia Museum of Art. Gift of
Mr. and Mrs. James Dermody.
1977-85-1
Plate 2

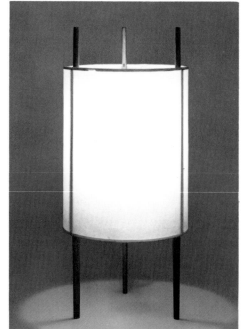

Isamu Noguchi American, born 1904
**IV-30 "Akari" hanging lamp, 1966
(from 1966)**
Mulberry-bark paper and wire, height
20" (50.8 cm)
Manufacturer: Kovacs
Philadelphia Museum of Art. Purchased

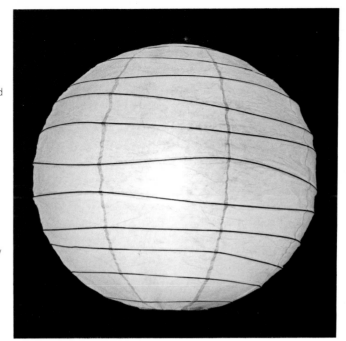

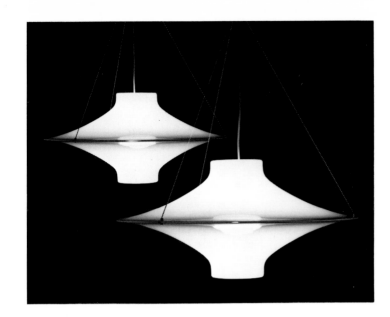

Yki Nummi Finnish, born China, 1925
**IV-31 "UFO" hanging lamp, 1960
(from 1960)**
Plastic, diameter 27½" (70 cm)
Manufacturer: Stockmann
Philadelphia Museum of Art. Gift of Oy
Stockmann AB

Richard Sapper Italian, born Germany,
1932
**IV-32 "Tizio" table lamp, 1972
(from 1972)**
ABS plastic and aluminum, height
(extended) 46½" (118.1 cm)
Manufacturer: Artemide
Prizes: Compasso d'Oro, 1979; Gold
medal, Ljubljana, Bio, 1981
Philadelphia Museum of Art. Gift of
Artemide Inc.

Gino Sarfatti Italian, born 1912
IV-33 Floor lamp, 1948
Metal, height (extended) 62" (157.5 cm)
Manufacturer: Arteluce
Flos S.p.A., Brescia, Italy, through
Atelier International, Ltd., New York

Gino Sarfatti Italian, born 1912
IV-34 Table lamp, 1966
Metal, height 11¹³/₁₆" (30 cm)
Manufacturer: Arteluce
Flos S.p.A., Brescia, Italy, through
Atelier International, Ltd., New York

Neal Small American, born 1937
**IV-35 "Miri" table lamp, c. 1970
(c. 1970–80)**
Acrylic and chromed steel, height 18"
(45.7 cm)
Manufacturer: Nessen
Philadelphia Museum of Art. Gift of
Nessen Lamps Inc. 1983-54-1

Kurt Versen American, born Sweden, 1901
IV-36 Floor lamp, c. 1946
Enameled metal, height (extended) 62"
(157.5 cm)
Manufacturer: Versen
Collection of Andrew B. Shapiro, Glen Mills, Pennsylvania

Vittoriano Viganò Italian, born 1919
IV-37 Floor lamp, 1960
Metal, height 62" (157.5 cm)
Manufacturer: Arteluce
Flos S.p.A., Brescia, Italy, through
Atelier International, Ltd., New York

Jean-Pierre Vitrac French, born 1944
IV-38 Floor lamp, 1970
Chromed metal, height (extended)
57¹/₁₆" (145 cm)
Manufacturer: Verre Lumière
Collection of the designer, Paris
Plate 42

Gilbert Watrous American, born 1919
IV-39 Floor lamp, 1950
Brass and steel, height (extended) 55"
(139.7 cm)
Manufacturer: Heifetz
Prize: First prize, New York, The
Museum of Modern Art, International
competition for floor lamp design, 1950
The Museum of Modern Art, New
York. Gift of the manufacturer. 465.51

Tapio Wirkkala Finnish, born 1915
**IV-40 "Wirkkala" hanging lamps
and holders, 1960 (from 1960)**
Glass and metal, length of longer
lamp 8¼" (21 cm)
Manufacturer: Airam (lamps); Idman
(holders)
Prize: Gold medal, Milan, Triennale,
1960
Philadelphia Museum of Art. Gift of Oy
Airam AB

Otto Zapf German, born 1931
**IV-41 "Light Column" floor lamp,
1972 (1972–77)**
Enameled aluminum, height 53⅛"
(135 cm)
Manufacturer: Zapf
Prize: Bundespreis "Gute Form," 1972
Philadelphia Museum of Art. Gift of
ZapfDesign

Metalwork   Introduction by Carl Pott

For some sixty years, Carl Pott has
designed cutlery and metal
tableware, produced by his own
firm in Solingen, West Germany,
which have been awarded
numerous design prizes. His factory
has also manufactured metalwork
created by other noted designers,
both German and foreign, which
has competed successfully with the
metalwork of Scandinavia, Great
Britain, and Italy on international
markets.

Metalware has really been my life for the past sixty years. In fact, silverware and table services have probably shaped me as much as I—from initial conception through handmade model to finished product—have shaped them.

Over these same years I have seen changes of many sorts, far-reaching developments both at home and abroad, reforms both internal and external. There have been remarkable innovations in society, in culture, and in public affairs—none of which has been without its impact on the whole range of industrial production.

Industrial design in my homeland was as good as nonexistent right after the Second World War. The industrial capacity of Germany had been all but wiped out, and quite apart from the widespread shortages, the focus was inevitably on procuring the necessities of food and housing. The task essentially was to rebuild the demolished and bombed-out factories, retool them for peacetime production, and out of the scraps and ashes of war, produce an urgently needed flow of basic consumer goods. It was a task that demanded the utmost, not from the designer's imagination but in technical and practical skill and effort.

Improvisation was the order of the day. Just as after the First World War, first simple handwork and then skilled labor were the chief forms of production; there was simply no other way to close the supply gaps and to meet not only the most basic of human needs but also cultural needs. Wherever factories had largely been spared devastation, it was possible to restore the prewar levels of production rather quickly, of course within the limits of prewar technological capacities. In actual practice even this relatively primitive level of restoration was achieved to only a modest degree, for industrial production also required a flow of raw materials, heavy equipment, and durable goods that had also to be produced and shipped. Government efforts to cope with the massive shortage of goods were barely able to provide the most basic necessities for the "average consumer."

Thus was the beginning of the postwar revival of West German life and its crucial market economy. Thus was the beginning also of a dynamic, profit-oriented process of ever-increasing expansion in production and consumption, in which industrial design was destined to play an important role. When the Federal Republic was once again restored to affluence, it seemed to take special delight in the effect of streamlining, from its kidney-shaped tables to its hip-roofed villas. Its new level of culture, though, was in many respects a historically conditioned and traditionally derived consumer culture. It reflected not a breakthrough on the part of people's desire for change and innovation but a return to artistic standards and consumer preferences that had long been familiar and accepted. Private consumption was rapidly met with the return of abundant supplies; it was also stylized by the promise of universal well-being confidently held out to consumers through all types of media advertising.

At first the need for disposable goods and luxury items seemed to have been met merely through reissuing the technical and artistic achievements of prewar industry. As the initial needs came to be satisfied, however, designers were given the task of developing new and different industrial products, items that would serve the changed marketplace not only in the sense of satisfying a growing demand but also in the sense of being aesthetically distinctive and appealing, or at least packaged in a fresh way.

The economic sphere is determined by the human spirit, by the choices and actions of people. As such, it is permeated by the culture of the people. We commonly speak of physical culture and of cultivating the mind and spirit; we can easily speak of cultural patterns in housing and in living, and there is what might be called an economic culture, a culture of the economy and of economic affairs. The production of goods in endless supply is not simply a matter of the economy and of technology; it involves also questions of design. When industry extols its creations with accolades such as "beautifully designed," indeed, when it brings into existence a wholly new profession, that of the designer, it does so because industry has realized the significance of form and beauty in successful marketing. When the Deutscher Werkbund and the Bauhaus began to combat ugliness in industrial products, they were really introducing a kind of cultural struggle into the sphere of industrial production. At stake was the improvement of the quality of the product, including its aesthetics, in order to save people from the mounting flood of ugliness being spewed forth by the machine.

The manufacture of cutlery and hollow ware is obviously influenced by such a host of preconditions and precedents, but these products are also an expression of changes in lifestyle. Formerly people washed their dishes piece by piece after every meal; today the entire task has been taken over by the ubiquitous dishwasher. Silver and silver plate are therefore no longer the most practical materials. Metals have to be much tougher, and utensils able to stand up to added abuse. Stainless steel, and then also steel mixed with nickel and chrome in special alloys, were introduced to meet these needs.

Eating habits have changed too. Women working outside the home have less time for cooking meals, and prepared foods, frozen meals, and canned items of all sorts are being ever more widely used. Accordingly, silverware is being made smaller and more versatile, adapted to a greater variety of uses. Scaled-down services have been created in which the forks have shorter, more widely spaced tines and contoured bowls for better handling of all sorts of foods. Silverware today has to do justice to the varied needs and habits of many different individuals. It has to serve people who are left-handed as well as those who are right-handed. It has to handle noodles of varying sizes and shapes. It has to cope with lobster as well as steak, not to speak of fruits and vegetables of every sort and description. It has to suit everyday meals and quick snacks, as well as the festive dinners with many courses that have become fashionable; accordingly, new silverware components and associated hollow-ware items have been developed which can equip even the most elaborate of tables.

Since today's silverware must be functional above all, and serve its purpose well no matter how people change the form, color, and display of their china and table decorations, I design my silverware without ornamentation. Smooth and plain shapes are the most universally compatible, and most easily cleaned anyway. Quality silverware that is both beautiful and practical seems to hold the greatest appeal for most people; it tends to be purchased by those who have experienced it first-hand, and thereby have become persuaded of its value. And despite all the impressive gains made in modern technology and in modern production processes, the silverware that is of the highest quality and the most appreciated is still that which is produced by the hands of skilled and dedicated craftspeople.

Folke Arström Swedish, born 1907
**V-1 "Focus de luxe" cutlery, 1956
(1956–c. 1973)**
Stainless steel and plastic, length of
knife 7⅞" (20 cm)
Manufacturer: Gense
GuldsmedsAktieBolaget GAB,
Eskilstuna, Sweden

Sergio Asti Italian, born 1926
V-2 "Boca" cutlery, 1976 (from 1976)
Stainless steel, length of knife 7¹³/₁₆"
(19.9 cm)
Manufacturer: Lauffer
Philadelphia Museum of Art. Gift of the
Pottery Barn. 1982-153-1–5
Plate 51

Carl Auböck Austrian, born 1924
V-3 Cocktail shaker, 1959
Chromed metal, height 8¼" (21 cm)
Manufacturer: Auböck
The Museum of Modern Art, New
York. Philip C. Johnson Fund.
699.59a–c

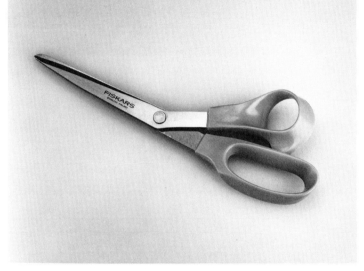

Olof Bäckström Finnish, born 1922
V-4 Scissors, 1963 (from 1967)
Stainless steel and ABS plastic, length
8½" (21.6 cm)
Manufacturer: Fiskars
Philadelphia Museum of Art. Gift of Oy
Fiskars. 1982-145-1

Gustav Beran Austrian, born 1912
V-5 "Dinette" kitchen tools, 1959
Steel and plastic, length of soup ladle
11⅛" (28.2 cm)
Manufacturer: Van Kempen & Begeer
Stedelijk Museum, Amsterdam

Nord Bowlen American, born 1909
V-6 "Contrast" cutlery, 1954
Sterling silver and nylon, length of
knife 9⁵/₁₆" (23.7 cm)
Manufacturer: Lunt
Lunt Silversmiths, Greenfield,
Massachusetts

Antonia Campi Italian, born 1921
V-7 "Neto" scissors, 1954 (from 1954)
Nickel-plated carbon steel, length 10¹³/₁₆" (27.5 cm)
Manufacturer: Ermenegildo Collini
Prize: Compasso d'Oro, 1959
Philadelphia Museum of Art. Purchased with funds contributed by COLLAB: The Contemporary Design Group for the Philadelphia Museum of Art. 1983-50-1

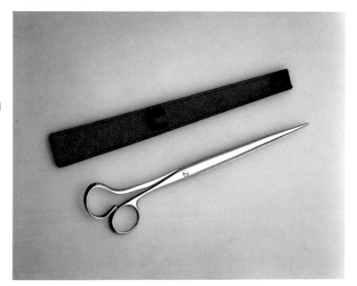

Karl Dittert German, born Austria, 1915
V-8 Nesting cooking set, 1960 (1960–c. 1970)
Stainless steel, height 8⅞" (22.5 cm)
Manufacturer: Kühn
Gebrüder Kühn, Schwäbisch Gmünd, West Germany

Tias Eckhoff Norwegian, born 1926
V-9 "Maya" cutlery and carving set, 1961 (from 1962)
Stainless steel, length of carving knife 13¹¹/₁₆" (34.8 cm)
Manufacturer: Norsk
Prize: Norwegian Design Centre emblem for good Norwegian design, 1965
Cutlery: Philadelphia Museum of Art. Gift of Norsk Stålpress
Carving set: Norsk Stålpress A/S, Bergen, Norway

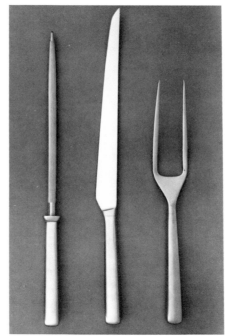

Ekco Products Company American, established Chicago, 1888
V-10 "Flint" kitchen tools, 1946 (from 1946)
Stainless steel and plastic, length of spatula 10¹¹/₁₆" (27.1 cm)
Manufacturer: Ekco
Ekco Housewares Company, Franklin Park, Illinois

Ergonomi Design Gruppen Swedish, established Bromma, 1979
V-11 "Eat and Drink" cutlery, 1980 (from 1981)
Metal and plastic, length of knife 9¼" (23.5 cm)
Manufacturer: RFSU Rehab
Philadelphia Museum of Art. Gift of RFSU Rehab

Bertel Gardberg Finnish, born 1916
V-12 "Canton" kettle, 1957
Stainless steel and teak, diameter 7⅞"
(20 cm)
Manufacturer: Hackman & Sorsakoski
Taideteollisuusmuseo, Helsinki

Annika Gudmundsson Swedish,
born 1951
**V-13 "Ergonova" kitchen tools, 1979
(from 1979)**
Stainless steel and plastic, width of
spatula 3⅜" (8.5 cm)
Manufacturer: Gense
GuldsmedsAktieBolaget GAB,
Eskilstuna, Sweden

Piet Hein Danish, born 1905
V-14 Tray, 1966 (from 1966)
Sterling silver, length 9¾" (24.8 cm)
Manufacturer: Jensen
Georg Jensen Sølvsmedie A/S,
Copenhagen

Erik Herløw, Danish, born 1913
V-15 Coffeepot, 1947 (from 1948)
Sterling silver, height 7¹³/₁₆" (19.8 cm)
Manufacturer: Michelsen
Georg Jensen Sølvsmedie A/S,
Copenhagen

Knud Holscher Danish, born 1930
**V-16 Salad servers and tongs, 1975
(from 1975)**
Stainless steel, length of fork 12³/₁₆"
(31 cm)
Manufacturer: Jensen
Georg Jensen Sølvsmedie A/S,
Copenhagen

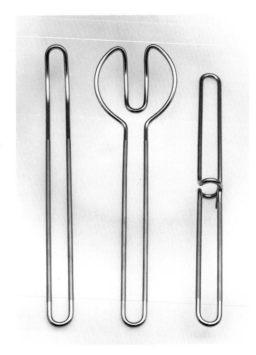

Arne Jacobsen Danish, 1902–1971
V-17 Cutlery, 1957 (from 1957)
Stainless steel, length of knife 7⅞"
(20 cm)
Manufacturer: Michelsen
Georg Jensen Sølvsmedie A/S,
Copenhagen

Arne Jacobsen Danish, 1902–1971
**V-18 "Cylinda Line" tableware, 1967
(from 1967)**
Stainless steel and nylon, height of
coffeepot 7½" (19 cm)
Manufacturer: Stelton
Prizes: ID Prize, Danish Society of
Industrial Design, 1967; A.I.D.
International Design Award, 1968
Philadelphia Museum of Art. Gift of
A/S Stelton
Plate 32

Søren Georg Jensen Danish, born
1917
V-19 Condiment set, 1951 (from 1951)
Sterling silver, height of mustard pot
2¹³⁄₁₆" (7.2 cm)
Manufacturer: Jensen
Philadelphia Museum of Art. Gift of
Mr. and Mrs. Louis Sherman.
1982-58-4a–c

Robert King American, born 1917
V-20 "Contour" cutlery, 1951
Sterling silver, length of knife 8⅞"
(22.5 cm)
Manufacturer: Towle
Philadelphia Museum of Art. Gift of
Towle Manufacturing Company.
1983-57-1–3

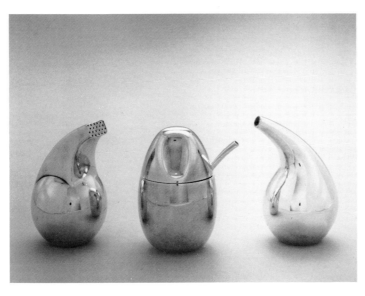

Henning Koppel Danish, 1918–1981
V-21 Teapot, 1954 (from 1954)
Sterling silver and ivory, height 4⅝"
(11.8 cm)
Manufacturer: Jensen
Georg Jensen Sølvsmedie A/S,
Copenhagen

Henning Koppel Danish, 1918–1981
V-22 Covered dish, 1954 (from 1954)
Sterling silver, length 28⅛" (71.5 cm)
Manufacturer: Jensen
Georg Jensen Sølvsmedie A/S,
Copenhagen

Henning Koppel Danish, 1918–1981
**V-23 Carving knife and fork, 1971
(from 1971)**
Stainless steel, length 12³/₁₆" (31 cm)
Manufacturer: Jensen
Georg Jensen Sølvsmedie A/S,
Copenhagen

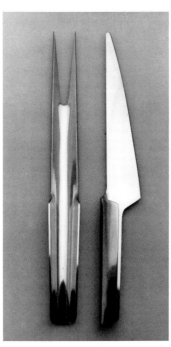

Herbert Krenchel Danish, born 1922
V-24 "Krenit" bowl, 1953
Enameled steel, diameter 7" (17.8 cm)
Manufacturer: Torben Ørskov
Prize: Gold medal, Milan, Triennale,
1954
Philadelphia Museum of Art. Purchased
with funds contributed by COLLAB: The
Contemporary Design Group for the
Philadelphia Museum of Art. 1983-50-2

Ennio Lucini Italian, born 1934
**V-25 "Tummy" covered saucepan,
1968 (from 1968)**
Stainless steel, height 8⅛" (20.6 cm)
Manufacturer: Barazzoni
Prize: Compasso d'Oro, 1979
Philadelphia Museum of Art. Gift of
Barazzoni S.p.A. 1983-3-1

Erik Magnussen Danish, born 1940
V-26 "Thermo" jug, 1977 (from 1977)
Stainless steel, height 11¹³/₁₆" (30 cm)
Manufacturer: Stelton
Prize: ID Prize, Danish Society of
Industrial Design, 1977
Philadelphia Museum of Art. Gift of
A/S Stelton. 1982-53-1a,b

David Mellor British, born 1930
V-27 "Thrift" cutlery, 1965
Stainless steel, length of knife 7¾"
(19.7 cm)
Manufacturer: David Mellor
Prize: Design Centre Award, 1966
Philadelphia Museum of Art. Gift of
the designer. 75-11-2

Sigurd Persson Swedish, born 1914
V-28 Vegetable dishes, 1953
Stainless steel, length 8⁷/₁₆" (21.5 cm)
Manufacturer: Silver & Stål
Philadelphia Museum of Art. Gift of
Silver & Stål. 1982-52-1,2

Sigurd Persson Swedish, born 1914
V-29 "Jet Line" cutlery, 1959
Stainless steel, length of knife 6⅞"
(17.5 cm)
Manufacturer: KF
Prize: Silver medal, Milan, Triennale,
1960
Philadelphia Museum of Art. Gift of
the designer. 1982-56-1–5

Arne Petersen Danish, born 1922
V-30 Bottle opener, 1975 (from 1975)
Stainless steel and brass, diameter 2½"
(6.3 cm)
Manufacturer: Jensen
Georg Jensen Sølvsmedie A/S,
Copenhagen

Carl Pott German, born 1906
V-31 Cutlery, 1952 (from 1952)
Silver plate, length of knife 8⁷/₁₆"
(21.4 cm)
Manufacturer: Pott
Prizes: Gold medal, Milan, Triennale,
1954; Gold medal, Brussels, Exposition
Universelle, 1958; Medal, Venice,
Biennale, 1978
Philadelphia Museum of Art. Gift of
C. Hugo Pott
Plate 14

Carl Pott German, born 1906
V-32 Cutlery, 1957 (from 1957)
Stainless steel, length of longer
knife 8¼" (21 cm)
Manufacturer: Pott
Prizes: Silver medal, Milan, Triennale,
1957; Gold medal, Brussels,
Exposition Universelle, 1958;
Bundespreis "Gute Form," 1973
Philadelphia Museum of Art. Gift of
C. Hugo Pott

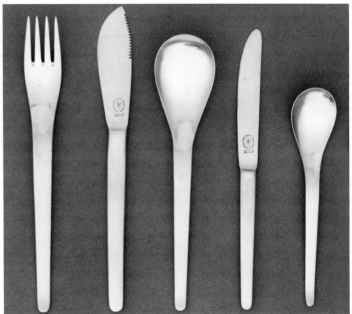

Peter Raacke German, born 1928
V-33 "Mono-a" cutlery, 1958 (from 1958); kitchen tools, 1965 (from 1965)
Stainless steel, length of carving knife 11⁵/₁₆″ (28.7 cm)
Manufacturer: Hessische Metallwerke
Prize: Bundespreis "Gute Form," 1973
Philadelphia Museum of Art. Gift of Hessische Metallwerke—Ziegenhain

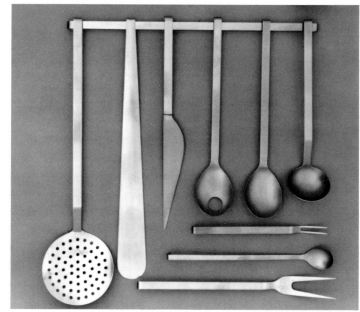

Börje Rajalin Finnish, born 1933
V-34 Teakettle, 1963 (1963–69)
Stainless steel and phenoplast, height 5³/₈″ (13.6 cm)
Manufacturer: Ja-ro
Philadelphia Museum of Art. Gift of Oy Ja-ro AB

Lino Sabattini Italian, born 1925
V-35 "Como" coffee and tea service, 1960 (1960–70)
Silver plate, height of coffeepot 8⁷/₁₆″ (21.5 cm)
Manufacturer: Christofle
Musée Bouilhet-Christofle, Saint-Denis, France

Lino Sabattini Italian, born 1925
V-36 "Eskimo" ice bucket, 1978 (from 1978)
Silver plate, height 6⅛″ (15.5 cm)
Manufacturer: Sabattini
Prize: Compasso d'Oro, 1979
Philadelphia Museum of Art. Gift of the designer

Roberto Sambonet Italian, born 1924
V-37 Fish serving dish, 1954 (from 1954)
Stainless steel, length 20" (50.8 cm)
Manufacturer: Sambonet
Prize: Compasso d'Oro, 1970
Philadelphia Museum of Art. Gift of Sambonet—Cutlery, Tableware & Holloware Manufacturers

Roberto Sambonet Italian, born 1924
V-38 "Center Line" cooking set, 1964 (from 1964)
Stainless steel, height (stacked) 7¹/₁₆" (18 cm)
Manufacturer: Sambonet
Philadelphia Museum of Art. Gift of Sambonet—Cutlery, Tableware & Holloware Manufacturers
Plate 38

Richard Sapper Italian, born Germany, 1932
V-39 Espresso pot, 1978 (from 1979)
Stainless steel, height 8¼" (21 cm)
Manufacturer: Alessi
Prizes: Compasso d'Oro, 1979; Honorable mention, Ljubljana, Bio, 1981
Philadelphia Museum of Art. Gift of Alessi S.p.A.

Timo Sarpaneva Finnish, born 1926
V-40 Covered cooking pot, 1959
Cast iron and wood, height 7¹/₁₆" (18 cm)
Manufacturer: Rosenlew
Taideteollisuusmuseo, Helsinki

Timo Sarpaneva Finnish, born 1926
V-41 Covered casserole, 1970 (from 1970)
Stainless steel, height 3¹⁵/₁₆" (10 cm)
Manufacturer: Opa
Philadelphia Museum of Art. Gift of Opa Oy. 1982-55-3a,b

Svend Siune Danish, born 1935
V-42 "Blue Shark" serving fork and spoon, 1965 (from 1965)
Stainless steel, length 8¹/₁₆" (20.5 cm)
Manufacturer: Jensen
Georg Jensen Sølvsmedie A/S, Copenhagen

Magnus Stephensen Danish, born 1903
V-43 Teapot, 1953 (from 1953)
Sterling silver and ivory, diameter 5¹³/₁₆" (14.8 cm)
Manufacturer: Jensen
Georg Jensen Sølvsmedie A/S, Copenhagen

Studio OPI Italian, established Milan, c. 1960s
V-44 Bar set, 1969 (from 1969)
Stainless steel, length of tongs 8¼" (21 cm)
Manufacturer: Cini & Nils
Philadelphia Museum of Art. Gift of Mr. and Mrs. Alan Gross. 1977-249-1a–f

Ilmari Tapiovaara Finnish, born 1914
V-45 "Polar" cutlery, 1963
Stainless steel, length of fork 9½" (24.1 cm)
Manufacturer: Hackman
Design Sammlung Bauer, Leonberg, West Germany

Lella Vignelli Italian, born 1930s
Massimo Vignelli Italian, born 1931
V-46 Bar set, 1971 (from 1971)
Sterling silver, length of strainer 6⅞" (17.5 cm)
Manufacturer: San Lorenzo
Philadelphia Museum of Art

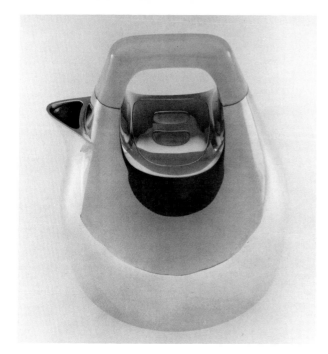

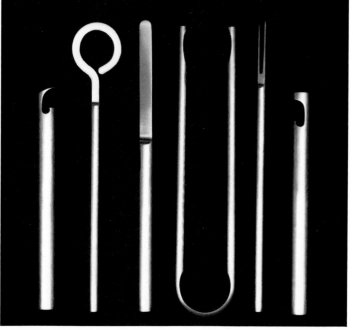

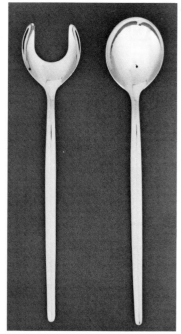

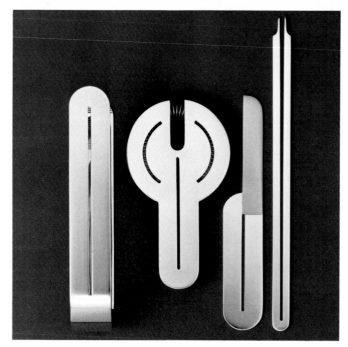

Wilhelm Wagenfeld German, born 1900
V-47 "Form 3600" cutlery, 1952
Stainless steel, length of knife 8"
(20.4 cm)
Manufacturer: WMF
Württembergische Metallwarenfabrik
AG, Geislingen, West Germany —WMF
of America

Wilhelm Wagenfeld German, born 1900
V-48 Stacking eggcup, 1954 (from 1954)
Stainless steel, length 5½" (14 cm)
Manufacturer: WMF
Philadelphia Museum of Art. Gift of
Württembergische Metallwarenfabrik
AG—WMF of America. 1983-59-3

Don Wallance American, born 1909
V-49 "Design 1" cutlery, 1954
Stainless steel, length of knife 7¹⁵/₁₆"
(20.1 cm)
Manufacturer: Pott
Prize: Gold medal, Milan, Triennale, 1954
Philadelphia Museum of Art. Gift of
C. Hugo Pott. 1982-152-22–25

Robert Welch British, born 1929
V-50 "Alveston" carving knife and fork, 1961 (from 1961); teapot, 1962 (from 1962)
Stainless steel, height of teapot 4⅜"
(11.1 cm)
Manufacturer: Old Hall
Prize: Design Centre Award, 1965
Philadelphia Museum of Art. Gift of
Old Hall Tableware Ltd. 74-149-1–7,
1983-9-1a,b
Plate 28

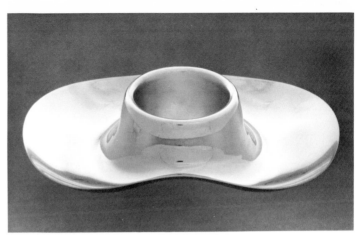

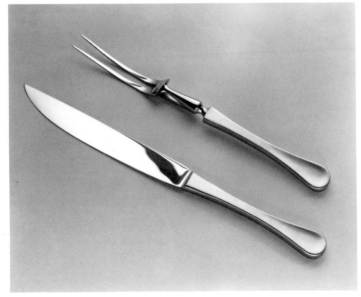

W. Archibald Welden American, born 1900s
V-51 Cooking pot, 1954
Stainless steel and copper, height 6¾"
(17.2 cm)
Manufacturer: Revere
Revere Ware Division, Revere Copper
and Brass Incorporated, Clinton, Illinois

Tapio Wirkkala Finnish, born 1915
V-52 "Composition" cutlery, 1963
Stainless steel, length of knife 8³/₁₆"
(20.8 cm)
Manufacturer: Rosenthal
Philadelphia Museum of Art. Gift of
Rosenthal AG. 1982-154-18–23
Plate 33

Tapio Wirkkala Finnish, born 1915
**V-53 "Puukko" knife, 1963 (from
1963)**
Stainless steel, polyamid, and brass,
length 7⅞" (20 cm)
Manufacturer: Hackman
Prize: Silver medal, Milan, Triennale,
1964
Philadelphia Museum of Art. Gift of
Oy Hackman. 1982-28-1a,b

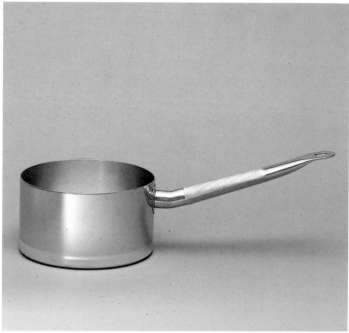

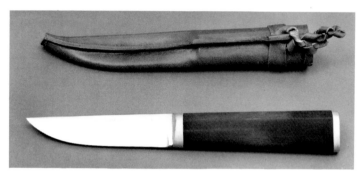

Plastics

Introduction by Bruno Danese

In their Milan firm, founded in 1957, Bruno Danese and his wife Jacqueline Vodoz have produced many of the most innovative objects in plastic by a number of Italy's most significant designers.

Objects for use or decoration, produced over the centuries, are always an important testimony of the cultural and economic evolution of the different civilizations of which they are expressions. These civilizations used natural materials, and their technologies of transformation were essentially manual. A close relationship existed between man and material, both with regard to objects of daily use, which were made in series, and precious objects—for which I use the term "ceremonial"—produced as unique pieces or in limited numbers.

By the beginning of this century, scientific research had given us the first plastic materials. Different groups worked on the employment of these new materials. Technicians designed the machines that produced the raw materials and the machines used in transforming them; industries evolved to manufacture the raw materials, and others, to transform them into the finished product. In the cycle of production the traditional relationship between man and the manufactured object was transformed, and the worker's involvement became marginal, offering no scope for creative participation. This was the industrial basis when the production of objects in plastic began, initially on quite a small scale, but developing rapidly in Europe after 1945.

At first, existing utilitarian objects made in traditional materials were imitated and produced in plastic. Having the means in hand to accelerate and expand production, manufacturers set their sights on mass consumption. The quality of the object, how long it would last, how it would stand up to use were unimportant; the chief requirement was a swift exchange in the market. Manufacturers backed a policy of low prices, thus instilling in consumers the idea that objects in plastic were commonplace things. Contrary to what is generally thought, however, plastic material of quality is not cheap; its production, when not overaccelerated and impoverished because of time and numbers, is not among the most economical.

To go beyond banal imitation and to rediscover the coherence that once existed between form, function, and realization—that is to say, the series of components that contribute to the creation of a "handsome object," however modest its function—a new "technician" had to be found who would be conversant with all the industrial problems and related production techniques as well as with all the characteristics and the possibilities for the use of this material. This capacity is found in the profession of designer, which beyond its creativity, offers itself as coordinator and mediator in the realization of truly relevant products.

Of the body of utilitarian plastic objects that have come on the market, those of significance are still few in number. Almost all have been realized in collaboration with designers, and many of the most interesting examples are shown in this section. From the beginning, however, the use of plastics has been much more consistently inventive in the area of technical products, in which interesting aesthetic results have also been obtained (see "Appliances"). Another important sector of production has been that of furniture, particularly from 1950 to 1970. This production, however, was publicized, and consequently accepted by the public, as an innovation rather than as a real alternative to traditional materials. It has not met with a lasting acceptance by the consumer and there have been few significant examples of plastic furniture of recent date.

With relation to our own experience at Danese, production of plastic objects has from the very beginning resulted from a close collaboration with the designers. These are all distinct objects with different characteristics, but they have in common a similar philosophy that underlies their design and production. A good design and consequently a good product are achieved when the use (function), quality of material, execution (technology), and form (aesthetics) are combined in perfect proportion. It has, in addition, always been specifically intended that our objects have characteristics that can be realized only in plastic. From this viewpoint, we believe that we have obtained very interesting results with such pieces as Enzo Mari's "Pago-Pago" flower vase (VI-12) and his "Java" container for table use (VI-13). With these principles in mind we have also turned our attention to the production of objects from plastic materials already industrially transformed into sheets or tubes, intervening subsequently with semi-industrial technologies, such as pressure molding and others that are closer to the methods of the handcraftsman.

To conclude, if there is something that distinguishes our objects, be it those produced in large quantities or those in small series, it stems from the quality of the designers' conceptions, from our commitment to the scrupulous realization of these projects, and from our rejection of any form of influence from the marketplace.

In proposing new materials and new realizations for objects of ordinary use, one must not forget that in every individual there exists the memory of "how things were" and that it takes time to become comfortable with something new and to assimilate it; increasing the pace may lead to momentary success, but also to a rapid decline. Very interesting things have already been done in the field of plastics but we are still in an early phase of its development. Plastic, if used correctly, can give even more exciting results.

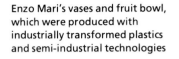

Enzo Mari's vases and fruit bowl, which were produced with industrially transformed plastics and semi-industrial technologies

Maria Benktzon Swedish, born 1946
Sven-Eric Juhlin Swedish, born 1940
(with Per-Olof Landgren)
**VI-1 Knife and cutting board, 1974
(from 1974)**
Plastic and steel, length 13¾" (35 cm)
Manufacturer: Gustavsberg
AB Gustavsberg, Gustavsberg, Sweden
Plate 50

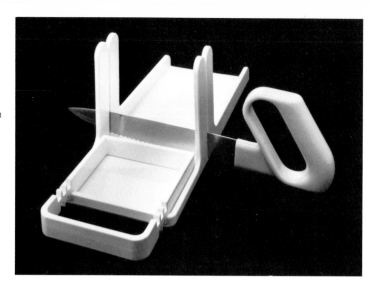

Sigvard Bernadotte Swedish,
born 1907
Acton Bjørn Danish, born 1910
**VI-2 "Margrethe" bowls, 1950
(from 1950)**
Melamine, height (stacked) 7½"
(19 cm)
Manufacturer: Rosti
Philadelphia Museum of Art. Gift of
Rosti (USA) Inc. 1983-56-1–5
Plate 11

Helen von Boch German, born 1938
Federigo Fabbrini Italian, born 1930s
**VI-3 "Bomba" picnic set, 1973
(1973–75)**
Melamine, height (stacked) 15½"
(39.3 cm)
Manufacturer: Villeroy & Boch
Philadelphia Museum of Art. Gift of
Villeroy & Boch

Carl-Arne Breger Swedish, born 1923
**VI-4 Covered bucket, 1959 (from
1959)**
Eten plastic, height 13³/₁₆" (33.5 cm)
Manufacturer: Gustavsberg
AB Gustavsberg, Gustavsberg, Sweden

Carl-Arne Breger Swedish, born 1923
**VI-5 Fruit juicer–pitcher, 1959
(1959–76)**
Propen plastic, height of smaller
pitcher 5¹¹/₁₆" (14.5 cm)
Manufacturer: Gustavsberg
AB Gustavsberg, Gustavsberg, Sweden

Anna Castelli Ferrieri (with Centrokappa) Italian, born 1920
VI-6 "Tabletop" service, 1979 (from 1979)
Methacrylate, diameter of largest bowl 13⅜" (34 cm)
Manufacturer: Kartell
Prize: Compasso d'Oro, 1979
Kartell USA, Easley, South Carolina

Gino Colombini Italian, born 1915
VI-7 Colander, 1962 (1962–73)
Polypropylene, diameter 10⅝" (27 cm)
Manufacturer: Kartell
Kartell USA, Easley, South Carolina

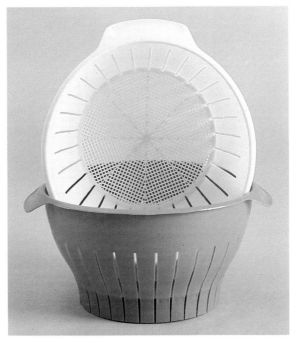

Ergonomi Design Gruppen Swedish, established Bromma, 1979
VI-8 "Eat and Drink" plate, 1980 (from 1981)
Melamine, diameter 7½" (19 cm)
Manufacturer: RFSU Rehab
Philadelphia Museum of Art. Gift of RFSU Rehab

Oskar Kogoj Yugoslavian, born 1942
VI-9 Cutlery, 1972 (from 1972)
Polyamide, length of knife 7⅞" (20 cm)
Manufacturer: Poligalant
Philadelphia Museum of Art. Gift of the designer. 1982-149-1–4

Stig Lindberg Swedish, 1916–1982
VI-10 Tray, 1970 (from 1970)
ABS plastic, width 19¹¹⁄₁₆" (50 cm)
Manufacturer: Gustavsberg
AB Gustavsberg, Gustavsberg, Sweden

Enzo Mari Italian, born 1932
**VI-11 "Tongareva" bowls, 1969
(from 1969)**
Melamine, diameter of largest bowl
11¹³/₁₆" (30 cm)
Manufacturer: Danese
Philadelphia Museum of Art. Gift of
Jacqueline and Bruno Danese

Enzo Mari Italian, born 1932
**VI-12 "Pago-Pago" vases, 1969 (from
1969)**
ABS plastic, height 11¹³/₁₆" (30 cm)
Manufacturer: Danese
Philadelphia Museum of Art. Gift of
Jacqueline and Bruno Danese
Plate 41

Enzo Mari Italian, born 1932
**VI-13 "Java" container, 1970 (from
1970)**
Melamine, height 2⅜" (6 cm)
Manufacturer: Danese
Philadelphia Museum of Art. Gift of
Jacqueline and Bruno Danese

Enzo Mari Italian, born 1932
**VI-14 "Ever-Ready" wastebasket,
1971 (from 1971)**
Polypropylene, height 16⅛" (41 cm)
Manufacturer: Danese
Philadelphia Museum of Art. Gift of
Jacqueline and Bruno Danese

Bruno Munari Italian, born 1907
**VI-15 "Cubo" ashtray, 1957 (from
1957)**
Melamine and aluminum, height
3⅛" (8 cm)
Manufacturer: Danese
Philadelphia Museum of Art. Gift of
Jacqueline and Bruno Danese

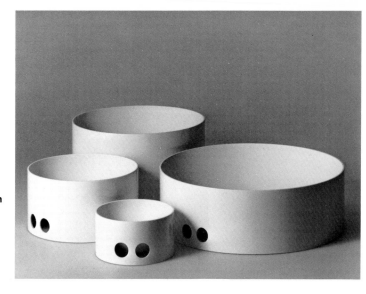

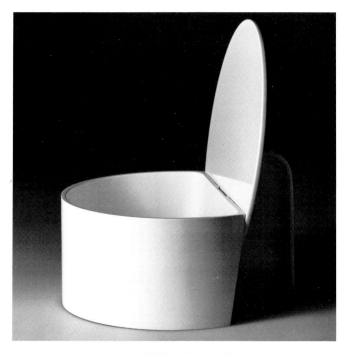

George Nelson American, born 1908
VI-16 "Florence Ware" service, 1955
Melamine, diameter of dinner plate 10"
(25.4 cm)
Manufacturer: Prolon
Collection of the designer, New York

David Harman Powell British,
born 1933
VI-17 Semi-disposable cutlery, 1970
ABS plastic, length of knife 7" (17.8 cm)
Manufacturer: Ekco Plastics
Prize: Council of Industrial Design
Award, 1970
Philadelphia Museum of Art. Gift of
Ekco Plastics Ltd. 74-148-1–6

Paolo Tilche Italian, born Egypt, 1925
**VI-18 "Pagoda" service, 1971
(from 1973)**
Dinnerware: Kostil (SAN), diameter of
dinner plate 9½" (24.1 cm); tumblers:
acrylic
Manufacturer: Guzzini
Prize: Compasso d'Oro, 1979
Philadelphia Museum of Art. Gift of
Fratelli Guzzini

Earl Tupper American, lives in Costa Rica, born c. 1908
VI-19 Cereal bowls and seals, c. 1949 (from c. 1949)
Polyolefin, diameter 6⅛" (15.6 cm)
Manufacturer: Tupper
Philadelphia Museum of Art. Gift of Tupperware Home Parties.
1982-156-1–6

Earl Tupper American, lives in Costa Rica, born c. 1908
VI-20 "Handolier" container, c. 1956 (from c. 1956)
Polyolefin, height 8⅞" (22.5 cm)
Manufacturer: Tupper
Philadelphia Museum of Art. Gift of Tupperware Home Parties. 1982-156-7
Plate 20

Kristian Vedel Danish, born 1923
VI-21 Bowls, 1960
Melamine, diameter of largest bowl 5⅝" (14.3 cm)
Manufacturer: Torben Ørskov
The Metropolitan Museum of Art, New York. Purchase, Edward C. Moore, Jr., Gift, 1961. 61.7.30, 31, 33

Massimo Vignelli Italian, born 1931
Lella Vignelli Italian, born 1930s
VI-22 Stacking service, 1964 (from 1971); mugs, 1972 (from 1972)
Dinnerware: melamine, diameter of dinner plate 9¾" (24.8 cm); mugs: polycarbonate resin
Manufacturer: Heller
Prize: Compasso d'Oro, 1964
Philadelphia Museum of Art. Gift of Heller Designs, Inc. 1982-146-1–17

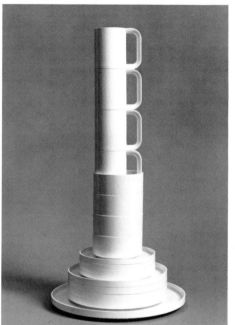

Jean-Pierre Vitrac French, born 1944
VI-23 Disposable picnic set, 1977 (1977–80)
Polystyrene, length 11" (28 cm)
Manufacturer: Diam
Philadelphia Museum of Art. Gift of Janet Kerr

Don Wallance American, born 1909
VI-24 "Design 10" cutlery, 1979 (from 1981)
Lexan polycarbonate, length of knife 7" (17.8 cm)
Manufacturer: Lauffer
Philadelphia Museum of Art. Gift of H. E. Lauffer Co., Inc. 1982-150-1–4

Textiles   Introduction by Jack Lenor Larsen

Textile designer, writer, and
teacher, Larsen has been director of
his own fabric concern since 1952.
His interest in the structure of
fabrics and in historic techniques
has led to a series of technical
innovations that have widely
influenced the international textile
industry.

It is difficult to explain the velocity with which design exploded out of the dim war years. Design then was a cause, allied with the optimism of a world to be made over in the light of the Four Freedoms. What a privilege it was to have been a design student when the solution was so simple and clear . . . and naïve! The new order would bring logic, coherence, beauty, and meaning to all those subscribing to it. Economics were hardly relevant. We had such kindly knights in George Nelson, Charles Eames, Eero Saarinen, and so many others; a mother church in New York's Museum of Modern Art; intense substantiation in design exhibitions across the country; and alliance with modern dance, modern art, and—of course—architecture, at last liberated from bourgeois Beaux-Arts traditions. This was Camelot, when design was *young.*

In 1983 it appears that then the pendulum had only swung more violently. The movement is mellow now, for some time conditioned by commerce and political disillusion, and long ago upstaged by the popular heyday of modern art.

The brave new years after the war were young and revolutionary in spirit, democratic in temper; "new design" was for anyone who cared about it. The Museum of Modern Art launched a vast public education program centering on the "Good Design" shows inaugurated by Edgar Kaufmann, Jr. These were shared by museums and galleries across the country; design competitions and exhibitions were frequent.

We liked clean, spare, logical solutions supported by common sense. The new architecture was primarily residential; so was the emphasis of furnishings. Storage was reconsidered. Overstuffed upholstery was *out*; so were flowers, wallpaper, clutter, polished surfaces, refinement, and any reference to ornament or the *ancien régime.* Window walls were draped out with a new fabric, the sheer casement. Color was primary and brash. We saw white walls for the first time, and black wrought-iron furniture floating on thin legs, free from alignment to a wall. The new wood was pale, lacquered birch.

If the spirit was democratic and revolutionary, the market was retail and residential. Stores with names containing the words "contemporary," "modern," or "design" mushroomed across the country, to serve as beacons for those making design pilgrimages. Later, when our lust for plain white china, Bertoia chairs, and bright geometry printed on white cotton abated, so did the enthusiasm of proprietors who were better as missionaries than shopkeepers. These same buzz words in firm names flagged possible credit risks.

In textiles the new textures were much sought after; we longed for surfaces that were "architectural" and "functional." For the most part these fabrics were inexpensive; so were the cotton, rayon, tow linen, and jute fibers with which they were woven. Novelty yarns emphasized texture; so did chenilles and, for the first time, Lurex.

For a decade Peruvian linens dyed luminous shades helped alleviate our appetite for visible texture. The Belgian, then Polish, linens that followed them were less durable. Everyday furnishing fabrics were cotton bark cloths and stubby "antique" satins. The square rush floor mat was the typical carpeting, almost as popular as the new white vinyl tile.

At the other end of the price scale, gutsy hand-weaves were locally woven for architects' houses. Patterns were printed, usually simple or simplistic, often with Swedish influence. The best of them were direct imports from Sweden, drawn by Scandinavian architects isolated and idle during the war. Whether abstractly free-form or geometric, they were graphic and—above all—architectural. Such leading American print designers as Angelo Testa and Ben Rose were centered in Chicago; in New York, Knoll Associates and Laverne Originals stressed freely drawn linear patterns, which at best were fresh and naïve, and sometimes humorous.

The great weavers of the period were led by Dorothy Liebes of San Francisco, who introduced over-scaled textures in finger-thick yarns and who reinvented, in her own terms, window blinds of heavy slats supported on warps striped with shimmering contrasts of matte and shiny, rough and smooth, and above all, flamboyantly colored materials. Marianne Strengell, weaving more naturalistic textures with a great variety of materials in a muted, Finnish palette, influenced both architectural designers and the many students she educated at the Cranbrook Academy of Art in Michigan. Anni Albers, who had moved from the Bauhaus to Black Mountain College in North Carolina, became the figurehead of the avant-garde. Her influence was philosophical, hard edged, pure. Although she had been involved with the rediscovery of texture, her work of this period tended to be in the area of architectonic pattern. Of the three, she was the writer and academician insistent upon clear thinking. She also helped to focus our attention on pre-Columbian weaving.

The best fabrics of the period were custom designed and handwoven for specific purposes. Knoll produced some simple power-woven textures by Toni Prestini and Marianne Strengell; they also imported hand-prints from the Nordiska Kompaniet in Sweden. There was not too much else from which to choose.

The 1950s were pivotal. Still a child in 1950, the first youth of modern design was spent before 1960. This was to be the last decade in which American design was dominant. We experienced the great impact of Abstract Expressionism and of the corporate-design client, and with it, the first alliances of design and the Establishment. We saw the acceptance of rich materials and surfaces, of fine craftsmanship, and—toward the end of the decade—of Edward Wormley's blend of old and new, of refinement within uncluttered architectural spaces. Together, Wormley and Edgar Kaufmann focused our attention on Art Nouveau and especially the art glass of Louis Comfort Tiffany. With this came a new penchant for craftsmanship, finished surfaces, studied composition, and a richness that matched our new acceptance of affluence. Sales emphasis switched from shops to showrooms. Florence Knoll led the transition from rush mats and vinyl tiles to velvety V'Soske carpets, from wrought iron to polished chrome and stainless steel. Our woods were oil-finished teak, walnut, and rosewood. This was the first decade of extensive travel, of the rediscovery of the Far East. With it came the first exotic imports. This was a heyday for Thai silks designed by the American architect Jim Thompson in Bangkok. With these simple, lustrous fabrics came glowing colors such as we had never before seen. Knoll imported the first honey-colored tussah silks, or silk burlaps, as they were known in those days. Small California fabric houses introduced Mexican hand-weaves and Norwegian woven straws. Grass cloths for walls were again imported. Jack Lenor Larsen developed hand-spun, wild cottons from Haiti, then hand-spun wools from Colombia and Mexico. Of the British design studios which geared up after the war, the most influential was Donald Brothers of Dundee, where Peter

Simpson developed the leno linen upholstery cloths so successful in Dan Cooper's showroom in New York. Although Lucienne Day, Marianne Straub, and Edinburgh Weavers led a movement to rationally designed, sensibly priced curtainings appealing to liberated tastes, few found their way to the American market.

In carpets Edward Fields and Stanislav V'Soske began using the electric pistol to tuft the first area rugs, often rich in color and pattern and in high relief. Machine-tufted carpets became available, first in cotton, but later displaced by nylon and the other "miracle fibers."

The influence of European design, particularly Scandinavian, was more and more felt. By the late 1950s we were reconsidering the prewar furniture forms of Thonet, Mies van der Rohe, Le Corbusier, and Breuer. Arundell Clarke reminded us of the fitness of such classic fabrics as velvet and plush and of horsehair and other such prewar structures.

Early in the decade Evelyn Hill and Eszter Haraszty worked with Rancocas to give Knoll an extraordinary upholstery collection of wools admixed with nylon monofilaments in the colors of peacocks and persimmons. Haraszty also introduced prints of durable interest, and two pivotal upholsteries: "Transportation Cloth," tightly woven of crisp viscose yarns, which for a while sustained the false promise of miracle fibers, and "Nylon Homespun" by Suzanne Huguenin, which gave us a cosier hand with considerable staying power. D. D. and Leslie Tillett introduced exotic hand-prints utilizing resists and drag boxes for free-flowing stripes and plaids. Alexander Girard developed for Herman Miller whole ranges of exotic geometry, both printed and woven, scintillating in dark-and-light contrasts or as vivid as Mexican folk art. Particularly in his Caribbean collection, Boris Kroll popularized the analogous iridescents we had learned to enjoy in the palettes of Dorothy Liebes and Jim Thompson. He also enriched our pattern vocabulary with sinuous Jacquards.

From Astrid Sampe and Viola Gråsten of the famous Nordiska Kompaniet studios in Stockholm came a series of printed linens and Jacquard domestics. We saw Vuokko's first fabrics for Marimekko— scintillating if simple prints in joyous colors. Marjatta Metsovaara of Helsinki was building up an extraordinary array of hand-weaves with the most incredible materials, some ultra-natural, others with plastic films and wire used as yarn. Although Finland's pioneer weaver Dora Jung is best remembered for her pictorial damask hangings, at this time she designed notable table linens for Jacquard damask looms. From Finland, too, came waves of monumental *rya* rugs with a presence and quality unique in postwar design. Marga Hielle-Vatter, of Rohi in West Germany, was developing wool upholstery fabrics for her dobby and Jacquard looms, often against striped backgrounds. By the late 1950s Larsen had managed to weave on power looms fabrics we had, up to that time, considered hand-weaves. He introduced a new palette of light and dark naturals plus earth tones and had started printing romantic patterns—often on cotton velvet.

The 1960s was a period of the new Establishment, of the rise of contract design, of the International Style, of the Miesian aesthetic, of accelerating interest in prewar furniture design often of chrome-plated tubes. There was considerable interest in controlling the glare and "night blackness" of the vast new windows of the modern houses and the curtain walls of the new high-rise towers. The casement fabric was ubiquitous, whether or not privacy was a requisite. Fiberglass was examined by Leslie Tillett and Ben Rose for its resistance to soil and flame and—in the beginning—dye and pigment. Jack Larsen developed warp knits of plastic films, which could be heat set to resist the sagging common to sheer curtains of the period.

As the large, unframed paintings in executive and residential interiors precluded competition from fabrics or carpets, heavy wool textures became more common. Because the hand-spun, undyed yarns were full of character in themselves, the weaves were simple. Stretch upholsteries were repeatedly explored to fit the new complex, compound curves of free-form furniture snugly. This was accelerated with the introduction of sculptural furniture by the French designers Olivier Mourgue and Pierre Paulin.

The influences of Art Nouveau and Tiffany continued, and the Japanese overtones of Elizabeth Gordon's *shibui* promotion were considerable. When we longed for humanizing elements, Alexander Girard filled this void with *popular artes* of Latin America. "Clutter" was *in.*

The American-European interchange grew with exhibitions and with the ever-increasing number of continental publications and design fairs. The new generation of Scandinavian fabric designers included Rolf Middelboe and Verner Panton for Unika-Vaev, Lis Ahlmann, Paula Trock, and others. In Great Britain, especially at Heal's and Edinburgh Weavers, vibrant prints appeared. By the late 1960s we saw the first Ambiente fabrics by Finland's Timo Sarpaneva, "hand painted" by robot automation in two large Finnish cotton mills, as well as a second wave of Marimekko prints, these in the larger repeats and sure hand of Maija Isola.

We also experienced the ravages of psychedelia, the youth revolution, the antiwar movement. Next came the breakdown of schools and civic institutions and with it a new freedom and abandon, most evidenced in apparel, but also in furnishings' patterns and color, and in a new emphasis on the low-cost informality of floor pillows, soft furniture, and unconventional seating on forms inflated with air or filled with plastic beans.

We saw for the first time a very considerable emphasis on highly styled domestics. Following Everett Brown's pioneering (and unacknowledged) collections for Fieldcrest, sheets and towels were *in,* and we were hard at work on the highly styled first designer collections. Martex achieved classics; Spring Mills, an extraordinary Emilio Pucci group, and, later, conservatively tasteful designs from the Bill Blass studio. We saw, too, a schizophrenic split between a youth-oriented, freewheeling residential market and the growing contract market, staid and Establishment in its point of view.

In the 1970s—the beige decade—we saw the popularization and exploitation of "natural" looks often inappropriate to the young families for which they were intended. There was a reaction against man-made fibers, and contract furnishings became so important as to dominate almost all new developments in furniture. We witnessed a national sophistication in which residents of even small towns experienced "gourmet" foods, modern dance, art films, and the effects of international travel.

In carpets we welcomed an end to the shag rug, the revival of smooth velvets and Wilton patterning, and—particularly in contract areas—the return to wools. There was a new sophistication in carpet making and patterning, and with it, the development of needle-punching and other postindustrial techniques. The carpet tile became part of our repertoire.

Too often came "designer collections" put together under the banner name of some famous couturier or movie star; we heard of "fashion impulses." Eclecticism was rampant, and so was a nostalgia strangely new, and the erasing of many of the barriers between modern and traditional design. We saw the return of silk as an important fiber, of smooth damasks, Egyptian cottons, superimposed patterns, and the increasing importance of Art Deco patterning.

Design leadership was fuzzy. Market focus, with increasingly important emphasis on best sellers, was on the minds of most designers and manufacturers. Increasingly we saw fabric collections distributed by furniture houses. A merger of European and American design was typified by the fresh new prints of Sven Fristedt of Sweden and the renewed popularity of Marimekko. Jack Larsen's first Thaibok silk collections introduced brocades, *ikats,* and discharge printing. The palette of the decade was low-keyed, soft, "adult," reflected on the mass market in too many undyed, soil-prone yarns.

Art fabrics—sometimes tapestries, but more often bold experiments wall hung, ceiling hung, or supported on pedestals—became important elements in public spaces. All through the decade we experienced environmental concerns, questions of reuse, recycling, and restoration. "Postindustrial" was a term heard more often. The galloping succession of movements and styles within the fine arts on the one hand, in mores and censorship on the other, was finally hastening the parade of architectural styles. What guise for Post-Modern furnishings?

The new decade brings a sense of perspective, giving us an overview of the twentieth century. With it comes the influence of such early progenitors as Frank Lloyd Wright, Gerrit Rietveld, Charles Rennie Mackintosh, and Josef Hoffmann, paralleled by a favorable appraisal of the Arts and Crafts movement, especially in its American phase. Interest in the early modern periods spills into the 1940s and 1950s. We see the revival, reissue, reproduction, and exhibition of prewar "moderne."

All of this is enhanced by a renewed focus on architectural restoration and reuse. After a half-century hiatus, architectural ornament returns to favor, as does the term and concept of decorative arts. The studio craft movement has, by now, gained such impact as to be of major influence. We witness new appreciation of such mid-century American craftsmen as Wharton Esherick, George Nakashima, and Maija Grotell in America, Meta Maas-Fetterstrom, Paolo Venini, and others in Europe.

We are aware of a new breed of studio craftsman content to produce a few signed pieces which acknowledge precedents. Sam Maloof and Wendel Castle are only the best known of a significant generation of furniture makers. Ed Moulthrop has created a new acceptance for ritual vessels turned from woods. The new art glass is spectacular. Ironworkers Brent Kington and Albert Paley build colossal torchiers and gates in iron and steel. Weavers as disparate as Richard Landis and Helena Hernmarck have led the art fabric back to the loom—and back to the wall.

The 1980s is a period of refinement, conservatism, and internationalism. Increasingly, furnishings houses are part of conglomerates, with more and more of them multinational. The relative stability and security of the American market brings more European firms to America for business and alternate bases of operations.

The loft syndrome of orchestrating open spaces according to need and income spills over into new structures. With it comes a further relaxation of parameters dividing interiors specifically into cooking, dining, and sleeping areas. Ever more formal and conservative elements are freely orchestrated in space—often with the *implied* separations of stagecraft. The multiple function/multiple mood aspect of Japanese residential architecture is reexamined for application to smaller, more open interior spaces—often in conjunction with lighting expertise adopted from the theater. Furnishings and the paraphernalia to particularize and personalize indifferent spaces become our "props." We search for the "feeling" of space and its effect on our collective psyche. It seems probable that—like the nineteenth century—the twentieth, which began with a classic and intellectual focus, will end with the emotional concerns of Romanticism.

The Deco influences which had superficially affected fabrics since the 1960s are apparent only in patterns neatly set against clear, colored grounds in notes of whimsy and visual pun, and in the preference for small, abstract, not necessarily geometric, patterns. Shadow lines creating a sense of *trompe l'oeil* relief have become common. Post-Modernism, so much in effect in architecture and particularly in the architecture press, will probably not affect fabrics as significantly as furniture and accessories—except in color. But expect more playful fabric treatments for windows: swags and valances may return. Shirred fabric walls and fluted or pleated fabrics will take advantage of thermoplastic properties.

Although exaggerated textures remain popular, there is a trend toward classic and formal surfaces. Generic and anonymous cloths become increasingly important. To the velvets and plushes carried over from the 1970s, add wool satins and billiard cloths, military serges and drills. Heavy, soft, aniline-dyed leathers become significant as upholstery covers; so do cane and wicker. Lacquer returns as a furniture surface. Wood is more popular than it has been since the 1950s, and we see less chromed-metal and plastic surfaces. Thick chenille yarns return to favor; silk appears more often than at any period in history.

Architects accept more pattern in their cloths and carpets. Plaids find new acceptance. More than any time since the 1930s, we witness orchestrations of pattern in graduated scales and the modulation of color with more carefully sought nuance. The new symmetry apparent everywhere from landscape architecture to mantel arrangements affects fabrics with regular, spotted motifs, patterns centered on upholstery cushions, and chairs with medallion motifs.

Finally, we see a renewed interest in design as an art form—just when the market and producers seem to have lost sight of it. Both here and abroad more museum exhibitions focus on design in general and on fabric design in particular. For the first time since the 1950s there is new impetus on design as a vocation, and with it, serious work in fabric structures. I expect a richly eclectic result, moving away from the superficial toward involvement with complex weaves and sophisticated surfaces and colorings. The new designers will be aware of both the past and the marketplace, and they will bring freshness to this oldest of industries.

Lis Ahlmann Danish, 1894–1979
Børge Mogensen Danish, 1914–1972
VII-1 Fabric, 1963 (from 1963)
Wool, width 51³/₁₆" (130 cm)
Manufacturer: C. Olesen
Fritz Hansens Eft. A/S, Allerød,
Denmark
Plate 4

Anni Albers American, born Germany,
1899
VII-2 Fabric, 1950
Cotton and linen, width 55" (139.7 cm)
Manufacturer: Anni Albers
Cranbrook Academy of Art/Museum,
Bloomfield Hills, Michigan. 1951.7

Hiroshi Awatsuji Japanese, born 1929
**VII-3 "Jitensha" art screen, 1982
(from 1982)**
Printed cotton, width 70¹/₂" (179 cm)
Manufacturer: Fujie
Fujie Textile Co., Ltd., Tokyo

Renata Bonfanti Italian, born 1929
VII-4 Fabric, 1956 (from 1956)
Cotton and linen, width 59" (149.9 cm)
Manufacturer: Renata Bonfanti
Philadelphia Museum of Art. Gift of
the designer

Barbara Brown British, born 1932
VII-5 "Spiral" fabric, 1970
Printed cotton, width 48" (122 cm)
Manufacturer: Heal
Prize: Council of Industrial Design
Award, 1970
Private collection

Eva Brummer Finnish, born 1901
VII-6 "Zebra" rug, 1951 (1982)
Wool and cotton, width 47⅝" (121 cm)
Manufacturer: Margit Ahlblad
The Friends of Finnish Handicraft,
Finland

California Drop Cloth American,
established Los Angeles, 1975
**VII-7 "Celebration" fabric, 1979
(from 1979)**
Hand-painted cotton, width 48½"
(123.2 cm)
Manufacturer: California Drop Cloth
California Drop Cloth, Incorporated,
Los Angeles
Plate 52

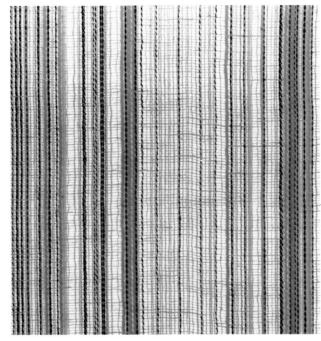

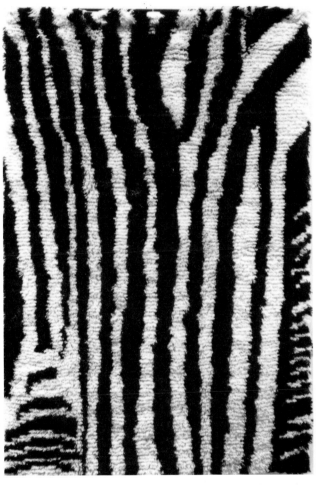

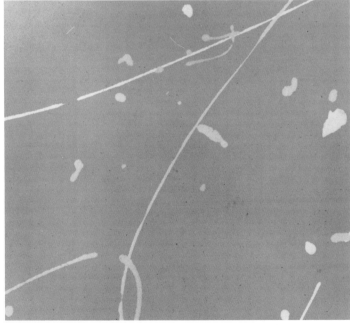

Fede Cheti Italian, 1905–1978
**VII-8 "Luna e Stelle" fabric, 1952
(from 1952)**
Cotton and Lurex, width 51³/₁₆"
(130 cm)
Manufacturer: Fede Cheti
Philadelphia Museum of Art. Gift of
Fede Cheti S.a.s. 1982-143-2

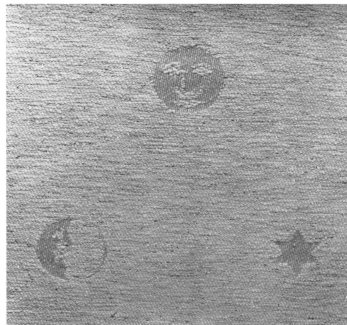

Shirley Craven British, born 1934
VII-9 "Five" fabric, 1968
Printed cotton and linen, width 48"
(122 cm)
Manufacturer: Hull Traders
Prize: Council of Industrial Design
Award, 1968
Philadelphia Museum of Art. Gift of
Hull Traders Ltd. 75-8-1

Lucienne Day British, born 1917
VII-10 "Calyx" fabric, 1951 (1951–56)
Printed linen, width 48" (122 cm)
Manufacturer: Heal
Prizes: Gold medal, Milan, Triennale,
1951; First A.I.D. International Design
Award, 1952
Heal Fabrics Limited, London
Plate 9

Antoinette de Boer German,
born 1939
VII-11 "Zazi" fabric, 1969 (1969–80)
Printed cotton, width 51⁵/₈" (131 cm)
Manufacturer: Stuttgarter
Gardinenfabrik
Stuttgarter Gardinenfabrik,
Herrenberg/Württ, West Germany

Nathalie du Pasquier French, lives in Italy, born 1957
VII-12 "Gabon" fabric, 1982 (from 1982)
Printed cotton, width 60" (152.4 cm)
Manufacturer: Rainbow
Philadelphia Museum of Art. Gift of Furniture of the Twentieth Century, Inc.

Vuokko Eskolin-Nurmesniemi
Finnish, born 1930
VII-13 "Rotti" fabric, 1954 (from 1954)
Printed cotton, width 54" (137.2 cm)
Manufacturer: Printex
Marimekko Oy, Helsinki

Alexander Girard American, born 1907
VII-14 "Rain" fabric, 1953 (1953–70)
Printed cotton, width 50" (127 cm)
Manufacturer: Herman Miller
Herman Miller, Inc., Zeeland, Michigan

Alexander Girard American, born 1907
VII-15 "Ribbons" fabric, 1957 (1957–70)
Printed cotton and linen, width 52" (132 cm)
Manufacturer: Herman Miller
Herman Miller, Inc., Zeeland, Michigan

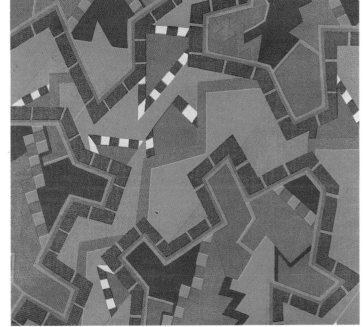

Viola Gràsten Swedish, born
Finland, 1910
**VII-16 "Hazels" fabric, 1958 (from
1958)**
Printed cotton, width 50³/₈" (128 cm)
Manufacturer: Nordiska
Philadelphia Museum of Art. Gift of
Nordiska Kompaniet

Eszter Haraszty American, born
Hungary, 1910s
VII-17 "Tracy" fabric, 1952
Printed silk, width 49" (124.5 cm)
Manufacturer: Knoll
Cranbrook Academy of Art/Museum,
Bloomfield Hills, Michigan. 1953.3

Sheila Hicks American, lives in France,
born 1934
**VII-18 "Badagara" fabric, 1968
(from 1968)**
Cotton, width 120" (304.8 cm)
Manufacturer: Commonwealth Trust,
Kerala, India
Collection of the designer, Paris

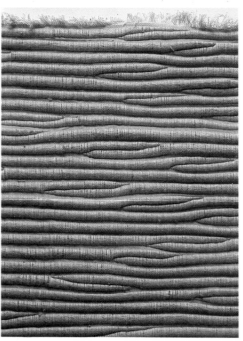

Marga Hielle-Vatter German, born
1913
**VII-19 "Alcudia" fabric, 1981 (from
1981)**
Wool and cotton, width 51" (129.5 cm)
Manufacturer: Rohi
Rohi Stoffe GmbH, Geretsried, West
Germany

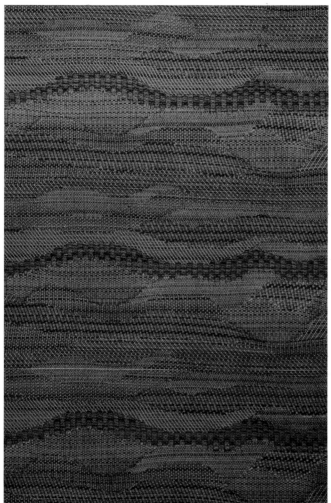

Margret Hildebrand German, born 1917
VII-20 "Empel" fabric, 1953 (1953–59)
Printed cotton, width 50¾" (129 cm)
Manufacturer: Stuttgarter Gardinenfabrik
Stuttgarter Gardinenfabrik, Herrenberg/Württ, West Germany

Evelyn Hill (Anselevicius) American, born 1925
VII-21 Fabric, 1951
Wool, viscose rayon, and synthetic raffia, width 34½" (87.6 cm)
Manufacturer: Evelyn Hill
Philadelphia Museum of Art. Gift of Mr. and Mrs. George Anselevicius. 1983-42-2

Evelyn Hill (Anselevicius) American, born 1925
VII-22 Fabric, 1953
Wool, width 36" (91.4 cm)
Manufacturer: Knoll
Prize: Second A.I.D. International Design Award, 1953
Philadelphia Museum of Art. Gift of Mr. and Mrs. George Anselevicius. 1983-42-1

Suzanne Huguenin Swiss, born 1930s
VII-23 "Nylon Homespun" fabric, 1958 (from 1958)
Nylon, width 50" (127 cm)
Manufacturer: Knoll
Collection of Florence Fink, Sag Harbor, New York

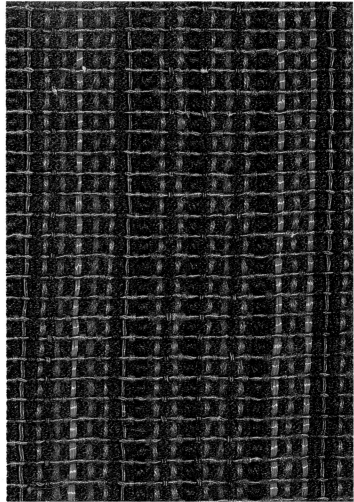

Fujiwo Ishimoto Japanese, lives in
Finland, born 1941
**VII-24 "Maisema" fabric, 1982
(from 1982)**
Printed cotton, width 54" (137.2 cm)
Manufacturer: Marimekko
Marimekko Oy, Helsinki

Maija Isola Finnish, born 1927
**VII-25 "Kivet" fabric, 1956 (from
1956)**
Printed cotton, width 54" (137.2 cm)
Manufacturer: Printex
Marimekko Oy, Helsinki

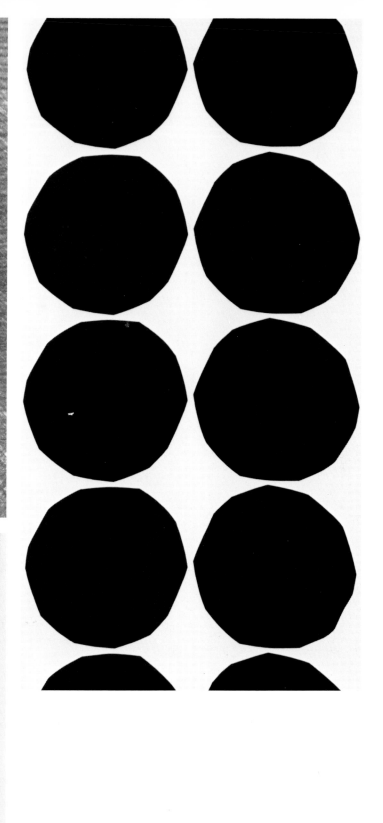

Maija Isola Finnish, born 1927
**VII-26 "Melooni" fabric, 1963 (from
1963)**
Printed cotton, width 54" (137.2 cm)
Manufacturer: Printex
Marimekko Oy, Helsinki
Plate 34

Dora Jung Finnish, 1906–1980
**VII-27 "Linenplay" tablecloth and
napkins, 1957**
Linen; length of tablecloth 106" (269.2
cm), width of napkins 20¼" (51.5 cm)
Manufacturer: Tampella
Prize: Grand prize, Milan, Triennale,
1957
Tablecloth: Jack Lenor Larsen, New
York
Napkins: Philadelphia Museum of Art.
Gift of Tampella Ltd. 1982-155-1, 2

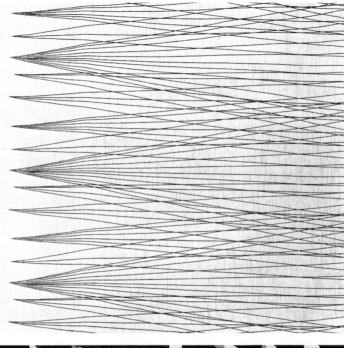

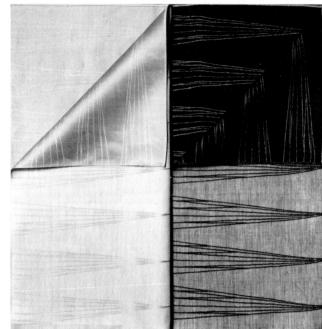

Masakazu Kobayashi Japanese,
born 1944
**VII-28 "Space Age" fabric, 1982
(from 1982)**
Printed cotton, width 47¼" (120 cm)
Manufacturer: Sangetsu
Collection of the designer, Kyoto

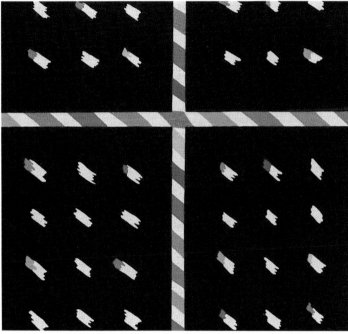

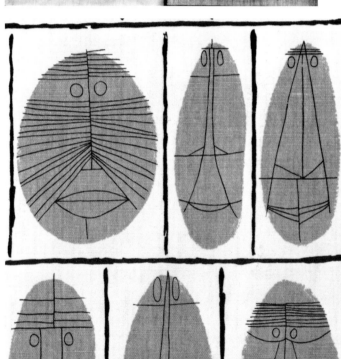

Ray Komai American, born 1918
**VII-29 "Masks" fabric, c. 1945 (from
c. 1945)**
Printed cotton and linen, width
50" (127 cm)
Manufacturer: Laverne
Laverne International Ltd., New York

Boris Kroll American, born 1913
VII-30 "Northern Lights" fabric, 1983
Wool, nylon, and rayon, width 54"
(137.2 cm)
Manufacturer: Boris Kroll
Boris Kroll Fabrics, Inc., New York

Hans Krondahl Swedish, born 1929
VII-31 "Spefåglar" fabric, 1959 (from 1959)
Printed cotton, width 53" (134.6 cm)
Manufacturer: NK-Inredning
Philadelphia Museum of Art. Gift of the designer

Jack Lenor Larsen American, born 1927
VII-32 "Remoulade" fabric, 1956 (1956–67)
Linen, cotton, rayon, wool, silk, metallics, jute, and other fibers, width 50" (127 cm)
Manufacturer: Larsen
Jack Lenor Larsen Incorporated, New York

Jack Lenor Larsen American, born 1927
VII-33 "Interplay" fabric, 1960 (from 1960)
Saran, width 48" (122 cm)
Manufacturer: Larsen
Philadelphia Museum of Art. Gift of Jack Lenor Larsen Incorporated

Jack Lenor Larsen American, born 1927
VII-34 "Magnum" fabric, 1970 (from 1970)
Cotton, vinyl, nylon, and polyester, width 55" (139.7 cm)
Manufacturer: Larsen
Jack Lenor Larsen Incorporated, New York
Plate 40

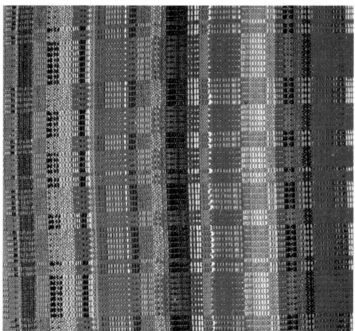

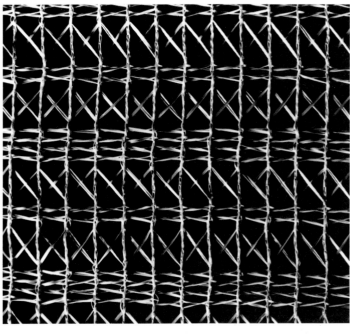

Jack Lenor Larsen American,
born 1927
**VII-35 "Quadrangle" carpet, 1973
(from 1973)**
Wool and acrylic, width 27" (68.6 cm)
Manufacturer: Larsen
Philadelphia Museum of Art. Gift of
Jack Lenor Larsen Incorporated

Jack Lenor Larsen American,
born 1927
**VII-36 "Pastorale" fabric, 1975
(from 1975)**
Polyester and cotton, width 118"
(299.8 cm)
Manufacturer: Larsen
Jack Lenor Larsen Incorporated,
New York

Dorothy Liebes American, 1899–1972
VII-37 Fabric, 1947
Leather, rayon, silk, and metallics,
width 50" (127 cm)
Manufacturer: Dorothy Liebes Design
Permanent collection, American Craft
Museum, New York. 73.2.13.6

Dorothy Liebes American, 1899–1972
VII-38 Fabric, c. 1947
Cotton, rayon, and metallics, width 50"
(127 cm)
Manufacturer: Dorothy Liebes Design
Permanent collection, American Craft
Museum, New York. 73.2.13.8

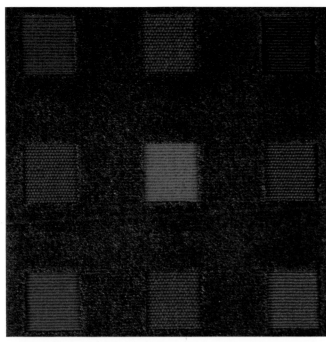

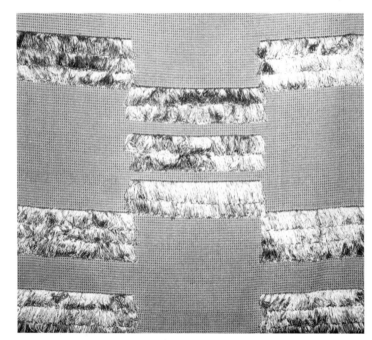

Dorothy Liebes American, 1899–1972
VII-39 Blinds, c. 1950
Bamboo splits, wooden dowels, rayon,
cotton, and metallics, widths 34"
(86.4 cm), 84" (213.3 cm)
Manufacturer: Dorothy Liebes Design
Collection of Bonnie Cashin, New York
Plate 7

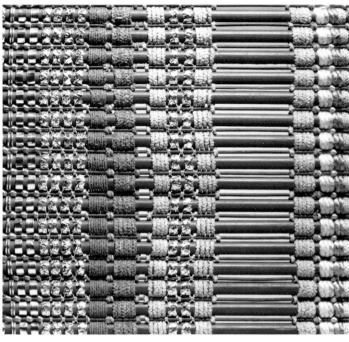

Dorothy Liebes American, 1899–1972
VII-40 Fabric, 1964
Orlon and metallics, width 50" (127 cm)
Manufacturer: Dorothy Liebes Design
Permanent collection, American Craft
Museum, New York. 73.2.13.12

Stig Lindberg Swedish, 1916–1982
**VII-41 "Apples" fabric, 1952 (from
1952)**
Printed cotton, width 50" (127 cm)
Manufacturer: Nordiska
Philadelphia Museum of Art. Purchased
with funds contributed by COLLAB:
The Contemporary Design Group for
the Philadelphia Museum of Art.
1983-50-3

Javier Mariscal Spanish, born 1950
**VII-42 "Ensaladilla" fabric, 1978
(from 1978)**
Printed cotton, width 63" (160 cm)
Manufacturer: Marieta
Philadelphia Museum of Art. Gift of
Marieta. 1983-8-1

Javier Mariscal Spanish, born 1950
**VII-43 "Floresta" fabric, 1981
(from 1981)**
Printed cotton, width 63" (160 cm)
Manufacturer: Marieta
Philadelphia Museum of Art. Gift of
Marieta. 1983-8-2

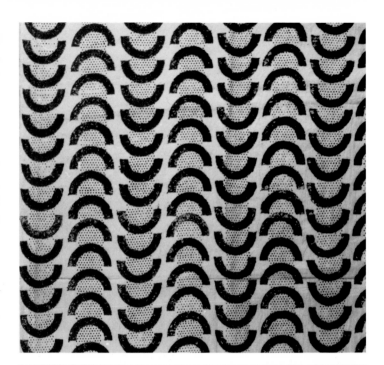

Enid Marx British, born 1902
VII-44 "Half-Moons" fabric, 1949
Printed cotton, width 35" (88.9 cm)
Manufacturer: Enid Marx
The Whitworth Art Gallery, University
of Manchester

Peter McCulloch British, born 1933
VII-45 "Cruachan" fabric, 1963
Printed cotton, width 48" (122 cm)
Manufacturer: Hull Traders
Prize: Design Centre Award, 1963
Philadelphia Museum of Art. Gift of
Hull Traders Ltd. 75-8-2

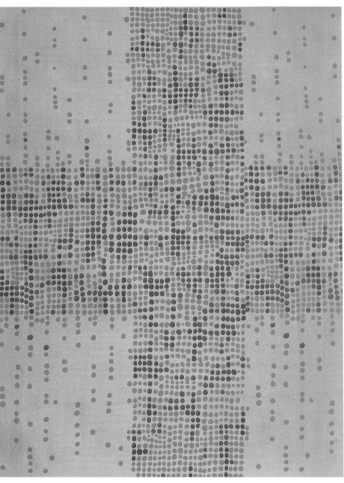

Marjatta Metsovaara Finnish,
born 1928
**VII-46 "King's Tweed" fabric,
1962 (1962–68)**
Wool and rayon, width 50" (127 cm)
Manufacturer: Metsovaara van Harere
Jack Lenor Larsen Incorporated,
New York

Rolf Middelboe Danish, born 1917
VII-47 "Unisol" wall hanging, 1957 (1957–69)
Printed cotton, width 41½" (105.4 cm)
Manufacturer: Unika-Vaev
Collection of the designer, Kolding, Denmark

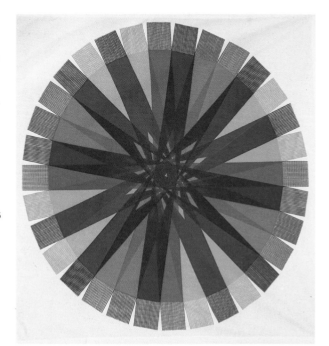

Verner Panton Danish, lives in Switzerland, born 1926
VII-48 "Bobinette Ring" fabric, 1966
Diolen, width 48" (122 cm)
Manufacturer: Unika-Vaev
Collection of the designer, Basel

Verner Panton Danish, lives in Switzerland, born 1926
VII-49 "Mira Columba" fabric, 1983 (from 1983)
Printed cotton, width 51" (129.5 cm)
Manufacturer: Mira-X
Philadelphia Museum of Art. Gift of Mira-X
Plate 60

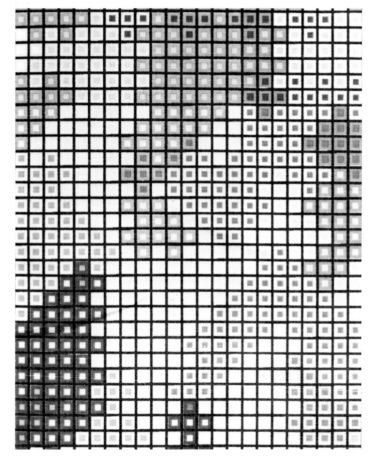

Benno Premsela (with Diek Zweegman) Dutch, born 1920
VII-50 Carpet, 1979 (from 1979)
Linen, width 39" (99 cm)
Manufacturer: Van Besouw
Van Besouw, Goirle, The Netherlands

Armi Ratia Finnish, 1912–1979
VII-51 "Faruk" fabric, 1952 (from 1952)
Printed cotton, width 54" (137.2 cm)
Manufacturer: Printex
Marimekko Oy, Helsinki

Maya Romanoff American, born 1941
VII-52 "Desert Root" fabric, 1978 (from 1978)
Dyed silk, width 46" (116.8 cm)
Manufacturer: Maya Romanoff
Philadelphia Museum of Art. Gift of the designer

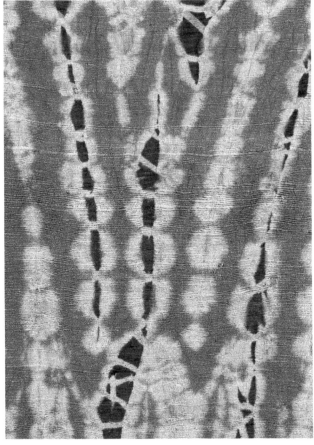

Astrid Sampe Swedish, born 1909
VII-53 "Linnelinjen" dish towel, 1955 (1955–c. 1970)
Linen, length 25¼" (64.1 cm)
Manufacturer: Almedahls
Philadelphia Museum of Art. Gift of the designer

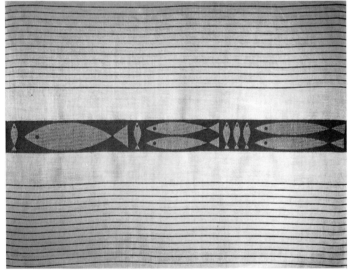

Timo Sarpaneva Finnish, born 1926
VII-54 "Bolero" fabric, 1968 (1968–75)
Printed cotton, width 51" (129.5 cm)
Manufacturer: Tampella
Jack Lenor Larsen Incorporated,
New York

Scot Simon American, born 1954
**VII-55 "Sunsquince" fabric, 1982
(from 1982)**
Nylon and polyester, width 45"
(114.3 cm)
Manufacturer: Scot Simon
Philadelphia Museum of Art. Gift of
the designer

Marianne Straub British, born
Switzerland, 1909
VII-56 "Surrey" fabric, 1951
Wool, cotton, and rayon, width 50"
(127 cm)
Manufacturer: Warner
Archive, Warner & Sons Ltd., London

Marianne Strengell American,
born Finland, 1909
VII-57 Fabric, 1959
Synthetic fibers, width 61" (155 cm)
Manufacturer: Chatham
Philadelphia Museum of Art. Gift of
the designer

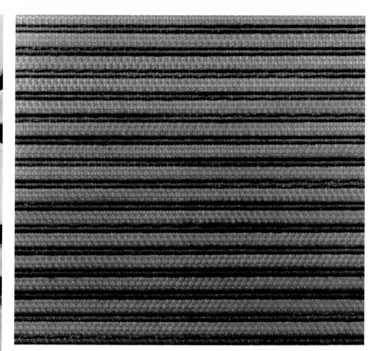

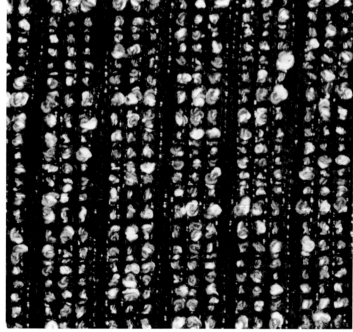

Angelo Testa American, born 1921
VII-58 "Textura Quatra" fabric, 1945
Printed linen, width 49¼" (125 cm)
Manufacturer: Angelo Testa
The Art Institute of Chicago. 1982-180

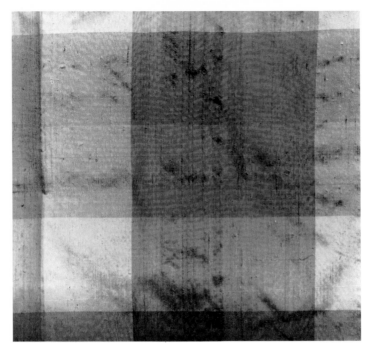

Jim Thompson American, 1906–1967?
VII-59 Fabric, 1960s
Silk, width 40" (101.6 cm)
Manufacturer: Jim Thompson Thai Silk
Philadelphia Museum of Art. Gift of
Jim Thompson Thai Silk Co.

D. D. Tillett American, born 1920s
**VII-60 "Queen Anne's Lace" fabric,
c. 1950 (from c. 1950)**
Printed cotton, width 48" (122 cm)
Manufacturer: D. D. and Leslie Tillett
Philadelphia Museum of Art. Gift of
D. D. and Leslie Tillett. 1983-12-1

Paula Trock Danish, 1889–1979
VII-61 Fabric, 1960 (from 1960)
Wool, width 39⅜" (100 cm)
Manufacturer: Spindegården
Prize: Gold medal, Milan, Triennale,
1960
Spindegården

Stanislav V'Soske American, 1900–1983
VII-62 "Romanesque" carpet, 1955–60
Wool, width 66" (167.7 cm)
Manufacturer: V'Soske
V'Soske, New York

Katsuji Wakisaka Japanese, born 1944
VII-63 "Ma" fabric, 1977 (from 1977)
Printed cotton, width 54³/₈" (138 cm)
Manufacturer: Wacoal
Philadelphia Museum of Art. Gift of Wacoal Interior Fabrics

Don Wight (with Larsen design studio) American, born 1924
VII-64 "Primavera" fabric, 1959 (from 1959)
Printed cotton velvet, width 48" (122 cm)
Manufacturer: Larsen
Jack Lenor Larsen Incorporated, New York

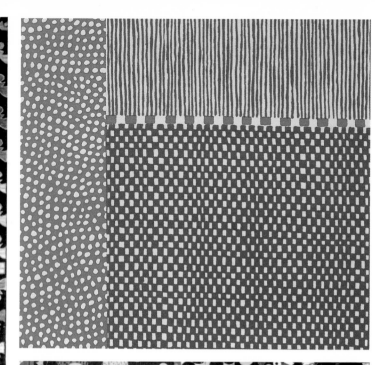

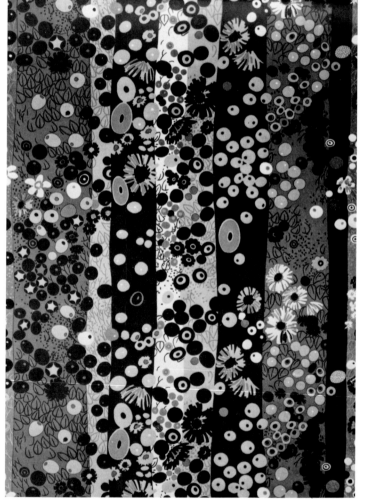

Wood

Introduction by Jens Quistgaard

The son of a sculptor and trained as a silversmith, Jens Quistgaard co-founded Dansk International Designs in 1954. As the firm's principle designer he has been responsible for the form of a great number of their objects, many in wood, which are both machine-made and handcrafted.

Wood is a standard by which man has measured his physical surroundings and which, aside from food, has been the most valuable element of his environment. From a historical point of view, there are very few things now made of steel, stone, glass, plastic, or bronze that have not at one time or another been made of wood.

I consider myself privileged because I have been involved with wood ever since I became aware of my surroundings, partly in my father's studio, where as a sculptor he worked with wood almost every day; partly in our garden and the surrounding woods, where we witnessed the lumbermen felling trees and planting them, and where we followed the growth of the trees from year to year; and partly in the workshops of the village, where everything that the small community needed was produced. That kind of experience instilled a deep understanding of the material and of how to handle it from the moment it is cut until it leaves the shop of the carpenter, cabinetmaker, turner, or wheelwright, each of whom has his own requirements as to the choice of wood; the manner of cutting, drying, aging, and storing it; and so forth.

This experience was also combined with the romantic associations of listening to the proud narratives of certain craftsmen about their beloved profession and their long travels as journeymen abroad. Little by little all these intimacies with wood were gathered into a capital which, together with my years of apprenticeship as a carpenter, sculptor, and architect, determined that wood would become a natural part of my profession. In my career as a designer, wood became my favorite material at a very early stage. I could not keep away from it; it fascinated me. And of course the knowledge of wood that I had picked up in my youth, and since, has always given me a great advantage. It also provided a foundation for my work in other mediums, such as clay, silver, steel, bronze, and iron. And it brought me to the conclusion that wood should be treated with much more respect than most often is the case. If, for example, you think of a tabletop cut in a single plank—if it is thirty inches across, the tree would have been growing for a couple of hundred years—is that not thought provoking? Such a table is a botanical wonder, which can last for generations, becoming more beautiful day after day. But if you mercilessly cut the same venerable tree into thin sheets of veneer, you may increase your profit, but you will get a much poorer table with a shorter life. This kind of mass production is a sort of pollution or wanton destruction of wood at the expense of nature and culture.

The craftsman who designs for mass production must first of all know and appreciate his material. And man must manage the result, not the machine. His models must be made out of the very same material as his product. He should create an object of sculptural worth with good proportions: He should determine the precise distribution of the material and the right weight in proportion to the size and breadth of the object, while not forgetting function as well as aesthetics and the appropriateness of its style. Some of the best objects being made of wood today are the traditional everyday goods of the Japanese, the work of modern Finnish designers, and the furniture of Danish craftsmen.

Industrialization has revolutionized the wood industry. My attitude regarding this has always been to make use of mechanical aids as far as possible, but without diminishing the quality of my product. Where the possibilities of the machine end, the rest has to be done by hand. I myself almost always work with solid wood, which in itself is a great advantage. It is much more difficult to produce a valuable and humane product in laminated wood (veneer); most often it will look artificial. Those technological solutions of bent, shaped veneer and squared profiles—chairs, for instance—would look like plexiglass or metal if they were arranged in a row with a matte, black-lacquered surface. One should be able to identify a good piece of craftsmanship as being made of wood even if it is covered in colored lacquer.

We live in the machine age, and are at the beginning of the electronics age. It is hoped that by means of these "tools," more people will be able to have well-manufactured wooden products at a reasonable price without reducing the demands of aesthetics and without ruthless exploitation and consumption of the forests.

Kay Bojesen Danish, 1886–1958
VIII-1 Double salad bowl with servers, 1949
Teak, diameter 14⁹/₁₆″ (37 cm)
Manufacturer: Bojesen
Collection of Mrs. Kay Bojesen, Copenhagen

Kay Bojesen Danish, 1886–1958
VIII-2 Salad bowl, 1949
Teak, diameter 11¹³/₁₆″ (30 cm)
Manufacturer: Bojesen
Collection of Mrs. Kay Bojesen, Copenhagen

Kay Bojesen Danish, 1886–1958
VIII-3 Salad bowl, 1949
Teak, diameter 11″ (28 cm)
Manufacturer: Bojesen
Collection of Mrs. Kay Bojesen, Copenhagen

Hermann Bongard Norwegian, born 1921
VIII-4 Salad servers, 1957
Plywood and teak, length 12¹¹/₁₆″ (32.2 cm)
Manufacturer: Glahn
Collection of the designer, Blommenholm, Norway

Finn Juhl Danish, born 1912
VIII-5 Salad bowl, 1950
Teak, width 14⁹/₁₆″ (37 cm)
Manufacturer: Bojesen
Collection of Mrs. Kay Bojesen, Copenhagen

James Prestini American, born 1908
VIII-6 Bowl, 1945
Mahogany, diameter 5¹/₁₆″ (12.8 cm)
Manufacturer: Prestini
Philadelphia Museum of Art. Gift of
the designer. 1979-167-2

James Prestini American, born 1908
VIII-7 Bowl, 1950
Chestnut, diameter 8⅝″ (21.9 cm)
Manufacturer: Prestini
Philadelphia Museum of Art. Gift of
the designer. 1979-167-8

Jens Quistgaard Danish, born 1919
**VIII-8 Ice bucket, 1960 (1961–73;
from 1983)**
Teak, height 19⅛″ (48.6 cm)
Manufacturer: Dansk
Philadelphia Museum of Art. Gift of
Dansk International Designs Ltd.
Plate 35

Jens Quistgaard Danish, born 1919
**VIII-9 Combination salt and pepper
shakers, 1972 (from 1972)**
Teak, height of taller shaker 9½″
(24.1 cm)
Manufacturer: Dansk
Philadelphia Museum of Art. Gift of
Dansk International Designs Ltd.

Tapio Wirkkala Finnish, born 1915
VIII-10 Platter, 1951
Plywood, length 29½″
(75 cm)
Manufacturer: Soinne
Taideteollisuusmuseo, Helsinki

Biographies of Designers

Kathryn B. Hiesinger
George H. Marcus

The quotations that appear in the biographies are the words of the designers. The appended dates refer not to the years in which the texts were written, but to the years of publication of the sources from which they were quoted. These citations may be found in the bibliographical listings following each biography. Where no date follows a quotation, the text has been taken from unpublished material in files of the Philadelphia Museum of Art.

Publications listed under Writings, Monographs, and References are meant to be selective; where a publication has an extensive bibliography, that is cited and should be consulted for additional bibliographical references.

A number of major prizes are regularly awarded in the field of design (see Introduction), and most of the designers have been recipients of them. No attempt has been made to give a comprehensive list of the design prizes or exhibition medals received by each designer.

Alvar Aalto
Finnish, 1898–1976

Architect, city planner, and designer of furniture, light fittings, textiles, and glass, Aalto is considered one of the greatest of modern architects, responsible for the humanization of the International Style through his emphasis on organic forms, on the use of wood as a medium, and on the relationship of architecture to nature. Aalto considered the applied arts as "architectural accessories," part of the "biology" of building, and his first mass-produced furniture and lighting were designed to furnish the sanatorium at Paimio, Finland (1929–33), which brought him international recognition. His laminated-wood chairs and tables in gently curving shapes were made by Huonekalutehdas Korhonen, which today still produces the now-classic furniture for Artek, the firm established in 1935 by Aalto. During the 1940s and 1950s Aalto continued to develop laminated-wood furniture (III-1) and light fittings specifically for his buildings —the floor lamp (IV-1) was designed in 1954 for the Public Pensions Institute in Helsinki—most of which were also incorporated into Artek's standard production.

Writings: Göran Schildt, ed., *Sketches: Alvar Aalto* (Cambridge, Mass., 1978).

Monographs: Paul David Pearson, *Alvar Aalto and the International Style* (New York, 1978); *Alvar Aalto: 1898–1976* (Helsinki, 1978); Malcolm Quantrill, *Alvar Aalto: A Critical Study* (New York, 1983).

Reference: "Aalto: Interior Architecture, Furniture and Furnishings," *Progressive Architecture*, vol. 58 (Apr. 1977), pp. 74–77.

Eero Aarnio
Finnish, born 1932

Interior and industrial designer, Aarnio studied at the Helsinki Institute of Industrial Arts (Taideteollinen oppilaitos) from 1954 to 1957, opening his own office in 1962. Best known outside Finland for his chair designs, Aarnio turned to plastics in 1960 and created two of the most notable chairs of the decade, the large environmental "Ball" or "Globe" chair (III-2), its upholstered interior often equipped with a telephone or stereo speakers, and the low, squashed, spherical "Gyro" or "Pastilli" chair (III-3). Both reflect Aarnio's preoccupation with geometric shapes, which he considered to be "the most comfortable forms to hold up the human body" (*New York Times*, 1970). Aarnio's one-man exhibition of fiberglass furniture in Helsinki

and Stockholm (1968) capped a decade of recognition, and he continued to exploit the possibilities of plastics, but more recently has returned to traditional materials, shown by his wooden "Viking" dining table and chairs for Polardesign (1982).

References: "A Designer's Home Is His Showcase, Too," *New York Times*, Dec. 16, 1970; London, Whitechapel Art Gallery, *Modern Chairs: 1918–1970* (July 22–Aug. 30, 1970), no. 89; Eileene Harrison Beer, *Scandinavian Design: Objects of a Life Style* (New York, 1975), pp. 74, 76–77, 79.

Gerald Abramovitz
British, born South Africa, 1928

An architect and industrial designer, Abramovitz studied architecture at the university of Pretoria (1949–51) and design at the Royal College of Art, London (1952–54). He has specialized in furniture, particularly seating, for Knoll (1961) and Hille (1966–67), and lighting (for Best & Lloyd), but has also designed appliances (for Frigidaire), play equipment, and prefabricated housing components. A molded-plastic armchair based on his earlier work for Knoll won a second prize in the London *Daily Mirror*'s 1963 international furniture-design competition (judged by CHARLES EAMES, ARNE JACOBSEN, Paul Reilly, and others) and his "Cantilever" desk lamp (IV-2), a Design Centre Award in 1966.

Reference: "Design Centre Awards 1966: 'Cantilever' Desk Lamp," *Design*, no. 209 (May 1966), pp. 40–41.

Lis Ahlmann
Danish, 1894–1979

A handweaver who in the 1950s began to design for commercial production, Ahlmann set standards of quality and craftsmanship for the Danish textile industry, which are still to be equaled. In 1953 she became artistic consultant for the Copenhagen firm of C. Olesen, collaborating with the furniture designer BØRGE MOGENSEN on

furnishing and upholstery fabrics (VII-1) in coordinated colors and interchangeable patterns. Drawing on the traditional plaids and stripes of her own weaving in muted, natural colors, Ahlmann first adopted these for simple power looms constructed like handlooms. Soon, however, encouraged by Mogensen, she introduced larger and richer patterns in bolder colors manufactured on more complicated machinery. The textiles she designed with Mogensen became the standard upholstery fabric on much of his furniture (III-52).

Monograph: Thomas Mogensen, *Lis Ahlmann Tekstiler* (Copenhagen, 1974).

References: Bent Salicath and Arne Karlsen, eds., *Modern Danish Textiles* (Copenhagen, 1959), pp. 12–15; Arne Karlsen, *Made in Denmark* (New York, 1960), pp. 72–79, 122–23; Arne Karlsen, *Furniture Designed by Børge Mogensen* (Copenhagen, 1968), *passim*.

Yūsuke Aida
Japanese, born 1931

Ceramic craftsman and designer, Aida was trained as a city planner at Chiba university and afterward studied ceramics with Ken Miyanohara. From 1961 to 1964 Aida worked in the United States as chief designer of the Bennington Potters in Vermont, creating the "Classic" series of tablewares—economical in detail and controlled in line—which is still produced by the company (II-1). On his return to Japan, Aida turned from the design of industrially produced tablewares to studio pottery. His work during the 1970s included large-scale ceramic wall panels for the Osaka Ina building and the Tourist Hotel in Nagoya. Aida has served as director of the Japanese Designer Craftsman Association (1972–74) and of its successor, the Japan Craft Design Association (since 1976).

Reference: Tokyo, Crafts Gallery, The National Museum of Modern Art, *Contemporary Vessels: How to Pour* (Feb. 10–Mar. 22, 1982), nos. 182–83.

Anni Albers
American, born Germany, 1899

Through the example of her work, her teaching, and her writings, Albers has been one of the most influential weavers of this century. She attended art school in Berlin and Hamburg and later studied at the Bauhaus (1922–30) with Wassily Kandinsky and Paul Klee. Specializing in textile design there, Albers was for a time both an instructor and acting head of the textile department. Between 1930 and 1933 she worked independently in Dessau and Berlin, and from 1933 to 1949, taught at Black Mountain College in North Carolina. Albers has been concerned consistently with both handweaving and production fabrics (for Knoll, from 1959; for Sunar, from 1978), her neat and elegant designs in geometric patterns (VII-2) a woven counterpart to the work of her late husband, the painter Josef Albers. She has viewed design as the strict organization of forms but acknowledges changes in style, for example, with texture, which is "one of the formal elements that has been of little or no interest for a long time but has again become one of today's stylistic components. . . . We like things today that are light—light as the opposite of heavy and light as the opposite of dark" (1965).

Writings: Anni Albers, *On Weaving* (Middletown, Conn., 1965); Anni Albers, *On Designing* (Middletown, Conn., 1971).

Monograph: Cambridge, Mass., Massachusetts Institute of Technology, *Anni Albers: Pictorial Weavings* (1959).

Franco Albini
Italian, 1905–1977

Trained as an architect at the Milan Politecnico, where he received a degree in 1929, Albini worked concurrently as architect, city planner, and designer of interiors, exhibitions, museum installations, furniture, and consumer products. As early as 1930 he exhibited furniture and objects at the Monza Biennale, and soon joined with the rationalist architects, who as a group were to present designs for interiors at the Milan Triennale of 1936. Drawn to the circle of the influential design magazine *Casabella*, he served as its editor in 1945–46. His furniture of the 1940s and 1950s clearly reveals the logic of its structure and method of manufacture (III-4), and is exceptionally strong in its sensitivity to materials, as, for example, his wicker and cane seating (III-5).

Other designs, some of which he executed with his associate (since 1951) Franca Helg, were done for such major manufacturers as Poggi, Bonacina, Arflex, Pirelli, Siemens, and Fontana Arte. His numerous awards include the Compasso d'Oro in 1955, 1958, and 1964.

Monograph: *Franco Albini: 1930–1970* (London, 1981) (biblio.).

Reference: Paolo Fossati, *Il design in Italia* (Turin, 1972), pp. 77–83, 163–78, pls. 1–63 (biblio.).

Winslow Anderson
American, born 1917

After graduating from the New York State College of Ceramics at Alfred University in 1946, Anderson was hired as the first designer at the Blenko glass company, remaining there until 1953. Although not a glass craftsman himself, he was able to design simple blown forms (II-2) directly in molten glass— rather than on paper or with models—through the close rapport he developed with the factory workers and his sensitivity to their skills and the medium. From 1953 to 1979 Anderson was a designer and design director for Lenox china.

Reference: Don Wallance, *Shaping America's Products* (New York, 1956), pp. 82, 105, 115–17.

John Andersson
Swedish, born 1900

Ceramic designer for the firm of Andersson & Johansson (now Höganäs; II-3), Andersson created in 1955 a highly successful series of modern ovenproof tablewares using the traditional earthenwares and the olive-green, manganese-brown, and mustard-yellow colors that had characterized pottery production in the town of Höganäs for more than a century. During the 1960s Andersson chiefly designed in stoneware bodies, combining a sculptor's sense of form with the craftsman's understanding of materials; in 1969–70 the firm abandoned production of earthenwares altogether in favor of the harder, nonporous ware.

Reference: Erik Zahle, ed., *A Treasury of Scandinavian Design* (New York, 1961), p. 268, no. 295.

Archizoom Associati
Italian, established Florence, 1966–1974

In 1966 four architects (Andrea Branzi, born 1938; Gilberto Corretti, born 1941; PAOLO DEGANELLO, born 1940; Massimo Morozzi, born 1941) and two industrial designers (Dario Bartolini, born 1943, and Lucia Bartolini, born 1944) formed a studio in Florence to design architecture, interiors, products, and exhibition installations. Polemical in speech and practice and characteristic of the period's social radicalism, Archizoom organized the "Center for Eclectic Conspiracy" at the 1968 Triennale in Milan, and declared the "right to go against a reality that lacks 'meaning' . . . to act, modify, form, and destroy the surrounding environment" (1972). Their "Mies" chair (III-6), with its uncompromising wedge shape and sloping diaphragm seat, is a well-known example of the firm's "counter-design," paying homage to the minimalist designs of the Bauhaus architect Mies van der Rohe, while their "AEO" chair for Cassina (1974), with its anchoring base and loose flapping back, was just as radical.

References: London, Whitechapel Art Gallery, *Modern Chairs: 1918–1970* (July 22–Aug. 30, 1970), no. 98; New York, Museum of Modern Art, *Italy: The New Domestic Landscape* (May 26–Sept. 11, 1972), pp. 101, 103, 108, 232–39; "Allestimento come informazione," *Ottagono*, no. 34 (Sept. 1974), pp. 82–83.

Folke Arström
Swedish, born 1907

A designer of flatware and hollow ware in silver, pewter, and stainless steel, Arström was trained at the Royal Academy of Fine Arts (Kungliga Konsthögskolan) in Stockholm. He opened his own design office in 1934, and in 1940 became head designer for the firm of Gense, which depended on him to launch a line of unadorned and well-modeled stainless-steel flatware that would overcome consumer prejudice against the material. "Thebe," his first pattern produced by Gense (1944), received critical acclaim, but it was not until over a decade later that his "Focus" cutlery (V-1) achieved international commercial success, especially in America, where it helped to set the fashion for quality stainless steel as an alternative to silver for formal dining.

References: Graham Hughes, *Modern Silver throughout the World* (New York, 1967), nos. 59, 61; Jay Doblin, *One Hundred Great Product Designs* (New York, 1970), no. 79.

Sergio Asti
Italian, born 1926

An architecture graduate of the Milan Politecnico (1953) and one of the founders of the Associazione per il Disegno Industriale (1956), Asti has designed exhibitions and interiors as well as a wide range of stylish products (furniture, china, cutlery, glassware, appliances, lighting) for numerous manufacturers. The versatility of his materials—glass, ceramic, plastic, marble, stainless steel, wood—mirrors the keen interest he takes in their particular qualities and in the details of design and manufacture. His forms are unusual, often oddly geometric and conceived above all for the pleasure of their abstract beauty, for example, his highly architectural line of vases for Knoll (1969–72), cutlery for Lauffer (V-2), and glassware for Salviati (II-4). But his work can also be coolly functional, be it a television for Brionvega (1974), Pyrex cookware for Corning France (1979, 1981–82), or his 1975 innovations in ski-boot design.

References: "Forme nuove per un'antica fornace," *Domus*, no. 421 (Dec. 1964), pp. 57–60; "Sergio Asti, tradition, recherches et dynamisme," *L'Oeil*, no. 190 (Oct. 1970), pp. 60–67; "Sergio Asti," *Interiors*, vol. 130 (Nov. 1970), pp. 120–21; "In Detail," *Industrial Design*, vol. 18 (Jan.–Feb. 1971), pp. 44–47; "From Italy: New Vases for Knoll International," *Domus*, no. 518 (Jan. 1973), pp. 36–37; "Le Design italien: Sergio Asti," *L'Oeil*, nos. 246–47 (Jan.–Feb. 1976), pp. 66–71; "Piccoli progetti ere ecologiche," *Modo*, no. 54 (Nov. 1982), pp. 46–48.

Carl Auböck
Austrian, born 1924

One of Austria's most prolific architects and designers, Auböck graduated from the Technische Hochschule in Vienna (1949) and studied at the Massachusetts Institute of Technology, Cambridge (1952). The range of his design work is extensive, including furniture, metal (V-3), wood, ceramics, and glass tableware (some produced and sold by his well-known family firm in Vienna), as well as machinery, scientific instruments, sports equipment, and packaging. Recent work reveals a looser, more eccentric combination of forms, as seen in his glassware designs and his enamel cooking set for Culinar.

Writings: Carl Auböck, "Design für Überfluss, Design für Not," in *Design ist unsichtbar* (Vienna, 1981), pp. 573–80.

Reference: Jocelyn de Noblet, *Design* (Paris, 1974), p. 252.

Gae Aulenti
Italian, born 1927

Architect and designer of interiors as well as of furniture and lighting, Aulenti studied architecture at the Milan Politecnico (1954), where she later taught (1964–69). Achieving first recognition in the late 1950s as a proponent of the controversial Neo-Liberty style—a revival of Art Nouveau forms that many critics saw as an abandonment of the ideals of progressive modernism—Aulenti epitomized the style in her bentwood "Sgarsul" rocking chair of 1961 (for Poltronova). She is best known for her lamps, designed in a variety of styles from 1964 (for Francesconi, Martinelli, Candle, Artemide, Kartell, and Stilnovo; IV-3), the "Faretti" series for Stilnovo winning a silver medal at the Milan Triennale of 1973. As an interior designer Aulenti has specialized in showroom design, from those for Olivetti in Paris (1967) and Buenos Aires (1968) to showrooms for Knoll in Boston (1968) and New York (1970) and for Fiat in Turin, Brussels, and Zurich (1970–71), developing a polished, dramatic style in which steps, platforms, and walled angular spaces establish areas for seating and display. Since 1975 Aulenti has designed stage sets in collaboration with the theater director Luca Ronconi, in Prato, Genoa, and Milan.

References: Los Angeles, Frederick S. Wight Art Gallery, University of California, *Design Process Olivetti 1908–1978* (Mar. 27–May 6, 1979), p. 254, and *passim*; Alfonso Grassi and Anty Pansera, *Atlante del design italiano: 1940–1980* (Milan, 1980), pp. 157, 166, 179, 188, 276.

Masakichi Awashima
Japanese, 1914–1979

After studying at the design department of the Japan Art School, Tokyo, Awashima worked from 1935 to 1946 for the craftsman Kozo Kagami, who had studied Western glass techniques in Germany. He became director of the industrial arts department of the Hoya glass factory in 1946, remaining until 1950, when he founded the Awashima Glass Design Research Institute. He developed mold-blown means for mass production, and in 1954 patented the process for *shizuku* ("dripping water") glass, which has since been used by the Awashima glass company (founded 1956) for its distinctively textured ware. It retains the feel and irregular forms of glass made in traditional ceramic molds, although it is produced with advanced techniques and metal molds (II-5). In 1956 he was awarded the Inventor's Prize by the Invention Society of Japan.

References: Dorothy Blair, *A History of Glass in Japan* (New York, 1973), pp. 254, 298–99, 319, pls. 37, 236; Tokyo, Crafts Gallery, The National Museum of Modern Art, *Modern Japanese Glass* (Tokyo, 1982), nos. 127–31.

Hiroshi Awatsuji
Japanese, born 1929

A textile and graphic designer, Awatsuji was graduated from the municipal art school in Kyoto (1950) and worked as a textile designer for Kanebo from 1950 to 1954. Since then he has designed independently, providing fabrics for industry (principally for Fujie textiles) and on commission, carpets (Government Hall, Expo '70, Osaka), furnishing fabrics (Tokyu Hotels, 1971–72), and tapestries (for IBM Japan, 1982). His bold and colorful printed textiles have signaled a departure in furnishing fabrics in Japan over the last decade. His recent "art screens," with which Awatsuji tries to create "one more window in the interior" (1982), are over-scale graphics responding to popular advertising imagery, printed as separate panels in the form of wide roll-up screens (VII-3).

References: "New Print Textile Designed by Hiroshi Awatsuji," *Japan Interior Design*, no. 252 (Mar. 1980), pp. 82–85; Chihaya Nakagawa, "'Art Screen' by Hiroshi Awatsuji," *Japan Interior Design*, no. 280 (July 1982), pp. 73–77.

Monica Backström
Swedish, born 1939

Educated at the School of Arts, Crafts and Design (Konstfackskolan) in Stockholm (1959–64), Backström has been a glass designer for Boda since 1965. Her work has taken an independent direction: she often incorporates metal—threads, nails, small flakes—into the molten glass body, and her bowls, plates, and candlesticks are often of distinctively original shapes (II-6), finished with enamel decoration on silvered surfaces. She has also carried out large-scale glass decorations for public and commercial buildings and a number of Swedish ocean liners.

References: Lennart Lindkvist, ed., *Design in Sweden* (Stockholm, 1972), pp. 16–18; Geoffrey Beard, *International Modern Glass* (London, 1976), pls. 112, 139, 329.

Olof Bäckström
Finnish, born 1922

A self-taught woodcarver, Bäckström was awarded a silver medal for wooden household objects at the Milan Triennale of 1957. Exploiting his gifts for sculpture, he was a cutlery designer for Fiskars from 1958 to 1980, designing in 1963 the first of the now well-known line of orange-handled, ergonomically conceived scissors (V-4). Bäckström won a second silver medal for his camping cutlery in Milan in 1960.

Reference: New York, Cooper-Hewitt Museum, *Scandinavian Modern Design: 1880–1980* (Sept. 14, 1982–Jan. 2, 1983), no. 255.

Jacob Bang
Danish, 1889–1965

Sculptor, architect, and industrial designer, Bang studied at the Royal Danish Academy of Fine Arts (Kongelige Danske Kunstakademie), Copenhagen, and in 1928 was appointed designer at the Holmegaard glassworks, serving as artistic director from 1928 until 1941. He then worked independently, designing ceramics for Nymølle and metalwork for Pan Aluminium and F. Hingelberg until 1957, when he became artistic director of the Kastrup glassworks (the firm merged with Holmegaard in 1965). Bang's functionalist (II-7) and decorative glasswares were simple and straightforward in shape and decoration.

Writings: Jacob E. Bang, "Lidt om Glasset i Hjemmet," in Sigvard Bernadotte, ed., *Moderne dansk boligkunst,* vol. 1 (Odense, 1946), pp. 255–60.

References: Corning, N.Y., The Corning Museum of Glass, *Glass 1959* (1959), nos. 55–57; Copenhagen, Kastrup & Holmegaard Glassworks, *150 Years of Danish Glass* (n.d.), nos. 181–208; Erik Lassen and Mogens Schlüter, *Dansk Glas: 1925–1975* (Copenhagen, 1975), pp. 21–31, 37–40, pls. A,B,D, figs. 15–66, 108–10, 114–16, 119–22.

Hans Theo Baumann
German, born Switzerland, 1924

Germany's leading designer of ceramics and glass, Baumann studied fine and applied arts (including glass painting) in Dresden and Basel. He opened his own studio in 1955 and has since designed ceramics for Rosenthal, Thomas, Schönwald, and Arzberg (II-8) and glassware for Gral, Rheinkristall, Rosenthal, Thomas, Daum, and Süssmuth. His range of designs has also included furniture, light fittings, and textiles, which are characterized by the same rounded, geometric shapes that have won him international recognition in the fields of ceramics and glass.

Monograph: Cologne, Kunstgewerbemuseum, *H. Th. Baumann Design* (Nov. 16, 1979–Jan. 27, 1980).

Alessandro Becchi
Italian, born 1946

Educated at the Istituto Statale d'Arte in Florence, Becchi began his collaboration with the firm of Giovannetti in 1969. In a series of sofas he designed (with Graziano Giovannetti as technical consultant) during the 1970s, Becchi transformed the standard convertible sofa into a soft structure. His "Anfibio" sofa bed (III-7), an all-soft pad without a frame, is constructed of expanded polyurethane foam wrapped in Dacron and upholstered in leather, vinyl, or fabric, and can be unrolled, folded, and refolded, or held together by means of straps.

Reference: "The Anfibio Collection," *Industrial Design,* vol. 19 (Apr. 1972), pp. 28–29.

Mario Bellini
Italian, born 1935

One of today's most diverse and important industrial designers, Bellini has served since 1963 as chief design consultant to Olivetti for microcomputers, calculators (I-2), typewriters (I-4), and copying machines. He has designed furniture for Cassina (III-8), C & B Italia, Bras, Bacci, Poggi, and Marcatré, electronic equipment for Brion-

vega (I-1), Minerva, Irradio, and Yamaha (I-3), lamps for Flos and Artemide (IV-4), and since 1978 has been consultant to Renault in the research and design of new automobile models. He received Compasso d'Oro awards in 1962, 1964, 1970, and 1979, and a gold medal at the Ljubljana biennial in 1968. Trained in architecture at the Milan Politecnico, Bellini continues to practice architecture and contribute to environmental projects: in 1975 he founded a workshop to research the relationship between man and his built environment; in 1981 he launched *Album,* an annual design magazine focusing on human activities rather than consumer products. Although known for their classical, even architectural sense of form, Bellini's products are equally celebrated from the point of view of their use and context: "I'm not interested in considering an object as an isolated item. It is part of a wider system of objects, structures, and spaces, that work together as part of our built environment as a whole. I consider design in a very broad sense as an activity to modify, to change, our physical nature" (1981).

References: "Mario Bellini per la Olivetti," *Domus,* no. 494 (Jan. 1971), pp. 32–42; Los Angeles, Frederick S. Wight Art Gallery, University of California, *Design Process Olivetti 1908–1978* (Mar. 27–May 6, 1979), pp. 255–56, and *passim;* Alfonso Grassi and Anty Pansera, *Atlante del design italiano: 1940–1980* (Milan, 1980), p. 277; "Talking with Four Men Who Are Shaping Italian Design," *Industrial Design,* vol. 28 (Sept.–Oct. 1981), pp. 30–35.

Maria Benktzon, *see Ergonomi Design Gruppen*

Gustav Beran
Austrian, born 1912

Educated at the Kunstgewerbeschule in Vienna under Josef Hoffmann and Eugen Mayer (1928–33), Beran worked in the Netherlands as a designer for the largest Dutch silverware manufacturer, Gerritsen & Van Kempen (later Van Kempen & Begeer), from 1934 to 1941, and after the war served for almost three

decades as its artistic director (1948–77). Beran often elegantly adapts traditional forms of metal objects, for example, the wide-bowled Dutch potato spoon, which appears frequently in his table services and kitchen tools (V-5).

Monograph: Fribourg, Galerie Mara, *Gustav Beran: Miniatures & Design* (Oct. 23–Nov. 20, 1982).

Reference: *Gold & Silber, Uhren & Schmuck,* no. 1 (Jan. 1963), pp. 30–31.

Sigvard Bernadotte
Swedish, born 1907

Son of King Gustav VI, and designer in many mediums, including silver, furniture, textiles, bookbindings, and stage sets, Bernadotte began his career with Georg Jensen in 1930, designing principally for that firm until 1947. His preference for hard, geometric forms and clean, functional lines was a departure from the soft contours of previous Jensen silver, and the work he produced for the firm over the next decades, as well as his leadership as a director of the company, helped establish its reputation for contemporary, International Style silver. With the Danish architect ACTON BJØRN, he opened an independent firm in Copenhagen in 1949 (later with offices in Stockholm and New York) structured along the lines of an American industrial design firm, supplying designs for a variety of products from cutlery and plastics (VI-2) to camping equipment and industrial machinery. Since 1964 he has headed his own design firm, one of Scandinavia's largest, and in 1967 became a director of the London consulting firm Allied Industrial Designers.

Writings: Sigvard Bernadotte, ed., *Moderne dansk boligkunst,* 2 vols. (Odense, 1946).

Monograph: Gotthard Johansson and Christian Ditlev Reventlow, *Sigvard Bernadotte sølvarbejder: 1930–1955* (Copenhagen, 1955).

References: "Designs from Abroad," *Industrial Design,* vol. 4 (Feb. 1956), pp. 76–79; Washington, D.C., Renwick Gallery, *Georg Jensen—Silversmithy: 77 Artists 75 Years* (Feb. 29–July 6, 1980), nos. 11–14; Jens Bernsen, *Design: The Problem Comes First* (Copenhagen, 1982), pp. 68–71.

Harry Bertoia
American, born Italy, 1915–1978

Sculptor, printmaker, and jewelry and furniture designer, Bertoia entered the Cranbrook Academy of Art, Bloomfield Hills, Michigan, on a scholarship in 1937, and in 1939 he set up a metal workshop and began to teach jewelry and metalworking there. In 1943 he joined his Cranbrook colleague CHARLES EAMES in California, contributing to the war effort with technical work on airplane and medical equipment for the Evans Product Company and experimenting there with Eames on molded-plywood seating. Encouraged by another Cranbrook associate, FLORENCE KNOLL, and her husband, Hans, he established a studio in Pennsylvania in 1950 and with their company's technicians, developed a series of furniture designs for them. His "Diamond" chair (III-9) of welded steel latticework on a pivoting mechanism, introduced in 1952, was quickly taken up by architects and designers as ideally fitting their new open plans. "When you get right down to it, the chairs are studies in space, form and metal too. If you will look at them, you will find that they are mostly made of air, just like sculpture. Space passes right through them" (London, 1970). Although Bertoia remained a consultant for Knoll, he ceased to contribute designs by the mid-1950s as he began to receive commissions that allowed him to devote himself to sculpture.

Monograph: June Kompass Nelson, *Harry Bertoia, Sculptor* (Detroit, 1970) (biblio.).

References: London, Whitechapel Art Gallery, *Modern Chairs: 1918–1970* (July 22–Aug. 30, 1970), no. 29; Eric Larrabee and Massimo Vignelli, *Knoll Design* (New York, 1981), pp. 66–71.

Max Bill
Swiss, born 1908

Architect, sculptor, painter, designer, and theorist, Bill was trained first as a silversmith at the Kunstgewerbeschule in Zurich and later at the Bauhaus school in Dessau (1927–29). Through the example of his own work and the influence of the "new Bauhaus," the Hochschule für Gestaltung in Ulm, West Germany, of which Bill

was co-founder, rector, head of the departments of architecture and product design, and architect (1950–56), he perpetuated the first Bauhaus ideal of designing industrial products that fulfilled their practical functions and maintained an ordered, primarily mathematical, aesthetic standard (see I-5, IV-5). A painter and sculptor, Bill moved to Zurich in 1929 and took up industrial design there in 1944. In his writings and the "Güte Form" exhibition that he organized for the Schweizerische Werkbund in 1949, Bill emphasized the equivalences of art and mathematics, of functional and aesthetic form: "Examining critically the shapes of objects in daily use, we invariably take as criterion the form of such an object, as a 'harmonious expression of the sum of its functions.' This does not mean an artificial simplification or an anti-functional streamlining. What we specifically perceive as form, and therefore as beauty, is the natural, self-evident, and functional appearance" (1955). In 1957 Bill returned to Zurich, where he still maintains a studio, principally for his painting and sculpture. A champion of pure form, he has based his solutions in product design on the study of human needs: "in the ideal case i should like to build a town with everything that goes with it, or on a smaller scale a civic centre including a museum presenting the development of culture—not only of art— and to design it thematically, that is to say, to create by design measures an environment which would be attractive, refreshing and socially constructive" (1978).

Writings: Max Bill, *Form—A Balance Sheet of Mid-Twentieth Century Trends in Design* (Basel, 1952); Max Bill, "The Bauhaus Idea: From Weimar to Ulm," in *The Architects' Year Book,* vol. 5 (1953), pp. 29–32.

Monographs: Tomás Maldonado, *Max Bill* (Buenos Aires, 1955); Margit Staber, *Max Bill* (London, 1964) (biblio.); Margit Staber, *Max Bill* (Saint Gall, 1971) (biblio.); Eduard Hüttinger, *Max Bill* (New York, 1978) (biblio.).

Acton Bjørn
Danish, born 1910

Trained as an architect and planner, Bjørn turned to industrial design during World War II. In 1949 he joined with SIGVARD BERNADOTTE in establishing Denmark's first industrial design firm, Bernadotte & Bjørn. A great variety of products for numerous manufacturers bear their signature, including metalwork, ceramics, office equipment (for Facit), sanitary fixtures, cutlery, plastics (for Rosti; VI-2), camping equipment, and industrial machinery. His "Beolit 500" transistor radio for Bang & Olufsen won the Danish ID award for 1966, when it was described as one of the first attempts to produce a radio that was just as simple as a telephone.

References: "Designs from Abroad," *Industrial Design*, vol. 4 (Feb. 1956), pp. 76–79; "Acton Bjorn," *Industrial Design*, vol. 14 (Oct. 1967), pp. 50–51; Jens Bernsen, *Design: The Problem Comes First* (Copenhagen, 1982), pp. 68–71.

Michael Boehm
German, born 1944

A glass designer associated since 1966 with Rosenthal, Boehm studied at the German national Glasfachschule in Hadamar (1959–62) and at the Hochschule für Bildende Künste in Cassel (1962–66). As a student Boehm traveled to Murano and Venice and brought back an interest in traditional Italian glassmaking techniques and materials, perhaps best seen in his limited "Reticelli" series for Rosenthal, blown with cotton twist threads in the manner of sixteenth-century Venetian examples. He has designed several lines of stemware for Rosenthal, among them the two-color "Snowflower" and "Papyrus" (II-9) series.

Reference: *Rosenthal: Mit Kunst leben* (Selb, n.d.), pp. 52–53.

Cini Boeri
Italian, born 1924

A graduate in architecture from the Politecnico in Milan (1951), Boeri worked as an interior designer in the studio of MARCO ZANUSO from 1952 to 1963. As an independent architect and industrial designer, and since 1979 as the head of her own design firm in Milan, she has been recognized for her achievement with Compasso d'Oro awards

in 1970 and 1979. Her component polyurethane seating without internal structure for Arflex—"Bobo" (1967), "Serpentone" (1971), "Strips" (1972; with Laura Griziotti)—demonstrates her conception of furniture as expandable, interrelated multiuse systems, rather than isolated elements, and her desire to effect economies through standardization of elements to make well-designed furnishings less expensive and thus more widely available. Among her other designs are the "Lunario" series of ellipsoid-based tables for Knoll; "Cubetto," a mobile storage unit for Arflex (1968); and plastic lighting for Arteluce (IV-6) and Stilnovo.

References: New York, Museum of Modern Art, *Italy: The New Domestic Landscape* (May 26–Sept. 11, 1972), pp. 29, 61, 121; Alfonso Grassi and Anty Pansera, *Atlante del design italiano: 1940–1980* (Milan, 1980), pp. 162, 165, 176, 187, 278.

Kay Bojesen
Danish, 1886–1958

Silversmith and wood craftsman, Bojesen trained with Georg Jensen in Copenhagen (1907–10), and afterward in France and Germany. Returning to Denmark in 1913, Bojesen established his own workshop in Copenhagen, where after producing ornamented silverwares in the manner of Jensen, he developed the smooth, functionalist style for which he became known from the late 1920s. To promote functional modern design, it was Bojesen's idea to establish a permanent exhibition of the best products of Danish craftsmanship and industrial design, and in 1931, Den Permanente, one of Europe's first design centers, opened in Copenhagen. A creator of simple, undecorated forms that rely for effect on beauty of proportion and material, Bojesen was a pioneer of the Danish "Modern" style. Nowhere is this style more evident than in the wooden objects he designed during the late 1940s and 1950s (VIII-1–3) for which he was awarded a gold medal at the 1954 Milan Triennale. In addition to his silverwork and wooden ware he also designed ceramics for Bing & Grøndahl (1930–31) and stainless-steel tablewares for Motala Verkstad and Universal Steel. His awards also include a grand prize and di-

ploma of honor in Milan in 1951 and 1954.

References: Edgar Kaufmann, Jr., "Kay Bojesen: Tableware to Toys," *Interiors*, no. 112 (Feb. 1953), pp. 64–67; Mary Lyon, "Master Plays Wide Field," *Craft Horizons*, vol. 13 (July 1953), pp. 26–31; "Kay Bojesen," *Design Quarterly*, no. 39 (1957), pp. 2–5; Erik Zahle, ed., *A Treasury of Scandinavian Design* (New York, 1961), p. 269, nos. 51, 105, 378–80.

Rodolfo Bonetto
Italian, born 1929

Designer of appliances, industrial machinery, and furniture, Bonetto began his career as a design consultant, working for Pininfarina and other automobile body manufacturers. His own firm (founded 1958) has supplied designs for many industrial clients, including Siemens, Brionvega, Driade, Autovox, Valextra, Bilumen, and Olivetti (since 1962). His much-admired "Sfericlock" (for Borletti), a rigorous redesign of the standard alarm clock, won a Compasso d'Oro in 1964; microfilm and office machines gained others in 1970 and 1979. While Bonetto believes in the basic honesty of design and durability of products, his work also exhibits a certain irony and humor: his linking, polyfoam "Boomerang" chair (1971) includes pockets for magazines, while his colorful plastic "Quattroquarti" sectional table (III-10) can be rearranged imaginatively into a variety of configurations. From 1961 to 1965 Bonetto taught in the product design department at the Hochschule für Gestaltung in Ulm, West Germany.

References: "Rodolfo Bonetto, Designer Italiano," *Domus*, no. 446 (Jan. 1967), pp. 43–50; New York, Museum of Modern Art, *Italy: The New Domestic Landscape* (May 26–Sept. 11, 1972), pp. 28, 33, 49, 71–72; Los Angeles, Frederick S. Wight Art Gallery, University of California, *Design Process Olivetti 1908–1978* (Mar. 27–May 6, 1979), p. 256, and *passim*.

Renata Bonfanti
Italian, born 1929

After studying weaving at the Istituto d'Arte in Venice and at the Kvinnelige Industriskole in Oslo, Bonfanti initially concentrated on handmade carpets and tapestries. In 1956 she began to design furnishing fabrics (VII-4) for mechanical production. The Compasso d'Oro (1962) cited her curtain fabric "JL" for its excellent technical and functional solution specifically through structural invention. She has continued to make carpets on commission and in series (for Danese) and has exhibited her tapestries and weaving widely.

References: Gio Ponti, "Milan: In Search for the New," *Craft Horizons*, vol. 21 (Mar. 1961), p. 34; "Tapetti di Renata Bonfanti," *Domus*, no. 382 (Sept. 1961), pp. 46–48; Milan, Palazzo delle Stelline, *Design & design* (May 29–July 31, 1979), pp. 87, 129.

Hermann Bongard
Norwegian, born 1921

One of Norway's outstanding graphic designers, Bongard has had a versatile career in other fields also—glass (II-10), wood (VIII-4), ceramics, textiles, silver, and monumental architectural decoration. Trained in lithography and commercial design at the National School of Crafts and Industrial Design (Statens Håndvaerks- og Kunstindustriskole) in Oslo, he worked from 1947 to 1955 as a designer at the Hadelands glassworks under his former teacher, the book illustrator and glass designer Sverre Pettersen. There Bongard created art glass with inventive forms and imaginative engraved decoration as well as more restrained glassware for table use, including "Ambassador" (1954), a service for Norwegian embassies. After 1955 he worked as a design consultant for various manufacturers, and since the mid-1960s has concentrated on graphics and the printed page.

Monograph: Oslo, Kunstindustrimuseet, *Tegneren Hermann Bongard* (Oslo, 1971) (biblio.).

Reference: "Thirtyfour Lunning Prize-Winners," *Mobilia* (special issue), no. 146 (Sept. 1967), n.p.

Nord Bowlen
American, born 1909

A graduate in industrial design from the Rhode Island School of Design, Providence, Bowlen headed the design department of Lunt silversmiths for over twenty-five years. Among his many flatware patterns was "Contrast" (1954), with black, injection-molded nylon handles (V-6). It was hoped that this bold, contemporary sterling-silver service would compete with stainless-steel cutlery then being imported from Europe, but it was not commercially successful.

Reference: "Annual Design Review," *Industrial Design*, vol. 3 (Dec. 1956), no. 148.

Artur Braun
German, born 1925

At the death of their father in 1951, Artur Braun and his brother Erwin took over the radio manufacturing firm Max Braun had founded in Frankfort in 1921. When Braun rebuilt the factory in 1945, he had diversified the firm's products with such household appliances as a portable flashlight and electric shaver. The Braun brothers, interested in modern design, embarked immediately on a completely new design program, emphasizing function as both the point of departure and goal of good design work. With FRITZ EICHLER, HANS GUGELOT, and Otl Aicher of the Hochschule für Gestaltung in Ulm, and later with DIETER RAMS, they developed a rational style for all Braun appliances based on the Bauhaus principles of austerity, simplicity, and the absence of decorative detailing. Extending their design philosophy into every aspect of the company, including logo, packaging, and advertising, the Brauns created a total corporate image that reflected the quality and appearance of their products. One of the first Braun appliances in the new style was a small table model radio designed by Artur Braun and Eichler (I-6), which was shown at the radio exhibition in Düsseldorf in 1955 as part of a complete radio and phonograph program.

Reference: François Burkhardt and Inez Franksen, eds., *Design: Dieter Rams &* (Berlin, 1980–81), *passim*.

Helen von Boch, *see* Villeroy & Boch

Carl-Arne Breger
Swedish, born 1923

An extremely prolific industrial designer, Breger attended the School of Arts, Crafts and Design (Konstfackskolan) in Stockholm (1943–48). From 1953 to 1957 he was a staff designer at Gustavsberg, designing sanitary fittings, tableware, and a wide range of utility plastics (VI-5), including a squared bucket (VI-4) called the best-designed plastic product for the years 1950 to 1960 by the Swedish Plastic Association. From 1957 to 1959 he worked as chief designer for the Bernadotte & Bjørn office in Stockholm, and since then has headed his own firm with offices in Malmö, Stockholm, and Rome. More recent designs include a metal handsaw, for which he won a Bundespreis "Gute Form" in 1975, and the "Diavox" telephone for Ellemtel.

Writings: Carl-Arne Breger, "The Story behind a Design," *Tele*, no. 2 (1979), pp. 12–15.

Reference: Stockholm, Nationalmuseum, *Gustavsberg 150 år* (1975), nos. 306, 309–10, 317.

Barbara Brown
British, born 1932

Textile and knitwear designer, Brown created a series of dramatic printed patterns for Heal fabrics that were related to Op art in their use of geometric forms and black and white, neutral, or closely ranged colors (VII-5). The illusionistic, three-dimensional patterns required careful overprinting where the separate areas of color met, and were given Council of Industrial Design awards (1968 and 1970) for their technical virtuosity as well as their style. Brown was educated at the Canterbury College of Art and at the Royal College of Art, London (1953–56), where she now teaches. She has always worked as an individual consultant designer, selling patterns to firms in France, Italy, Germany, and America, as well as in Britain.

References: Manchester, Whitworth Art Gallery, *Brown/Craven/Dodd: 3 Textile Designers* (1965), pp. 6–10; "Furnishing Fabrics: Heal's Chevron, Complex and Extension," *Design*, no. 233 (May 1968), pp. 42–43; London, Heal & Son Limited, *Classics* (Spring 1981), no. 119.

Axel Brüel
Danish, 1900–1977

After working at his own pottery from 1928, Brüel became art consultant to the porcelain manufacturer Danmark in 1956, turning from the heavy forms of his own ceramics to the crisper lines required by the thinner body used. Working with the factory's technicians, he incorporated new materials and techniques in his designs, such as flame-resistant porcelain for cookware, while his handleless "Thermodan" coffee service (II-11) had double walls.

Reference: Arne Karlsen, *Made in Denmark* (New York, 1960), pp. 64–71.

Eva Brummer
Finnish, born 1901

A textile artist specializing in the weaving of *rya* (*ryijy*) rugs, Brummer was trained at the Institute of Industrial Arts (Taideteollisuuskeskuskoulu), Helsinki (1925). In 1929 she established an independent studio to revive the traditional Finnish *rya*, a thick hand-knotted tapestry used either as a carpet (VII-6), marriage-bed cover, or wall hanging. Known first for her brilliant colors, Brummer later adopted a more subdued palette, using an unevenly cut pile to give a relief effect. She has been associated throughout her career with the Friends of Finnish Handicraft, exhibiting in that organization's competitions and providing designs to be woven on commission. Much premiated even for her earliest work, Brummer received the grand prize, diploma of honor, and gold medal at the Milan Triennale in 1951, 1954, and 1957, respectively.

References: Oili Mäki, ed., *Finnish Designers of Today* (Helsinki, 1954), pp. 14–18; Erik Zahle, ed., *A Treasury of Scandinavian Design* (New York, 1961), p. 270, no. 188; Anja Louhio, *Modern Finnish Rugs* (Helsinki, 1975), pp. 42–45.

California Drop Cloth
American, established Los Angeles, 1975

Using paint pigments, not dyes, nor silkscreen or other printing techniques, but the hands of artist-craftsmen, California Drop Cloth produces a line of fabrics for upholstery and wall coverings, custom printed in individually chosen color combinations. Among the earliest of its some seventy patterns, "Drop Cloth" and "Celebration" (VII-7) resemble the random effects of the painter's drop cloth, but each, though hand painted and "redesigned" as executed, remains within a loose, predetermined design structure. Other patterns include stripes, foliage, and abstract motifs set against broad areas of flat background tones. California Drop Cloth was founded in 1975 by Leonard Polikoff, an interior designer and graduate of the University of California at Los Angeles, who sees his innovative approach as providing "unstructured design for structured placement in an environment" (1980).

Reference: Les Gilbert, "Happenings West: Drop Cloths Turn to Fabric Art," *Home Fashions Textiles*, vol. 1 (June 1980), pp. 63, 65.

Antonia Campi
Italian, born 1921

An independent designer of ceramics and household objects, Campi has created works for such Italian firms as Richard Ginori and Ermenegildo Collini. Her elegantly formed scissors (V-7) and poultry shears have received particular notice, winning respectively the Compasso d'Oro (1959) and an award from the National Industrial Design Council of Canada (1964).

Reference: Carlo Bestetti, ed., *Forme nuove in italia* (Rome, 1962), p. 109.

Anna Castelli Ferrieri
Italian, born 1920

Art consultant (since 1966) and later art director for Kartell, Castelli Ferrieri is an architect, urban planner, and industrial designer with a degree in architecture from the Milan Politecnico (1942). In 1951 she received a gold medal for modular kitchen units (with Eugenio Gentili) at the Milan Triennale. From 1959 to 1973 she was an associate of the architect Ignazio Gardella, with whom she collaborated on architecture and the design of products, among them a series of plastic tables for Kartell. Several of her own designs, which include plastic kitchen shelving, and storage systems (III-12), modular furniture, kitchen and tableware (VI-6), and stacking storage units (III-11), were awarded the Compasso d'Oro in 1979. Castelli Ferrieri was a founding member of the Associazione per il Disegno Industriale (1956) and its president from 1969 to 1971.

References: Milan, Palazzo delle Stelline, *Design & design* (May 29–July 31, 1979), pp. 130–31, 157; Alfonso Grassi and Anty Pansera, *Atlante del design italiano: 1940–1980* (Milan, 1980), pp. 141, 153, 280.

Achille Castiglioni
Italian, born 1918

Castiglioni has led postwar Italian design in both the variety and stylish vitality of the forms and illumination effects he has created (in association with his older brothers PIERGIACOMO and, occasionally, LIVIO). He has championed industrial design through his participation in the organization of the Milan Triennale exhibitions, his activity as a founder of the Associazione per il Disegno Industriale, his part in the organization of the Compasso d'Oro awards (which he and Piergiacomo themselves won five times between 1955 and 1979), and his teaching (since 1969, in the schools of architecture in Turin and Milan). After receiving an architecture degree at the Milan Politecnico (1944), he and Piergiacomo began their quarter century of collaboration in 1945, concentrating on exhibition and product design more than on architecture, and concerning themselves constantly with a sense of context and function in the objects they created. The Castiglioni name is most immediately associated with a vast array of inventive lighting (IV-7-13; principally for Flos) in metal, glass, and plastics, but his products are wide-ranging: radios, televisions, and record players (for Brionvega, Nova Radio), appliances (I-7), silver (for Bacci), ceramics and glass (including glass tableware for Danese, 1983), flatware (for Alessi), furniture (for Kartell, Bernini, Beylerian, Zanotta, Gavina; III-13, 14), and plastics.

References: Paolo Fossati, *Il design in Italia* (Turin, 1972), pp. 122–27, 224–33, pls. 310–54 (biblio.); Daniele Baroni, *L'Oggetto lampada* (Milan, 1981), pp. 128–37, figs. 292–321.

Livio Castiglioni
Italian, 1911–1979

Castiglioni worked principally as a lighting designer, at times collaborating with his brothers ACHILLE and PIERGIACOMO (until about 1952), at times with others, or else on his own. A graduate in architecture from the Politecnico of Milan (1936), he and Piergiacomo founded a design studio in 1938, which was taken over by Piergiacomo and Achille after the war. His work frequently used industrial materials and new types of bulbs, in inventive settings and combinations and often undisguised, as in the "Boalum" (IV-14), designed with GIANFRANCO FRATTINI.

References: Sylvia Katz, *Plastics: Designs and Materials* (London, 1978), p. 75; Alfonso Grassi and Anty Pansera, *Atlante del design italiano: 1940–1980* (Milan, 1980), p. 279.

Piergiacomo Castiglioni
Italian, 1913–1968

Although overshadowed by his brother ACHILLE, with whom he collaborated throughout his career, Castiglioni had a distinct personality and presence within the Italian design community. An architect, he was among the founders of the Associazione per il Disegno Industriale (1956), won numerous prizes at the Milan Triennale and Compasso d'Oro awards (with Achille), and taught in the school of architecture at the Milan Politecnico. He first collaborated with his brother LIVIO in a design firm from 1938 to 1940, creating with him (and Luigi Caccia Dominioni) a landmark in appliance design, the first Italian plastic radio (1939). After the war he reopened the studio in partnership with Achille, collaborating with him on the design of lighting (IV-7-11), furniture (III-13), appliances (I-7), plastics, exhibitions, and architecture.

References: Paolo Fossatti, *Il design in Italia* (Turin, 1972), pp. 122–27, 224–33, pls. 310–54 (biblio.); Vittorio Gregotti, "Ricordo di Pier Giacomo Castiglioni," *Ottagono*, no. 12 (Jan. 1969), pp. 20–23; Agnoldomenico Pica, "Piergiacomo Castiglioni," *Domus*, no. 470 (Jan. 1969), pp. 1–2.

Fede Cheti
Italian, 1905–1978

For almost half a century, the rich and famous flocked to the Milan showroom of Fede Cheti for the drapery and upholstery fabrics (VII-8) that would turn their houses into fashionable interiors. Having established her own firm in 1930, Cheti exhibited at the Monza Biennale that same year (and again in Milan in 1933), and she was discovered, and subsequently encouraged, by GIO PONTI. Over the next decade her name began to be known outside Italy, with her initial American acclaim coming in 1938. Her chintzes, silks, and velvets printed and painted in many colors with large original motifs drawn from nature—flowers, shells, landscapes, figures—were very popular in the 1950s, after she had won a first prize at the Venice Biennale in 1950 for her "art fabrics." Cheti also issued fabrics designed by well-known artists, including Giorgio de Chirico and Raoul Dufy, as well as Ponti, but all bore her name except those by the French designer René Gruau.

References: Milan, Museo Poldi Pezzoli, *Milano 70/70: Un secolo d'arte*, vol. 2, *Dal 1915 al 1945* (Apr. 28–June 10, 1971), p. 195; Maria Vittoria Alfonsi, *Donne al vertice* (Milan, 1975), pp. 41–43.

Wells Coates
British, born Japan, 1895–1958

Credited with introducing International Style architecture to England (in his Lawn Road Flats in Hampstead, 1933), Coates had gained experience in the office of Le Corbusier after graduating with a degree in engineering from the University of London (1924). One of a number of architects and designers commissioned by the E. K. Cole company to design their radios, he integrated engineering and styling in his streamlined, circular plastic table model in 1934, which soon became the best-known radio in Britain. A restyled version was issued immediately after the war, but in 1947 Coates totally rethought the product in his portable "Princess" model (I-8), with its colorful plastic housing and adjustable, clear handle. At this time he was designing aircraft interiors, and he was later involved in the Festival of Britain exhibition (1951). In his last years he moved to Canada to pursue transportation (monorail and catamaran) studies and a town-planning scheme, which did not succeed.

Writings: "Wells Coates 1895–1958: An Address to the 1957 Graduation Banquet, School of Architecture, University of British Columbia," *Journal of the Royal Architectural Institute of Canada*, vol. 36 (June 1959), pp. 205–11.

Monograph: Sherban Cantacuzino, *Wells Coates* (London, 1978).

Reference: J. M. Richards, "Wells Coates 1893–1958," *Architectural Review*, vol. 124 (Dec. 1958), pp. 357–60.

Luigi Colani
German, born 1928

Educated in Berlin and Paris, Colani has studied subjects as varied as sculpture and aerodynamics and designed products ranging from speedboats to ladies' garments. His reputation as one of Germany's most progressive and unconventional designers masks his serious concerns for human comfort and use: His "Drop" porcelain service for Rosenthal (II-12), awarded the Gute Industrieform prize in Hanover in 1972, is designed with the handle near the teapot's center of gravity so that the pot can be poured without effort, in thin porcelain so that the drink is not too quickly cooled, and with footed cups, which do not collect liquids from the saucer. Colani has also designed a tea service for Melitta (1981).

References: Hanover, Kestner-Museum, *Rosenthal: Hundert Jahre Porzellan* (Apr. 29–June 13, 1982), pp. 171–72, no. 102; "Moderne Klassiker, pt. 13: Geschirr, Besteck, Glas," *Schöner Wohnen* (Feb. 1982), p. 174; Tommaso Trini, "Il Design post-diluviano di Luigi Colani," *Domus*, no. 636 (Feb. 1983), pp. 48–49.

Gino Colombini
Italian, born 1915

As head of the technical department of the plastics manufacturer Kartell from its establishment in 1949, Colombini brought a conscious concern for good design to domestic objects in plastic, from buckets to kitchen utensils (VI-7). Awarded the Compasso d'Oro in 1955, 1957, 1959, and 1960, his products were cited for their innovation in the field of plastics, respect for materials, completely new forms, and exploration of the aesthetic possibilities of a medium otherwise prized only for its economy.

References: Gillo Dorfles, *Il disegno industriale e la sua estetica* (Bologna, 1963), figs. 133, 136, 138; Milan, Palazzo delle Stelline, *Design & design* (May 29–July 31, 1979), pp. 44, 60, 69, 74.

Joe Colombo
Italian, 1930–1971

An ingenious designer of furniture, glass, lighting, and interiors, Colombo led progressive Italian design in the 1960s with a series of products in new materials and systems that combined a variety of domestic services into one compact assembly. His design innovations included one of the first one-piece injection-molded plastic chairs (III-16), an acrylic lamp that reflects light from a fluorescent element in its base (IV-15), and a complete kitchen on wheels containing range, refrigerator, drawers, cupboard, chopping block, and a stove cover that doubles as a serving tray (I-9). Although Colombo's objects won international recognition for their high level of technical and aesthetic accomplishment (three medals at the Milan Triennale in 1964, Compasso d'Oro awards in 1967 and 1970, and the A.I.D. International Design Award in 1968), they were conceived for economy and versatility. Colombo studied painting at the Accademia di Belle Arti di Brera (1949) and architecture at the Politecnico in Milan (1950–54). Founder of the Nuclear painting movement and a member of the Concrete art movement during the 1950s, Colombo turned to industrial design only in 1962, when he opened his own office in Milan. Among his first commissions were a series of glasses for Arnolfo de Cambio and an air-conditioning unit for Rheem Safim. His many later clients were to include Bayer ("Visiona '69"), Bernini, Candy, Comfort, Elco, Kartell (III-15), Sormani (III-17), Stilnovo, O-Luce (IV-16), and Italora. In the 1972 exhibition of Italian design at the Museum of Modern Art in New York, he (with Ignazia Favata) was represented by the prototype of a "Total Furnishing Unit," which, with his early death, became a posthumous summation of his ideas.

References: "Una nuova concezione dell'arredamento: Joe Cesare Colombo," *Lotus*, vol. 3 (1966–67), pp. 176–95; London, Whitechapel Art Gallery, *Modern Chairs: 1918–1970* (July 22–Aug. 30, 1970), nos. 61, 79, 80, 91; M. Pia Valota, "Joe C. Colombo," *Casabella*, vol. 35, no. 358 (1971), pp. 46–48; Milan, Museo Poldi Pezzoli, *Milano 70/70: Un secolo d'arte*, vol. 3, *Dal 1946 al 1970* (from May 30, 1972), p. 296; New York, Museum of Modern Art, *Italy: The New Domestic Landscape* (May 26–Sept. 11, 1972), pp. 30, 40, 45, 53, 62, 116–17, 123, 170–79.

Andries Copier
Dutch, born 1901

As artistic director of the Royal Leerdam glassworks and head of the Leerdam glass school, Copier was a leading force in European glass design and manufacture for more than four decades. Taking charge of design for the factory in 1927, he oversaw both the "Unica" series of one-of-a-kind pieces, and the "Serica" line of table glass, both of which were artistically and commercially successful. His own household wares—tumblers, pitchers, and stemware—as well as his "Primula" pressed-glass tableware (II-13) are basic forms in clear glass, severe and unadorned. His recent work at Murano, Italy, begun after almost a decade of inactivity (he left Leerdam in 1970), is more experimental, with etched and colored decoration and freer forms. Designed as unique objects, they are nevertheless conceived as repeatable in series.

Monographs: Rotterdam, Museum Boymans–van Beuningen, *A.D. Copier: Glas* (Apr. 5–May 19, 1963) (biblio.); The Hague, Gemeentemuseum, *A.D. Copier* (July 10–Sept. 26, 1982).

References: Geoffrey Beard, *International Modern Glass* (London, 1976), pls. 74, 129, 250, 262; D. U. Kuyken-Schneider, "The Old Man—Andries Dirk Copier," *Neues Glas* (Feb. 1982), pp. 102–3.

Shirley Craven
British, born 1934

A textile designer, Craven created printed fabrics for Hull Traders during the 1960s that were given awards by the Council of Industrial Design—in 1961 for "Le Bosquet," in 1964 for "Division," "Sixty-Three," and "Shape," and in 1968 for "Simple Solar" and "Five" (VII-9). Craven studied painting, sculpture, and textile design, first at Kingston upon Hull, then at the Royal College of Art, London (from 1955 to 1958), and joined Hull Traders as consultant art director in 1960, commissioning work from other designers; in 1963 she became a director of the firm. After Hull Traders dissolved in 1972, Craven returned to painting and teaching.

References: Ken Baynes, *Industrial Design and the Community* (London, 1967), pp. 57–59; "Furnishing Fabrics: Hull Traders' Simple Solar, Five," *Design*, no. 233 (May 1968), pp. 30–31.

Gunnar Cyrén
Swedish, born 1931

Cyrén turned to glass design in 1959 after having studied gold- and silverwork at the School of Arts, Crafts and Design (Konstfackskolan) in Stockholm from 1951 to 1956, and at the Cologne Werkschule. As a designer at the Orrefors glassworks from 1959 to 1970 and since 1976, he has concentrated on ornamentation, employing cutting, engraving, acid etching, the company's own special *graal* technique, and for a period, vivid color (II-14). His work, which includes unique art glass, tableware, and cut-glass lighting fixtures, won him the Lunning Prize in 1966. He has also continued to work independently as a silversmith.

References: "Thirtyfour Lunning Prize-Winners," *Mobilia* (special issue), no. 146 (Sept. 1967), n.p.; Eileene Harrison Beer, *Scandinavian Design: Objects of a Life Style* (New York, 1975), pp. 98–99; New York, Cooper-Hewitt Museum, *Scandinavian Modern Design: 1880–1980* (Sept. 14, 1982–Jan. 2, 1983), nos. 239, 302; Skien, Sweden, Ibsenhuset, *Aktuell Svensk Form* (Oct. 3–21, 1982), pp. 24–27.

Lucienne Day
British, born 1917

Joining with her husband, ROBIN DAY, in a design firm in 1948, Lucienne Day soon became known for her boldly colored textiles in abstract patterns (for Heal Fabrics, Edinburgh Weavers, Cavendish). Her "Calyx" pattern of 1951 (VII-10) was judged the best textile design on the American market in 1952, when she received the First Award from the American Institute of Decorators. She won a gold medal at the Milan Triennale of 1951 and a grand prize in 1954; three Council of Industrial Design awards were added in the 1950s and 1960s. Her other work includes wallpapers, table linens, carpets, and porcelain (for Rosenthal, 1957–69), and she has recently focused on the design of individual, abstract wall hangings, which she calls silk mosaics. A graduate of the Royal College of

Art in London, Day was named a Royal Designer for Industry in 1963.

References: "8 British Designers," *Design Quarterly* (special issue), no. 36 (1956), pp. 9–10; "Furnishing Fabrics: Heal's Chevron, Complex and Extension," *Design*, no. 233 (May 1968), pp. 42–43; Fiona MacCarthy, *British Design since 1880* (London, 1982), figs. 17, 165.

Robin Day
British, born 1915

Robin Day achieved international recognition as a furniture designer when the tapered wooden and tubular-metal storage units he designed with Clive Latimer won a first prize in the 1948 competition for low-cost furniture at the Museum of Modern Art in New York. The following year he began a long association with the British furniture manufacturer Hille, conceiving plastic, plywood, and upholstered seating with an eye to ease of manufacture, comfort, and cost. Day's pioneering stacking "Polyprop" chair (1963), with an injection-molded polypropylene seat on a tubular-steel frame (III-18), is inexpensive and quickly made, and has become one of the most successful chairs ever produced. His contract work has included seating for many public buildings, among them Royal Festival Hall (1951) and the Barbican Arts Centre (from 1968) in London. Other designs include aircraft interiors, exhibitions, appliances (for Pye), cutlery, and carpets. Designs for Hille won him the gold medal at the Milan Triennale in 1951, to which were since added six Design Council awards (*see* p. 40). Day was named a Royal Designer for Industry in 1959.

References: Edgar Kaufmann, Jr., *Prize Designs for Modern Furniture* (New York, 1950), pp. 34–41; Richard Carr, "Design Analysis: Polypropylene Chair," *Design*, no. 194 (Feb. 1965), pp. 33–39; Sutherland Lyall, *Hille: 75 Years of British Furniture* (London, 1981), *passim*; Fiona MacCarthy, *British Design since 1880* (London, 1982), figs. 146–47, 169, 178, 183.

Antoinette de Boer
German, born 1939

A student of MARGRET HILDEBRAND at the Hochschule für Bildende Künste in Hamburg (1957–61), de Boer became a textile designer for Stuttgarter Gardinenfabrik in 1963, and succeeded her teacher as its artistic director in 1975. Specializing in printed patterns, she believes that textile design should be proportionately related to architecture

and interior decoration, and for her brightly colored "Zimba" and "Zazi" (VII-11) series of 1969 she drew inspiration from the forms and colors of Italian interiors. De Boer founded her own firm in 1973.

References: "Antoinette de Boer et ses dessins de tentures aux tendances nouvelles," *Meubles et Décors* (Nov. 1969); "Textil-Design ist keine Kunst," *Meubles et Décors* (Apr. 1976).

Paolo Deganello
Italian, born 1940

Architect and furniture designer, Deganello completed his study of architecture at the university of Florence in 1966; between 1963 and 1974 he worked as an urban planner, and he has taught at the university of Florence, the Architectural Association in London (1971–72, 1974), and the university of Milan (1976). A theorist and founder of the radical ARCHIZOOM group (1966–1974), Deganello established in 1975 the "Collettivo Technici Progettisti" with Gilberto Corretti, an Archizoom associate (and others). If the self-conscious intellectualism of Archizoom's designs (for example, the "Mies" chair; III-6) has been replaced in Deganello's work by more practical concerns for function, the qualities of innovation and daring remain. Deganello recognizes a "widespread demand for subjectivity and the imaginary" and declares his belief "that it is this very same demand for the imaginary which must be incorporated in the productive process" (1981). Transposing these ideas into visual form, Deganello has created furniture (for Cassina) marked by color, decoration, radical shapes, and historicizing references (III-19).

Writings: Paolo Deganello, "Post-Modern Boulevard," *Domus*, no. 614 (Feb. 1981), pp. 9–10.

References: Cristina Morozzi, "Incastro simmetrico," *Modo*, no. 56 (Jan.–Feb. 1983), pp. 48–49; "Colloqui di Modo: Il progetto sulle spine," *Modo*, no. 57 (Mar. 1983), pp. 26–30.

De Pas, D'Urbino, Lomazzi
Italian, established Milan, 1966

An architecture and design firm whose image projected the unconventional attitudes of the 1960s, De Pas, D'Urbino, Lomazzi (Jonathan De Pas, Donato D'Urbino, Paolo Lomazzi, all born 1930s) gained a reputation for independence of thinking with their colored inflatable-plastic "Blow" chair (III-20) designed in

1967. It was further reinforced in 1970 with their witty but practical "Joe," a Pop leather chair in the form of a baseball glove (III-21). During the 1970s they focused on flexibility (III-22) and interchange-ability, especially in their modular foam seating and their plywood and plastic furniture and storage systems (for Driade, BBB Bonacina, Palina); but they have also designed more luxurious furniture (for Poltronova and Zanotta) and light fittings (for Stilnovo).

Writings: J. De Pas, D. D'Urbino, and P. Lomazzi, "I nuostri buoni propositi," in Milan, Museo Poldi Pezzoli, *Milano 70/70: Un secolo d'arte*, vol. 3, *Dal 1946 al 1970* (from May 30, 1972), pp. 166–67.

References: New York, Museum of Modern Art, *Italy: The New Domestic Landscape* (May 26–Sept. 11, 1972), pp. 34, 44, 57, 95, 114; Gerd Hatje, *New Furniture 11* (New York, 1973), nos. 103, 168–69, 354–55, 390–93, 424–25; Alfonso Grassi and Anty Pansera, *Atlante del design italiano: 1940–1980* (Milan, 1980), p. 299.

Freda Diamond
American, born 1905

A designer, consultant, and stylist whose inexpensive tableware and furniture brought "good taste" to the average consumer during the 1950s, Diamond was retained by Libbey glass in 1942 to survey the glassware market and offer a program for its postwar domestic production. Her sales-oriented recommendations—theme glassware in boxed sets sold through national advertising campaigns (some of which featured Diamond herself)—and her own designs proved successful for the company as it turned to automated production methods, which allowed it to sell its glasses widely at a reasonable price. Few of the many lines she originated were as simple and devoid of decoration as the "Classic Crystal" series of tumblers (II-15), which was included in the "Good Design" exhibition at the Museum of Modern Art in New York in 1950, but she repeatedly spoke out against the gaudy decorations then thought necessary for the sale of inexpensive merchandise. A graduate of Cooper Union in New York, Diamond served as advisor on design and marketing to many manufacturers and retailers.

Writings: Freda Diamond, *The Story of Glass* (New York, 1953).

References: "Designer for Everybody," *Life*, vol. 36 (Apr. 5, 1954), pp. 69–70; Carl U. Fauster, *Libbey Glass since 1818* (Toledo, 1979), pp. 100, 133, 140–41, 161, 186.

Karl Dittert
German, born Austria, 1915

Trained as a silversmith, Dittert has had his own industrial design firm in Schwäbisch-Gmünd since 1950. His work has ranged widely from office furniture systems to household products, notably in silver and in stainless steel, such as his nesting cooking set with burner (1960) for Kühn (V-8), his "Classica" kitchen cutlery series (1966) for Felix Gloria-Werk, and his food slicer (1981) for Ritter.

References: Graham Hughes, *Modern Silver throughout the World* (New York, 1967), nos. 83–86, 101; *Industrial Design*, vol. 28 (Nov.–Dec. 1981), p. 23.

Nanna Ditzel
Danish, lives in England, born 1923

Designer of furniture, metalwork, ceramics, and textiles, Ditzel has created a wide variety of objects distinguished by their rational planning and attention to surface texture. Trained at the School of Arts and Crafts (Kunsthånd-vaerkerskolen), Copenhagen, she opened her first design office with her husband Jørgen Ditzel in 1946, working in collaboration with him until his death in 1961. The Ditzels won numerous awards for their jewelry (for Michelsen and Jensen) and were the recipients of the Lunning Prize in 1956. Together they created an early, experimental modular furniture system with geometric blocks of polyester foam (1952), and during the 1950s and 1960s Ditzel herself designed furniture of strong, simple shapes, including a series of cane and basketwork chairs (for Wengler) that exploited the handsome fabriclike character of the material (III-23). Ditzel opened an office in London in 1970, continuing, however, to design for Danish firms. Her recent work includes furniture for Scandus (1976) and Kruger (1980), and a range of wooden tablewares for Den Permanente (1981). In 1981 she was named chairman of the Design and Industries Association, London.

Writings: Nanna Ditzel and Jørgen Ditzel, eds., *Danish Chairs* (Copenhagen, 1954).

References: Bent Salicath and Arne Karlsen, eds., *Modern Danish Textiles* (Copenhagen, 1959), pp. 28–29; "Nanna Ditzel: An Exhibition," *Interiors*, vol. 123 (Dec. 1963), pp. 102–3; "Thirtyfour Lunning Prize-Winners," *Mobilia* (special issue), no. 146 (Sept. 1967), n.p.; Washington, D.C., Renwick Gallery, *Georg Jensen—Silversmithy: 77 Artists 75 Years* (Feb. 29–July 6, 1980), nos. 25–29.

Henry Dreyfuss
American, 1904–1972

One of the pioneer American industrial designers and founders of the profession (with Norman Bel Geddes, RAYMOND LOEWY, and Walter Dorwin Teague), Dreyfuss designed a great deal of the American scene, from airplanes and plows to telephones and coffee cups, during a career that began in the late 1920s. Among his most-noted designs were transportation equipment, the *20th Century Limited*, the *Constitution* and her sister ship, the *Independence*, the interior of the Boeing 707 (for American Airlines); telephones (for Bell Laboratories; I-10); farm equipment (for John Deere); and numerous household appliances. Dreyfuss was a pioneer believer and experimenter in ergonomics, and the author of a popular account of the subject, *Designing for People* (1955), and of numerous technical charts published as *The Measure of Man* (1960). The latter included two life-size diagram-figures of "Joe and Josephine," the average man and woman, with meticulous measurements and plots of the human body's structure and movements. Throughout Dreyfuss's work there is a persistent interest in people and in relating all design projects to the human scale: "We bear in mind that the object being worked on is going to be ridden in, sat upon, looked at, talked into, activated, operated, or in some other way used by people individually or en masse. When the point of contact between the product and the people becomes a point of friction, then the industrial designer has failed. On the other hand if people are made safer, more comfortable, more eager to purchase, more efficient—or just plain happier—by contact with the product, then the designer has succeeded" (1955). Dreyfuss opened his first industrial design office in New York in 1928 and subsequently maintained offices both in New York and Pasadena. In 1969 he retired from the concern, which continued under the name of Henry Dreyfuss Associates.

Writings: Henry Dreyfuss, *Designing for People* (New York, 1955); Henry Dreyfuss, *Industrial Design: A Pictorial Accounting, 1929–1957* (New York, 1957); Henry Dreyfuss, *The Measure of Man* (New York, 1960).

References: "Henry Dreyfuss 1904–1972," *Industrial Design*, vol. 20 (Mar. 1973), pp. 37–43; Jeffrey L. Meikle, *Twentieth Century Limited: Industrial Design in America, 1925–1939* (Philadelphia, 1979), *passim*.

Nathalie du Pasquier
French, lives in Italy, born 1957

A self-taught artist, du Pasquier has designed textiles for clothing (for Rainbow) and furnishings (for Memphis, produced by Rainbow and Lipstick) in brilliant allover patterns (VII-12). Her work, more sophisticated for its seeming naïveté, is inspired by the intense colors and compositional freedom of the arts of Africa, India, and Australia, where she traveled for four years. She has also designed objects, and furniture for Memphis.

Reference: Barbara Radice, "Mosaici Morbidi," *Modo*, no. 54 (Nov. 1982), p. 68.

Charles Eames
American, 1907–1978

One of the most influential designers of the twentieth century, Eames had far-ranging achievements: films, toys, buildings, fabrics, machinery, exhibition and interior designs, and the revolutionary series of chairs for which he is best known. He studied architecture at Washington University in Saint Louis and in 1936 accepted a fellowship, and later a teaching post, at the Cranbrook Academy of Art in Bloomfield Hills, Michigan; among his colleagues there were FLORENCE KNOLL, HARRY BERTOIA, and EERO SAARINEN, who were to affect profoundly the development of Eames's career. With the help of Ray Kaiser (from 1941 his wife and partner), Eames and Saarinen collaborated on a molded-plywood chair with complex curves that won two first

prizes in the Museum of Modern Art's organic furniture competition in 1940. During the war the Eameses moved to southern California, where they continued their research on low-cost plywood molding techniques, and designed equipment for the Navy department based on these experiments. Out of this work came Eames's classic chair with separate molded-plywood back (III-24), which was exhibited along with his other plywood furniture at the Museum of Modern Art in New York in 1946 and produced shortly thereafter, first by Evans and then by Herman Miller. Eames's interest in new materials and techniques led to experiments with fiberglass-reinforced plastics and the development in 1948 of the one-piece fiberglass-shell chair (III-25), which was to be much admired at the Museum of Modern Art's International Competition for Low-cost Furniture Design, where it shared second prize. Other notable and influential chair designs by Eames include a group of wire-based furniture (1951), a lounge chair and ottoman in laminated rosewood (1956; III-26), and a die-cast aluminum lounge chair (1958). Equally influential was the house he designed for himself in 1949 in Pacific Palisades, California, a steel-frame building made with standard prefabricated parts. Throughout his career Eames was concerned with uniting utmost economy of means with intrinsic quality, and defined his job as "getting the most of the best to the greatest number of people for the least."

Writings: Charles Eames, "General Motors Revisited," *Architectural Forum*, vol. 134 (June 1971), pp. 21–27; Charles Eames, *A Computer Perspective* (Cambridge, Mass., 1973).

Monographs: Arthur Drexler, *Charles Eames: Furniture from the Design Collection* (New York, 1973); Los Angeles, Frederick S. Wight Art Gallery, University of California, *Connections: The Work of Charles and Ray Eames* (Dec. 7, 1976—Feb. 6, 1977); "Eames Celebration," *Architectural Design* (special issue), vol. 36 (Sept. 1966).

References: Don Wallance, *Shaping America's Products* (New York, 1956), pp. 177–81; London, Whitechapel Art Gallery, *Modern Chairs: 1918–1970* (July 22–Aug. 30, 1970), nos. 27, 30, 51, 74, 103.

Tias Eckhoff
Norwegian, born 1926

Designer of ceramics and metalwork, Eckhoff was trained as a potter at the National School of Crafts and Industrial Design (Statens Handvaerks- og Kunstindustriskole) in Oslo. He joined the Porsgrund porcelain works in 1949, serving as head designer from 1952 to 1957. He has since worked independently, while remaining as a consultant to the firm. During his years at Porsgrund, Eckhoff created a series of new products that earned him his first international honors (at the Milan Triennale in 1954, 1957, and 1960), and brought the factory considerable commercial success. In 1953 Eckhoff won first prize for silver cutlery ("Cypress") in Georg Jensen's inter-Scandinavian competition and launched his next considerable achievement in the field of flatware. Marked by disciplined economy of form and decoration, his designs include silver for Jensen, and stainless-steel tablewares, especially "Fuga" and "Opus" flatware for Dansk and "Maya" (V-9) for Norsk.

Writings: Tias Eckhoff, "Keramiske materialer i husholdningen," *Bonytt*, vol. 15 (1955), pp. 183–85.

Monograph: Alf Bøe, *Industridesigneren Tias Eckhoff* (Oslo, 1965).

Reference: Alf Bøe, *Porsgrunds porselaensfabrik: 1885–1965* (Oslo, 1965), *passim*.

Fritz Eichler
German, born 1911

Program director and member of the board of directors of Braun, Eichler was trained in art history and drama in Berlin and Munich (1931–35) and worked in theater design from 1945 to 1963. In 1954 he joined Erwin and ARTUR BRAUN in the direction of their family firm, and was responsible, with them, for commissioning a series of radio (I-6) and phonograph sets from the Hochschule für Gestaltung in Ulm. These sets established the formal characteristics of Braun design as balanced, ordered, and rational: "It was in 1955 at the Radio Exhibition in Düsseldorf that we presented an entire radio program in a 'revolutionary'-looking design (maybe it was at that).... Very concrete patterns set the style, and they were to become the basis for our future developments" (1980–81).

In his capacity as coordinator of the various Braun departments, Eichler has been responsible for the firm's highly consistent design policy and for the fact that Braun's corporate image is closely related to the character of its products.

References: "Braun's Guiding Light," *Design*, no. 180 (Dec. 1963), p. 61; Paris, Centre de Création Industrielle, *Qu'est-ce que le design?* (Oct. 24–Dec. 31, 1969), n.p.; Jocelyn de Noblet, *Design* (Paris, 1974), pp. 265–66; François Burkhardt and Inez Franksen, eds., *Design: Dieter Rams &* (Berlin, 1980–81), pp. 11–16.

Ekco Products Company
American, established Chicago, 1888

Long a manufacturer of rather ordinary kitchen tools, Ekco decided toward the end of the war to upgrade the look and quality of its merchandise. With no designer then on staff, the company turned to its own employees—engineers, moldmakers, marketing personnel, executives—for the concept and form the redesign would take. While a number of names (including engineers Myron J. Zimmer, James Chandler, and Walter Lueneberg; industrial designer James Hvale, who was hired in 1944; and the company head Arthur Keating) have been connected with the set of "Flint" kitchen tools introduced in 1946 (V-10), this must stand as an example *par excellence* of successful design by committee. Based on long experience with the product, the team retained the standard forms of the tools themselves, but introduced the flat shafts, riveted, black plastic handles, and polished surfaces that give this line its distinctive look. The tools were conceived as sets with a metal holder and packaged by RICHARD LATHAM, head designer for Raymond Loewy Associates in Chicago. Latham again worked with Ekco in the 1950s on product planning and marketing for Ekco's entire line of kitchen products.

References: Eliot Noyes, "The Shape of Things: Good Design in Everyday Objects," *Consumer Reports* (Jan. 1949), p. 27; "The Change at Ekco: Merchandising Bows to a Unique Planning Group," *Industrial Design*, vol. 3 (Oct. 1956), pp. 103–5; Don Wallance, *Shaping America's Products* (New York, 1956), pp. 129–31; Jay Doblin, *One Hundred Great Product Designs* (New York, 1970), no. 46.

Ergonomi Design Gruppen
Swedish, established Bromma, 1979

An amalgamation of two Swedish firms (Designgruppen and Ergonomi Design) founded in the late 1960s, the Ergonomi Design Gruppen creates and develops ergonomic products based on knowledge of the human body, its construction, patterns of movement, muscular functions, postures, and psychological reactions. The projects of this group are partly research and development assignments financed by state organizations (The Swedish Work Environment Fund, The National Board for Occupational Health and Safety) and partly commissions for manufacturing companies in such fields as mechanical engineering, building equipment, plastics (Gustavsberg), and medical technology. Achieving simple and practical solutions for industrial production, the fourteen-member group, one of the largest design offices in Sweden, has designed equipment for people with limited strength and movement ability (for example, combination cutlery for those with only one functioning hand; V-11) and printing and welding machinery that improves work patterns and reduces accident risks and unsuitable methods of use. Of the group, Maria Benktzon (Swedish, born 1946) and Sven-Eric Juhlin (Swedish, born 1940), both graduates of the Stockholm School of Arts, Crafts and Design (Konstfackskolan), have specialized in the design of technical aids for the handicapped (VI-1, 8). Before joining the group Juhlin worked as a plastics designer for Gustavsberg from 1967 to 1976.

References: Stockholm, Nationalmuseum, *Gustavsberg 150 år* (1975), nos. 302, 313–16, 318–20, 322–24, 332–34, 336, 338–39; Skien, Sweden, Ibsenhuset, *Aktuell Svensk Form* (Oct. 3–21, 1982), pp. 52–55.

L M Ericsson Company
Swedish, established Stockholm, 1876

In 1940 the L M Ericsson company, Sweden's first and largest manufacturer of telephone sets, decided to create a new table model for their international market, smaller and lighter than the conventional two-piece telephone. The single element telephone (I-11), with fewer components, simpler electrical connections, and smaller and lighter transmitter and receiver insets and induction coils, was designed and engineered over a fourteen-year period (1940–54) by Hugo Blomberg, Ralph Lysell, and Gösta Thames. The initial conception of the "Ericofon," which for three decades was the world's most popular one-piece set, was Blomberg's, assisted by Lysell. From 1949 Thames was responsible for the development of the telephone's design as well as its mechanical construction. Blomberg (Swedish, born 1897), who graduated from the technical university in Stockholm as an electrical engineer (1920), joined Ericsson in 1929 and served as head of the technical department and later chief engineer and head of development. Lysell (Swedish, born 1907) studied in the United States and worked there and in Germany as an industrial designer before joining Ericsson in 1939, where he worked until 1945. Thames (Swedish, born 1916), an engineer and designer, was employed by Ericsson from 1938 to 1981, serving as deputy technical manager of the telephone instrument engineering department.

Reference: Hugo Blomberg, "The Ericofon—The New Telephone Set," *Ericsson Review*, vol. 33, no. 4 (1956), pp. 99–109.

Vuokko Eskolin-Nurmesniemi
Finnish, born 1930

Trained as a ceramist at the Institute of Industrial Arts (Taideteollinen oppilaitos), Helsinki (1952), Eskolin-Nurmesniemi briefly designed ceramics and glass for Arabia and Nuutajärvi (winning a gold medal for glasswares at the Milan Triennale of 1957), but turned to textile design when she became associated with Marimekko (originally Printex) in 1953. As Marimekko's chief designer (1953–60) she was responsible for designing fabrics and clothing, adding a warm range of colors to the geometric prints first popularized by the firm (VII-13). During this period she also designed printed and woven fabrics for Borås (Sweden) and Pausa (Germany). In 1964 she founded the firm Vuokko, producing ready-to-wear clothing, accessories, and

textiles from her own designs. Her many awards include the grand prize at the Milan Triennale of 1964 (with her husband ANTTI NURMESNIEMI), the Lunning Prize (1964), and the Pro-Finlandia medal (1968).

References: "Thirtyfour Lunning Prize-Winners," *Mobilia* (special issue), no. 146 (Sept. 1967), n.p.; Marja Kaipainen, "Some Call Them Purists," *Form Function Finland*, no. 2 (1981), pp. 13–16; Charles S. Talley, *Contemporary Textile Art: Scandinavia* (Stockholm, 1982), pp. 136–38.

The Eureka Company
American, established Detroit, 1909

By 1927, through door-to-door sales, the Eureka company accounted for one-third of the vacuum cleaners sold annually in America. Specializing in versatile and lightweight machines, Eureka has depended on a large research and design department for innovations in the field, and today has some forty models available, including the "Mighty Mite" (I-12). Sleek and compact, and with a brightly colored plastic housing, it was developed by Eureka's chief industrial designer (since 1964), Samuel Hohulin (American, born 1936), with Kenneth Parker (American, born 1957).

Reference: Wolf von Eckardt, "Fashionable Is Not Enough," *Time*, vol. 121 (Jan. 3, 1983), pp. 76–77.

Federigo Fabbrini, *see* Villeroy & Boch

Elsa Fischer-Treyden
German, born Russia, 1901

Best known as a designer of ceramics and glass, in 1918 Fischer-Treyden moved from Russia to Berlin, where she worked as an independent textile designer and studied at the Hochschule für Bildende Künste under WILHELM WAGENFELD (1925–32). Awarded medals for metalwork at the Milan Triennale in 1951 and 1954, and for

porcelain at the Triennale of 1957, Fischer-Treyden began to work for Rosenthal in 1953, designing stoneware, porcelain, and glass. Her "Fuga" glass series (II-16) was awarded the Bundespreis "Gute Form" in 1969.

Reference: Hanover, Kestner-Museum, *Rosenthal: Hundert Jahre Porzellan* (Apr. 29–June 13, 1982), pp. 174–75, nos. 90, 103, 111–12.

Kaj Franck
Finnish, born 1911

One of this century's most influential designers of everyday ceramics and glass, Franck revolutionized the ceramic tablewares industry in 1952 with his inexpensive, multipurpose "Kilta" series (II-17). Franck has been responsible for the high artistic standards of utility wares, in glass (II-18, 19) as well as ceramics, combining originality and brilliant imagination in design with a fundamental understanding of industrial manufacture. Trained as an interior designer at the Institute of Industrial Arts (Taideteollisuuskeskuskoulu), Helsinki (1929–32), Franck designed lighting fixtures, furniture, and textiles until 1945, when he was employed by the Arabia ceramics factory; until 1977 he worked as a full-time designer and, sporadically, artistic director with the Wärtsilä group, comprising the Arabia ceramics factory, the Nuutajärvi glassworks, and production plants for sanitary porcelain and enamel. His first glasswares were designed in 1951, when the Nuutajärvi glassworks merged into the Wärtsilä group, and although a sometime designer of art glass, Franck concentrated on the production of utility wares, striving to combine economy with quality aesthetic design. His recognitions include a gold medal at Milan in 1951, a grand prize there in 1957, the Lunning Prize in 1955, and the Compasso d'Oro in 1957. Since his retirement from Wärtsilä in 1978, Franck has continued to teach and to work as an independent designer; his recent work includes a series of plastic bowls and plates for Sarvis.

Writings: Kaj Franck, "Finland," *Craft Horizons*, vol. 16 (July 1956), pp. 24–25; Kaj Franck, "Anonymity," *Craft Horizons*, vol. 27 (Mar. 1967), pp. 34–35; Kaj Franck, "The Arabia Art Department," *Ceramics and Glass*, nos. 1–2 (1973) pp. 47–57; Kaj Franck with Eeva Siltavuori, "Constructive Thinking in Finnish Design: Our Organic Heritage," *Form Function Finland*, no. 2 (1981), pp. 51–57.

References: Erik Zahle, ed., *A Treasury of Scandinavian Design* (New York, 1961), p. 273, nos. 207–9,

232–35, 325–28, 343–46; Helsinki, Finnish Society of Crafts and Design, *Finland: Nature, Design, Architecture* (1980–81), pp. 60–66.

Gianfranco Frattini
Italian, born 1926

Architect and interior and industrial designer, Frattini received his diploma from the Milan Politecnico in 1953 and worked in the office of GIO PONTI from 1952 to 1954. Establishing his own firm, he turned to industrial design when objects that would satisfy the requirements of his interiors were not available commercially. His designs have included lacquered wood, plastic, wicker, and upholstered furniture (for Bernini, Cassina, C & B Italia), metalware, as well as lighting (for Artemide), including the flexible "Boalum" (IV-14) in collaboration with LIVIO CASTIGLIONI.

Reference: Alfonso Grassi and Anty Pansera, *Atlante del design italiano: 1940–1980* (Milan, 1980), pp. 178, 224, 282.

Saburō Funakoshi
Japanese, born 1931

A graduate of the crafts division of the Tokyo University of Arts (1954), Funakoshi worked in the design department of the Shizuoka Prefectural Industrial Test Institute before joining the Hoya corporation as a glass designer in 1957. Presently head of Hoya's Musashi factory design department, Funakoshi has designed a wide variety of crystal objects for mass production by his company; these are generally simple in shape and structure and made both by hand and automation, including hand-pressed dishes with sand-blasted decoration (1976), geometrically rounded "capsules" (1981), and such useful wares as soy sauce bottles (II-20, 21). In 1969 an exhibition of Funakoshi's work was held at the Matsuya department store and in 1970 he was awarded the Osaka Design House prize.

References: Corning, N.Y., The Corning Museum of Glass, *New Glass: A Worldwide Survey* (Apr. 26–Oct. 1, 1979), p. 255, no. 63; Tokyo, Crafts Gallery, The National Museum of Modern Art, *Modern Japanese Glass* (Tokyo, 1982), no. 142; Tokyo, Crafts Gallery, The National Museum of Modern Art, *Contemporary Vessels: How to Pour* (Feb. 10–Mar. 22, 1982), nos. 189–90.

Bertel Gardberg
Finnish, born 1916

Known principally as a silversmith, jeweler, and designer of stainless steel, Gardberg is also a craftsman in wood and stone whose works preserve the nature of the materials he uses. His metalwork won him gold and silver medals at the Milan Triennale in 1954, 1957, and 1960 as well as the Lunning Prize in 1961. From 1966 to 1971 Gardberg served as artistic director of the Kilkenny Design Workshop in Dublin, working to revive the country's decorative arts and to promote craftsmanship in local workshops. Trained at the goldsmiths' school and the Institute of Industrial Arts (Taideteollisuuskeskuskoulu), Helsinki (1938–41), Gardberg maintained a studio in Helsinki between 1949 and 1966, where he modeled cutlery and stainless steel for industry (for Fiskars, Hopeatehdas, and Hackman; V-12), domestic and ecclesiastical silver, and wooden objects for Noormarkun Kotiteollisuus. Gardberg established a metal and woodworking studio at Pohja in southwest Finland in 1973, continuing the style of jewelry set with precious and semiprecious stones that he had developed in Ireland.

References: Erik Zahle, ed., *A Treasury of Scandinavian Design* (New York, 1961), p. 273, nos. 327, 343–44, 368, 374, 400–401, 405, 408, 410–11; John Haycraft, *Finnish Jewellery and Silverware* (Helsinki, 1962), pp. 38–47; Barbro Kulvik, "Craftsmanship Is a Way of Life," *Form Function Finland*, no. 1 (1983), pp. 34–39.

Gatti, Paolini, Teodoro
Italian, established Turin, 1965

Since 1965 Piero Gatti (born 1940), Cesare Paolini (born 1937), and Franco Teodoro (born 1939) have worked together as architects and industrial and graphic designers, concerned then as now with breaking down the confining structures of traditional living spaces and the restricting forms of standard furnishings. Perhaps no other example of postwar furniture is as universally adaptable as their "Sacco" chair (III-27). A leather bag without rigid internal structure, containing millions of tiny polystyrene beads, it adapts to any form, can be used in any position, is light and portable, and is sold at a low price.

References: London, Whitechapel Art Gallery, *Modern Chairs: 1918–1970* (July 22–Aug. 30, 1970), no. 94; Victor Papanek, *Design for the Real World* (New York, 1974), pp. 103–4.

Frank O. Gehry
American, born Canada, 1929

Like his buildings, which he views as sculptural objects and constructs of inexpensive and unexpected materials, the furniture Gehry designed in 1972 was both boldly plastic in form and made of an unusual substance—corrugated cardboard. A West Coast architect, Gehry studied architecture at the University of Southern California in Los Angeles (1954) and the Graduate School of Design at Harvard University in Cambridge, Massachusetts (1956–57), and has had his own design office in Los Angeles since 1962. The cardboard furniture, which he called "Easy Edges" (parodied in 1982 by his exhibition pieces "Rough Edges"), was extremely strong and versatile, adapted to both rectilinear and curvilinear (III-28) use. Produced in limited numbers in 1972, the series was reissued in 1982.

References: "Paper Currency," *Industrial Design,* vol. 19 (May 1972), p. 53; New York, Whitney Museum of American Art, *Shape and Environment: Furniture by American Architects* (New York, 1982), pp. 34–35, fig. 23.

Alexander Girard
American, born 1907

An architect specializing in interior and exhibition design, Girard is also known as a graphic artist and a designer of a wide variety of consumer products, most notably textiles (VII-14, 15), many of which were inspired by the visual richness, figural simplicity, and joyous spirit of his vast folk art collection. In his fabrics and wallpapers for Herman Miller (since 1952), his interiors such as that of the New York restaurant La Fonda del Sol (1959–60), and his corporate design program for Braniff airlines, including brightly painted planes (1965), Girard displays a keen feeling for color and ornament and an ability to orchestrate and manipulate textures and patterns. Trained as an architect in London and Rome, Girard practiced architecture in Florence before opening his own office in New York in 1932. In 1937 Girard moved to Detroit, where he executed important interior design commissions for the Ford (1943) and Lincoln motor companies (1946) and served as exhibition designer of "Design for Living" at the Detroit Institute of Arts (1949) and as color consultant for the General Motors Research Center (1951–52). In 1953 Girard settled permanently in Santa Fe, where among other projects he directed the fabric division of Herman Mil-

ler, which popularized his simple geometric patterns and vibrant colors for a wide American market.

Writings: Alexander H. Girard, *The Magic of a People* (1968).

References: "Out-Maneuvering the Plain Plane," *Interiors,* vol. 125 (Feb. 1966), pp. 99–105; Jack Lenor Larsen, "Alexander Girard," in *Nelson/ Eames/Girard/Propst: The Design Process at Herman Miller, Design Quarterly* (special issue), nos. 98–99 (1975), pp. 31–40, 61–62 (biblio.); Charles Lockwood, "A Perfectionist at Play," *Connoisseur,* vol. 212 (Jan. 1983), pp. 92–98.

Giorgetto Giugiaro
Italian, born 1938

With some two hundred employees, engineers, computer specialists, as well as designers, Giugiaro's firm, Ital Design (founded 1968), has developed a wide range of consumer and industrial products. Their well-conceived designs, from the viewpoint of both manufacture and use, include sports equipment, cameras, appliances (I-13), street furniture (for the city of Turin), and transportation, especially automobiles (recently, the Fiat "Panda"). Giugiaro himself studied at the Accademia di Belle Arti in Turin and began his career in the design department of Fiat. He left to work with the sports car designer Nuccio Bertone and then for Ghia, continuing his collaboration after the establishment of Ital Design, and creating, within seven years, some twenty-five cars, from Volkswagens to Maseratis.

References: Alfonso Grassi and Anty Pansera, *Atlante del design italiano: 1940–1980* (Milan, 1980), pp. 94, 243, 300; Steve Braidwood, "Taxi to Turin," *Design,* no. 386 (Feb. 1981), p. 27; Wolf von Eckardt, "Creation, Italian-Style," *Time,* vol. 119 (Feb. 22, 1982).

Giuliana Gramigna
Italian, born 1929

As an associate of the architect SERGIO MAZZA (since 1961), Gramigna has collaborated with him in the fields of interior architecture, furniture (for Cinova, Frau, and Full), lighting (for Quattrifolio), and industrial design. Independently, she has designed ceramics (for Gabbianelli), including wall tiles and the 1969 "Pomona" tableware serv-

ice (II-22). She has also served as editor of the architectural and interiors magazine *Ottagono* since its founding in 1966.

References: New York, Museum of Modern Art, *Italy: The New Domestic Landscape* (May 26–Sept. 11, 1972), pp. 35, 77; "Sergio Mazza e Giuliana Gramigna," *Interni,* no. 282 (Sept. 1978), pp. 54–57; Alfonso Grassi and Anty Pansera, *Atlante del design italiano: 1940–1980* (Milan, 1980), pp. 168, 290.

Kenneth Grange
British, born 1929

An industrial designer with an exceptional range of experience, Grange trained at the Willesden School of Arts and Crafts, and worked for several architects and designers before establishing his own firm in London in 1958. His design for consumers has been mainly in the areas of domestic appliances (for Ronson, Bendix, Kenwood; I-14), furniture, such small items as pens (for Parker) and disposable razors (for Wilkinson), and photographic equipment (for Kodak); but he has also worked on industrial products—transportation (for British Rail), office machinery, and furnishing systems. The recipient of eight Design Council awards, Grange received the Duke of Edinburgh's Prize for Elegant Design in 1963 for his "Courier" electric shaver (*see* p. 41), and was named a Royal Designer for Industry in 1969. Grange is a founder-partner of the Pentagram Design Partnership, established in 1972.

Monograph: London, The Conran Foundation, *Kenneth Grange at the Boilerhouse: An Exhibition of British Product Design* (May 1983).

Reference: Peter Gorb, ed., *Living by Design: Pentagram Design Partnership* (London, 1978), esp. pp. 224–83.

Viola Gråsten
Swedish, born Finland, 1910

One of Sweden's influential colorists and designers of printed textiles, Gråsten was trained at the Institute of Industrial Arts (Taideteollisuuskeskuskoulu), Helsinki. Her first works in Sweden were colorful, long-pile *rya* rugs that drew their inspiration from Finnish folk art. From 1945 to 1956 she designed both figurative and geometric pat-

terns for printed textiles for Nordiska in Stockholm (VII-16). From 1956 through the end of the next decade, she served as artistic director of Mölnlycke textiles in Göteborg; during the 1970s, as a freelance designer, Gråsten created prints for Borås and Kasthall.

References: Erik Zahle, ed., *A Treasury of Scandinavian Design* (New York, 1961), p. 174, nos. 143, 149, 302; Stockholm, The Swedish Institute, *Design in Sweden* (1972), p. 69.

Michael Graves
American, born 1934

Architect, painter, sculptor, and furniture designer, Graves was considered one of the "New York Five" architects during the early 1970s (with Richard Meier, John Hejduk, Peter Eisenman, and the partnership of Charles Gwathmey and Robert Siegel), each of whom in individual ways attempted to construct a new Post-Modern architectural language out of pure International Style forms. Inspired by classical and academic examples ranging from Roman triumphal arches to visionary French designs of the eighteenth century, Graves has moved away from the austere white formalism associated with the five architects toward an original, highly decorative style that is frankly symbolical and historicizing and which relies for its effect on color and ornament. Graves, with a degree from the Graduate School of Design at Harvard University (1959), has taught architecture at Princeton University since 1962, and until the construction of his first large architectural commission, the Public Services building in Portland, Oregon (1982), was known principally for his elegantly colored architectural fantasy drawings. Although furniture designs appear in Graves's sketchbooks of the 1970s and certain of his residential commissions included built-ins and custom pieces, his first furniture was produced independently only in 1980–81: the "Plaza" dressing table (for Memphis) and a table and chair series designed for Sunar. Borrowing form and decoration from sources as diverse as ordinary mass-produced tin-top tables of the 1930s and 1940s, the Wiener Werkstätte, and early nineteenth-century Neoclassical designs (III-29), Graves's furniture is similar in line

and color to his architecture, and offers the same rich eclecticism.

Monograph: *Michael Graves,* Architectural Monographs 5 (New York, 1979) (biblio.).

Reference: Paul Goldberger, "Architecture of a Different Color," *New York Times Magazine* (October 10, 1982), pp. 42–44, 48–52, 65–66.

Annika Gudmundsson
Swedish, born 1951

A student in the industrial design department of the university of Göteborg (1971–75), Gudmundsson joined the Industridesign Kunsult group in Göteborg in 1977, designing graphics and products in various mediums, including metal and plastic for Guldsmeds (V-13). Since 1981 she has worked as an industrial designer at Made Arkitektkontor in Stockholm.

Hans Gugelot
Swiss, born Indonesia, 1920–1965

Architect and industrial designer, Gugelot headed the department of product development at the Hochschule für Gestaltung in Ulm, West Germany, from 1955 until his death, and through the example of his teaching and the works he created for Braun, Bofinger, Pfaff, Kodak, and other firms, was chiefly responsible for the widespread influence of functionalism on mid-century design. Gugelot taught that a product should function well and display its function without disguise or ornamentation. One of his first commercially successful products, the combination radio and phonograph designed with DIETER RAMS (I-35), exhibits all the characteristics of style that were to become so firmly identified with Braun: logic of form, economy of materials, and function expressed with clarity. Gugelot was trained as an architect at the Eidgenössischen Technische Hochschule in Zurich (1946) and continued to practice architecture while designing for industry.

References: *Industrial Design Heute* (Hamburg, 1966), p. 100; Herbert Lindinger, "Was wir Hans Gugelot verdanken," in *Zeitgemässe Form: Industrial Design International* (Munich, 1967), pp. 204–5.

Eszter Haraszty
American, born Hungary, 1910s

Designer of fabrics, clothing, and interiors, Haraszty was director of Knoll textiles from 1949 to 1955, responsible for assembling the group of designers that made the firm's furnishing fabrics among the most innovative of the period. These included handwoven designs by MARIANNE STRENGELL and EVELYN HILL, which were translated into machine-loomed upholstery, and prints created for Knoll by ANGELO TESTA and imported from such Scandinavian designers as STIG LINDBERG, Sven Markelius, and ASTRID SAMPE. Haraszty's own designs (VII-17), including "Knoll Stripes" in 1951 and "Fibra" in 1953, were presented regularly in the Museum of Modern Art's "Good Design" exhibitions; in 1956 "Triad" won an A.I.D. International Design Award. Educated in Hungary, Haraszty established a screen-printing studio in Budapest in the 1930s, which she managed to re-open after the war; faced with the shortage of materials, she printed on sheets, window shades, and other salvage. In 1947 she came to the United States, working first as a consultant to Knoll; by 1958 Haraszty had opened an independent studio in New York.

References: "The Exhilarated World of Eszter Haraszty," *Interiors*, vol. 114 (May 1955), pp. 92–99; Eric Larrabee and Massimo Vignelli, *Knoll Design* (New York, 1981), pp. 92–93.

Marc Harrison
American, born 1936

An industrial designer trained at the Pratt Institute of Arts, New York, and the Cranbrook Academy of Art, Bloomfield Hills, Michigan (1959), Harrison has taught industrial design at the Rhode Island School of Design in Providence since 1959, specializing in ergonomics and human-factor engineering, concerns reflected in his product design. At the same time he has maintained an independent practice, particularly in the fields of medical and industrial equipment, where he holds patents for the Red Cross blood collecting system (1972), now widely used throughout the United States, and subway equipment designed for the Massachusetts Bay Transit Authority. Since 1978 Harrison has served as principal designer for Cuisinarts, and his redesign of that firm's food proc-

essing machine (I-15) is noteworthy for its consideration of the physically and visually impaired, with its large and prominent warning labels and controls that can be operated by gross motions.

Writings: Marc Harrison, "Design for the Donor," *Industrial Design*, vol. 20 (Nov. 1973), pp. 20–29.

Reference: "Product Portfolio," *Industrial Design*, vol. 28 (July–Aug. 1981), p. 20.

Cedric Hartman
American, born 1929

A designer of lighting and furniture, Hartman manufactures his own products in a small factory in Omaha. His floor lamp (IV-17), designed in 1966, has a counterbalanced base and a mirror-polished reflector that rotates effortlessly in a full circle for proper adjustment of light for reading.

Reference: "The 25 Best-Designed Products," *Fortune*, vol. 95 (May 1977), p. 271.

Edith Heath
American, born 1911

Trained as a painter and sculptor at the Art Institute of Chicago (1934–40), in 1941 Heath moved to California, where she studied ceramics at the California School of Fine Arts in San Francisco (1942) and ceramic chemistry at the Univeristy of California. Opening her own workshop at home, she began to experiment with pottery, producing (with a number of assistants) a line of hand-thrown dinnerware that was offered for sale in a San Francisco department store. In 1947 she gave up hand throwing each piece and (with her husband) established a small factory to manufacture the ovenproof "Coupe" stoneware service (II-23). Although much of the manufacturing process was organized for the production line, some elements, such as the

casserole handles, continued to be made by hand, while the variation in the muted glazes called attention to the handmade origins of the design. In 1960 Heath Ceramics entered the field of tile manufacture, supplying tiles for architectural construction, including the sheathing of the Pasadena Art Museum.

Writings: Edith Heath, "Pottery and Dinnerware," *Arts and Architecture*, vol. 66 (Sept. 1949), pp. 38–39.

Reference: Don Wallance, *Shaping America's Products* (New York, 1956), pp. 93–96.

Piet Hein
Danish, born 1905

Familiar throughout Scandinavia under his pen name Kumbel as the author of thousands of popular epigrammatic poems, which he calls "grooks" (*see* p. 120), Hein is also a mathematician, scientist, artist, and designer. Drawn into urban design in the 1960s as a consultant on the planning of the Sergels square in Stockholm, Hein projected its form as a "super-ellipse," a shape that mediates between oval and rectangle, which solved the problem of traffic patterns in the area. The success of this satisfying shape led to other applications—tables (III-48) and chairs (developed with BRUNO MATHSSON), lighting, metal (V-14), china, glass, and textiles.

References: Carl E. Christiansson, "Bruno Mathsson: Furniture Structures Ideas," *Design Quarterly*, no. 65 (1966), pp. 5–9; Washington, D.C., Renwick Gallery, *Georg Jensen—Silversmithy: 77 Artists 75 Years* (Feb. 29–July 6, 1980), nos. 48–49.

Poul Henningsen
Danish, 1894–1967

Industrial designer, architect, and writer, Henningsen is best known for the series of elegant and functional "PH" light fittings he developed for Poulsen from the mid-1920s. The series consists of a number of shades shaped and placed to conceal the bulb and to transmit, diffuse, and reflect the beam of light (IV-18, 19).

Henningsen served with Kaare Klint, one of the pioneers of functionalism in Denmark, as editor of *Kritisk Revy* (1926–28), where he attacked the artistic pretentiousness and lack of thought for practical use in the Danish ceramic and furniture industries. Trained at the Danish College of Technology (Danmarks Tekniske Højskole), Copenhagen, Henningsen practiced architecture in Copenhagen, designing houses, theater interiors, and part of the Tivoli gardens.

References: Erik Zahle, ed., *A Treasury of Scandinavian Design* (New York, 1961), p. 276, nos. 49–50; *Mobilia*, no. 295 (1980), pp. 14–17, and poster.

Robert Heritage
British, born 1927

A consultant designer who has produced notable models for Race furniture—including the technically innovative cast-aluminum "QE2" chair (1968–69)—Heritage has had his own design agency since 1953. His earlier furniture designs for Archie Shine followed the simple, understated tradition of his teacher at the Royal College of Art, R. D. Russell. Heritage has also designed cutlery (for Yote), high-tech lighting (IV-20), and appliances. He has won more Design Council Awards than any other person, and was named a Royal Designer for Industry in 1963. Since 1974 he has taught in the school of furniture design at the Royal College of Art, London, while retaining his own practice in partnership with his wife Dorothy.

References: Race Furniture Limited, "Race: Case Histories" (Submitted to the Royal Society of Arts . . . 1969), pp. 19–25; London, Whitechapel Art Gallery, *Modern Chairs: 1918–1970* (July 22–Aug. 30, 1970), no. 45; Fiona MacCarthy, *British Design since 1880* (London, 1982), figs. 184, 199, 208, 221.

Erik Herlow
Danish, born 1913

As architect of several official exhibitions of Danish design (Milan Triennale, 1951; "Design in Scandinavia," United States and Canada, 1954; "Formes Scandinaves," Paris, 1958), as co-founder of the Danish Industrial Design Society (1954), and as head of the industrial design department at the Royal Danish Academy of

Fine Arts (Kongelige Danske Kunstakademi), Copenhagen (since 1959), Herløw has been a strong force behind the development and recognition of industrial design in his country. His own work is primarily in metal, and includes jewelry, for Jensen (since 1959), and sterling-silver, stainless-steel, and aluminum cooking – and tablewares, for Michelsen (V-15), Dansk Aluminium, and Universal Steel ("Obelisk" cutlery, 1954). A graduate in architecture of the Royal Danish Academy of Fine Arts (1941), Herløw opened his own firm in 1945. He has served as artistic director for Royal Copenhagen porcelain since 1955.

References: Arne Karlsen, *Made in Denmark* (New York, 1960), pp. 13, 86–93, 114–15; Copenhagen, The Danish Society of Arts and Crafts and Industrial Design, *Contemporary Danish Design* (1960), pp. 17, 58, 87, 90–91, 94.

Sheila Hicks
American, lives in France, born 1934

Textile artist and designer, Hicks has been one of the most influential creators of wall hangings since the late 1960s, combining ancient weaving techniques with modern technology in her fiber reliefs. Hicks studied painting with Josef Albers, and later Rico Lebrun, at Yale University in New Haven (1954–58). Traveling and living in Mexico (1960–63), elsewhere in Central and South America, and in India (1966–67), Hicks began to weave, inspired both by traditional processes and by the constructivist principles of Albers. In South India she worked with a handloom factory to create commercial textiles, notably her "Badagara" (VII-18), a strong, double-sided cloth with thick meshes of cotton embedded in the weaving to give it deep relief; used as a wall covering, this cloth is still in production. In 1967 she established a studio in Paris, the Ateliers des Grands Augustins, but has continued to work and teach throughout the world in regions of traditional handcrafts, including Chile, Morocco, and Israel, where she has promoted local weaving production while remaining faithful to indigenous methods. At the same time, principally from her Paris studio, Hicks has created a number of large hangings and reliefs for such interiors as the main conference room of the Ford Foundation building, New York (1966–68, with WARREN PLATNER); the conference center for the United Arab League, Mecca, Saudi Arabia (1969); and the entrance of the CB 12 tower for IBM at La Défense, Paris (1972).

Monograph: Monique Lévi-Strauss, *Sheila Hicks* (New York, 1974).

Reference: Mildred Constantine and Jack Lenor Larsen, *Beyond Craft: The Art Fabric* (New York, 1973), pp. 172–93.

Marga Hielle-Vatter
German, born 1913

Educated in Dresden and Vienna, Hielle-Vatter has designed fabrics for her own mill since 1933. Awarded a silver medal at the Milan Triennale of 1957, she has specialized in weaving complex geometric patterns with long repeats, such as "Alcudia" (VII-19).

Reference: Jack Lenor Larsen and Jeanne Weeks, *Fabrics for Interiors* (New York, 1975), pp. 72–73.

Margret Hildebrand
German, born 1917

Educated at the Staatliche Kunstgewerbeschule in Stuttgart and at the Kunstschule für Textilindustrie in Plauen, Hildebrand served as design director of Stuttgarter Gardinenfabrik from 19ʳ6 to 1966. Adapting the functionalist lessons of integrity of design and materials to the realities of mass production, Hildebrand became Germany's best-known fabric designer in the early postwar years and was awarded a gold medal for her work (VII-20) at the Milan Triennale of 1954. Since 1966 she has taught textile design at the Hochschule für Bildende Künste in Hamburg.

Writings: Margret Hildebrand, "Der tapfere Käufer," in *Zeitgemässe Form: Industrial Design International* (Munich, 1967), pp. 109–11.

Monograph: *Margret Hildebrand, Schriften zur Formebung* (Stuttgart, 1952).

Evelyn Hill (Anselevicius)
American, born 1925

Textile artist and designer, Hill studied with Josef Albers at Black Mountain College in North Carolina, and at the Institute of Design in Chicago. During the 1950s she designed fabrics for Knoll and Cohama, introducing brilliant color combinations and wool and monofilament structures to commercial furnishing textiles (VII-21, 22): "There are no inhibiting factors regarding the use of pure color in fabric design. Color is used relatively, as it is in painting. Even radiant pinks and orange may be used if used in proportion to the surrounding space—and in relation to the surrounding colors. Colors often remind me of sounds—high and low, loud and soft" (1953). From the 1960s, as Evelyn Anselevicius, she worked as an independent weaver in San Miguel de Allende, Mexico, but recently moved to Albuquerque.

References: "Evelyn Hill," *Everyday Art Quarterly,* no. 25 (1953), pp. 18–19; Mildred Constantine and Jack Lenor Larsen, *Beyond Craft: The Art Fabric* (New York, 1973), pp. 108–11.

David Hills
American, born 1923

A graduate of the Pratt Institute of Arts, New York, Hills worked as a glass designer for Steuben from 1948 to 1952, creating more than twenty production pieces—vases, urns, candlesticks, pitchers, and glasses—and several examples of Steuben exhibition glass. His heavy blown-glass bud vase (II-24), with an air bubble trapped in its base, led Steuben's popular-priced line during the 1950s, and is still being produced today.

Reference: Mary Jean Madigan, *Steuben Glass: An American Tradition in Crystal* (New York, 1982), pp. 98, 101, 103, 196, 227–28, 262, 265, 267, 270, 274, 278, 279–80.

Pavel Hlava
Czechoslovakian, born 1924

Hlava studied glass techniques at the industrial training school for glassmaking in Železný Brod (1939–42) and at the Academy of Applied Arts in Prague (1943–48). His production includes both decorative and utilitarian designs in heavy glass (II-25), some with deeply cut or engraved decoration (techniques he has attempted to revive), brilliant colors, and in large-scale geometrical forms. From 1952 to 1958 he was associated with the Art Center for Glass Industry in Prague, and since then, with the Institute for Interior and Fashion Design. He has also designed glass tableware for the Rosenthal Studio Line (since 1969).

References: Frankfort, Museum für Kunsthandwerk, *Modernes Glas* (May 15–June 27, 1976), p. 181, nos. 191-95; Corning, N.Y., The Corning Museum of Glass, *Czechoslovakian Glass: 1350–1980* (May 2–Nov. 1, 1981), p. 167, nos. 106, 120–21.

Knud Holscher
Danish, born 1930

Holscher completed architectural studies at the Royal Danish Academy of Fine Arts (Kongelige Danske Kunstakademi), Copenhagen (where he has taught since 1968), and for five years was associated with ARNE JACOBSEN, acting as supervising architect for his St. Catherine's College project in Oxford (1960–64). He has won numerous competitions for schools, universities, sports pavilions, and town centers throughout Scandinavia and abroad. His design work has included lines of sanitary fittings and hardware (his "Modric" series, with Alan Tye, won several British design awards in 1966), lighting (for Følsgaard), and metalwork (for Georg Jensen, beginning 1974; V-16). Since 1967 he has been a partner in the architecture and design firm of Krohn & Hartvig Rasmussen.

References: "'Modric' Architectural Ironmongery," *Design,* no. 209 (May 1966), pp. 36–37; Washington, D.C., Renwick Gallery, *Georg Jensen—Silversmithy: 77 Artists 75 Years* (Feb. 29–July 6, 1980), nos. 54–55.

Saara Hopea
Finnish, born 1925

After studying interior design at the Institute of Industrial Arts (Taideteollisuuskeskuskoulu) in Helsinki (1943–46), Hopea worked as an independent designer of interiors (1946–49), furniture (for Majander, 1946–48), and lighting (for Taito, 1948–52). In 1952 she joined the Nuutajärvi glassworks as assistant to KAJ FRANCK, designing decorative and utility glassware (including the earliest Finnish nesting series, in mold-blown glass in various colors, 1951; II-26); she also worked in ceramics under Franck for Arabia, another company in the Wärtsilä group. Since 1967, after living abroad for seven years, she has concentrated on jewelry design and enameling for her family firm Ossian Hopea (in Porvoo), for which she is also artistic director. Hopea won silver medals at the Milan Triennale in 1954 and 1957 for her glassware, and a diploma of honor in 1960 for jewelry design.

References: "15 Contemporary Finnish Designers," *Design Quarterly* (special issue), no. 37 (1957), pp. 12–13; Tuula Koli, "Saara Hopea-Untracht—Tapio Yli-Viikäri," *Form Function Finland,* no. 3 (1982), pp. 12–14; New York, Cooper-Hewitt Museum, *Scandinavian Modern Design: 1880–1980* (Sept. 14, 1982—Jan. 2, 1983), nos. 173, 329.

Suzanne Huguenin
Swiss, born 1930s

Head of Knoll textiles from 1955 to 1963, Huguenin joined the firm in 1952 as apprentice-assistant to ESZTER HARASZTY, whom she succeeded as division director. Huguenin was responsible for developing the upholstery fabric known as "Nylon Homespun" (VII-23)—an exceptionally strong cloth with a homespunlike texture, actually made with nylon carpet yarns, which until then had been available only in filament yarns and with a slick and shiny appearance. Since 1964 Huguenin has worked as an independent textile consultant with studios in both New York and Mensingen, Switzerland.

Reference: Eric Larrabee and Massimo Vignelli, *Knoll Design* (New York, 1981), p. 93.

Peter Hvidt
Danish, born 1916

Architect and furniture designer, Hvidt was trained as a cabinet-maker and designer at the School of Arts and Crafts (Kunsthandvaerkerskolen) in Copenhagen, where he later taught (1942–45). In 1944 Hvidt opened an office in partnership with ORLA MØLGAARD-NIELSEN, designing furniture for such firms as Fritz Hansen, France, and Søborg. In 1950 Hvidt and Mølgaard-Nielsen developed the "Ax" series of chairs and tables (III-31), which pioneered the use of both laminate glueing (a process borrowed from tennis rackets) and knock-down construction in Danish furniture production. The "Ax" series did much to establish the international reputation of Danish mass-produced (as opposed to handcrafted) furniture; it was exhibited in 1951 in the "Good Design" exhibition at the Museum of Modern Art in New York and won the firm diplomas of honor at the Milan Triennale in 1951 and 1954.

References: Esbjørn Hiort, *Danish Furniture* (New York, 1956), pp. 11–12, 86–93; Erik Zahle, ed., *A Treasury of Scandinavian Design* (New York, 1961), p. 277, nos. 40–41; London, Whitechapel Art Gallery, *Modern Chairs: 1918–1970* (July 22–Aug. 30, 1970), no. 75.

I. D. Two
American, established Palo Alto, 1979

Founded as a California branch of Bill Moggridge's London-based industrial design firm, Design Developments, I. D. Two has specialized in computer design, counting among its American clients Grid Systems, Conversion Technologies, and Decision Data. The "Compass" computer, which I. D. Two designed for Grid in 1982 (I-16), was one of the first portable computers on the market, a high-density unit housed in a lightweight magnesium case. Moggridge (British, born 1943) was trained at the Central School of Art and Design, London (1965), and opened his own office in 1969, designing scientific and consumer products for Hoover, Pitney Bowes, and American Sterilizer. In 1977 Moggridge established Industrial Design Models in London to produce models and prototypes, and in 1979 founded Design Developments, under which I. D. Two and Industrial Design Models now operate. Stephen Hobson (American, born 1942), a principal in the firm, studied at Stanford University (1969) and worked for Norse Micrographics, Coates & Welter, and Hewlett-Packard before joining I. D. Two in 1980 as project coordinator.

References: London, Central School of Art and Design, *Central to Design, Central to Industry* (1983), pp. 95–96; ''The Compass Computer: The Design Challenges Behind the Innovation,'' *Innovation* (Winter 1983), pp. 4–8.

Vittorio Introini
Italian, born 1935

A graduate of the school of architecture of the Milan Politecnico (1961), where he now teaches, Introini is an architect, city planner, and industrial designer. Since 1963 he has worked with Saporiti, and later also with its affiliate, Proposals, designing furnishings —the steel component library system (III-32)—as well as their showrooms (Saporiti, New York, 1975).

References: Enrichetta Ritter, *Design italiano mobili* (Milan, 1968), p. 175; ''Saporiti Italia on Fifth Avenue,'' *Interior Design,* vol. 47 (Feb. 1976), pp. 142–43.

Fujiwo Ishimoto
Japanese, lives in Finland, born 1941

Trained as a graphic designer at the National University of Arts in Tokyo, Ishimoto designed textiles for Ichida from 1964 to 1970. In 1971 he went to Finland, and since 1974 has created printed fabrics for Marimekko. His early work was generally restricted to black and white; while his geometric patterns recalled the example of MAIJA ISOLA, they were distinguished by visible brushstrokes in the manner of calligraphy. By the early 1980s Ishimoto's prints were both more subtly colored and distinctly Japanese in feeling, but in such series as his ''Landscapes'' (1983), he also drew inspiration from the Finnish countryside (VII-24).

References: ''Marimekko Oy,'' *Domus,* no. 599 (Oct. 1979), pp. 76–77; Ullamaria Pallasmaa, ''The Spirit of Things,'' *Form Function Finland,* nos. 3–4 (1981), pp. 22–30; Bella Obermaier, ''Castle of the Winds,'' *Mobilia,* no. 298 (1981), pp. 25–32; Marja-Terttu Vuorimaa, ''Marimekko Exports Know-How,'' *Form Function Finland,* no. 2 (1983), pp. 10–11.

Maija Isola
Finnish, born 1927

Painter and designer of printed textiles, Isola was educated at the Institute of Industrial Arts (Taideteollisuuskeskuskoulu), Helsinki, and in 1949 joined Printex, where she created many of the bold, brightly colored patterns that gained the firm's distinctive international recognition in the 1950s and 1960s. Using ordinary cotton sheeting, she gave the strong, inexpensive material remarkable elegance through her silkscreen-printed designs, both in the furnishing fabrics of Printex and, from 1951, in the clothing of Marimekko. Isola's earliest works were nonfigurative prints, embodying huge abstract designs (VII-25, 26), followed by a series of more densely patterned ornamental prints reflecting both Byzantine decorations and traditional folk motifs of Karelia, in eastern Finland. These fabrics anticipated the folk-inspired patterns and peasant-derived styles popular in textile design during the 1970s.

References: Erik Zahle, ed., *A Treasury of Scandinavian Design* (New York, 1961), p. 277, nos. 193, 197–99; David Davies,''Fabrics by Marimekko,'' *Design,* no. 236 (Aug. 1968), pp. 28–31; ''Marimekko Oy,'' *Domus,* no. 599 (Oct. 1979), pp. 76–77; Charles S. Talley, *Contemporary Textile Art: Scandinavia* (Stockholm, 1982), pp. 130–31.

Arne Jacobsen
Danish, 1902–1971

Jacobsen approached design through his architecture, the simply stated International Style structures (built often, however, of traditional materials) that brought him to a leading position among Scandinavian architects in the 1950s. His vision—even the first buildings he designed after graduating from the school of architecture of the Royal Danish Academy of Fine Arts (Kongelige Danske Kunstakademi), Copenhagen, in 1928—took in every detail, including furnishings, and many of the objects for which he is now so well known (III-34, 35) were originally conceived for a specific interior. He achieved his most complete statement of the integration of architecture, interior furnishings, and utilitarian objects in the glass-sheathed S.A.S. Air Terminal and the Royal Hotel, Copenhagen (1959). About 1950 he also began to design furnishings for larger-scale factory production; his earliest product (and still his most successful), the 1951 three-legged stacking chair in plywood and steel (III-33), was conceived with the total consideration for materials and industrial techniques and the close rapport with its manufacturer that would characterize his furniture (for Fritz Hansen), lighting (for Louis Poulsen; IV-21), silver and stainless steel (for Stelton and Michelsen; V-17), and textiles (for Grautex, Aug. Millech, and C. Olesen) throughout his career. His ''Cylinda Line'' hollow ware (V-18) and his ''Vola'' bathroom fittings (for I. P. Lunds) won the Danish ID prize in 1967 and 1969, respectively.

Monographs: London, Royal Institute of British Architects, *Arne Jacobsen: Architecture, Applied Art* (Feb. 25–Mar. 25, 1959); Tobias Faber, *Arne Jacobsen* (New York, 1964); Poul Erik Shriver and E. Waade, *Arne Jacobsen* (Copenhagen, 1976).

References: Arne Karlsen, *Made in Denmark* (New York, 1960), pp. 94–103, 147; ''Arne Jacobsen: Immeuble de la S.A.S. à Copenhague,'' *L'Architecture d'Aujourd'hui,* nos. 91–92 (1960), pp. 56–62; Rebecca Tarschys and Henry End, ''Arne Jacobsen: From Stainless Flatware to the Royal Hotel in Copenhagen,'' *Interiors,* vol. 122 (Oct. 1962), pp. 112–21; The Danish Society of Industrial Design, *ID Prizes 1965–1969* (Copenhagen, 1970), pp. 38–39, 42–43.

Jakob Jensen
Danish, born 1926

Jensen has been a designer of audio equipment for Bang & Olufsen since the late 1960s. He conceived its distinctive and very successful marketing image, and implied through the sleek, refined lines of its products, a sense of the company's high performance standards and engineering advances (such as the now widely used tangential pick-up arm, introduced in the ''Beogram 4000'' in 1972; I-18). His ''Beosystem 1200'' (I-17)—radio/amplifier, record player, and tape recorder components—won the Danish ID prize in 1969, when the judges commented that in its form, materials, and graphic style it achieved a fine balance between ''apparatus'' and ''furniture.'' A graduate of the School of Arts and Crafts (Kunsthåndvaerkerskolen) in Copenhagen (1952), where he studied industrial design, Jensen served as chief designer under SIGVARD BERNADOTTE from 1952 to 1959. While working in Chicago and teaching at the University of Illinois (1959–61), he joined with RICHARD LATHAM and several others in an international design firm, opening a Copenhagen office on his return in 1961.

References: Svend Erik Moller, ''A Non-Specializing Specialist,'' *Danish Journal,* vol. 76 (1973), pp. 30–32; Jens Bernsen, *Design: The Problem Comes First* (Copenhagen, 1982), pp. 90–95.

Søren Georg Jensen
Danish, born 1917

Sculptor and silversmith, Jensen was the second youngest son of the noted silversmith Georg Jensen and apprenticed in 1936 in the firm founded by his father. He studied sculpture at the Royal Danish Academy of Fine Arts (Kongelige Danske Kunstakademi), Copenhagen (1945), and while traveling on fellowships to France and Italy. Jensen has pursued his interests in both sculpture and silverwork, heading the design department of Jensen from 1962 until 1974, when he retired to devote full time to his sculpture. His utilitarian wares demonstrate the sculptor's concern for strong, geometric shapes (V-19).

References: Graham Hughes, *Modern Silver throughout the World* (New York, 1967), no. 19; Washington, D.C., Renwick Gallery, *Georg Jensen—Silversmithy: 77 Artists 75 Years* (Feb. 29–July 6, 1980), nos. 82–84.

Willy Johansson
Norwegian, born 1921

Son of a craftsman at the Hadelands glassworks, Johansson followed the trade of his father, entering the firm's glassmaking workshop in 1936. He remained there throughout his career, except for the years 1939–42, when he studied at the National School of Crafts and Industrial Design (Statens Håndvaerks- og Kunstindustriskole), Oslo. Art director since 1947, Johansson has designed unique works and production pieces in pressed and blown glass, whose simple outlines are given authority by their solidity of form (II-27). His best-known works are of clear or smoked glass, finished with a white rim, his ''trademark.''

References: ''Revolution in Scandinavian Design: Willy Johansson,'' *Craft Horizons,* vol. 18 (Mar. 1958), p. 32; Eileene Harrison Beer, *Scandinavian Design: Objects of a Life Style* (New York, 1975), pp. 116–18, 120.

Lisa Johansson-Pape
Finnish, born 1907

Interior designer and exhibition architect, Johansson-Pape was trained at the Institute of Industrial Arts (Taideteollisuuskeskuskoulu) in Helsinki (1927). Working as a furniture and textile designer, and as an interior designer for Stockmann from 1937, Johansson-Pape became designer for the Stockmann-Orno lamp company in 1949, developing the specialization in light fittings for which she is best known. Rational in form and executed in practical modern materials— ''When we started out, there was just wood, yarn, and clay, but soon there was a flood of materials. . . . Industry gave us unlimited scope for experimentation with different colors and materials'' (1982)—her lamps in acrylic and metal (IV-22) were awarded medals at the Milan Triennale in 1951, 1954, and 1960.

References: Erik Zahle, ed., *A Treasury of Scandinavian Design* (New York, 1961), p. 278, nos. 99, 101; Marja Kaipainen, ''Lisa Johansson-Pape—Lauri Anttila,'' *Form Function Finland,* no. 3 (1982), pp. 6–11.

Finn Juhl
Danish, born 1912

It was through Juhl that Danish design first came to international attention in the late 1940s, although the sculptural forms and abstract patterns of his furniture were quite distinct from the functionally defined designs of his well-known countrymen HANS WEGNER and ARNE JACOBSEN. After studying architecture under Kaare Klint at the Royal Danish Academy of Fine Arts (Kongelige Danske Kunstakademi) in Copenhagen, Juhl, in 1937, began a longstanding collaboration with the cabinetmaker Niels Vodder, who superbly handcrafted his furniture (III-36); their pieces consistently won prizes in the Copenhagen Cabinetmakers' Guild exhibitions over the next decade. His seating was particularly innovative, for example, what appear to be "floating" seats, suspended not on the frame but on one or two crossbars (III-37). In 1951 Baker introduced in the United States a wide range of Juhl-designed furniture, mass-produced but crafted to the designer's standards and shown at the "Good Design" exhibitions in New York and Chicago; other lines were later issued in Europe by Bovirke and France. Juhl has designed houses and interiors, including the Trusteeship Council Chamber at the United Nations building in New York (1951), as well as glassware (for Jensen), porcelain (for Bing & Grøndahl), appliances, lighting, carpets (for Unika-Vaev), and a series of handsomely carved wooden bowls for Bojesen (VIII-5).

References: Edgar Kaufmann, "Finn Juhl of Copenhagen," *Interiors,* vol. 108 (Nov. 1948), pp. 96–99; "Finn Juhl," *Interiors,* vol. 110 (Sept. 1950), pp. 82–91; "Finn Juhl," *Interiors,* vol. 111 (Nov. 1951), pp. 84–93; George Nelson, ed., *Chairs* (New York, 1953), pp. 30–31, 96–101, 156; Esbjørn Hiort, *Danish Furniture* (New York, 1956), pp. 8–9, 52–65; Enzo Frateili, "Finn Juhl: Architect and Designer," *Zodiac,* no. 5 (1960), pp. 106–15.

Sven-Eric Juhlin, *see* Ergonomi Design Gruppen

Dora Jung
Finnish, 1906–1980

Weaver and textile designer, Jung specialized in damask weaving, both in production patterns for Tampella and in the individual tapestries and curtains she created for such interiors as those of the National Bank of Finland, the Finnish National Theater, and Finlandia Hall, in Helsinki. She developed new tools and techniques to create hitherto unknown effects in damask, including the use of full-scale cartoons, changes in the structure of the loom itself, and variations in the color and texture of yarns, which created different fields in the same pattern. Trained at the Institute of Industrial Arts (Taideteollisuuskeskuskoulu), Helsinki, Jung established her own studio in Helsinki in 1932. Her first international success came at the Paris international exhibition in 1937, where she was awarded a gold medal; during the 1950s she received three grand prizes at the Triennale in Milan (1951, 1954, 1957). Among her award-winning fabrics was "Linenplay" (1957; VII-27), a machine-woven damask linen, which, with bleached warp and black weft, is characteristic of Jung's discreet and refined color treatment and precise and economical design.

References: Benedict Zilliacus, *Finnish Designers* (Helsinki, 1954), n.p.; Erik Zahle, ed., *A Treasury of Scandinavian Design* (New York, 1961), p. 279, nos. 123–25, 127, 181–82, 344, 408; Eeva Siltavuori, "I Never Tire of Watching a Gull's Glide," *Form Function Finland,* no. 2 (1981), pp. 58–63; Enid Marx, [Obituary], *Journal of the Royal Society for the Encouragement of Arts, Manufactures and Commerce* (Mar. 1981), p. 264; Charles S. Talley, *Contemporary Textile Art: Scandinavia* (Stockholm, 1982), pp. 107–13.

Arne Jon Jutrem
Norwegian, born 1929

Trained as a painter and graphic artist at the National School of Crafts and Industrial Design (Statens Håndvaerks- og Kunstindustriskole) in Oslo, and in Paris with Fernand Léger (1952), Jutrem designed graphics, furniture, textiles and carpets, ceramics, metalwork, and principally glass from 1950 to 1967. His work as a staff designer at the Hadelands glassworks (1950–62), along with WILLY JOHANSSON and HERMANN BONGARD, and as a freelance designer for Holmegaard in Copenhagen (1962–64) encompassed a range of decorative and utilitarian glass—vases (II-28), bowls, plates, pitchers, stemware—with engraved decoration, strong colors, or muted, matte finishes. Jutrem was awarded a gold medal for his glassware at the Milan Triennale in 1954 and the Lunning Prize in 1959. In the late 1960s he returned to painting as a full-time occupation.

Monograph: Oslo, Kunstindustrimuseum, *Arne Jon Jutrem* (Aug. 23–Sept. 16, 1979).

Reference: "Thirtyfour Lunning Prize-Winners," *Mobilia* (special issue), no. 146 (Sept. 1967), n.p.

Wilhelm Kåge
Swedish, 1889–1960

A designer at Gustavsberg from 1917 to 1960 (and chief artist until 1949), Kåge had perhaps more influence on Swedish ceramics of this century than any other artist. Trained as a painter and known as a poster designer, Kåge was brought to Gustavsberg by the Swedish Association of Arts and Crafts (Svenska Slöjdföreningen) in its crusade for the beautification of everyday objects through the employment of artists in industry. His tablewares set standards for Swedish ceramics; he introduced stacking china, heat-treated dinnerware, simple functionalist forms, and open-stock purchasing—and many of his services were made for those with modest incomes. Among the art pottery that Kåge designed concurrently for production was his own type of molded stoneware, heavy forms showing strong Chinese and Mexican influence (II-29), which he called "Farsta" after the island on which Gustavsberg is located.

Monographs: Nils Palmgren, *Wilhelm Kåge: Konstnär och Hantverkare* (Stockholm, 1953); Stockholm, Nationalmuseum, *Wilhelm Kåge, Gustavsberg* (Apr. 17–May 14, 1953).

References: Stockholm, Nationalmuseum, *Gustavsberg 150 år* (1975), *passim;* New York, Cooper-Hewitt Museum, *Scandinavian Modern Design: 1880–1980* (Sept. 14, 1982–Jan. 2, 1983), nos. 73–74, 102–4, 132, 134, 161.

Katavolos-Littell-Kelley
American, established New York, 1949–1955

In 1949 three graduates of the Pratt Institute of Arts in New York, William Katavolos (American, born Greece, 1924), Ross Littell (American, born 1924), and Douglas Kelley (American, born c. 1924), began a six-year partnership designing furniture, textiles, and dinnerware for Laverne Originals (*see* ERWINE AND ESTELLE LAVERNE). Working as a team, they conceived the "New Furniture Group," chairs and tables in leather, chrome, glass, and marble. Their elegant "T" chair (1952; III-38), a three-legged dining chair made of four T-shaped elements, shows their concern for logic of structure and unity of form. Their furniture was shown in the "Good Design" exhibitions at the Museum of Modern Art in New York in 1953 and 1955, and won the A.I.D. award for the best furniture design in the United States in 1952. Textiles for Laverne by Littell and by Katavolos were also shown in the "Good Design" exhibitions.

References: "Good Design," *Interiors,* vol. 113 (Aug. 1953), pp. 88–89, 146–48; Roberto Aloi, *Mobili tipo* (Milan, 1956), pp. 97, 121, 187, 216; Clement Meadmore, *The Modern Chair* (New York, 1975), pp. 98–101.

Perry King
British, born 1938

Concerned principally with graphics and typeface design, King has been design coordinator for the corporate identity service of Olivetti since 1972. After studying at the Birmingham College of Art, he became a consultant for Olivetti in 1965, collaborating with ETTORE SOTTSASS, JR. (until 1970) on the design of office equipment and furniture (including the "Valentine" typewriter; I-47). Since 1977 he has worked with Santiago Miranda in Milan; together they have designed graphics, furniture ("Cable," an office system for Marcatrè), and industrial and home lighting (many with Giancarlo Arnaldi, for Flos and Arteluce), and have thoughtfully considered their own role in the design process: "A particular design for a light fitting can slot nicely into somebody's environment and life-style, it can modify them, or it can simply have no effect. But design clearly must comprehend not only technology and economics, but sociology, too. This leads us to the conclusion that designers must have a political or philosophical model on which to base their work—something which can at the very least explain the mismatch between their aims and their achievements" (1983).

References: "Due nuove macchine per scrivere," *Domus,* no. 475 (June 1969), pp. 35–38; "When Is a Dot not a Dot?," *Design,* no. 317 (May 1975), p. 22; Los Angeles, Frederick S. Wight Art Gallery, University of California, *Design Process Olivetti 1908–1978* (Mar. 27–May 6, 1979), p. 260, and *passim;* James Woudhuysen, "Priests at Technology's Altar," *Design,* no. 410 (Feb. 1983), pp. 40–42.

Robert King
American, born 1917

A student of silversmithing and enameling at the School for American Craftsmen at the Rochester Institute of Technology (1947–49), King joined Towle silversmiths in 1949 as a designer, working first on the models of flatware in a contemporary style that would be issued in 1951 as the "Contour" line (V-20). He designed cutlery and hollow ware at Towle until 1962, when he began to work for International Silver (until 1977), continuing throughout this time to create handcrafted jewelry, enamels, and silver table pieces.

Reference: Lee Nordness, *Objects: U.S.A.* (New York, 1970), p. 178.

Toshiyuki Kita
Japanese, born 1942

Furniture and interior designer, Kita studied at the University for Design in Osaka and in 1964 opened an independent design office there. After traveling in Italy (where he collaborated with Silvio Coppola, Bepi Fiori, and Giotto Stoppino for Bernini), Kita began to design furniture that combined both traditional Japanese and European forms with a new boldness of expression and vibrant use of color, as in his "Wink" chair for Cassina (III-39). In 1975 Kita was awarded the Japan Interior Design prize for his furniture.

Reference: "Arredi su dimensioni modulari," *Ottagono,* no. 38 (Sept. 1975), pp. 110–15.

Poul Kjaerholm
Danish, 1929–1980

Designer of furniture and interiors, Kjaerholm studied at the School of Arts and Crafts (Kunsthandvaerkerskolen) in Copenhagen (1949). Despite his traditional training as a cabinetmaker, Kjaerholm designed furniture exclusively for industrial production (for E. Kold Christensen), combining stainless- or chromed-steel frames with natural materials—woven cane, canvas, leather, wood, and rope. Like the Bauhaus designers with whom he is sometimes compared, Kjaerholm was uncompromising in his insistence on structural clarity and technical quality. However, his personal concern for comfort and everyday use—the pliant wickerwork in a version of his 1956 chair (III-40) is deliberately thickened at the back and edge of the seat to pad the stiff steel rails—did much to domesticate and popularize the austere functionalist style with which he was associated. His distinctions have included the grand prize at the Milan Triennale of 1957 and the Lunning Prize in 1958.

References: London, Whitechapel Art Gallery, *Modern Chairs: 1918–1970* (July 22–Aug. 30, 1970), nos. 34, 38, 88, 118; "One Hundred Great Danish Designs," *Mobilia* (special issue), nos. 230–33 (Dec. 1974), nos. 12–14; Per Mollerup, "Poul Kjaerholm's Furniture," *Mobilia*, nos. 304–5 (1982), pp. 1–24.

Esben Klint
Danish, 1915–1969

Son of the furniture designer and theorist Kaare Klint, Esben studied at the Royal Danish Academy of Architecture, Copenhagen, trained with several Danish and Swedish architecture firms, and worked as an industrial designer for Philips in the Netherlands (1938–39). Among his industrial designs was a project for school furniture with BØRGE MOGENSEN (1962) and folded-paper lighting (IV-23) for the small family firm Le Klint. The firm, begun in the 1940s, developed a sort of local art form based on turn-of-the-century prototypes that generated models from many members of the family and other designers.

References: Arne Karlsen, *Furniture Designed by Børge Mogensen* (Copenhagen, 1968), pp. 116–19; Svend Hansen, "Le Klint," *Mobilia*, no. 206 (1972), n.p.

Florence Schust Knoll
American, born 1917

Furniture and interior designer, Knoll was a pioneer in American furniture manufacture during the 1950s and 1960s. As a partner in Knoll Associates with Hans Knoll (whom she married in 1946), she helped to popularize the International Style through the firm's editions of classic Bauhaus designs (particularly those of Mies van der Rohe) from the late 1940s. As important, through the Knoll planning unit, which she headed, she commissioned a series of new furniture designs from architects and designers that were themselves to become modern classics, including the "Diamond" chair by HARRY BERTOIA (III-9) and the pedestal series of EERO SAARINEN (III-79, 80). She also developed a textile division of the company, and the woven fabrics designed by ANNI ALBERS, EVELYN HILL (VII-22), ESZTER HARASZTY (VII-17), and SUZANNE HUGUENIN (VII-23) in the 1950s added a new vocabulary of textural richness and variety to institutional spaces. Knoll was personally responsible for such interiors as those of the Connecticut General Life Insurance Company, Hartford (1954–57), and the CBS Headquarters building, New York (1964–65); her own functionalist furniture (III-41) appeared regularly in the Museum of Modern Art's "Good Design" exhibitions and won an A.I.D. First International Design Award in 1954. Trained at the Cranbrook Academy of Art in Bloomfield Hills, Michigan, with both Eliel and Eero Saarinen, Knoll studied architecture at the Architectural Association in London and with Mies van der Rohe at the Illinois Institute of Technology in Chicago (1941). She worked in the architectural offices of Walter Gropius and Marcel Breuer in Cambridge, Massachusetts, and of Harrison and Abramovitz in New York, and then joined Knoll in 1943. Following the death of her husband in 1955, she served as president of Knoll; in 1959 she sold her interest in the firm, but remained as design director until her retirement in 1965.

Monograph: Washington, D.C., Renwick Gallery, *A Modern Consciousness: D. J. De Pree, Florence Knoll* (Apr. 11–Nov. 9, 1975).

References: Paris, Musée des Arts Décoratifs, *Knoll au Louvre* (Jan.–Mar. 1972), n.p.; Eric Larrabee and Massimo Vignelli, *Knoll Design* (New York, 1981), esp. pp. 76–89.

Ray Komai
American, born 1918

An industrial, interior, and graphic designer, Komai studied at the Art Center College of Los Angeles. In 1944 he moved to New York, where he worked in advertising and opened a design office (with Carter Winter) in 1948. His furniture designs (for the J.G. Furniture company) include tables, upholstered seating, and an early (1949)

Masakazu Kobayashi
Japanese, born 1944

A graduate of the University of Arts in Kyoto, Kobayashi worked as a textile designer for Kawashima from 1966 to 1975. In both his production fabrics and, since the 1970s, his large-scale studio fiberworks, he evokes traditional Japanese textile arts: the pattern of stripes and short lines repeated evenly over the surface of the fabric "Space Age" (VII-28) suggests the textile-dyeing technique known as *komon*, which uses paper patterns with tiny designs; his hangings "W³W to the Third Power" (1977) and "Meditation" (1979) include threads suspended in frames in the manner, if not the style, of traditional weavings.

Reference: Mildred Constantine and Jack Lenor Larsen, *Beyond Craft: The Art Fabric* (New York, 1973), pp. 20–21, 42–43, 190, 197, 263.

Oskar Kogoj
Yugoslavian, born 1942

A graduate of the industrial design program at the Istituto Statale d'Arte in Venice (1966), Kogoj first became known when his "Red Object"—a plastic wagon-toy—won an *Abitare* magazine design award in 1969. He has continued to design children's toys, furniture, cutlery (VI-9), tools, and kitchenware, mainly in plastic with strongly organic forms. His ergonomic concerns are evident in the "Gondola" series of easy chairs, based on a seating shell derived from impressions of the human body at rest, and in his curved and channeled plastic cutlery.

Monograph: Ljubljana, Moderna Galerija, *Oblikovalec Oskar Kogoj* (1972) (biblio.).

References: "Design in Action: Prototype Plastic Flatware," *Industrial Design*, vol. 19 (Oct. 1972), pp. 60–61; "Child Care," *Industrial Design*, vol. 24 (May 1977), pp. 49–51.

molded-plywood chair with a slit, one-piece seat (III-42). He has also designed wallpapers and textiles with figurative (VII-29) and abstract patterns.

References: W. J. Hennessey, *Modern Furnishings for the Home*, vol. 1 (New York, 1952), pp. 115, 272, 278; George Nelson, ed., *Chairs* (New York, 1953), pp. 59, 92, 155.

Henning Koppel
Danish, 1918–1981

Trained as a sculptor at the Royal Danish Academy of Fine Arts (Kongelige Danske Kunstakademi), Copenhagen (1936–37), and at the Académie Ranson in Paris (1938), Koppel designed jewelry, glass (for Orrefors, 1971), ceramics (for Bing & Grøndahl, 1961), and lighting and clocks (for Louis Poulsen, 1967). Most importantly, however, it was the metalwork that Koppel created for Georg Jensen over a period of thirty-five years that made his reputation (V-21–23). A refugee in Stockholm during the German occupation of Denmark, Koppel returned to Copenhagen and a position with Jensen in 1945. His first designs were for silver jewelry, whose abstract, softly rounded sculptural shapes represented a new departure for the firm. Koppel brought this personal, expressive style to maturity during the 1950s with a series of hollow-ware pieces and flatware that won him the Lunning Prize in 1953 and gold medals at the Milan Triennale in 1951, 1954, and 1957. He said of his approach to silverwork: "In the days of functionalism it was often declared that any practical thing was beautiful. . . . For the life of me I cannot see any disadvantage in a thing that is really handsome to look at. . . . If you decide to use silver for an article of everyday use, besides being useful it simply must also be a joy to behold" (1972).

Writings: Henning Koppel, in Copenhagen, Danish Society of Arts and Crafts and Industrial Design, *D B & D* (1972), pp. 7–10.

Monograph: Viggo Sten Møller, *Henning Koppel* (Copenhagen, 1965).

References: Arne Karlsen, *Made in Denmark* (New York, 1960), pp. 38–43, 141, 150, 152; Graham Hughes, *Modern Silver throughout the World* (New York, 1967), p. 237, pls. 22–31; Washington, D.C., Renwick Gallery, *Georg Jensen—Silversmithy: 77 Artists 75 Years* (Feb. 29–July 6, 1980), nos. 88–97.

Herbert Krenchel
Danish, born 1922

Trained as a civil engineer at the Danish College of Technology (Danmarks Tekniske Højskole) in Copenhagen, Krenchel established an office in 1953 as an industrial designer, working both independently and for such firms as Torben Ørskov. His "Krenit" bowls (V-24) were produced from millimeter-thin steel plate, which was machine-pressed cold and enameled, a marriage of industrial process and rational form unparalleled then by other domestic wares. The bowls were awarded a gold medal at the Milan Triennale of 1954.

Reference: Erik Zahle, ed., *A Treasury of Scandinavian Design* (New York, 1961), p. 281, no. 52.

Boris Kroll
American, born 1913

One of the largest textile manufacturers in America, Kroll has specialized in fabrics woven on a Jacquard loom, creating unique tapestries of his own design along with complex and subtly colored patterns for the mass market (VII-30). He apprenticed with his brother Hammond, a furniture designer, and in 1938 established his own firm, Cromwell Designs, to provide modern furnishing fabrics. In 1946 he established Boris Kroll Fabrics in New York and later showrooms in other major cities.

References: "A New Home for the House of Boris Kroll," *Interiors*, vol. 111 (Dec. 1951), pp. 115–18, 180–81; New York, Fashion Institute of Technology, *Boris Kroll—Tapestries & Textiles* (Nov. 4, 1980–Jan. 10, 1981).

Hans Krondahl
Swedish, born 1929

Known principally as a textile artist and designer of patterns for printed textiles, Krondahl was trained at the School of Arts, Crafts and Design (Konstfackskolan), Stockholm (1955–60), and opened his own studio in Brösarp in 1960. From 1959 to 1975, as a studio craftsman and freelance designer for Nordiska Kompaniet, Krondahl developed pictorial weavings and tapestries, and series of printed interior fabrics in cotton, fiberglass, and velvet, for which he was awarded the Lunning Prize in 1965. Krondahl's patterns are often in a large geometric or stylized figurative format (VII-31) and bright in color—characteristics that also appear in his paintings and studio work. Krondahl has taught and worked both in Scandinavia and the United States (in 1974–75 as a designer for Argos in Oak Grove Village, Illinois) and served as a United Nations advisor in Indonesia (1979–80).

Writings: Hans Krondahl, "Swedish Design," *Handwoven* (Mar.–Apr. 1983), pp. 29–33.

Monograph: Borås, Museet Kulturhuset, *Hans Krondahl* (May 23–Sept. 5, 1982) (biblio.).

References: "Thirtyfour Lunning Prize-Winners," *Mobilia* (special issue), no. 146 (Sept. 1967), n.p.; Charles S. Talley, *Contemporary Textile Art: Scandinavia* (Stockholm, 1982), pp. 73–76.

Nils Landberg
Swedish, born 1907

Trained at the school of glass engraving at Orrefors from 1925 to 1927, Landberg joined its design staff, where he worked until 1972, producing tableware, art pieces, and architectural decoration. His preference was for freely blown glass—often in very thin and delicate, attenuated forms. His subtly toned "Tulip" wineglasses (1956; II-30), with their eccentric bowls, long, drawn stems, and turned rims, stand as a summation of his intense, creative beliefs. Landberg received a gold medal at the Milan Triennale of 1954.

References: "Nils Landberg," *Design Quarterly*, no. 34 (1956), pp. 16–17; Erik Zahle, ed., *A Treasury of Scandinavian Design* (New York, 1961), p. 281, nos. 220, 228; Eileene Harrison Beer, *Scandinavian Design: Objects of a Life Style* (New York, 1975), pp. 90, 93, 96.

Gerd Lange
German, born 1931

Educated at the Hochschule für Gestaltung in Offenbach (1952–56), Lange has practiced interior and exhibition design, opening his own design studio and workshop in Kapsweyer in 1961. Since 1962 Lange has designed furniture for Thonet, Bofinger, Schlapp, and Drabert, and lighting systems for Staff and Kartell. His multipurpose chairs with legs and shell of different materials (III-43) combine formal simplicity and technical ingenuity. Made small and light for domestic purposes, they stack and gang in contract use. His chairs were awarded the Bundespreis "Gute Form" in 1969.

References: London, Whitechapel Art Gallery, *Modern Chairs: 1918–1970* (July 22–Aug. 30, 1970), no. 70; "A Chair for All Seasons from Thonet," *Contract Interiors*, vol. 136 (July 1977), p. 20.

Jack Lenor Larsen
American, born 1927

One of today's most distinguished textile designers, Larsen is principal designer of his own firm, as well as a writer and teacher, known for the technical ingenuity of his fabrics and his adaptations of traditional styles and processes (VII-32, 35, 36). His innovations include the first printed velvet upholstery fabrics, the first stretch upholstery (1961), and the development of warp-knit casements (most notably in "Interplay," a saran monofilament, 1960; VII-33). Using handspun natural yarns and synthetics, and both handlooms and power looms, Larsen bases his designs on the functionalist principle that fabrics should evolve from the specific characteristics of their fibers. Trained at the University of Washington in Seattle, where he first became interested in weaving (1945–50), and at the Cranbrook Academy of Art, Bloomfield Hills, Michigan (1950–51), Larsen opened a studio in New York in 1952 and the same year received his first major commission, draperies for New York's Lever House. At the same time he began to power-weave "handwoven" fabrics, using the random repeats and handspun yarns that have since been so widely imitated. In 1953 Larsen reorganized his firm into its present form and in 1958 he established the Larsen Design Studio to develop new materials and processes and expand the firm's operation as fabric consultants and designers for large-scale architectural projects. His varied commissions have included upholstery fabrics for Pan Am and Braniff (1969; 1972–78); theater curtains for the Filene Center for the Performing Arts, Wolf Trap Farm Park, Vienna, Virginia (1971; handwoven of handspun mohair in Swaziland), and the Phoenix (Arizona) Civic Plaza concert hall ("Magnum," 1970; VII-34); quilted silk banners for the Sears bank in the Sears Tower, Chicago (1974); and upholstery collections for Cassina (1981; III-19) and Vescom. Larsen's distinctions range from a gold medal at the 1964 Milan Triennale to nomination as a Royal Designer for Industry in 1982.

Writings: Jack Lenor Larsen and Azalea Thorpe, *Elements of Weaving* (New York, 1967); Mildred Constantine and Jack Lenor Larsen, *Beyond Craft: The Art Fabric* (New York, 1973); Jack Lenor Larsen and Jeanne Weeks, *Fabrics for Interiors* (New York, 1975); Jack Lenor Larsen et al., *The Dyer's Art: Ikat, Batik, Plangi* (New York, 1976); Jack Lenor Larsen and Mildred Constantine, *The Art Fabric: Mainstream* (New York, 1981).

Monograph: Paris, Musée des Arts Décoratifs, *Jack Lenor Larsen: 30 Years of Creative Textiles* (Sept. 24–Dec. 28, 1981).

References: Larry Salmon, "Jack Lenor Larsen in Boston," *Craft Horizons*, vol. 23 (Apr. 1971), pp. 14–23; Mildred Constantine, "Jack Lenor Larsen: The First 25 Years," *American Fabrics and Fashions* (special issue), no. 113 (Summer 1978).

Richard Latham
American, born 1920

Trained in engineering and design (under Mies van der Rohe), Latham was a product designer for RAYMOND LOEWY from 1940 to 1955, heading the design team of the Chicago office for much of that period and including among his work Hallicrafters radios and televisions (I-20, 21). With Loewy he designed as well as conceived the marketing techniques for a line of moderately priced "contemporary" dinnerware for Rosenthal specifically for the American market (II-31). In 1955 Latham joined with several designers (including JAKOB JENSEN) in the firm of Latham Tyler Jensen, with offices in Chicago, Long Beach, California, and Copenhagen, which counted Xerox, Argus cameras, Ampex, and Bang & Olufsen among its clients. Latham has also designed glassware for the Rosenthal Studio Line.

Writings: Richard S. Latham, "Is This Change Necessary?," *Industrial Design*, vol. 5 (Feb. 1958), pp. 66–70; Richard S. Latham, "The Artifact as a Cultural Cipher," in Laurence B. Holland, ed., *Who Designs America?* (New York, 1966), pp. 257–80; Richard S. Latham, "Der Designer in USA: Stilist, Künstler, Produktplaner?," *Form*, no. 34 (1966), pp. 28–31.

References: Don Wallance, *Shaping America's Products* (New York, 1956), pp. 47–50; Hanover, Kestner-Museum, *Rosenthal: Hundert Jahre Porzellan* (Apr. 29–June 13, 1982), nos. 83 A–D, 94 B, 96 B.

Erwine Laverne
American, born 1909
Estelle Laverne
American, born 1915

Students of painting under Hans Hofmann at the Art Students' League of New York, Erwine and Estelle Laverne founded Laverne Originals about 1938. Their first designs were fabrics and wall coverings, including the very successful "Marbalia" series of marblelike murals, inspired by Erwine's studies of decorative arts during his travels abroad. A number of their works were exhibited at the "Good Design" exhibitions at the Museum of Modern Art in New York in the early 1950s, along with textiles and the "New Furniture Group" (III-38), designed for them by KATAVOLOS-LITTELL-KELLEY, who had teamed up with them in 1949. This was followed in 1957 by the Lavernes' own "Invisible" group, see-through plastic furniture designed to be as unobtrusive as possible, giving a sense of greater space to the environment. Early examples of plastic furniture, the "Invisible" line was produced with methods and techniques developed by the Lavernes, which they later licensed to other manufacturers.

Reference: New York, The American Federation of Arts, *Please Be Seated* (1968), no. 68.

Michael Lax
American, born 1929

A graduate of the New York State College of Ceramics at Alfred University, Lax studied in Finland and in Rome (as winner of a Prix de Rome in industrial design) and heads his own design firm in New York. His interest has been divided between exhibition, environmental, and graphic information systems and the design of products —cast-iron cookware, cutlery, sanitary fittings, glassware, wall coverings, and lighting (the "Lytegem" high-intensity lamp; IV-24)—for such companies as Copco, Corning, Dunbar (glass bowls shown at the "Good Design" exhibition at the Museum of Modern Art in 1952), Formica, Kimberley-Clark, Lightolier, and Salton.

Reference: Jay Doblin, *One Hundred Great Product Designs* (New York, 1970), no. 99.

Fabio Lenci
Italian, born 1935

Designer of interiors, furniture, lighting fixtures, textiles, and appliances, Lenci was trained in Rome, where he established a shop for contemporary furniture. At the same time he began to explore the possibility of using new plastic materials and manufacturing techniques in his own furniture designs—notably the "chain" armchair with rolls of upholstered foam suspended between plate-glass sheets (for Bernini). In his recent "Aquarius" series of bath and sanitary fixtures fitted with storage compartments (I-19), Lenci has introduced a brightly colored methacrylate.

Reference: Sylvia Katz, *Plastics: Designs and Materials* (London, 1978), p. 96.

Cesare Leonardi-Franca Stagi
Italian, established Modena, 1962

Graduates in architecture from the university of Florence (1970) and the Milan Politecnico (1962), respectively, Cesare Leonardi (Italian, born 1935) and Franca Stagi (Italian, born 1937) have been partners in a design firm in Modena since 1962. They have specialized in architecture and urban planning, particularly parks, swimming pools, and other public spaces in Modena, as well as in industrial design: furniture (for Bernini, Fiarm, Peguri), plastics (for Elco), and lighting (for Lumenform). Their 1967 rocking chair (III-45), with its organic fiberglass form perfectly expressing its movement, has become a classic of Italian sculptural design.

References: London, Whitechapel Art Gallery, *Modern Chairs: 1918–1970* (July 22–Aug. 30, 1970), no. 119;

"Tavolini da Soggiorno in Vetro-resina, Impignabili," *Domus,* no. 483 (Feb. 1970), pp. 43–44.

Dorothy Liebes
American, 1899–1972

One of the first American textile designers to adapt hand techniques to mass production, Liebes did much to create a youthful, optimistic image in the industry in the early postwar years. Her innovative works (VII-37–40) were distinguished by bright colors in unusual combinations and by unconventional yarns and other materials, including ticker tape, sequins, plastics, grass, and strips of leather and bamboo. Educated at the University of California at Berkeley and Columbia University in New York, Liebes opened her first studio in San Francisco in 1930, specializing in custom handwoven work for architects and decorators. Her first involvement with large-scale production came in 1940, when she was engaged as a designer by Goodall Fabrics in Sanford, Maine; later she received commissions from such firms as du Pont (1955), Bigelow-Sanford (1957), and Sears Roebuck (1969). In 1948 Liebes moved her design studio to New York and a decade later terminated custom work in order to concentrate on industrial consulting and designing for mass production.

Monograph: New York, Museum of Contemporary Crafts, *Dorothy Liebes* (Mar. 20–May 10, 1970).

Stig Lindberg
Swedish, 1916–1982

Although Lindberg designed plastics (VI-10), enamels, textiles (VII-41), glass, appliances, and graphics, it was principally as a ceramics designer that he was known. Trained at the Stockholm School of Arts, Crafts and Design (Konstfackskolan) (1935–37), where he later taught (1957–72), Lindberg was employed by Gustavsberg in 1937; the work of the firm's then-artistic director, WILHELM KÅGE, proved highly influential for the sprightly, softly rounded table services that Lindberg designed a decade later. In 1949 he succeeded Kåge as chief artist at Gustavsberg, a position he held until 1956, and again from 1972 to 1980. Lindberg designed both decorative and useful ceramics (II-32, 33) and provided painted decorations for the firm's enamelwares. He also created large-scale mural paintings and ceramic wall decorations, which counted among his last public works.

Monograph: Dag Widman, *Stig Lindberg—Swedish Artist and Designer* (Stockholm, 1962).

References: "Stig Lindberg," *Everyday Art Quarterly,* no. 25 (1953), pp. 14–15; Kim Taylor, "Stig Lindberg," *Graphis,* vol. 15 (July 1959), pp. 308–15; Stockholm, Nationalmuseum, *Gustavsberg 150 ar* (1975), *passim.*

Raymond Loewy
American, born France, 1893

Loewy is one of a handful of designers who in the early 1930s virtually created the profession of industrial design, stamping the entire decade with their streamlined vision. Trained in France as an engineer, but working in New York as a graphic and theatrical designer, Loewy opened his own design firm in 1930, recognizing the value of public relations and styling to give products a competitive stance in the marketplace. His redesign in 1934 of the "Coldspot" refrigerator for Sears Roebuck is a classic success story in the field, the first of many that would build his reputation and make his name a household word. His firm expanded widely, with hundreds of employees and offices in many cities, and his work reached into all areas of industrial and graphic design, from Pennsylvania Railroad locomotives to the Coca Cola bottle and the Lucky Strike package. His sphere of activity in the 1940s and 1950s was so broad that an estimated three out of every four Americans came into contact with at least one of his products or designs each day. In 1944 he formed Raymond Loewy Associates (with four partners), and the company was renamed Raymond Loewy/William Snaith in 1961. In the postwar period Loewy set the course for the American automotive industry with his designs for Studebaker—the controversial 1947 "Champion," the 1953 European-styled "Starline" coupe, and the 1962 "Avanti." His work in transportation, packaging, product (I-20, 21; II-31), and interior design (Lever House, New York) has continued to pervade all areas of life on earth—and in space, through his "habitability" studies for NASA and his design of the interiors of Skylab. While he has often been unjustly criticized as being a mere stylist, he has justified even that: "Good design keeps the user happy, the manufacturer in the black, and the esthete unoffended" (1953).

Writings: Raymond Loewy, *Never Leave Well Enough Alone* (New York, 1951); Raymond Loewy, *Industrial Design* (New York, 1979).

Monograph: Washington, D.C., Renwick Gallery, *The Designs of Raymond Loewy* (Aug. 1–Nov. 16, 1976).

References: C.F.O. Clarke, "Raymond Loewy Associates: Modern American Industrial Designing," *Graphis,* vol. 2 (Jan.–Feb. 1946), pp. 94–97; David Pleydell-Bouverie and Alec Davis, "Popular Art Organised: The Manner and Methods of Raymond Loewy Associates," *Architectural Review,* vol. 110 (Nov. 1951), pp. 319–26; *Current Biography* (1953), *s.v.*

Heinrich Löffelhardt
German, 1901–1979

Germany's most premiated designer of ceramics and glass since the war, Löffelhardt succeeded Hermann Gretsch as artistic director of the Arzberg and Schönwald porcelain factories in 1952, a position he held until 1971. From 1954 to 1977 Löffelhardt was also design director of the Jenaer Glaswerk Schott & Gen in Mainz and its affiliate, the Vereinigte Farbenglaswerke in Zwiesel. In his first highly successful works for the porcelain companies (for example, "Arzberg 2000," 1954; II-34), Löffelhardt depended closely on Gretsch's prewar models, distinguished by their functional forms and undecorated surfaces. However, with the "Arzberg 2050" service (1959; II-36), he realized an independent style of elegant, elongated forms for which he was awarded a grand prize at the Milan Triennale of 1960 and international prizes in 1961 and 1962 at the Salone Internazionale della Ceramica in Vicenza. At the Jenaer glassworks, Löffelhardt was similarly successor to the prewar work of WILHELM WAGENFELD. His thoughtful redesign of Wagenfeld's heat-resistant dishes (II-35) was also recipient of a grand prize at the Triennale in 1960. If the adoption of automated processes caused a number of Löffelhardt's successful glass designs to be withdrawn from production, it allowed mass marketing of others: by 1978 the Vereinigte Farbenglaswerke had sold 240 million white-wine glasses from his "Neckar" series. Löffelhardt first trained in the design department of the silverware manufacturer P. Bruckmann in Heilbronn (1920–23) and later studied sculpture with Georg Kolbe in Berlin (1924–28), followed by independent work as a sculptor in Stuttgart (1929–36). From 1937 to 1941 Löffelhardt worked with Wagenfeld at the Vereinigte Lausitzer glassworks in Weisswasser; it was Wagenfeld who, after the war, arranged for Löffelhardt's appointment as director of design at the District Trade and Craft Offices (Landesgewerbeamt) in Stuttgart.

Monograph: Karlsruhe, Badisches Landesmuseum, *In Memoriam. Heinrich Löffelhardt, 1901–1979: Design für die Glas- und Porzellanindustrie* (Oct. 11–Nov. 16, 1980) (biblio.).

Ennio Lucini
Italian, born 1934

A packaging and graphics designer who served as art director and designer of covers for *Domus* (1975–80), Lucini is also a creator of small-scale objects for the home, principally ceramics and glass (for Gabbianelli) and metalware (for Barazzoni). He applies the formal concerns of his graphics to product design, his hemispherical "Ponte di Brera" glasses (II-37) based rigorously on a composition of circles, his "Tummy" series of stainless-steel cookware (V-25)—awarded a Compasso d'Oro in 1979—on the purity of outline of traditional pottery forms.

References: "Designers d'oggi: Ennio Lucini," *Interni* (Apr. 1979), pp. 54–55; Carla Caccia, "Parliamo di design con . . . Ennio Lucini," *Arredorama* (Jan. 1983), pp. 9–14.

Per Lütken
Danish, born 1916

Glass, according to Lütken, who studied painting at the School of Arts and Crafts (Kunsthandvaerkerskolen), Copenhagen, "demands collaboration: intimate, imperative and exciting collaboration based on mutual, personal acquaintanceship between designer and glassmaker. . . . Movements of the glassmaker are rhythmically beautiful and deliberate and hold great fascination and interest, just like the glass itself. And it seems to me that the more the finished piece of glass tells us about this process and bears witness to it through the vigour of its form, the better" (1972). Organic expression remains very much evident in the ample, flowing forms of the blown-glass vases, bowls (II-38), decanters, and drinking glasses Lütken has designed at the Holmegaard glassworks (since 1942), where he succeeded JACOB BANG as artistic director, continuing in that position to this day.

Writings: Per Lütken, in Copenhagen, Danish Society of Arts and Crafts and Industrial Design, *D B & D* (1972), pp. 21–22.

References: Arne Karlsen, *Made in Denmark* (New York, 1960), pp. 50–55, 119; Erik Lassen and Mogens Schlüter, *Dansk Glas: 1925–1975* (Copenhagen, 1975), *passim;* Copenhagen, Kastrup & Holmegaard Glassworks, *150 Years of Danish Glass* (n.d.), nos. 209–37.

Vico Magistretti
Italian, born 1920

Trained as an architect (1945), Magistretti entered the architectural office established by his father in Milan, specializing in urban planning and interior design. His architectural projects have included town planning and designing a civic center for Campana, Argentina (1955), the Torre del Parco office building in Milan (1956), and the Hispano Olivetti training center in Barcelona (1970). Although Magistretti began designing consumer products independently only about 1960, he had often created furnishings for his interiors, including a number of bookcases, most notably a ladder-like shelf system designed to lean against a wall (1950). Awarded the Compasso d'Oro for the "Eclisse" lamp (1967) and "Gaudi" chair (1979) for Artemide, the "Atollo" lamp (1977; IV-25) for O-Luce, and the "Maralunga" chair (1973; III-46) for Cassina, Magistretti was one of the first Italian designers in the 1960s to use plastics, and considered the material highly suitable for use in quality mass-production through the use of completely mechanized systems.

References: Milan, Museo Poldi Pezzoli, *Milano 70/70: Un secolo d'arte,* vol. 3, *Dal 1946 al 1970* (from May 30, 1972), pp. 304–5; "Vico

Magistretti," in Prague, The Museum of Decorative Arts, *Design and Plastics* (Oct.–Dec. 1972); Los Angeles, Frederick S. Wight Art Gallery, University of California, *Design Process Olivetti 1908–1978* (Mar. 27–May 6, 1979), p. 261; Alfonso Grassi and Anty Pansera, *Atlante del design italiano: 1940–1980* (Milan, 1980), p. 283.

Erik Magnussen
Danish, born 1940

Trained as a ceramist at the School of Arts and Crafts (Kunsthåndvaerkerskolen) in Copenhagen (graduated 1960), Magnussen also designs glass, metal hollow ware and cutlery, and furniture. Since 1962 he has been a designer for Bing & Grøndahl and since 1978, for Georg Jensen. Practicality is one of his chief concerns—reducing to essentials the variety and forms of pieces in a service, making them interchangeable and stackable (II-39), and giving them temperature-retaining forms (V-26). Magnussen was awarded the Lunning Prize in 1967, and has twice received the Danish ID prize.

References: "Thirtyfour Lunning Prize-Winners," *Mobilia* (special issue), no. 146 (Sept. 1967), n.p.; New York, Cooper-Hewitt Museum, *Scandinavian Modern Design: 1880–1980* (Sept. 14, 1982—Jan. 2, 1983), nos. 260, 331.

Angelo Mangiarotti
Italian, born 1921

A graduate in architecture from the Milan Politecnico (1948), Mangiarotti taught at the Illinois Institute of Technology in Chicago (1953–54), and has worked in Milan as an architect and industrial designer since 1955. His "Secticon" clock of 1962 (I-22) is a development of the series he designed with Bruno Morassutti (with whom he collaborated between 1955 and 1960); it shows his concern for strong plastic form in everyday objects (like the armchair he designed for Cassina in 1963) and for a simple but singular graphic presentation, in which the time indicators increase in width as they range from one to twelve. Mangiarotti has designed a great variety of objects, from collapsible furniture and metalwork to glasswares and marble objects (for Knoll).

Writings: Angelo Mangiarotti and Bruno Morassutti, "Secticon," *Stile Industria,* no. 28 (Aug. 1960), pp. 3–10.

References: Gillo Dorfles, *Il disegno industriale e la sua estetica* (Bologna, 1963), figs. 67–71, 68–81; Andrea Branzi and Michael De Lucchi, eds., *Il design italiano degli anni '50* (Milan, 1981), pp. 72, 104, 106, 264, 267, 274.

Pio Manzù
Italian, 1939–1969

Interested primarily in transportation design and theory, Manzù applied the rigorous devotion to formal purity of his studies at the Hochschule für Gestaltung at Ulm, West Germany, to his automobile, taxi, and tractor design (for Fiat) and to his critical writings (for *Form, Industrial Design, Style Auto, Interiors*). His other work includes appliances, packaging (for Olivetti), and lighting, most notably the "Parentesi" lamp (IV-12), completed after his untimely death by ACHILLE CASTIGLIONI, which won a Compasso d'Oro in 1979.

Reference: Alfonso Grassi and Anty Pansera, *Atlante del design italiano: 1940–1980* (Milan, 1980), pp. 91, 177, 244, 305.

Enzo Mari
Italian, born 1932

A designer whose studied, elegant work has stood apart from the successive stylistic turns in postwar Italy, Mari has created graphics, toys, and furniture for children; a series of household objects of great poise, primarily in plastic; and provocative exhibition and installation designs. An artist and theoretician also, Mari studied at the Accademia di Belle Arti di Brera in Milan (1952–56), and about the same time initiated research into psychology and the perception of space, color, and volume; he later taught courses in the methodology of design (most recently at the Politecnico in Milan) and published his research and design theory in *Funzione della ricerca estetica* (1970). Concerned also for the role of the designer and industrial design in society, Mari refused to create an environment for the 1972 "Italy: The New Domestic Landscape" exhibition at the Museum of Modern Art in New York, providing instead a socioeconomical "anti-design" statement: "The only correct undertaking for 'artists' is that of language research—that is, critical examination of the communications systems now in use. . . . [They] must not confine themselves to experimenting and devising new modes of expression but must show a fundamental concern for the manner in which the substance and implications of their research are communicated and received." Continuing to design, however—because "the profession to which I belong must rely solely on formal quality for its patronage, and hence for its survival" (New York, 1972) —Mari consistently provides serious solutions to those design problems he attacks; he has collaborated extensively with Danese since the 1950s (VI-11–14), but has also designed for other manufacturers including Driade (textiles and furniture) and Gabbianelli (notably, his "Elementare" wall tiles, 1979). Mari was awarded a Compasso d'Oro in 1967 for his research in the area of design and in 1979 for his "Delfina" chair (for Driade).

Writings: Enzo Mari, *Funzione della ricerca estetica* (Milan, 1970).

Monographs: Max Bill and Bruno Munari, *Enzo Mari* (Milan, 1959); Arturo Carlo Quintavalle, *Enzo Mari* (Parma, 1983) (biblio.).

References: Paolo Fossati, *Il design in Italia* (Turin, 1972), pp. 141–46, 243–49, pls. 450–508 (biblio.); New York, Museum of Modern Art, *Italy: The New Domestic Landscape* (May 26–Sept. 11, 1972), pp. 54, 76–77, 83, 89–91, 262–65; "Colloqui di Modo: Artigianato non esiste," *Modo,* no. 56 (Jan.–Feb. 1983), pp. 22–25.

Javier Mariscal
Spanish, born 1950

Designer of graphics, textiles, furniture, and interiors, Mariscal studied at the Escuela de Grafismo Elisava in Barcelona (1971) and during the 1970s worked independently as a graphic designer. His cartoons have been published in various Spanish and American periodicals, and his posters of the 1970s include one for the city of Barcelona conceived in three sections as a pictogram of the word BAR ("bar")/CEL ("sky")/ONA ("wave") (1979). In 1978 Mariscal began designing printed textiles for Marieta (VII-42, 43) with the same inventiveness and fluent brushwork that characterize his graphic designs. The brightly colored and asymmetrical barstools he created for the Bar Duplex in Valencia in 1981 have been paralleled by similarly unconventional designs (III-47).

References: "Global New Waves in 70s—Spain," *Gurafuikki Dezain/ Graphic Design,* no. 76 (Dec. 1979), p. 52; Barbara Radice, ed., *Memphis: The New International Style* (Milan, 1981), pp. 39–40.

Enid Marx
British, born 1902

A member of the UTILITY FURNITURE DESIGN PANEL, Marx designed most of the utility furnishing fabrics used in Britain late in the war and during the postwar recovery period. From 1944 to 1948, within the severe restrictions in material (until 1946 only four colors were available in two types of cotton yarn) and scale (a small pattern repeat was required for economical piecing of upholstery), she provided muted textile designs in abstracted patterns—chevrons, stripes, stars, circles—that were both rich in their texture and serviceable. Marx studied at the Central School of Art as well as at the Royal College of Art, London, and from 1925 to 1939 designed and hand printed cottons, linens, and velvets in simple patterns, which gained her the reputation that brought her to the attention of the design panel chairman Gordon Russell. She has also designed fabrics for Edinburgh Weavers and for Morton Sundour (including a fabric used in the Royal Pavilion at the Festival of Britain in 1951) in addition to those she has printed herself (VII-44).

Monograph: London, Camden Arts Centre, *Enid Marx* (Oct. 3–Nov. 25, 1969).

References: London, Geffrye Museum, *CC 41: Utility Furniture and Fashion, 1941–1951* (Sept. 24–Dec. 29, 1974), pp. 30–31; Jacqueline Herald, "A Portrait of Enid Marx," *Crafts,* no. 40 (Sept. 1979), pp. 17–21.

Bruno Mathsson
Swedish, born 1907

The prototypical designer of "Swedish Modern" furniture, which first came to be admired abroad in the late 1930s, Mathsson based his work on his country's handcraft tradition—favoring natural wood, principally beech, and flowing organic lines—and on his anatomical research into the physiology of seating. Like ALVAR AALTO he experimented with laminated woods bent into complex curves, and developed lightweight elegant chairs with firm cloth or leather webbing. Much of his furniture has been custom made at the family factory in Värnamo, originally owned by his father, Karl, where he received his training as a cabinetmaker; his later designs have been for Dux Mobel. In the early 1960s Mathsson collaborated with PIET HEIN on adapting Hein's "super-ellipse" to furniture and on developing a widely applicable self-clamping leg (III-48). Consistently focusing on his basic concerns—"the business of sitting never ceases to fascinate me" (1966)—Mathsson adapted his forms and design principles to tubular-steel construction, designing in the 1960s the cloth-upholstered "Jetson" chair and the leather-cushioned "Karin" chair. Mathsson is also an interior designer and architect, having pioneered with glass-wall construction in Sweden after an enthusiastic trip to the United States just before the war.

Monograph: *Design Quarterly* (special issue), vol. 65 (1966).

References: Erik Zahle, ed., *A Treasury of Scandinavian Design* (New York, 1961), p. 284, nos. 3-4, 33; London, Whitechapel Art Gallery, *Modern Chairs: 1918–1970* (July 22–Aug. 30, 1970), nos. 20, 111.

Roberto Sebastian Matta
French, born Chile, 1911

A painter linked in the 1930s to Surrealism, and then to machine and astral, fantastic imagery, Matta was trained as an architect in Santiago and in the 1930s apprenticed in the office of Le Corbusier in Paris. In the mid-1960s he collaborated with the avant-garde Italian furniture firm Gavina to design his "Malitte" component cushion system (III-49), soft, upholstered polyurethane foam "puzzle" pieces that stack in a square but can be arranged into several seating elements.

Reference: Eric Larrabee and Massimo Vignelli, *Knoll Design* (New York, 1981), pp. 172, 176, 178–79.

Sergio Mazza
Italian, born 1931

Designer and interior architect, Mazza received a degree from the school of architecture in Lausanne in 1954. He opened his own design studio in Milan in 1956, and has designed interiors, furniture (for Artemide, Saporiti, Cinova, and Formica), lighting (for which he won a Compasso d'Oro in 1960), and ceramics (for Cedit). His range of products for Artemide in plastic and metal includes the highly sculptural, molded "Toga" armchair (1968), the low, fitted, "Bacco" mobile bar (1969; III-50), shelving units, mirrors, and lighting. Since 1961 he has been associated with GIULIANA GRAMIGNA, with whom he has collaborated on product design in their Studio SMC Architettura and on *Ottagono,* the magazine he founded in 1966.

References: New York, Museum of Modern Art, *Italy: The New Domestic Landscape* (May 26–Sept. 11, 1972), pp. 35, 56; "Sergio Mazza e Giuliana Gramigna," *Interni,* no. 282 (Sept. 1978), pp. 54–57; Alfonso Grassi and Anty Pansera, *Atlante del design italiano: 1940–1980* (Milan, 1980), pp. 162, 168, 290.

Paul McCobb
American, 1917–1969

America's most successful furniture designer of the 1950s, McCobb was featured repeatedly in furniture advertisements and represented in the "Good Design" exhibitions at the Museum of Modern Art in New York. He was well known to professionals and to the public, who admired his furniture and accessories in department stores across the country, including Bloomingdale's in New York, where in 1957 the Paul McCobb Shop featured fifteen room settings with 348 items. He is credited with the creation of an entirely new American interior style—with clean, low lines, natural wood, and trim foam cushions—and with popularizing modular furniture, room dividers, and wall systems (which he called "living walls"). He believed firmly in giving the consumer good value, and a product that would relate to contemporary spaces, be durable, and not go out of style. Having studied painting and worked as a interior and display designer and in an industrial design office, McCobb formed his own firm in 1945, and began to develop his designs for furniture groups. With a furniture distributor, B. G. Mesberg, McCobb went into the low-cost furniture market in 1950, launching his immediately popular modular "Plan-

ner" group (III-51), followed by other, somewhat more expensive furniture systems, the "Directional," "Predictor," "Linear," and "Perimeter" groups, which he also distributed and merchandised.

References: "McCobb's Predictor Solves Many Problems Simultaneously," *Interiors,* vol. 111 (Oct. 1951), pp. 126–29; "An Interior View: Paul McCobb," *Art Digest,* vol. 26 (Sept. 15, 1952), p. 19; George Nelson, ed., *Storage* (New York, 1954), pp. 32, 48, 60, 62, 67, 76, 92; *Current Biography* (1958), *s.v.;* Jay Doblin, *One Hundred Great Product Designs* (New York, 1970), no. 60.

Peter McCulloch
British, born 1933

A textile designer, McCulloch trained at the Glasgow School of Art and in the early 1960s taught at the Falmouth School of Art. His "Cruachan" fabric (VII-45), based on experiments with contrasting colors applied in small dots to form patterns suggestive of a computer's printed circuit, was produced by Hull Traders. Forward-looking and experimental designs such as "Cruachan," which was given a Design Centre Award in 1963, were fostered by SHIRLEY CRAVEN, design consultant to the company.

Reference: "Design Centre Awards 1963," *Design,* no. 174 (June 1963), pp. 44–45.

Manfred Meinzer
German, born 1943

Chief designer of Studer Revox since 1965, Meinzer studied industrial design at the Art Center College, Los Angeles, and then worked for Ford (in Cologne) and Telefunken (in Berlin) before taking up his present position. Meinzer's high-fidelity equipment for Revox substituted transistors for vacuum tube electronics and was designed with modular components like the "family" systems of DIETER RAMS. Sharing with Braun products a functionalist aesthetic, Meinzer's stereo tape recorder (I-23), his first important unit for Revox, presents its function openly and minimizes the display of its operating controls.

David Mellor
British, born 1930

Silversmith and industrial designer, Mellor combines both activities in the workshop he opened in Sheffield in 1954, where designs for commercial and government clients (from bus shelters to disposable polystyrene cutlery) as well as unique silver pieces are created. Among the several sets of his cutlery that have become classics of English tableware are "Pride" (1954), a simplified interpretation of traditional forms in silver plate, which was given one of the first Design Council Awards (1957); and two sets originally commissioned by the Ministry of Public Building and Works, "Embassy" (1963), a "modern"-style silver service for use in British embassies (*see* p. 40), and "Thrift" (1965), a stainless-steel set for government canteens, hospitals, and prisons designed for economy of form and production (V-27). Since 1969 he has manufactured various lines of cookware, woodenware, hardware, and textiles, which are sold in his London shop: "The designer's special talent is relating art to life. In a world where an awful lot of people spend their time doing jobs they don't particularly like, manufacturing products no one specially wants, it could very well be argued that designers are not entrepreneurs enough" (1977). He was named a Royal Designer for Industry in 1962.

References: Graham Hughes, *Modern Silver throughout the World* (New York, 1967), nos. 122, 384–89, 424–25; *Design,* no. 342 (June 1977), p. 47; London, Heal & Son Limited, *Classics* (Spring 1981), nos. 15–16, 44; Fiona MacCarthy, *British Design since 1880* (London, 1982), figs. 153, 166, 185–86, 193, 211.

Marjatta Metsovaara
Finnish, born 1928

Textile artist and designer, Metsovaara was trained at the Institute of Industrial Arts (Taideteollinen oppilaitos) in Helsinki (1949) and established a workshop there in 1954. Working on a handicraft basis with both traditional and synthetic materials, Metsovaara has been particularly interested in creating rich effects of texture and color (VII-46). In addition to her studio fabrics, Metsovaara has designed both woven and printed furnishing fabrics for Uniwool and Tampella, and dress fabrics for Finn-Flare, the fashion company she established in 1963 with Maj Kuhlefelt. Metsovaara also produces, in her own studio, wool and mohair stoles and lap rugs, *rya* rugs, and carpets. For the quality and variety of her work, she was awarded medals at the Milan Triennale in 1957 and 1960.

Floris Meydam
Dutch, born 1919

Meydam's glass, both the freely formed unique pieces and the tableware series produced at the Leerdam glassworks in the Netherlands, focuses on the simple crystalline qualities of the material itself, spare in form and unadorned (II-40). Meydam was selected in 1935 as an assistant by Leerdam's artistic director ANDRIES COPIER and in 1943 he became a trainee at the Leerdam glass school. The following year he started to teach there, and also returned to the factory, becoming its chief designer in 1949, a position he has held since then. In 1953 his work was included in the "Good Design" show at the Museum of Modern Art in New York.

Reference: Geoffrey Beard, *International Modern Glass* (London, 1976), pls. 91, 93, 253.

Grethe Meyer
Danish, born 1918

Educated as an architect, Meyer joined BØRGE MOGENSEN in his research into the standardization of elements for consumer products, co-designing both the "Boligens Byggeskabe (B. B.)" and "Øresund" furniture systems. Her stacking glassware (designed with IBI TRIER MØRCH) for Kastrup glassworks (II-41), and her "Blue Line" ceramic tableware (II-42) and oven-to-table "Firepot" series (1976), both for Royal Copenhagen, exemplify her reductive simplicity of form and careful analysis of use. The "Blue Line" was awarded the Danish ID prize for 1965.

References: Arne Karlsen, *Made in Denmark* (New York, 1960), pp. 118–19; Arne Karlsen, *Furniture Designed by Børge Mogensen* (Copenhagen, 1968), *passim;* Jens

References: Erik Zahle, ed., *A Treasury of Scandinavian Design* (New York, 1961), p. 285; Eileene Harrison Beer, *Scandinavian Design: Objects of a Life Style* (New York, 1975), pp. 137, 139, 146–47, 155.

Rolf Middelboe
Danish, born 1917

A graphic designer and textile printer with his own workshop (since 1941), Middelboe has also provided designs for printed and woven textiles for a number of Danish firms, including Spindegården and Unika-Vaev (VII-47). His regular, screen-printed patterns of simple geometric motifs are given heightened interest by the variety of their arrangement and color and by the use of positive/negative alternations.

References: Arne Karlsen, *Made in Denmark* (New York, 1960), pp. 80–85; Erik Zahle, ed., *A Treasury of Scandinavian Design* (New York, 1961), p. 285, no. 158.

Elmer Miller
American, 1901–1960

Son of a glass craftsman (the maker of the first piece produced by the New Martinsville, Virginia, glass company, 1901), Miller began to work in the factory at the age of fourteen. A moldmaker by trade, later superintendent of the plant, Miller designed several elegant glass objects for New Martinsville (later the Viking glass company), including a pitcher with an elongated lip (II-43) and a candleholder similarly complex in its production technique.

Reference: Corning, N.Y., The Corning Museum of Glass, *Glass 1959* (1959), no. 289.

Børge Mogensen
Danish, 1914–1972

A student (1938–41) and then assistant of Kaare Klint—whose school of furniture design at the Royal Danish Academy of Fine Arts (Kongelige Danske Kunstakademi) in Copenhagen inspired much of Danish design of this period—Mogensen fully realized in production furniture the functional experiments of his teacher. His storage

Bernsen, *Design: The Problem Comes First* (Copenhagen, 1982), pp. 64–67.

units and sectional furniture, the "Boligens Byggeskabe (B.B.)" and "Øresund" systems, designed with another Klint follower GRETHE MEYER, were based on extensive investigation into the standardized measurements and ideal proportions of objects intended for daily use. Trained as a craftsman, Mogensen favored wood almost exclusively, combining it with leather and simple fabrics, which he designed along with LIS AHLMANN for C. Olesen (VII-1), for which he began to work as artistic consultant in 1953. His modest utilitarian pieces, designed first as head of the Danish Co-operative Wholesale Society (1942–50) and then independently, rely on a broad international furniture tradition, from Windsor chairs and Shaker forms to Chinese furniture. Conceived as durable, mass-market items for use in middle-class homes, they were practical and popular, and many are still in production (III-52).

Monograph: Arne Karlsen, *Furniture Designed by Børge Mogensen* (Copenhagen, 1968).

References: Bent Salicath and Arne Karlsen, eds., *Modern Danish Textiles* (Copenhagen, 1959), pp. 12–15; Arne Karlsen, *Made in Denmark* (New York, 1960), pp. 104–27.

Orla Mølgaard-Nielsen
Danish, born 1907

Trained as a cabinetmaker and furniture designer at the School of Arts and Crafts (Kunsthåndvaerkerskolen) in Copenhagen, Mølgaard-Nielsen also studied in that city at the Royal Danish Academy of Fine Arts (Kongelige Danske Kunstakademi) with the cabinetmaker and theorist Kaare Klint. In 1944 he formed a partnership with PETER HVIDT, and immediately after the war the firm achieved considerable success with a sectional furniture series that recalled Klint's own storage designs, but which could be easily and economically disassembled for shipment. In 1950 Mølgaard-Nielsen and Hvidt created the "Ax" series of chairs and tables for Fritz Hansen (III-31), which further developed the knock-down principle and introduced laminate glueing and plywood to the Danish furniture industry. Other clients have included France and Søborg.

References: Esbjørn Hiort, *Danish Furniture* (New York, 1956), pp. 11–12, 86–93; Erik Zahle, ed., *A Treasury of Scandinavian Design* (New York, 1961), p. 277, nos. 40–41; London, Whitechapel Art Gallery, *Modern Chairs: 1918–1970* (July 22–Aug. 30, 1970), no. 50.

Carlo Mollino
Italian, 1905–1973

The furniture of Mollino and his students at the university of Turin (from which he received a degree in architecture in 1931) stands apart from the rigorous rationalism of the Milanese school, which dominated design in Italy in the 1950s. Responding to the work of CHARLES EAMES, and perhaps inspired by the spatial concerns of Henry Moore, he developed a series of glass tables with one-piece plywood bases pierced and bent into complex curves, chairs sculptured into organic forms (III-53), and upholstered seating pieces with eccentric stances, which forcefully expressed his belief that everything is "permissible, as long as it is fantastic" (1951). Mollino was also active as an architect, interior designer, and urban planner, and wrote widely in the fields of art and architecture.

References: Roberto Aloi, *Esempi di Arredamento* (Milan, 1950), vols. 1–4, *passim*; "Across the Seas Collaboration for the New Singer Collection," *Interiors*, vol. 111 (Dec. 1951), pp. 120–29, 158; L. L. Ponti and E. Ritter, eds., *Mobili e interni di architetti italiani* (Milan, 1952), pp. 4, 21, 36–41, 68, 73, 91; "Nuovi Mobili di Mollino," *Domus*, vol. 270 (1952), pp. 50–53.

Ibi Trier Mørch
Danish, born 1910

Trained as an architect at the Royal Danish Academy of Fine Arts (Kongelige Danske Kunstakademi), Copenhagen, Mørch works as an industrial designer in the mediums of silver and glass. She has collaborated with ERIK HERLØW (1951–60), and with GRETHE MEYER on the "Stub" series of stacking glassware for the Kastrup glassworks (II-41).

References: "One Hundred Great Danish Designs," *Mobilia* (special issue), nos. 230–33 (Dec. 1974), no. 47; Stockholm, Nationalmuseum, *Danskt 50 Tal: Scandinavian Design* (Oct. 7–Nov. 29, 1981), p. 36, no. 126.

Olivier Mourgue
French, born 1939

Designer of furniture, textiles, environments, and toys, Mourgue is a serious inventor of new forms and a whimsical observer of contemporary life: his distinctly human "Bouloum" lounge chairs (III-55), used also as signposts in the French pavilion at Expo '70 in Osaka, and his "play seats" (*sièges jouets*) with kite frames and butterfly-wing at-

tachments (1973, 1974), reflect his concern that furniture, while functional and multipurpose, should also create an atmosphere of spontaneity and joy. Trained in interior design at the Ecole Boulle (1954–58) and the Ecole Nationale Supérieure des Arts Décoratifs (1958–60) in Paris, Mourgue achieved international recognition with his "Djinn" series for Airborne (1965; III-54), the first furniture to move toward sculptural and flowing forms, using urethane foam over tubular-steel frames, and considered so futuristic as to furnish the space-station interiors in Stanley Kubrick's film *2001: A Space Odyssey* (1968). His success won him the Eurodomus and A.I.D. awards in 1968, and commissions to design the interiors of the French government pavilions in Montreal in 1967 as well as in Osaka in 1970. Mourgue has also been concerned with problems of space and mobility. In a domestic environment created for Bayer's "Visiona 3" (1971), Mourgue developed a modular system based on the concept of open, undivided living space with movable room dividers; he has also developed a two-wheeled design studio (1970) for himself, designed an all-soft-surfaced plastic bathroom suite (1970), and prepared studies for Renault (1977) on interior space and color in automobiles. In 1976 Mourgue moved from Paris to Brittany, where he teaches at the Ecole d'Art in Brest.

References: London, Whitechapel Art Gallery, *Modern Chairs: 1918–1970* (July 22–Aug. 30, 1970), no. 117; Paris, Centre de Création Industrielle, *Design Français* (Oct.–Dec. 1971), no. 138; "Visiona 3," *Industrial Design*, vol. 19 (May 1972), pp. 42–45; J. Roger Guilfoyle, "An Atelier for Living," *Industrial Design*, vol. 20 (Oct. 1973), pp. 28–32.

Gerd Alfred Müller
German, born 1932

Apprenticed as a joiner (1952), Müller was trained as an interior designer at the Werkkunstschule in Wiesbaden and employed directly thereafter by Braun (1955). Subscribing to the functionalist aesthetic that the company was then developing, Müller designed some of Braun's best-known products of the later 1950s, including the kitchen machine (I-24) and electric razors, their solid undecorated forms creating an image of order and rational design. Since 1960 Müller has worked independently as an industrial and graphic designer in Eschborn.

Reference: *75 Jahre Deutscher Werkbund* (Frankfort, 1983), n.p.

Bruno Munari
Italian, born 1907

Known since the war as a graphic and industrial designer as well as a theorist and writer, Munari began his career as a painter and sculptor, exhibiting in Futurist exhibitions in Milan between 1928 and 1931 and designing constructions that he called useless machines in 1933 and 1945. Munari's earliest designs for industry were produced in the 1950s—a toy monkey for Pigomma, which won a Compasso d'Oro in 1954, an ice bucket for Tre A in 1955, which also won a Compasso d'Oro, and an ashtray for Danese in 1957 (VI-15), thus beginning a long association with the firm that continues to the present, and which has included objects as various as plastic lamps and wooden puzzles. During the 1970s Munari developed larger constructions in metal—a space-frame environment (1971) and a hanging bookshelf (for Robots), both awarded a Compasso d'Oro in 1979. As his career has been divided between the fine and applied arts so Munari has continuously explored through his writings and design practice the relationship between aesthetics and function. "Beauty as conceived of in the fine arts, a sense of balance comparable with that of the masterpieces of the past, harmony, and all the rest of it, simply make no more sense in design. If the form of an object turns out to be 'beautiful' it will be thanks to the logic of its construction, and to the precision of the solutions found for its various components. It is 'beautiful' because it is just right. An exact project produces a beautiful object, beautiful not because it is like a piece of sculpture, even modern sculpture, but because it is only like itself" (1971).

Writings: Bruno Munari, *Design As Art* (Baltimore, 1971).

References: Paolo Fossati, *Il design in Italia* (Turin, 1972), pls. 78–94 (biblio.); Alfonso Grassi and Anty Pansera, *Atlante del design italiano: 1940–1980* (Milan, 1980), p. 274.

Peter Murdoch
British, born 1940

An industrial designer and consultant (with his own firm since 1969), Murdoch is known for graphic, signage, and corporate identity programs, among them the graphics for the 1968 Olympics in Mexico City (with Lance Wyman). His fiberboard child's chair "Spotty" (III-56), which he designed as a student at the Royal College of

Art, London, and produced in America in 1964–65, was the first of its kind to be commercially marketed (albeit in small quantities). A redesigned line of brightly colored, plastic-coated, laminated-paperboard children's furniture, sold flat and at low cost by Perspective Designs in 1967, achieved wide distribution in Britain and abroad and received a Council of Industrial Design award in 1968.

References: "Children's Table, Chair and Stool: Perspective Design's Those Things," *Design*, no. 233 (May 1968), p. 33; London, Whitechapel Art Gallery, *Modern Chairs: 1918–1970* (July 22–Aug. 30, 1970), no. 69.

George Nakashima
American, born 1905

America's foremost furniture craftsman, Nakashima studied architecture at the University of Washington in Seattle and at the Massachusetts Institute of Technology in Cambridge. From 1934 to 1939 he practiced architecture with the firm of Antonin Raymond in Tokyo and India, returning to the United States in 1940 shortly before the outbreak of war in the Pacific. During 1941–42 Nakashima established his first furniture workshop in Seattle; following his internment in a war relocation center, Nakashima settled in New Hope, Pennsylvania, in 1943, and three years later built his present craft-furniture studio there. A designer of both production furniture and unique pieces, Nakashima uses machine tools and production methods as far as is possible without compromising the intrinsic qualities of the material: "Our approach is to realize a synthesis between the hand and the machine working as a small unit. It is a return to the business methods of the early American craftsman who made chairs, tables and cabinets, and put them in carts for transporting and selling directly to the customers who wanted them" (1981). Nakashima's original, graceful, and sturdy furniture (III-57) reflects influences of the Windsor chair, Shaker craftsmanship, Japanese woodworking, contemporary forms, and above all, the qualities and spirit of wood: "We work with wood, in a sense an eternal material, for without a tree there would be no human life. And we work with solid wood, not veneer, the better to search for its soul" (1981).

Writings: George Nakashima, *The Soul of a Tree: A Woodworker's Reflections* (Tokyo, 1981) (biblio.).

Nason & Moretti
Italian, established Venice, 1923

The firm of Nason & Moretti has depended on the experience of its own directors, rather than on outside designers, for the development of designs and models for the glass tablewares it has produced for some sixty years. The winner of a Compasso d'Oro in 1955, Umberto Nason's series of white bowls and glasses with brilliant colors on their interiors were cited for bringing a new direction and a new aesthetic to Murano glass (II-44).

Reference: Milan, Palazzo delle Stelline, *Design & design* (May 29–July 31, 1979), p. 42.

George Nelson
American, born 1908

Architect, industrial and interior designer, writer, and teacher, Nelson has been, with CHARLES EAMES, among the foremost American designers of the past forty years, an insistent, influential voice for rational, functional design and planning. Trained as an architect at Yale University in New Haven (1928–31), Nelson won the Prix de Rome in architecture in 1932, and as a fellow of the American Academy in Rome (1932–34), met the architects of the International Style, whom he wrote about in a series of articles in *Pencil Points* (1936–37). On his return to New York he became an editor of, and later consultant to, *Architectural Forum* (1935–44; 1944–49), and opened his first office in partnership with William Hamby (1936–41). During the early 1940s, Nelson developed two visionary ideas: "Grass on Main Street" (1942), a proposal for the now-familiar pedestrian mall, and the "storage wall" (1945), a combination storage unit and room divider that became ubiquitous in various forms from the late 1940s. In 1946 Nelson was appointed first design director of Herman Miller, beginning a long association with the firm, which continues to the present and has included designing and developing products ("Basic" storage components, 1946; "Comprehensive" storage system, 1958; "Catenary" furniture group, 1959; "Sling" sofa, 1964, III-58; "Action Office," 1964; "Executive Office" group, 1971) as well as interiors (Herman Miller showrooms in Chicago, 1948; New York, 1953, 1966; Washington, D.C., 1964), and architecture (Herman Miller factory, Zeeland, Michigan, 1962, 1966). In 1947 Nelson established an industrial design firm and an associated architecture firm in partnership with

Gordon Chadwick. Working independently, he has designed a broad range of well-known products, from his "Bubble" lamps (IV-27) and clock (I-25) for Howard Miller to plastic dinnerware for Prolon (VI-16). Nelson designed the American national exhibition in Moscow for the United States Information Agency (1959), the Chrysler exhibition and Irish pavilion at the New York World's Fair (1964), and "USA '76: The First Two Hundred Years," an exhibition for the American Revolution Bicentennial Administration (1976). Nelson's work and writings have mirrored the issues that have faced the design profession in the last decades—from his early concerns for space-saving furnishings in postwar houses to the notion of a total work environment and a consideration of the social aspects of recent urban planning.

Writings: George Nelson and Henry Wright, *Tomorrow's House* (New York, 1945); George Nelson, ed., *Living Spaces* (New York, 1952); George Nelson, ed., *Chairs* (New York, 1953); George Nelson, ed., *Display* (New York, 1953); George Nelson, ed., *Storage* (New York, 1954); George Nelson, *Problems of Design* (New York, 1957); George Nelson, *How to See* (Boston, 1977); George Nelson, *George Nelson on Design* (New York, 1979).

Reference: Olga Gueft, "George Nelson," in *Nelson/Eames/Girard/Propst: The Design Process at Herman Miller, Design Quarterly* (special issue), nos. 98–99 (1975), pp. 11–19.

Greta von Nessen
American, born Germany, c. 1900–c. 1978

After the death in 1942 of her husband, Walter von Nessen, a Bauhaus-trained architect and designer, Greta von Nessen directed the lighting company he had founded in 1927. She continued to market his many lamps, including his classic swing-arm series of 1927; introduced new models by other designers; and designed lamps herself. Her "Anywhere" lamp (IV-28) was exhibited in 1952 at the "Good Design" exhibition at the Museum of Modern Art in New York. An extremely versatile design, its pivoting dome on an aluminum frame allowed it to be hung, mounted on a wall, or set on a tabletop.

Reference: "Market Spotlight," *Interior Design*, vol. 42 (Mar. 1971), p. 68.

Aldo van den Nieuwelaar
Dutch, born 1944

Trained at the Akademie für Bildende Künste St. Joost in Breda, van den Nieuwelaar worked for architecture and design offices in Amsterdam before establishing his own firm there in 1969. During the 1970s van den Nieuwelaar designed exhibitions, light fittings, and furniture (III-59); he also served as a consultant to the Dutch lighting industry and designed lighting for the courtyard of the Frans Hals Museum, Haarlem (1974), and for the Bijenkorf company, Amsterdam (1978–79). His work is conceived graphically, using pure geometric forms: "Products with nothing to add to existing products have no right to exist, in my opinion. In my work I try to capture the essence of a utility product with a minimum of materials and means. Industrial design is a visual realization of that process" (1981).

Reference: Amsterdam, Visual Arts Office for Abroad, *Design from the Netherlands* (1981), pp. 38–41.

Marcello Nizzoli
Italian, 1887–1969

One of the most noted industrial designers of the twentieth century, Nizzoli was responsible for the elegant, functional styling of Olivetti products with a series of adding machines; calculators—"Summa 40" (1940), "Elettrosumma 14" (1946; I-26), and "Divisumma 14" (1948); and typewriters—"Lexicon 80" (1948; I-27) and "Lettera 22" (1950; I-28). He studied architecture, painting, and decoration at the Accademia di Belle Arti in Parma and exhibited in 1914 with the "Nuove Tendenze" group, which included the architect Antonio Sant'Elia. He was associated with rationalist architects and designers of the 1920s and 1930s, such as Giuseppe Terragni and Edoardo Persico, and it was with the latter, then editor of *Casabella*, that in 1931 Nizzoli did his first work for Olivetti: graphics for a newspaper advertisement. In 1938 Nizzoli was hired as a graphic designer in Olivetti's advertising office, but already by 1940 he had designed the first of the adding machines (in collaboration with engineers Natale Capellaro and Giuseppe Beccio). He was to serve the company also as its architect (and exhibition designer), and was responsible for its headquarters, Palazzo Olivetti, in Milan (with Bernasconi and Fiocchi). His inde-

pendent work included two well-known sewing machines for Necchi, cigarette lighters for Ronson (1959), furniture for Arflex, and a gasoline distributor and kitchen stove for Agip (1960). The Necchi "Supernova BU" and "Mirella" (I-29) sewing machines both won Compasso d'Oro awards, in 1954 and 1957, respectively, as did the Olivetti "Lettera 22," also in 1954.

Monograph: Germano Celant, *Marcello Nizzoli* (Milan, 1968) (biblio.).

References: Jay Doblin, *One Hundred Great Product Designs* (New York, 1970), nos. 3, 63, 83; Los Angeles, Frederick S. Wight Art Gallery, University of California, *Design Process Olivetti 1908–1978* (Mar. 27–May 6, 1979), p. 262, and *passim*; Alfonso Grassi and Anty Pansera, *Atlante del design italiano: 1940–1980* (Milan, 1980), p. 268.

Isamu Noguchi
American, born 1904

One of the most distinguished modern American sculptors, Noguchi has also designed furniture and lamps since the early 1940s. His 1944 free-form coffee table with glass top and detachable wooden base (for Herman Miller) was one of the most advanced "organic" furniture designs and, like his rocking stool-table of 1954 (for Knoll), widely imitated. Among his product designs, his lamps are perhaps best known. Evolving from experimental "Lunar" sculptures—thin, hollow, "light" sculptures of magnesite illuminated from within—the first lamp designed by Noguchi consisted of a simple cylinder supported by three legs and concealing a light bulb (IV-29). The relation of Noguchi's lamps to traditional Japanese forms grew more marked in the series of white-paper shades he developed from 1951. Made in Japan of mulberry-bark paper, they are produced in a wide variety of shapes (IV-30) from simple spheres to intricate twists, and called "Akari." "'Akari' means light in Japanese, its written ideograph the sun and the moon. In olden days it was customary to say 'bring an "Akari"' just as we would say 'bring a light.' 'Akari' also suggests lightness in the same way as 'light' does. This is why I named my lanterns 'Akari.' 'Akari' are light in weight, they bring lightness and light together, but what is of even greater significance to me is the quality of the light they shed. Due to the paper (handmade) there is a human warmth which we miss in our too perfect modern materials" (1954). Born in Los Angeles, Noguchi spent his childhood in Japan, returning to the United States in 1918. He studied art in New York, and in Paris with the sculptor Constantin

Brancusi (1927–28). His first major commission, a large relief sculpture for the Associated Press building in Rockefeller Center, New York, came in 1938.

Writings: Isamu Noguchi, "Japanese Akari Lamps," *Craft Horizons*, vol. 14 (Sept. 1954), pp. 16–18; Isamu Noguchi, "Akari," *Arts and Architecture*, vol. 72 (May 1955), pp. 14, 31.

Monographs: New York, Whitney Museum of American Art, *Isamu Noguchi* (1968); Minneapolis, Walker Art Center, *Noguchi's Imaginary Landscapes* (Apr. 23–June 18, 1978).

Eliot Noyes
American, 1910–1977

As consultant director of design for IBM from 1956 until his death, Noyes set its much-respected design policy and made it the first major American corporation to have an integrated and readily identifiable line of products and an architectural and graphic image. Dedicated to clear, clean design and the "obvious solution," Noyes preferred to "develop things which have a relation to people, things which people use and look at a lot" (1977). He saw his office as "the conscience in design for the client. We try to relate our work to a philosophy of design worked out to reflect the client and how he wants to be seen and known in society" (1966). A graduate of Harvard University (1932) in Cambridge, Massachusetts, with a master's degree in architecture from the Harvard Graduate School of Design, he first worked in the Cambridge office of the architects Marcel Breuer and Walter Gropius, but on the latter's recommendation, became the first director of the department of industrial design at the Museum of Modern Art in New York. He was responsible for the landmark 1940 "Organic Design in Home Furnishings" exhibition, which introduced the work of CHARLES EAMES and EERO SAARINEN. After the war Noyes became design director for Norman Bel Geddes, and began work on a typewriter design for IBM, a project he continued after he opened his own office in 1947. Noyes himself designed a number of IBM's best-known products, including the "Executive" (1959) and "Selectric" (1961; I-30) typewriters and many of its corporate office structures and interiors; he was also responsible for the appointments of Paul Rand as coordinator of graphics for IBM and Eames as designer of films and exhibitions. Noyes concurrently worked for other major corporations—Westinghouse, Mobil (from 1964, in charge of its total design program), Pan American World Airways, Xerox—and independently designed technically innovative structures and award-winning buildings, including his own house in New Canaan, Connecticut (1955). From 1947 to 1954 Noyes wrote a column on design for *Consumer Reports,* and from 1965 to 1970 he was president of the International Design Conference in Aspen, Colorado.

Writings: Eliot F. Noyes, *Organic Design in Home Furnishings* (New York, 1941).

References: Walter McQuade, "An Industrial Designer with a Conspicuous Conscience," *Fortune* (Aug. 1963), pp. 135–38, 183–88, 190; Scott Kelly, "Eliot Noyes and Associates," *Design,* no. 210 (June 1966), pp. 38–43; Jay Doblin, *One Hundred Great Product Designs* (New York, 1970), no. 93; "Eliot F. Noyes (1910–1977)," *Industrial Design,* vol. 24 (Sept.–Oct. 1977), pp. 42–43.

Yki Nummi
Finnish, born China, 1925

Born in China where his Finnish parents were missionaries, Nummi studied mathematics and physics in Helsinki and Turku (1945–47) and decorative painting at the Institute of Industrial Arts (Taideteollinen oppilaitos), Helsinki (1946–50). Specializing in the design of light fittings and color planning, Nummi designed light fixtures for Stockmann from 1950 to 1975, using innovative materials in various combinations and colors, including white (IV-31) and colored acrylics, opaline glass, enameled aluminum, and brass, for which he was awarded gold medals at the Milan Triennale in 1954 and 1957. In 1958 Nummi joined the paint manufacturer Schildt & Hallberg as head of the color planning department, and during the early 1960s designed a color plan for the Helsinki cathedral. Nummi has designed light fixtures for numerous Finnish institutions, and in 1971 was awarded the Pro-Finlandia Medal in recognition of his work.

Reference: Erik Zahle, ed., *A Treasury of Scandinavian Design* (New York, 1961), p. 287, no. 100.

Antti Nurmesniemi
Finnish, born 1927

Nurmesniemi trained as an interior designer at the Institute of Industrial Arts (Taideteollinen oppilaitos), Helsinki (1950), and worked for the architect Viljo Rewell before starting his own firm in 1956. He has designed numerous interior spaces (public and corporate offices, banks, restaurants, hotels) and for one of the first, the Palace Hotel, Helsinki (1952), he created the rustic horseshoe-shaped sauna stool (III-60) that was widely praised and awarded a silver medal at the Milan Triennale in 1964. Among his many exhibition installations was the characteristically spare Finnish section of the Triennale, which he arranged with his wife, textile designer VUOKKO ESKOLIN-NURMESNIEMI. As an industrial designer he has worked in many mediums: furniture (for Artek, Lifjaama, Merivaara, and his own studio), metal (his "Finel" coffeepot in colored enamel, 1958, for Wärtsilä, is a basic item in Finnish homes), glass, wallpaper, textiles, lighting, and transportation (with BÖRJE RAJALIN, the projection and prototype for the Helsinki Metro). Nurmesniemi was awarded the Lunning Prize in 1959 and is president of Ornamo, the Finnish Association of Designers.

References: Erik Zahle, ed., *A Treasury of Scandinavian Design* (New York, 1961), p. 287, nos. 19–20, 332; "Thirtyfour Lunning Prize-Winners," *Mobilia* (special issue), no. 146 (Sept. 1967), n.p.; London, Whitechapel Art Gallery, *Modern Chairs: 1918–1970* (July 22–Aug. 30, 1970), no. 35; Marja Kaipainen, "Some Call Them Purists," *Form Function Finland,* no. 2 (1981), pp. 12–16.

Sven Palmquist
Swedish, born 1906

A glass craftsman and designer in many forms (studio glass, tableware, lighting, architectural decoration) and techniques (engraving, cutting, layering), Palmquist was engaged in the craft even as a schoolboy, when he assisted glassblowers in a factory in his native province of Småland. He trained first at the engraving school of the Orrefors glassworks (beginning in 1928), then in Stockholm at the School of Arts, Crafts and Design (Konstfackskolan) (1931–33) and the Royal Academy of Fine Arts (Kungliga Konsthögskolan) (1934–36). He studied abroad, in Germany and Czechoslovakia (1936) and in France, Italy, and the United States (1937–39). From 1936 to 1972 he was a designer at Orrefors, where he developed two new styles—"Ravenna," a boldly colored glass with simple

mosaiclike inlays (II-45), and "Kraka," a white or colored glass with fishnetlike patterns—as well as a method of forming bowls from molten glass by centrifugal force, which eliminated the need for hand finishing (II-46).

References: "Sven Palmquist," *Design Quarterly,* no. 34 (1956), pp. 21–23; Erik Zahle, ed., *A Treasury of Scandinavian Design* (New York, 1961), p. 287, nos. 217, 219, 231; New York, Cooper-Hewitt Museum, *Scandinavian Modern Design: 1880–1980* (Sept. 14, 1982–Jan. 2, 1983), nos. 141, 147.

Verner Panton
Danish, lives in Switzerland, born 1926

Over the past thirty years Panton has been credited with truly innovative furniture design verging on the futuristic, as he wrestled with new technologies and expanded formal possibilities through the use of new materials: "I try to forget existing examples even though they may be good, and concern myself above all with the material. The result then rarely has four legs, not because I do not wish to make such a chair, but because the processing of materials like wire or polyester calls for new shapes" (1970). An architect as well as a designer, Panton studied at the Royal Danish Academy of Fine Arts (Kongelige Danske Kunstakademi) in Copenhagen and worked as an associate with ARNE JACOBSEN (1950–52) before starting his own firm in 1955. Throughout his career he has doggedly pursued the single-form chair, from his 1960 plastic design, the earliest to succeed in commercial production (issued by Herman Miller in 1967; III-61), and his 1965 "S-Chair," made of one sheet of plywood, to recent jigsawed plywood models (1982), cut out in abstract and natural shapes and painted in delicate colors. He has also designed exhibitions ("Visiona 2," for Bayer), lighting (for Louis Poulsen), rugs, and textiles (VII-48, 49).

References: "Experimentator im Design," *Form* (May 1969), pp. 2–7; Paris, Centre de Création Industrielle, *Qu'est-ce que le design?* (Oct. 24–Dec. 31, 1969), n.p.; London, Whitechapel Art Gallery, *Modern Chairs: 1918–1970* (July 22–Aug. 30, 1970), no. 56; Sylvia Katz, *Plastics: Designs and Materials* (London, 1978), pp. 87, 138, 142–43, 156, 169.

Pierre Paulin
French, born 1927

Like his compatriot OLIVIER MOURGUE, Paulin designed a succession of boldly sculptural furniture in the mid-1960s, with an inner structure of steel tubing, covered in foam and upholstered in stretch fabric (for Artifort). His "Ribbon" chair (III-62) and stacking chair (III-63) were totally new in form and a particularly striking departure from the upholstered seating on black tubular-metal legs that he had designed in the 1950s (for Thonet) and which had been marketed very successfully throughout Europe. Paulin collaborated in 1968 with the Mobilier National on the study of new furniture forms, developing the prototype of a snakelike "endless" sofa of rigid foam, which was manufactured (by Alpha) in 1971. His other work for the Mobilier has included important government commissions: special seating for the French government pavilion at Expo '70 in Osaka, furniture and interiors for the Elysée palace in Paris, and visitor seating for the Louvre. Since the mid-1960s Paulin has headed his own industrial and interior design firm, designing automobile interiors (for Simca), telephones (for L M ERICSSON), and packaging (for Christian Dior) in addition to furniture.

References: Paris, Musée des Arts Décoratifs, *Les Assises du siège contemporain* (May 3–July 29, 1968), nos. 221–28; London, Whitechapel Art Gallery, *Modern Chairs: 1918–1970* (July 22–Aug. 30, 1970), nos. 82–83; Paris, Centre de Création Industrielle, *Design Français* (Oct.–Dec. 1971), nos. 120–22, 140.

Inger Persson
Swedish, born 1936

Persson studied at the School of Arts, Crafts and Design (Konstfackskolan) in Stockholm and in 1959 began to design ceramic table services and decorative objects for Rörstrand. The winner of a gold medal at the international ceramic exhibition in Faenza in 1969, she opened her own workshop in 1971, but has since returned to Rörstrand. Her "Pop" service, designed in 1972 (II-47), combines the vitality of new forms and colors more often found in earthenware with the authority of traditional dinnerware in porcelain.

Reference: Lennart Lindkvist, ed., *Design in Sweden* (Stockholm, 1972), p. 39.

Sigurd Persson
Swedish, born 1914

A silver craftsman and independent designer, Persson is best known for his handcrafted jewelry and his simple, functional silver, stainless-steel flatware, hollow ware (V-28), and cooking utensils. He has also designed plastics, glassware, furniture, electrical equipment, and graphics. Trained first with his father, a silversmith, and then at the Akademie für Angewandte Kunst, Munich (1937–39), and the School of Arts, Crafts and Design (Konstfackskolan), Stockholm (1942), he opened a silver studio in 1942, and also undertook industrial design, producing in 1953 cutlery for the Cooperative Society of Sweden (Kooperativa Förbundet). His first prize in a 1959 competition for cutlery for Scandinavian Airlines (V-29) won him the commission for the entire in-flight tableware, and later for other airplane furnishings.

Writings: Sigurd Persson, *Modern Swedish Silver* (Stockholm, 1951).

Monograph: Malmö, Malmö Museum, *Sigurd Persson Design* (1961).

References: Erik Zahle, ed., *A Treasury of Scandinavian Design* (New York, 1961), p. 287, nos. 394, 397, 418; Graham Hughes, *Modern Silver throughout the World* (New York, 1967), nos. 137, 167–87.

Gaetano Pesce
Italian, born 1939

Like a number of other Italian designers, Pesce has recently begun to narrow his horizons, designing for a specialized audience and for small-scale production by small manufacturers: "There is a new phenomenon. In the past the designer's attitude was to design for the whole society. I prefer to study something for someone who is like me, for a little part of society" (*Industrial Design,* 1981). His means, however, have remained very much within mainstream Italian design, as he creates innovative forms in today's materials, generally plastics, by new methods (III-65). In 1969, working with the technical staff of C & B Italia, he devised a totally new furniture concept in his "Up" series: fabric-covered flexible polyurethane-foam seating without internal rigid structure, which was shipped flat in a vacuum vinyl container but expanded to its full form and density on being removed from the packing envelope (III-64). An artist who has worked in various kinetic, participatory, and conceptual mediums, Pesce began his design activity in 1962, after having attended the schools of architecture (1958) and industrial design (1959) in Venice and having worked at the Hochschule für Gestaltung in Ulm, West Germany (1961).

Writings: Gaetano Pesce, "Der Kollektive Schiffbruch," in *Design ist unsichtbar* (Vienna, 1981), pp. 299–304.

Monograph: Paris, Musée des Arts Décoratifs, *Gaetano Pesce: "The Future Is Perhaps Past"* (Jan. 8–Mar. 9, 1975) (biblio.).

References: New York, Museum of Modern Art, *Italy: The New Domestic Landscape* (May 26–Sept. 11, 1972), pp. 35, 97–98, 212–22; "Talking with Four Men Who Are Shaping Italian Design," *Industrial Design*, vol. 28 (Sept.–Oct. 1981), pp. 30–35.

Arne Petersen
Danish, born 1922

Petersen learned the trades of silversmith and goldsmith at the firm of C. C. Herman in Copenhagen, and since 1948 has been employed by Georg Jensen, joining the hollow-ware department in 1976. Among his designs is the ovoid stainless-steel and brass bottle opener of 1975 (V-30).

Reference: Washington, D.C., Renwick Gallery, *Georg Jensen—Silversmithy: 77 Artists 75 Years* (Feb. 29–July 6, 1980), no. 118.

Philco
American, established Philadelphia, 1892

Using assembly-line procedures, Philco introduced the first popular-priced radio receivers in 1929, and in the following years the company became one of the leading manufacturers of audio equipment, adding refrigerators, air conditioners, stoves, and other appliances over the next years. Its

first commercial television set, marketed in 1947, was followed by a series of models in conservative wooden cabinets, with technological features and larger screens added in pace with the industry. In 1958, however, the company departed from standard styling to bring out the "Predicta" line, which, according to its advertising, "for the first time in television history . . . freed the tube from the chassis." With a fully finished, brass-trimmed housing, the screen could swivel on its chassis in the floor or table (I-31) model, or be moved freely about a room in the portable model, connected to the chassis only by a thick wire.

Reference: "15 Years of Industrial Design," *Industrial Design*, vol. 16 (April 1969), p. 50.

Ezio Pirali
Italian, born 1921

An electromechanical engineer and managing director of Zerowatt, an Italian manufacturer of electrical appliances, Pirali has worked on developing the company's products and contributed to their distinctive styling, as demonstrated by his 1954 table fan (I-32), awarded a Compasso d'Oro that same year.

Reference: Milan, Palazzo delle Stelline, *Design & design* (May 29–July 31, 1979), p. 29.

Giancarlo Piretti
Italian, born 1940

A graduate of the Istituto Statale d'Arte in Bologna, Piretti immediately went to work for Castelli, where he became director of research and design. He developed furniture systems, primarily seating, with prefabricated and modular elements, suited to the industrial clients and assembly-line operation of this large-scale furniture manufacturer. His much-admired "Plia" chair (1969; III-66), an updated aluminum and plastic version of the traditional folding chair refined into pure visual geometry, spawned the "Plona" folding armchair (1970) and the "Platone" folding desk (1971), in similar materials and construction. His more recent work (with Emilio Ambasz) includes two series of ergonomically conceived seating, the "Dorsal" and "Vertebra" systems for Open Ark,

licensed to Castelli.

References: Adalberto Dal Lago, "Italian Look" (Milan, 1972), n.p.; London, Heal & Son Limited, *Classics* (Spring 1981), no. 71; "Vertebra Seating System," *Domus*, no. 572 (June 1977), pp. 38–39.

Warren Platner
American, born 1919

A graduate of the Cornell University School of Architecture in Ithaca, New York (1941), Platner worked in the offices of RAYMOND LOEWY, EERO SAARINEN, I. M. Pei, and Kevin Roche and John Dinkeloo before setting up his own design studio in North Haven, Connecticut, in 1967. Between 1953 and 1967, with the help of a grant from the Graham Foundation, Platner developed a line of sculptural wire furniture for Knoll (III-67), both creating the graceful single-form design itself and devising the tooling and elaborate methods for its production, which for an easy chair required 1,400 separate welds. He has continued to design furniture, especially for offices (for Knoll and Lehigh), and has worked on major architectural commissions and contract interiors, lighting, and furnishings, including the Georg Jensen Design Center and the Windows on the World restaurant in the World Trade Center in New York and Water Tower Place in Chicago.

Writings: Warren Platner, "Designing in Steel," *Industrial Design*, vol. 16 (June 1969), pp. 62–66.

References: "Prototypes and Principles," *Industrial Design*, vol. 17 (Sept. 1970), pp. 54–59; Barbaralee Diamonstein, *Interior Design: The New Freedom* (New York, 1982), pp. 238–43.

Flavio Poli
Italian, born 1900

As head designer for Seguso since 1934, Poli has been responsible for the high quality of new production of this Murano firm and the postwar introduction of its line of undecorated blown glass in simple shapes. His heavy vases (II-48), bowls, and glasses, particularly the cased glass of the late 1950s in several bold contrasting colors, achieve

both a satisfying sense of traditional harmony of form and an aura of contemporaneity.

References: Corning, N.Y., The Corning Museum of Glass, *Glass 1959* (1959), nos. 182–87; Gio Ponti, "Alta Fedeltà: Vetro di Flavio Poli," *Domus*, no. 410 (1964), pp. 50–52.

Gio Ponti
Italian, 1891–1979

For more than half a century Ponti was a champion of modern design both through the buildings and products he conceived and through the influential architecture and design magazines he directed: *Domus*, which he founded in 1928 and with the exception of six years, edited until his death, and *Stile*, which he directed from 1941 to 1947. His impact on the activity of Italian design circles was wide, be it through his participation in the organization of the Biennale of Monza (later the Milan Triennale), his work toward the institution of the Compasso d'Oro award, or his involvement in the founding of the Associazione per il Disegno Industriale. The architect of numerous buildings in Europe and worldwide, he left a strong mark on the skyline of his native Milan with the faceted concrete Pirelli tower of 1956 (with ALBERTO ROSSELLI and Antonio Fornaroli, his partners from 1950 to 1970, and others), considered one of the finest postwar buildings. His design activity was far-reaching, characterized by a personal and poetic expressiveness: His furniture of the 1940s and 1950s (for Cassina, Arflex, Singer, and the Nordiska Kompaniet) exhibits the same penchant for exaggerated lines and eccentric shapes seen in the articulation of his architectural surfaces, while his elaborate espresso-coffee machine for La Pavoni served as an icon of a new style. However, his toilet for Ideal Standard (I-33), considered the classic in its field, shows a simple purity of design, and his "Superleggera" chair (III-68) is a lightened, streamlined version of a traditional Italian form. He also produced a great deal of decorative work—ceramics for Richard Ginori, enamels for Paolo di Poli, mosaics for Gabbianelli, printed textiles, even stage designs for La Scala, Milan—that is of seizing imagery and brilliant colors. Indeed, the sheer range and extent of his output are extraordinary, especially considering that he was also an active professor of architecture at the Milan Politecnico and wrote nine books and three hundred studied articles.

Writings: Gio Ponti, "Come e perchè ho disegnato nuove forme," *Rivista Ideal Standard* (Jan.–Mar. 1959), pp. 47–49.

Monographs: "Espressione di Gio Ponti," *Aria d'Italia* (special issue), vol. 8 (1954); Nathan H. Shapira, "The Expression of Gio Ponti," *Design Quarterly* (special issue), nos. 69–70 (1967) (biblio.).

Reference: Jay Doblin, *One Hundred Great Product Designs* (New York, 1970), no. 74.

Carl Pott
German, born 1906

Successor to the metalwares firm founded by his father, Pott studied design and metallurgy at the technical school in Solingen and at the Forschungsinstitut und Probieramt für Edelmetalle in Schwäbisch-Gmünd. Determined to acquire proficiency as a metal craftsman, Pott specialized in damascening and galvanizing, passing master craftsman examinations in both fields before entering his father's business. Caught up in the ideas of the Deutscher Werkbund, the Bauhaus, and other progressive design movements in Germany during the 1920s, Pott completely altered the style of the firm's products, substituting his own simple, functional designs for the heavily ornamented work then still popular. His first recognition came in 1937 with a diploma of honor at the Paris exposition, followed by a silver medal at the 1940 Milan Triennale. Since the war Pott cutlery—silver, silver-plated, and stainless-steel designs both by Carl Pott himself (V-31, 32) and by the distinguished designers whose work he commissioned—has become the most premiated of modern flatware, repeatedly winning awards in Milan, Düsseldorf, Brussels, and Ljubljana. The designers who have collaborated with Pott include Josef Hoffmann, Hermann Gretsch, Elisabeth Treskow, and WILHELM WAGENFELD.

References: Heinz Georg Pfaender, "Der Designer Carl Hugo Pott," *Architecture und Wohnform*, vol. 74 (1966), pp. 372–74; Graham Hughes, *Modern Silver throughout the World* (New York, 1967), pls. 63–76.

David Harman Powell
British, born 1933

As chief designer of Ekco Plastics of Southend since 1960, Powell has been responsible for design innovation for the company's industrial and consumer products, including the injection-molded plastic stacking tableware "Nova," the winner of the Duke of Edinburgh's Prize for Elegant Design in 1968; "Ekcoware" kitchen storage containers; and a line of carefully engineered semi-disposable cutlery (VI-17). His technical experience in plastic processes was gained in the product design unit of British Industrial Plastics (1954–60), where he worked on the development of melamine tableware. Since 1968 he has worked independently, and served as the first tutor in molded plastics in the school of industrial design at the Royal College of Art, London.

References: John Heyes, "Getting It Right the First Time," *Design,* no. 217 (Jan. 1967), pp. 47–53; "Disposable Plastics Cutlery," *Design,* no. 258 (June 1970), p. 45.

Ambrogio Pozzi
Italian, born 1931

Successor to his family's ceramic factory in Gallarate, Pozzi redesigned the firm's traditional products in accordance with modern functional principles, winning two Compasso d'Oro awards in 1970 for his "Compact" coffee service and "TR 113" tableware series. Concerned with efficiency of production methods and use, he designed "Compact" entirely for machine manufacture and in three sizes unified in section and equal in diameter, which are thus capable of stacking. Pozzi also designed tablewares for Alitalia, and the "Duo" service for Rosenthal (II-49), the latter distinguished by the broad circular shape of the bowl which is repeated throughout in the design of the handles.

References: *Premio Compasso d'Oro* (1971), pp. 122–25; Faenza, Palazzo delle Esposizioni, *Arte e design* (July 27– Oct. 5, 1980), n.p.

Benno Premsela
Dutch, born 1920

Designer of textiles distinguished for their range of subtle colors and of exhibitions, Premsela was trained as an interior designer at the Nieuwe Kunstschool in Amsterdam (1937–41). He worked first in the furniture department of Bijenkorf, Amsterdam's largest department store (1949–51), later becoming head of display there (1956–63). Between 1951 and 1953 he worked in Italy designing and printing textiles, and was awarded bronze and silver medals for his fabrics at the Milan Triennale in 1954 and 1957, and first prize for carpet design in an Amsterdam competition of 1956. In 1963 Premsela established a partnership with the architect Jan Vonk, which has continued to the present (since 1973 as the firm Premsela Vonk). He has been responsible for design and product development of carpets for Van Besouw (since 1967; VII-50), wall coverings for Vescom (since 1972), and upholstery fabrics for Gerns & Gahler (since 1975).

Monograph: Amsterdam, Stedelijk Museum, *Benno Premsela onder anderen* (Dec. 12, 1981–Feb. 7, 1982).

Reference: Amsterdam, Visual Arts Office for Abroad, *Design from the Netherlands* (1981), pp. 50–51.

James Prestini
American, born 1908

America's most distinguished designer of wooden objects from the 1930s through the 1950s, Prestini was trained as a mechanical engineer at Yale University, New Haven (1930), and worked as a research engineer at the Armour Research Foundation, Chicago (1943–53). In connection with his work at Armour, he was one of a team that submitted a pioneering design for a one-piece molded-plastic chair to the low-cost furniture competition at the Museum of Modern Art in New York in 1948. Prestini had become interested in woodworking in 1933, and during the summer of 1938 had served an apprenticeship in furniture design with Carl Malmsten in Stockholm. For Prestini, turning wooden bowls was a way of studying the design process. Skilled also in metalworking techniques, he turned objects whose delicately thin, symmetrical shapes were derived from metal spinning and whose purity of form was much admired by proponents of functional modernism (VIII-6, 7). Prestini inspired a generation of American woodturners, who developed his semimechanical products into pure handcraft. Prestini has taught design continuously, including work at the Institute of Design, Illinois Institute of Technol-

ogy, Chicago (1939–46; 1952–53), and the University of California, Berkeley (1956 to present), and has served as a design education consultant to the governments of West Germany (1962) and India (1962–63), as well as the United States (1964). Between 1953 and 1956 Prestini studied sculpture in Italy, and continues to the present to work as a sculptor.

Monograph: Edgar Kaufmann, Jr., *Prestini's Art in Wood* (New York, 1950).

References: Edgar Kaufmann , Jr., *Prize Designs for Modern Furniture* (New York, 1950), pp. 44–47; Don Wallance, *Shaping America's Products* (New York, 1956), p. 152; John Kelsey, "The Turned Bowl," *Fine Woodworking* (Jan.–Feb. 1982).

Ulla Procopé
Finnish, 1921–1968

Educated at the Institute of Industrial Arts (Taideteollisuuskeskuskoulu), Helsinki, Procopé designed useful ceramic wares for Arabia from 1948, the year of her graduation, working as a model planner under the direction of KAJ FRANCK. Among her designs were "Liekki" (1957) and "Ruska" (1960; II-50), the first, a flameproof stackable series with lids that can be used as serving dishes, the second, a set combining craftsmanlike effects of texture with a strong, warm-brown stoneware glaze. Procopé was awarded a diploma of honor at the Milan Triennale of 1957 and gold medals at ceramic exhibitions in Sacramento (1962, 1963), San Francisco (1963), and Utrecht (1963).

References: Erik Zahle, ed., *A Treasury of Scandinavian Design* (New York, 1961), p. 288, nos. 331, 333; Benedict Zilliacus, "Discreet and Important," *Ceramics and Glass,* no. 1 (1969), pp. 2–3; Leena Maunula, "A Hundred Years of Arabia Dishes," *Ceramics and Glass* (special issue) (Nov. 1973), p. 20.

Jens Quistgaard
Danish, born 1919

Designer of objects in wood, glass, and metal, Quistgaard apprenticed at the Georg Jensen silversmithy and opened an independent design studio in Copenhagen after the war. Specializing in metalwares, Quistgaard achieved his first recognition in 1954, when he was awarded both the Lunning Prize and gold and silver medals at the

Milan Triennale (for enameled cast-iron cooking pots for De Forenede Jernstøberier and for flatware). In the same year, with the American Ted Nierenberg, Quistgaard founded Dansk International Designs, for which he has served as principal designer of tablewares, including wooden objects (VIII-8, 9), enameled cookware, cutlery, ceramics, and glass. Strongly sculptural though economical of form, Quistgaard's designs exploit the inherent nature of the materials he uses, whether they are natural wood, unglazed stoneware, or cast metal.

References: Arne Karlsen, *Made in Denmark* (New York, 1960), pp. 116–17; "Thirtyfour Lunning Prize-Winners," *Mobilia* (special issue), no. 146 (Sept. 1967), n.p.

Peter Raacke
German, born 1928

Trained in enamel-, gold-, and silverwork at the Staatliche Zeichenakademie in Hanau and as a metal and glass artist at the Werkschule in Cologne, Raacke has designed metal cutlery, kitchen tools, and cookware for Hessische Metallwerke, notably his "Mono-a" series (V-33), with cutlery issued in stainless steel and in sterling. He also designed a range of cardboard furniture, his "Papp" series (1967)—modular seating, tables, and storage units in hexagonal format, as well as stacking easy chairs (III-69)—produced by highly automated methods by Faltmöbel Ellen Raacke.

References: "Technologia del Provvisorio: Papp, Mobili di Carta," *Casabella,* no. 323 (Feb. 1968), pp. 55–56; "Paper for Parents and Children," *Design,* no. 232 (Apr. 1968), p. 65; Nuremberg, Gewerbemuseum, *Gold & Silber, Schmuck & Gerät* (Mar. 19–Aug. 22, 1971), n.p.

Ernest Race
British, 1913–1963

Race was consistently innovative in the materials (aluminum, steel, plastics) and techniques that he used for his furniture. In 1945, with a background in interior design at the Bartlett School of Architecture of the University of London, he founded Ernest Race Ltd. (later Race Furniture) with a tool-and-die manufacturer who wanted to apply

engineering techniques to furniture production. Restricted to metal (no wood or fabric was permitted the young company by the Board of Trade in postwar Britain), Race designed the "BA" chair (III-70) to be sand-cast from re-smelted aluminum alloy from aircraft salvage; shown at the "Britain Can Make It" exhibition in 1946 (see p. 39), it became his most successful single product. Other original furniture followed, including a metal-framed wing chair (1947); a design for component storage units, awarded an honorable mention in the 1948 international competition for low-cost furniture design at the Museum of Modern Art in New York; outdoor furniture produced for the 1951 Festival of Britain (see p. 39; III-71); and the "Sheppey" series, component chairs and settees (1963). Race continued as director of design at the firm until 1954, after which he became a freelance designer.

Monograph: Hazel Conway, *Ernest Race* (London, 1982).

References: "Design Review: Trends in Factory Made Furniture by Ernest Race," *Architectural Review,* vol. 103 (May 1948), pp. 218–20; L. Bruce Archer, "Theory into Practice: Design and Stress Analysis," *Design,* no. 101 (May 1957), pp. 18–21; Gillian Naylor, "Ernest Race," *Design,* no. 184 (Apr. 1964), pp. 54–55; Race Furniture Limited, "Race: Case Histories" (Submitted to the Royal Society of Arts . . . 1969), pp. 3–13; London, Whitechapel Art Gallery, *Modern Chairs: 1918–1970* (July 22-Aug. 30, 1970), nos. 26, 50.

Börje Rajalin
Finnish, born 1933

Rajalin graduated from the Helsinki Institute of Industrial Arts (Taideteollinen oppilaitos) in 1955 and the following year opened his own studio, working in the fields of consumer, exhibition, and interior design. He has designed technical and transportation equipment (a train for the Helsinki Metro, 1972, with ANTTI NURMESNIEMI), plastic fittings, cutlery, and stainless-steel table- and cookware (V-34). Rajalin is also a silversmith, having worked for BERTEL GARDBERG and provided jewelry designs for Kalevala Koru since 1956. A large silver screen won him a gold medal at the Triennale in Milan in 1960 and the A.I.D. International Design Award in 1961. He received the Lunning Prize in 1963 for Scandinavian achievement.

References: Erik Zahle, ed., *A Trea-*

sury of Scandinavian Design (New York, 1961), p. 288, nos. 371–72; Graham Hughes, *Modern Silver throughout the World* (New York, 1967), no. 137.

Dieter Rams
German, born 1932

Germany's most important industrial designer of the postwar period, Rams developed the modern design program at Braun, which he joined in 1955 and where he has served as chief designer and head of product design. Responsible for many of the austerely beautiful and functional appliances (I-37) that transformed the Braun product range in the 1950s and 1960s, Rams also created the system of "product families" in which several products are interconnected and combined with one another over a period of years. One of the first of these was series of hi-fi units, beginning with a combined radio and phonograph (with HANS GUGELOT, 1956; I-35) and including the "Atelier 1" unit (1957), which for the first time separated a loudspeaker from the chassis, the separated loudspeaker also usable as a supplementary speaker for the original model. Rams simultaneously developed a series of portable radios that included the "Transistor 1" (1956; I-34) and the "T3-T4" (1958) pocket receiver, which was combined with a small record player as a portable phonograph and radio combination (1959; I-36). For Rams "the aesthetic requirement of an industrial product is that it should be simple, carefully made, honest, balanced and unobtrusive. . . . I regard it as one of the most important and most responsible tasks of a designer today to help clear the chaos we are living in" (1978). Rams studied architecture and interior design at the Werkkunstschule in Wiesbaden (1947). By 1956 he had abandoned architecture for product design at Braun and in 1957 designed his first furniture for what was to become the Vitsoe furniture factory. His furniture program of modular storage units and seating (III-72) reflects the same concern for fitness and order that characterizes his work for Braun.

Writings: Dieter Rams, "And That's How Simple It Is to Be a Good Designer," *Designer* (Sept. 1978), pp. 12–13; Dieter Rams, "Die Rolle des Designers im Industrieunternehmen," in *Design ist unsichtbar* (Vienna, 1981), pp. 507–16.

Monograph: François Burkhardt and Inez Franksen, eds., *Design: Dieter Rams &* (Berlin, 1980–81) (biblio.).

Hans Rath
Austrian, 1904–1968

Great-grandson of the founder of Lobmeyr, the noted Viennese manufacturer and distributor of crystal tableware and chandeliers, Rath studied art history in Munich and entered the firm in 1924, becoming its chief designer in 1938. He was instrumental in the postwar revival of the Austrian glass industry and brought back to Lobmeyr prestigious chandelier commissions for public buildings, theaters, and opera houses (Metropolitan Opera House in Lincoln Center, New York, 1966; John F. Kennedy Center for the Performing Arts in Washington, D.C., 1968, designed by his son Peter), such as the firm had enjoyed during the nineteenth century. His designs for table crystal include the "Alpha" service of 1952 (II-51), its simple outline following the tradition of the crystal designed by Josef Hoffmann for Lobmeyr about 1920.

References: Corning, N.Y., The Corning Museum of Glass, *Glass 1959* (1959), no. 2; Abby Rand, "The Lights of Lobmeyr," *Town & Country* (Dec. 1981), pp. 266–67, 331–34.

Armi Ratia
Finnish, 1912–1979

Founder of Marimekko, Ratia developed the concept of printed textiles in bold, nonfigurative patterns and strong, saturated colors, which broke with traditional furnishing and dress fabrics. Trained in textile design at the Institute of Industrial Arts (Taideteollisuuskeskuskoulu), Helsinki (1935), Ratia maintained a weaving shop in Vyborg, where she sold *rya* rugs of her own design (until 1939). A decade later, in 1949, Ratia joined her husband's company, Printex, which manufactured oilcloth, and immediately reorganized the factory for silkscreen printing by hand on cotton sheeting. Ratia encouraged a number of designers to realize their graphic ideas in the textile medium, including MAIJA ISOLA and VUOKKO ESKOLIN-NURMESNIEMI. To popularize Printex's new cotton

fabrics, Ratia conceived the idea of introducing them into a range of made-up dresses, first presented in 1951 under the name Marimekko ("A little dress for Mary"), which later became the trading name for the whole of the organization's activities. The first prints were small abstract patterns, which became increasingly large in scale (VII-51); during the 1960s, principally through Isola, Marimekko introduced more densely patterned prints and brightly colored oversize bird and flower designs. Marketed most successfully in northern Europe and the United States, Marimekko products were diversified during the 1960s and 1970s and ranged from cotton, jersey, and wool fabrics to paper goods, laminated plastics, and table coverings. For Ratia, "colors have always been the subject of our interest and study. The color experiments are merciless. If a general concept is correct from the start, if a fashion or pattern is well thought out right away, it will be good for twenty years" (1975).

References: David Davies, "Fabrics by Marimekko," *Design*, no. 236 (Aug. 1968), pp. 28–31; "The Finn-Tastics," *Sphere* (Mar. 1975); Ristomatti Ratia, "The Legacy of Armi Ratia," *Form Function Finland*, nos. 1-2 (1980), pp. 10–11.

Carlos Riart
Spanish, born 1944

A designer of interiors, exhibitions, and furniture, Riart studied industrial design and cabinetry, and taught industrial design at the Escuela de Diseño Eina in Barcelona (1976–78). His furnishings of the 1970s and 1980s—tables, chairs (III-73), cabinets, lighting, and mirrors—for Snark, Tecmo, Ecart, and Knoll, allude to historical and 1950s forms in their highly individual but decidedly Post-Modern style.

References: "A Barcelona Workshop," *Domus*, no. 546 (May 1975), p. 28; "Knoll Presents: Three Diverse Furniture Groups," *Interior Design*, vol. 53 (Dec. 1982), pp. 134–35.

Claus Josef Riedel
Austrian, born 1925

Member of the Riedel family, whose glassmaking factories were expropriated and lost during the war, Riedel studied chemistry in Innsbruck (1947–50) and afterward worked for Ginori at the Cristalleria Nazionale in Naples, becoming the factory's technical director. In 1956 Riedel, together with his father, established an independent factory in

Kufstein, and by 1958 had won the first of what was to be a long series of prizes for distinguished glassware of his design, ranging from silver medals at the 1960 Milan Triennale for glasses to the Bundespreis "Gute Form" for "Genova" in 1982. In 1969 Riedel opened a second factory at Schneegattern, which was notable at the time for its modern production methods, and in 1972 established a lead crystal grinding shop in Matrei. Although he declared himself a glassmaker rather than an artist, the elegant, clean lines of his glasses, such as "Exquisit" (II-52) and "Monaco," have been universally considered models of functional design.

References: Corning, N.Y., The Corning Museum of Glass, *Glass 1959* (1959), no. 5; Corning, N.Y., The Corning Museum of Glass, *New Glass: A Worldwide Survey* (Apr. 26–Oct. 1, 1979), p. 267, nos. 194–95; "Moderne Klassiker, pt. 13: Geschirr, Besteck, Glas," *Schöner Wohnen* (Feb. 1982), p. 183.

Gastone Rinaldi
Italian, born 1920

A graduate of the Istituto Tecnico Superiore, Padua, Rinaldi began his career as a designer in 1948, specializing in metal furniture (for Rima) that won him a Compasso d'Oro in 1954 for its style and quality of execution. His recent work for Thema, of which he is also a partner, includes the "Aurora" stacking chair and the "Dafne" folding chair (1979; III-74).

References: Ernst Erik Pfannschmidt, *Metallmöbel* (Stuttgart, 1962), pp. 26–28, 32, 39, 44, 60, 101; Milan, Palazzo delle Stelline, *Design & design* (May 29–July 31, 1979), p. 28.

Nick Roericht
German, born 1932

A student (1955–59) and later faculty member (1964) of the Hochschule für Gestaltung in Ulm, West Germany, Roericht achieved notable success with his senior diploma project of 1959, a widely imitated design for stacking dinnerware (II-53), which has been produced by Thomas since 1961. Following the Ulm curriculum, which

included a basic design exercise in modular stacking elements, Roericht has since been a designer of systems and environments rather than isolated forms. After teaching industrial design at Ohio State University, Columbus (1966–67), Roericht opened an independent design office in Ulm in 1967–68, specializing in visual communication and research and design of product programs. From 1967 to the present he has worked for Lufthansa, designing color systems for aircraft, lounge furnishings, interiors, and graphic displays, including passenger information charts. Roericht's other major commissions have included the conception and design of visitor and participant facilities, among them desk systems and stadium seating, for the Munich Olympic Games (1972), and studies of working environments for Wilkhahn (1971) and Eüro-Landschaft (1977). Since 1977 Roericht has taught industrial design at the Hochschule der Künste, Berlin.

Reference: Gillo Dorfles, *Il disegno industriale e la sua estetica* (Bologna, 1963), no. 97.

Maya Romanoff
American, born 1941

During the 1970s Romanoff introduced the concept of textile environments, both in one-of-a-kind pieces executed on commission and in coordinated wall and floor coverings and upholstery fabrics. After graduating from the University of California at Berkeley and traveling in North Africa and India, he began experiments with his then-wife Rebecca in resist-dyeing, using their fabrics first for hand-dyed clothing collections, and then for furnishings. Through technical experimentation and innovation, Romanoff has brought these traditional techniques into the industrial world, devising methods of repeating them consistently over long runs of yardage (VII-52). In his first fabric environment, "Garden Room," commissioned by *House and Garden* (1971), he executed a resist-dyed canvas floor covering, an idea that he introduced to the trade in 1976, winning a Resources Council award for the best technological innovation in American home furnishings. He has also devised methods of resist-dyeing leather and suede, and introduced quilting into furnishing materials.

Monograph: New York, The Arsenal, *Maya Ramanoff: Fabric Impressionist* (1979).

Alberto Rosselli
Italian, 1921–1976

Founder and editor of *Stile Industria* (1953–63), Rosselli was an organizer and first president (1956) of the Associazione per il Disegno Industriale. With a degree in architecture from the Politecnico of Milan (1947), where he later taught (from 1963), Rosselli joined with his father-in-law GIO PONTI and Antonio Fornaroli in an architecture and design firm (Studio PFR) organized in 1950, collaborating (until 1970) on many buildings, including the Pirelli tower in Milan (1956). He also worked independently, beginning in 1955, designing transportation (for Fiat-Orlandi), appliances, furniture (for Kartell, Arflex, Bonacina, and Saporiti), lighting (for Fontana Arte), metalwork, ceramics (for Cesame), and glass (for Salviati). His plastic furniture (III-75) responds to the flexibility and multiplicity of function required in modern environments and shows a willingness to go beyond rigid categories and develop a vocabulary of forms with new technology and materials.

Monograph: Giovanni Klaus Koenig et al., *Stile Industria: Alberto Rosselli* (Parma, 1981).

Reference: Paolo Fossati, *Il design in Italia* (Turin, 1972), pp. 128–38, pls. 355–403 (biblio.).

David Rowland
American, born 1924

Son of a museum director and a violinist, Rowland studied briefly with László Moholy-Nagy at Mills College in Oakland, California (1940), and at the Cranbrook Academy of Art, Bloomfield Hills, Michigan (1950–51). After working for Norman Bel Geddes in New York (1952–53), Rowland opened his own design office there in 1955. A tireless experimenter, he has devoted his career to exploring the use of steel and plastic finishes in seating, developing two innovative, widely premiated chairs—the "40-in-4" lightweight stacking and ganging chair (forty chairs can be stacked in a height of four feet) of steel-wire rod and sheet steel (1964; III-76), and the "Sof-Tech" chair of tubular steel and vinyl-coated steel-wire springs (1979; III-77). "Steel wire fits a concept which I believe to be fundamental to good design—to accomplish the most with the least. . . . A small amount of wire can furnish great strength with very little weight or bulk. It can provide rigidity, but also resiliency. And wire suggests intriguing visual ideas: its openness, for example, and its literally infinite variety of forms" (1965).

References: "United States Steel," *Industrial Design,* vol. 12 (Nov. 1965), pp. 7–9; Olga Gueft, "Thonet Sof-Tech Stacker," *Interiors,* vol. 139 (Aug. 1979), pp. 66–67, 84; "David Rowland Designs the Sof-Tech Chair for Thonet," *Interior Design,* vol. 50 (Aug. 1979), p. 167.

Eero Saarinen
American, born Finland, 1910–1961

Perhaps the greatest architect of his generation and himself the son of a gifted architect (Eliel Saarinen), Eero Saarinen created highly original works, daring in concept and sculptural in form. They epitomized a free, organic style that challenged functionalist architecture during the 1950s and included the Jefferson National Expansion Memorial (Gateway Arch) in Saint Louis (completed 1964), Trans World Airlines terminal, John F. Kennedy airport, New York (1962), and the terminal building, Dulles International airport, Washington, D.C. (1963). Saarinen was equally important as a furniture designer, and collaborated with CHARLES EAMES on a revolutionary body-molded plywood-shell chair that won two first prizes in the Museum of Modern Art's organic design competition of 1940, anticipating both his own work with molded plastic shells—the 1946 upholstered "Womb" chair (III-78) and the 1956 pedestal series (III-79, 80)—as well as that of Eames (III-25). Saarinen developed the possibilities and richness of plastic form in smooth-flowing classic shapes (III-78) that recall his boyhood ambition to be a sculptor. In 1923 Saarinen moved with his family from Finland to Bloomfield Hills, Michigan, where his father designed, and later became president of, the Cranbrook Academy of Art. Saarinen studied architecture at Yale University in New Haven, served briefly on the Cranbrook faculty, and practiced architecture from 1936 until his death in 1961.

Writings: Eero Saarinen, "Function, Structure and Beauty," *Architectural Association Journal,* vol. 73 (July–Aug. 1957), pp. 40–51; Aline B. Saarinen, ed., *Eero Saarinen on His Work* (New Haven, 1968).

Monographs: Allan Temko, *Eero Saarinen* (New York, 1962); Robert A. Kuhner, *Eero Saarinen: His Life and Work* (Monticello, Ill., 1975).

Reference: Detroit, Detroit Institute of Arts, *Cranbrook: The Saarinen Years* (forthcoming).

Lino Sabattini
Italian, born 1925

One of Italy's leading silversmiths, Sabattini educated himself in Como during the war by reading *Domus,* by studying the techniques and materials of metalworking at the brasswares shop where he worked, and by serving an informal apprenticeship with a refugee German potter, Rolando Hettner. By 1955 Sabattini had moved to Milan and established contact with GIO PONTI and the young architects around him. Between 1956 and 1963 he worked in Milan, and in Paris, where he served as director of design for Christofle; in 1964 he established his own factory at Bregnano, near Como. Original, independent, and inventive, Sabattini combines technical understanding of the nature of his materials with a gift for fantasy (V-35, 36).

Monograph: Enrico Marelli, *Lino Sabattini: Intimations and Craftsmanship* (Mariano Comense, 1979).

Roberto Sambonet
Italian, born 1924

An industrial and graphic designer as well as a painter, Sambonet studied architecture at the Politecnico in Milan (1942–45). He painted professionally, and worked at the Museu de Arte in São Paulo, Brazil (1948–53), and with ALVAR AALTO in Finland (1953) before joining his family firm in Vercelli in 1954 as a designer of stainless-steel cutlery and cooking wares. His elegant fish serving dish in the form of a bivalve shell (V-37), his flatware, and his series of nesting containers—including the eight concentric "Center Line" saucepans and frying pans (V-38)—were new designs for the company, establishing Sambonet as a distinguished inventor of forms and bringing the designer such awards as the Compasso d'Oro (1956, 1970) and gold medals (1957, 1973) and a grand prize (1960) at the Milan Triennale. Sambonet has elaborated his interest in rational, abstract forms: "I project, for pure research, a new spider web, a square example according to a 'Max-Billian' scheme. I derive from it a result never seen before, although formalist, one that is very different instead if I add more, identical spider webs, or ones with different diameters in a modular progression, intersecting, projecting into three-dimensional space" (Grassi and Pansera, 1980). Along such lines he has reduced the series of "Center Line" containers to a single geometrical structure through the modulated alteration of their proportions and profiles, and has extended this concept to his work in other mediums, including glasswares for Baccarat (1977; II-54) and Seguso (1979) and ceramics for Bing & Grøndahl (1974) and Richard Ginori (1979). Sambonet served as art director of the Italian periodical *Zodiac* (1957–60) and taught design in Rio de Janeiro, São Paulo, and Carrara (1980).

Monograph: Milan, Palazzo Bagatti Valsecchi, *Roberto Sambonet: Design grafica pittura '74–'79* (1980) (biblio.).

References: Paolo Fossati, *Il design in Italia* (Turin, 1972), pp. 135–40, 239–42, pls. 404–49 (biblio.); Alfonso Grassi and Anty Pansera, *Atlante del design italiano: 1940–1980* (Milan, 1980), p. 287.

Astrid Sampe
Swedish, born 1909

Textile artist and designer, Sampe has been influential as a pattern designer and colorist, and through the innovative policies she pursued from 1937 to 1972 as head of the textile design workshop of the Nordiska Kompaniet, Stockholm. In 1946 she introduced glass cloth to Sweden, and during the 1950s, in cooperation with the Kasthall and Wahlbeck rug factories, was responsible for the revival there of industrially woven carpets. In 1955 Sampe created a series of household linens in geometric and folk-inspired prints that, like other contemporary tablewares, could be used interchangeably (VII-53). Trained at the Stockholm School of Arts, Crafts and Design (Konstfackskolan) and at the Royal College of Art, London, Sampe was named a Royal Designer for Industry in 1949 and has received many awards for her work, including a gold medal at the Milan Triennale of 1954 and a silver medal at the Triennale of 1960. Since 1972 she has worked in Stockholm as an independent interior and textile designer.

Writings: Astrid Sampe, *Swedish Textile* (Stockholm, 1981).

References: Erik Zahle, ed., *A Treasury of Scandinavian Design* (New York, 1961), p. 290, nos. 112, 115; Lennart Lindkvist, ed., *Design in Sweden* (Stockholm, 1972), pp. 66–67.

Ludovico de Santillana
Italian, born 1931

Director of Venini International, de Santillana took over the firm in 1959 with Ginette Venini, when his father-in-law, PAOLO VENINI, died. Among the first works presented by the new administration at the Venice Biennale in 1960 was the "Battuto" series, which de Santillana himself designed in collaboration with TOBIA SCARPA (II-55). His other works include the "Faraono" eggs (1963) and a series of vases, bowls, and accessories designed for Pierre Cardin (1969). De Santillana has continued Venini's tradition of developing new forms and techniques in collaboration with outstanding international architects and designers, such as, from the 1960s, Toni Zuccheri, TAPIO WIRKKALA, and the American studio-glass artists Dale Chihuly and Richard Marquis. In 1965 de Santillana started a new glass manufacturing unit, V-Linea and Ve-Art, which employ semiautomatic production systems and commercial applications of handblown techniques. Of major importance to the Ve-Art and V-Linea group in the 1970s and 1980s have been architectural lighting commissions, which support the free, handblown art glass for which the Venini factory is best known. De Santillana is a graduate of the school of architecture in Venice (1955), where he taught architectural design from 1959 to 1968.

Reference: Washington, D.C., Smithsonian Institution, *Venini Glass* (1981).

Richard Sapper
Italian, born Germany, 1932

Trained in engineering and economics, Sapper worked as a designer for Daimler-Benz (1956) in Germany before moving to Italy in 1958. Specializing in high technology products—particularly in the field of consumer electronics—Sapper worked in Milan first in the office of GIO PONTI and then, until 1977, often in collaboration with

MARCO ZANUSO, with whom he designed a series of award-winning products for Brionvega (I-51, 52, 54). In 1968 he was co-organizer of an exhibition of advanced technology at the Milan Triennale, and from 1970 to 1976 served as a consultant to Fiat and Pirelli on the development of experimental vehicles and automobile equipment. In 1972 he collaborated with GAE AULENTI on an investigation of new systems of urban transport, which was developed as an exhibition for the 1979 Triennale in Milan. In 1980 Sapper was appointed industrial design consultant to IBM for all product design work. His widely premiated domestic products for Kartell (III-96), Artemide, and Alessi (V-39) are as well engineered as their industrial counterparts, and range from the "Tizio" lamp (IV-32), its arms designed to act as counterweights, to a series of timing devices (I-38).

References: Paolo Fossati, Il design in Italia (Turin, 1972), p. 219 (biblio.); Alfonso Grassi and Anty Pansera, Atlante del design italiano: 1940–1980 (Milan, 1980), p. 289, and passim; Jane Lott, "Interview: Fifties Fantasist Turned Design Houdini," Design, no. 381 (Sept. 1980), p. 37.

Gino Sarfatti
Italian, born 1912

Sarfatti was the moving force behind the development of innovative lighting in Italy immediately after the war, dominating the field in the 1950s through his own models and those of other designers—FRANCO ALBINI, VITTORIANO VIGANÒ, Ico Parisi, GIANFRANCO FRATTINI, MARCO ZANUSO—manufactured by his firm Arteluce (founded in 1939). Initially producing brass and lacquered metal lamps of a functionalist style (IV-33), Sarfatti soon became more adventurous, experimenting with a variety of new materials and forms, including exposed neon tubes, plastics, and movable elements (IV-34); he pioneered halogen lamps for home use, producing the first halogen table lamp in 1971. He won the Compasso d'Oro two years running, in 1954 and 1955 (the first two years of the award), as well as a prize at the Milan Triennale. Most of his later individual work was done for the hotels, schools, offices, and ships designed by advanced architects, including the fixtures in the *Michelangelo* and *Raffaello* ocean liners, the Olivetti building in Barcelona, and the Hilton Hotel in Rome. He brought to his work a passionate dedication to all technical aspects of production that admitted no compromise, and when

eventually his company was bought by Flos, Sarfatti severed himself from all designing activity.

References: "Cause for Applause: Lightolier's Italian Lamps and Wormley Decor," *Interiors*, vol. 110 (Nov. 1950), pp. 130–32; Andrea Branzi and Michele De Lucchi, eds., Il design italiano degli anni '50 (Milan, 1981), pp. 221, 223, 225–27, 229, 232; Daniele Baroni, L'Oggetto lampada (Milan, 1981), pp. 126–27, figs. 268–69, 271–72, 274–85.

Timo Sarpaneva
Finnish, born 1926

Designer of graphics, textiles, glass, ceramics, metalwork, and exhibitions, Sarpaneva is an innovator of forms and technical processes: for his Ambiente fabric series in 1968 (VII-54) Sarpaneva invented a process by which the design is printed on both sides of the fabric simultaneously by computerized robot; at Iittala, in the mid-1960s, Sarpaneva developed a technique for blowing glass sculptures in wooden molds that burn during the procedure, giving the glass a special, textured surface (*see* pp. 100–101). His elegant, studied works display a sureness of line and proportion that suggests Sarpaneva's training as a draftsman, between 1946 and 1949, at the Institute of Industrial Arts (Taideteollisuuskeskuskoulu), Helsinki, where he later taught textile composition and printing. In 1950 he began his long association with Iittala as an independent glass artist (II-56, 57), the profession that brought him wide recognition as a major creative artist and grand prizes (1954, 1957) and a gold medal (1960) at the Triennale in Milan. Sarpaneva established his own office in 1962 and has since designed award-winning products in a wide range of materials for both Finnish and international firms: Porin Puuvilla, Rinnasand, Opa, and Rosenthal (II-58). In each instance his approach has been the same, to get a thorough mastery of process on the factory floor, talking at the sides of the machines to the most experienced technicians, who will ultimately turn his ideas into reality.

Monograph: Benedict Zilliacus, *Timo Sarpaneva* (forthcoming).

References: Erik Zahle, ed., A Treasury of Scandinavian Design (New York, 1961), pp. 290–91, nos. 210,

212–13, 349; "Timo Sarpaneva," *Interiors*, vol. 128 (Jan. 1969), pp. 128–31; "Two Faced Textiles," *Industrial Design*, vol. 16 (Mar. 1969), pp. 52–53; Geoffrey Beard, *International Modern Glass* (London, 1976), pls. 111, 145, 271, 299.

Afra Scarpa
Italian, born 1937
Tobia Scarpa
Italian, born 1935

Trained as a designer in Venice, Tobia Scarpa, son of noted designer Carlo Scarpa, worked for Venini in Murano from 1957 to 1961 (II-55), designing lamps and other glass objects which were exhibited in the Milan Triennale of 1960. In that year he opened an independent office in Montebelluna (Treviso) in collaboration with his wife Afra. Designing furniture and lighting for such firms as Cassina (III-81), B & B, Flos, and Gavina, the Scarpas developed a "classical" personal style of solid geometric shapes executed in steel, wood, and leather—a series of monumental objects designed to convey absolute values for a small, luxury market. Since the collapse of the plastic furniture industry in the mid-1970s, the use of rare hardwoods with secondary wood inlays by the Scarpas has brought them particular notice.

References: "Afra e Tobia Scarpa, 1964–1966," *Domus*, no. 453 (Aug. 1967), pp. 23–27; Barbara Allen, "Italy's New Idiom," *Industrial Design*, vol. 14 (Oct. 1967), p. 39; Jocelyn de Noblet, *Design* (Paris, 1974), p. 338.

Peter Schlumbohm
American, born Germany, 1896–1962

An inventor, not a designer—"Inventors are original, noncompromising pioneers; designers are parasitic politicians" (1960)—Schlumbohm nevertheless won recognition from the design community for his functionally determined designs, many of which he not only engineered himself but also manufactured and zealously promoted. The holder at the time of his death of more than three hundred patents, Schlumbohm received a doctorate in chemistry from the university of Berlin at the age of thirty and began to market his inventions, first in the field of refrigeration, which brought him to the United States in 1931. Ten years later he created his best-known product, the hourglass-shaped Chemex coffeemaker, whose success and that of the company he founded to

produce it may be partly attributed to Schlumbohm's crusade for the benefits of the filtered coffee it made. This was followed by other domestic products, among them a frying pan that did not require washing, a quick water boiler (1949; II-59), and an ingenious air-filtering fan (1951; I-39).

References: "Two Inventors," *Industrial Design*, vol. 7 (Nov. 1960), pp. 72–75; Ralph Caplan, "Chemex and Creation," *Industrial Design*, vol. 9 (Dec. 1962), pp. 121–22; Victor Papanek, *Design for the Real World* (New York, 1974), pp. 105–6.

Richard Schultz
American, born 1926

A member of the Design Development Group of Knoll, Schultz joined the firm in 1951, working first with HARRY BERTOIA on the development and production of Bertoia's wire "Diamond" chair (III-9). Schultz's own designs for Knoll included the "Petal" table (1960); a steel-wire lounge (1961); and the "Leisure Collection," aluminum and Dacron-webbed chairs and lounges (III-82), introduced by Knoll in 1966 to be used indoors or out, and given the A.I.D. International Design Award the following year. A graduate of Iowa State University and the Illinois Institute of Technology in Chicago, Schultz has continued to explore the possibilities of outdoor furniture with a series introduced in 1981.

References: London, Whitechapel Art Gallery, *Modern Chairs: 1918–1970* (July 22–Aug. 30, 1970), no. 84; Eric Larrabee and Massimo Vignelli, *Knoll Design* (New York, 1981), pp. 158–59, 292–93.

Scot Simon
American, born 1954

Trained as a painter at Carnegie-Mellon University, Pittsburgh (1974), and at the San Francisco Art Institute (1976), Simon painted in San Francisco and New York until 1977, when he began designing jewelry and belts in New York, both independently and for Accessocraft. Fascinated by man-made materials and by the possibilities of using

natural materials in new ways, Simon has worked with rubber, vinyls, and plastics, and recently has designed handmade wallpapers with embossed decorations and fabric applications. Since 1980 Simon has designed tablewares and table linens both independently and for Mikasa, and at the same time began to develop the textiles (VII-55) and wall coverings that now occupy him exclusively.

Reference: "Scot Simon," *American Fabrics and Fashions*, no. 128 (1983), pp. 11–17.

Clive Sinclair
British, born 1940

An electronics "genius," Sinclair has consistently led the field of miniaturization in home electronics, personally developing the required new computer technology that allowed him to reduce the scale of his products and market them at low cost. In 1972 Sinclair, whose company Sinclair Radionics had been selling miniature radios and amplifiers by mail for a decade, introduced the first pocket-size calculator, the "Executive" (I-40), designed with his brother Iain, which immediately brought him to the forefront of the industry and won him a Design Council Award in 1973; his luxury "Sovereign" calculator and his miniature "Microvision" television (1976; I-41) won Design Council Awards in 1977 and 1978, respectively. The small, inexpensive personal computers that Sinclair's new firm, Sinclair Research, has marketed since 1980 have sold in greater numbers throughout the world than any other home computer, and lately in ever-increasing numbers after they were licensed for distribution by Timex in the United States. Sinclair has developed, for 1983 introduction, a cigarette-package-size "Microvision" pocket television incorporating his radical flat-screen picture tube. The "ZX 81" personal computer won a Design Council Award in 1982.

References: "Clive Sinclair's New Leaf," *Design*, no. 389 (May 1981), pp. 26–27; Myron Magnet, "Clive Sinclair's Little Computer That Could," *Fortune*, vol. 105 (Mar. 8, 1982), pp. 78–84.

Harold Sitterle
American, born 1910s

Trudi Sitterle
American, born 1920s

From 1949 to the early 1970s, the Sitterles designed and manufactured in a small workshop a line of elegant porcelain table accessories—candleholders, pitchers, creamers, sugar bowls, serving utensils (II-61), and most notably, the hourglass-shaped pepper mill and its accompanying salt dish (II-60). Harold, a graphic designer for *McCall's*, joined his ceramist wife Trudi in developing the pepper mill in response to a suggestion by a magazine colleague of the need for a ceramic version that would marry well with white dinnerware. Shown in 1950 at the "Good Design" exhibition at the Museum of Modern Art in New York, the pepper mill immediately was published widely and became the best-selling design in their newly formed porcelain business. Repeatedly cited as examples of successful designer-craftsmen, they encouraged others to work on their own: "Though it is difficult for a designer or potter to make a living producing, by hand, the things in which he believes, we feel there is still a good chance to do this today. A craftsman has the chance to grace a material with personal skill and art, the two things which will always be free of machine competition. The art and spirit in various crafts and industries are being greatly depreciated by over-emphasizing rationalizations such as 'functionalism,' 'uniformity,' 'durability,' 'profit,' and 'efficiency.' These values are very often over-emphasized for the sake of mass production because they are so well suited to machines" (1957).

References: "Manufacturing in Microcosm: Sitterle Ceramics," *Industrial Design*, vol. 2 (Apr. 1955), pp. 78–81; Don Wallance, *Shaping America's Products* (New York, 1956), pp. 159–61; "Trudi and Harold Sitterle," *Design Quarterly*, no. 39 (1957), pp. 24–27.

Svend Siune
Danish, born 1935

A graduate of the School of Arts and Crafts (Kunsthåndvaerker-skolen) in Copenhagen (1961), Siune was a free-lance advertising artist from 1961 to 1976 and a designer of furniture and both metal and plastic cutlery. His forged stainless-steel "Blue Shark" cutlery (1965; V-42) in deep, generalized shapes won the Jensen cutlery contest in 1966.

Reference: Washington, D.C., Renwick Gallery, *Georg Jensen—Silversmithy: 77 Artists 75 Years* (Feb. 29–July 6, 1980), no. 137.

Hans Erich Slany
German, born 1926

One of Germany's most distinguished and prolific industrial designers, Slany studied engineering in Eger (1941–44) and Esslingen (1948), working first for Ritter Aluminium in Esslingen (1948–55) as a specialist in metal, plastics, and product development. In 1956 he opened an independent design office in Esslingen, working through 1957 under the direction of HEINRICH LÖFFELHARDT in the field of ceramic and glass design. Since 1957 Slany has created a wide variety of products in various materials, ranging from medical equipment to electronic components for a rocket and including such consumer products as power tools, plastics, and domestic appliances (for Leifheit, I-42; and Progress, from 1957). A founding member of the German Designers' Association (VDID; 1959) and a jury-member of the Bundespreis "Gute Form" in 1969 and 1971, Slany was himself awarded the prize for his plastic tablewares (for Deutsche Ornapress, 1973) and his "Panther" and "Dubelblitz" power tools (for Bosch, 1975). "I want to create good products that are functionally flawless and aesthetically pleasing. They should be accessible at the most favorable price to a wide group of consumers and not to a small exclusive circle. . . . Functionally correct execution, scientifically correct finishing methods and the application of the best adaptable materials seem equally important as aesthetic considerations" (1966).

Monograph: Essen, Haus Industrieform, *E. H. Slany: Auswahl Designarbeiten 1953 bis 1965* (1965).

References: "Der Designer E. H. Slany: 10 Fragen," *Form*, no. 33 (Mar. 1966), pp. 35–39; Darmstadt, Rat für Formgebung, *Prämiierte Produkte* (June 19–July 24, 1977), pp. 14, 17.

Neal Small
American, born 1937

An inventive designer in acrylic plastic in the 1960s as well as a sculptor, Small bent, folded, and molded sheets of the transparent material, sometimes in combination with chromed steel, in furniture, lighting, and glasswares that were produced both by his own firm, Neal Small Designs, and by other manufacturers including Nessen (IV-35). "For a long time people thought acrylic plastic was only good for displays. Of course in the thirties there was a trend to Lucite because of the novelty of it. But now, I think, we've gotten more adult in our design ideas about it. . . . I had used Plexiglas as a lampshade material originally, but then I began to think of using it in other ways" (1967). Small opened his own design office in New York in 1965–66, moving to Pine Bush, New York, when the firm stopped its manufacturing activities in 1973. Since that time (from 1978, again in New York, as president of Squire and Small), he has concentrated on conceptual sculpture and product design for such clients as Brueton, Sigma, and Kovacs.

References: Lisa Hammel, "He's a One-Man Furniture Craft Guild," *New York Times* (November 7, 1967); Jocelyn de Noblet, *Design* (Paris, 1974), pp. 340–41.

The Sony Corporation
Japanese, established Tokyo, 1945

By exporting high-quality audio and video equipment in the 1950s and 1960s, the Sony corporation combated the poor image that others had of postwar Japanese products. Founded by Masaru Ibuka in 1945 and incorporated with Akio Morita in 1946 as the Tokyo Telecommunications Engineering Corporation (changed to Sony in 1958), the company capitalized first on magnetic tapes and then on transistors, building its reputation through the consistent quality of its products, its emphasis on miniaturization and the development of imported technology, and its aggressive consumer education and marketing techniques. Receiving a license in 1954 to manufacture transistors in Japan, the company created the world's first mass-produced transistor radio in 1955

and the first all-transistor television in 1959 (I-43); since then, among its "firsts," Sony has introduced the home video recorder (1964) and the "Trinitron" color television system (1968). Sony design, which now claims a leading position in the industry, is an all-company involvement: engineers and product-design groups work in conjunction with the communications division, which maintains design consistency and corporate identity in all Sony products (I-44-46). Sony has manufacturing plants in Tokyo, San Diego, Cologne, and Bridgend (Wales).

Monograph: London, The Boilerhouse at the Victoria and Albert Museum, *Sony Design* (London, 1982).

Reference: Wolfgang Schmittel, *Design Concept Realisation* (Zurich, 1975), pp. 169–96.

Ettore Sottsass, Jr.
Italian, born Austria, 1917

Two seemingly contradictory strands weave through the career of Sottsass: the cool, functional designs conceived for his corporate clients (Olivetti, for example, for whom he has been a design consultant since 1957) and the imaginative and symbolic expressions of his painting, sculpture, and many of his products—furniture (for Knoll, Abet, Memphis, Studio Alchymia, Poltronova; III-83), plastics, lighting (for Arredoluce), metalware (for Alessi), and ceramics. In all his work, however, personal expression is constantly implied, and even his appliances and office equipment —a typewriter or a computer— display bold color and referential shapes, if not the symbolic imagery of his other endeavors. Sottsass was a participant in the "anti-design" movement of the 1960s, and more recently, with his Memphis group, he has been among those who have reasserted the validity of patterns and colors and introduced totally new forms into product design (III-84) in an effort to vitalize and enrich domestic surroundings. The son of an architect, Sottsass received an architecture degree from the Turin Politecnico in 1939, and in 1947 opened an office in Milan, participating in postwar reconstruction and interior and exhibition design, but then concentrating on the design of products. In 1956 he spent a year in America working in the studio of GEORGE NELSON, and has traveled widely. His work for Olivetti, including the "Elea" computer series (1959), adding machines, and typewriters—"Praxis" (1963), "Valentine" (1969; I-47)—as well as total office systems, won him the Compasso d'Oro in 1959 and 1970. In 1980 he formed a design firm, Sottsass Associati, in

partnership with several younger architects.

Writings: Federica Di Castro, ed., *Sottsass's Scrap-Book* (Milan, 1976).

Monographs: Paris, Centre de Création Industrielle, *Ettore Sottsass, Jr: De l'objet fini à la fin de l'objet* (Oct. 21–Jan. 3, 1977); Penny Sparke, *Ettore Sottsass Jnr* (London, 1982).

References: Pier Carlo Santini, "Introduction to Ettore Sottsass, Jr.," *Zodiac*, no. 11 (1963), pp. 79–128; Paolo Fossati, *Il design in Italia* (Turin, 1972), pp. 114–21, 220–23, pls. 250–74, 296–309 (biblio.); Los Angeles, Frederick S. Wight Art Gallery, University of California, *Design Process Olivetti 1908–1978* (Mar. 27–May 6, 1979), p. 267, and *passim*; Marco Zanini, "A Well Travelled Man," in *Design ist unsichtbar* (Vienna, 1981), pp. 464–74; Christine Colin, "Memphis a encore frappé," *Décoration Internationale*, no. 51 (Dec. 1982–Jan. 1983), pp. 54–57, 206.

Magnus Stephensen
Danish, born 1903

Stephensen has had a long career as an architect and a designer, working in metal, ceramics, and furniture, for which he received three gold medals (1954 and 1957) and two grand prizes (1954) at the Triennale in Milan. His designs for Kay Bojesen (1938–52) and for Georg Jensen (from 1950) include excellent stainless-steel and silver hollow ware (V-43) and cutlery, remarkable for the attention paid to both function and finish. His early oven-to-table ware in several colors for Royal Copenhagen and Aluminia (1957; II-62) led Danish ceramics manufacturers to follow the trend developing elsewhere toward multiuse and interchangeable services.

References: Arne Karlsen, *Made in Denmark* (New York, 1960), pp. 114–15, 119, 122; Erik Zahle, ed., *A Treasury of Scandinavian Design* (New York, 1961), p. 292, nos. 275, 387, 412; Washington, D.C., Renwick Gallery, *Georg Jensen—Silversmithy: 77 Artists 75 Years* (Feb. 29–July 6, 1980), no. 140.

Nanny Still McKinney
Finnish, lives in Belgium, born 1925

An independent designer of handcrafted and industrial objects, Still McKinney graduated from the Institute of Industrial Arts (Taideteollinen oppilaitos) in Helsinki in 1949. She first worked in glass, producing both blown and molded decorative and utility pieces—often in idiosyncratic shapes with textured surfaces—for Riihimäen Lasi (1949–76), for which she is still best known (II-63). Gradually she branched out into other fields: wood (for which she was awarded a diploma of honor at the Milan Triennale in 1954), lighting (for Raak), porcelain, cutlery (for Hackman), and jewelry. Since 1977 she has also designed glass and ceramics for the Rosenthal Studio Line.

Monograph: Bruges, Huidevettershuis, *Nanny Still Design* (Sept. 22–Oct. 13, 1963).

References: Erik Zahle, ed., *A Treasury of Scandinavian Design* (New York, 1961), p. 292, nos. 242–43; Geoffrey Beard, *International Modern Glass* (London, 1976), pls. 97, 119, 137.

Marianne Straub
British, born Switzerland, 1909

Having studied at the Kunstgewerbeschule in Zurich (1928–31), Straub began to weave at home and to train in industrial techniques in a small cotton mill. Upon moving to England, she attended Bradford Technical College (1932–33), spent nine months in the workshop of the weaver Ethel Mairet, and designed cloth for the Welsh Woolen Mills. In 1937 she became head designer for Helios (a division of Barlow & Jones), handweaving on a dobby loom textured prototypes for many of their furnishing fabrics. From 1950 to 1970 she worked for Warner (successor to Helios), in 1951 producing designs for the Festival Pattern Group. This was a program set up by the Council of Industrial Design to coordinate flat-pattern motifs in the Festival of Britain exhibition. Following the requirements of Festival Pattern designs, her curtain material "Surrey" (VII-56) was based on the structure of crystals as seen through a microscope—natural repetitive patterns being heralded then as a promising new source of inspiration for design—and produced by Warner under the Council's licensing arrangements with twenty-six manufacturers. Straub also worked for Tamesa and Heal fabrics, and taught in many schools, including the Central School of Art

and the Royal College of Art, London. She was appointed a Royal Designer for Industry in 1972.

Writings: Marianne Straub, *Hand Weaving and Cloth Design* (London, 1977).

References: Michael Farr, *Design in British Industry* (Cambridge, 1955), pls. XXXIII, XXXV 2, XXXVI 1; Warner & Sons Limited, *A Choice of Design: 1850–1980* (London, 1981), pp. 64–65, nos. 244, 248.

Marianne Strengell
American, born Finland, 1909

One of America's most distinguished weavers and textile designers, Strengell was trained at the Institute of Industrial Arts (Taideteollisuuskeskuskoulu), Helsinki (1929), and afterward worked as a designer of rugs and furnishing fabrics for Hemflit-Kotiahkeruus (1930–36) and Bo Atieselskab, Copenhagen (1934–36). In these years she became co-owner of her own firm, Koti-Hemmet, for which she designed interiors and furniture as well as textiles (1934–36). Coming to the United States in 1936, Strengell served as an instructor of weaving at the Cranbrook Academy of Art, Bloomfield Hills, Michigan (1937–42), and from 1942 to 1961 headed the weaving and textile design department there. At Cranbrook, using handlooms as well as power looms, Strengell developed pilots for machine-woven fabrics, emphasizing the textures that she created with new synthetic materials and combinations of synthetic and natural fibers. Through the wide influence of her work and teaching, the appearance of handwoven fabrics entered the commercial American textile industry beginning in the 1940s, with her own designs ranging from drapery and upholstery fabrics for Knoll (from 1947) to automobile upholstery fabrics in tweeds and Jacquard filaments for Chatham (VII-57). Strengell also designed handwoven and power-loomed textured fabrics for architectural interiors such as the General Motors Technical Center by EERO SAARINEN (1946–56) and fiberglass fabrics for the Owens Corning Fiberglas building in New York. In recent years she has continued to weave and design for industry and for architectural interiors, and has served as a consultant

on weaving programs to various government agencies in Jamaica (1967), Appalachia (1968 to present), and Saint Croix (1969–71).

References: Don Wallance, *Shaping America's Products* (New York, 1956), p. 183; Eric Larrabee and Massimo Vignelli, *Knoll Design* (New York, 1981), pp. 91, 272.

Studio OPI
Italian, established Milan, c. 1960s

Studio OPI designers Franco Bettonica (Italian, born 1927) and Mario Melocchi (Italian, born 1931) created bar (V-44), smoking, and desk accessories in the 1960s and 1970s. Their cool, sleek designs in stainless steel and plastic have been produced by Melocchi's associated firm Cini & Nils.

Reference: New York, Museum of Modern Art, *Italy: The New Domestic Landscape* (May 26–Sept. 11, 1972), pp. 80–81, 84.

Richard Süssmuth
German, born 1900

After studying at the Akademie für Kunsthandwerk in Dresden, in 1924 Süssmuth founded a glass factory in Penzig, whose products were widely exhibited and premiated in Milan, Berlin, and Paris during the 1930s. Reestablishing his factory after the war in Immenhausen, Süssmuth manufactured art and stained glass along with glass tablewares in a variety of styles, including the heavy, cylindrical "Capitol" series he designed in 1948 (II-64). His work was shown in New York at the "Good Design" exhibitions at the Museum of Modern Art in the 1950s.

Reference: Corning, N.Y., The Corning Museum of Glass, *Glass 1959* (1959), no. 147.

La Gardo Tackett
American, born 1911

Tackett studied sculpture and art history at Claremont College in California after the war, and then opened his own pottery studio, which he maintained until 1954. As an instructor at the California School of Design in Los Angeles in 1948, Tackett developed his earliest outdoor pottery planters with his students as a class project, which

led to the founding of the Architectural Pottery company to produce them (1950). Over the next decade he introduced glazed and unglazed planters for interior and outdoor spaces in hemispherical, cylindrical (II-65), and hourglass shapes, which were widely imitated. Among his other work was a line of ceramic dinnerware for Schmid International (1957) produced in Japan. In 1963 he became manager of the Objects Division of Herman Miller.

Writings: La Gardo Tackett, "A New Casual Structure for Ceramic Design," *Art and Architecture,* vol. 72 (Apr. 1955), pp. 14–15, 30.

References: "New Solutions to Planting Problems," *Interiors,* vol. 115 (Feb. 1956), pp. 114–15; Norbert Nelson, "The Marketplace," *Industrial Design,* vol. 10 (Mar. 1963), pp. 74–76.

Roger Tallon
French, born 1929

One of the few industrial designers practicing in France after the war, Tallon joined Technès in Paris in 1953, becoming director of research in 1960. French industry was slow to accept the professional designer, and although Tallon was to create such products as cameras for SEM (1957, 1961), a coffee grinder for Peugeot (1957–58), and a typewriter for Japy (1960)—the last winning a silver medal at the 1960 Milan Triennale—his principal commissions were foreign: from 1957 to 1964 he was a consultant designer to General Motors for their Frigidaire refrigerators. During the 1960s Tallon experimented with new materials and techniques, most notably in the furniture series for Lacloche upholstered in heavily textured polyester foam (III-85). His recent work has included innovative lighting fixtures for Erco (1977), and he has been a consultant designer for the French rail system (SNCF) since 1970.

References: "Da Parigi: Design e idee di Roger Tallon," *Domus,* no. 452 (July 1967), pp. 40–45; Paris, Centre de Création Industrielle, *Qu'est-ce que le design?* (Oct. 24–Dec. 31, 1969); Xavier Gilles, "Le Design selon Tallon," *L'Oeil,* no. 244 (Nov. 1975), pp. 57–59; Catherine Millet, "Un Designer à Paris," in Paris, Centre Georges Pompidou, *Paris 1937–1957* (May 28–Nov. 2, 1981), pp. 446–52.

Ilmari Tapiovaara
Finnish, born 1914

One of the pioneers of knock-down furniture design in the late 1940s and early 1950s, Tapiovaara entered the low-cost furniture design competition at the Museum of Modern Art in New York in 1948 with a lightweight, stacking, wood and fabric or leather chair that could be easily dismantled and packed for overseas shipment. A functionalist who believed that the principles and details of construction should be readily apparent, Tapiovaara developed his ideas in a series of chairs that were awarded gold medals at the Milan Triennale in 1951, 1954, 1957, and 1960. Since the 1960s he has extended his interests to product design in fields other than furniture, notably the "Polar" cutlery for Hackman (V-45) and radio and stereo equipment for Centrum (1972–74); to color planning for the paint manufacturer Winter & Co. (1974–80); and to wall paintings, tapestries, and a "stabile" construction executed during the 1970s in, respectively, Udine, Italy; Quatre Bornes, Mauritius; and Rauma-Repola, Finland. Trained in both industrial and interior design at the Institute of Industrial Arts (Taideteollisuuskeskuskoulu), Helsinki (1937), Tapiovaara worked for ALVAR AALTO in Artek's London office (1935–36), for Le Corbusier in Paris (1937), and for Mies van der Rohe in Chicago (1952–53), opening his own office in Helsinki in 1950. Interior design has remained a constant occupation for Tapiovaara, with projects such as student hostels in Helsinki (1947, 1949); offices, cinemas, and theaters, including the Leningrad concert hall, in the Soviet Union (1955–73); aircraft interiors for Finnair (1960s); and the Intercontinental Hotel in Helsinki (1973).

Writings: Ilmari Tapiovaara, "The Idea Was More Important Than the Product," *Form Function Finland* (1983), pp. 17–19.

References: Benedict Zilliacus, *Finnish Designers* (Helsinki, 1954), n.p.; Erik Zahle, ed., *A Treasury of Scandinavian Design* (New York, 1961), p. 293, nos. 21–24.

Angelo Testa
American, born 1921

The first graduate of the Institute of Design in Chicago (1945), Testa had already created a fabric with an abstracted figural design, "Little Man" (1942), that was reproduced widely, heralded as a new direction in textile design. He introduced abstract and nonobjective patterns into commercial American printed cottons, considering this a necessary response to contemporary furniture and architecture: "The role of the printed fabric has been made more important by the simplicity and spaciousness of the floor plan, abundant use of materials of different textures, and the extensive use of soft gray tones for walls. . . . By the use of thick and thin lines, combinations of solid and outline forms, a freer articulation of positive and negative space is brought into play. By the use of pure linear elements undreamed of vibrations and effects are created which, when properly controlled, are made subtle enough to reveal beautiful and exciting space experiences. With the use of clearly defined abstract forms and linear elements, there also comes a chance to use clean, pure colors" (1946). His textiles, with names such as "Diagonals," "Space Dashes," "Forms within Forms," "Line in Action," and "Experiment in Space" that underlined the formal concerns of his designs, were produced by his own factory (VII-58)—some with matching wallpapers—and by Greeff, Forster, Cohn-Hall-Marx, and Knoll. He has also produced designs for plastic laminates, fiberglass panels, and vinyls, and is himself a painter and sculptor.

Monograph: Chicago, College of Architecture, Art and Urban Planning Gallery, *Angelo Testa* (Apr. 13–May 6, 1983).

References: "Textiles," *Arts and Architecture,* vol. 62 (Oct. 1945), pp. 42–43; "Angelo Testa," *Arts and Architecture,* vol. 63 (July 1946), pp. 42–43; "Angelo Testa," *Everyday Art Quarterly,* no. 25 (1953), pp. 16–17.

Jim Thompson
American, 1906–1967?

Once a practicing architect in New York, Thompson created the modern silk industry in Thailand through the Thai Silk company, which he founded in Bangkok in 1948. Thompson first visited Thailand during World War II, sent by the Office of Strategic Services, and stayed there permanently. By 1967 he had developed the country's production of silk into a network of twenty-thousand cottage weavers, with export sales of over one million dollars. Although his weavers retained many of the methods of their native handicraft, Thompson replaced traditional, fugitive vegetable dyes with high-quality colorfast dyes from Switzerland and added faster, foot-operated shuttles to the looms. A gifted colorist, Thompson introduced a brilliantly iridescent and often audacious

palette in his silks (VII-59), which sold with great success during the 1950s and 1960s.

Monograph: William Warren, *The Legendary American: The Remarkable Career and Strange Disappearance of Jim Thompson* (Boston, 1970).

Paolo Tilche
Italian, born Egypt, 1925

A graduate of the architectural school of the Milan Politecnico, Tilche has designed numerous offices, industrial plants, and private residences in Italy. His prolific design work, often extremely inventive in shape and in the combination of functions within one object or component set, includes furniture (for Arform), sanitary fittings (for Ideal Standard), blown-glass lamps (for Barbini), glass tableware, plastics (for Guzzini; VI-18), and ceramics.

Reference: Milan, Palazzo delle Stelline, *Design & design* (May 29– July 31, 1979), p. 150.

D. D. Tillett
American, born 1920s

In 1946 designer D. D. (Doris) Tillett joined with her husband Leslie, who had a background in textile production and color technology, in establishing a laboratory and workshop for the design and production of printed textiles in New York. Taking advantage of available equipment and technology and exploring the subtleties of textile printing by insisting on designing with dyes on fabric (rather than with watercolor on paper), the Tilletts introduced many lines of textiles both for their own custom production and for industry (for J. C. Penney, Covington, and Leacock). The sources for their richly detailed designs were widespread; they chose abstract patterns and took inspiration from nature ("Queen Anne's Lace," VII-60; in production for more than thirty years) and from history—ancient Peruvian art, medieval tapestries, nineteenth-century sporting prints—varying their output by using a multiplicity of printing techniques and issuing patterns in many different colors and fabrics. In 1954 the Tilletts undertook the production of printed fiberglass for Owens Corning.

References: "Pilot Printing Plant," *Interiors,* vol. 108 (June 1949),

pp. 104–11; "New Glass Curtains for New Glass Houses," *Interiors,* vol. 113 (May 1954), pp. 120–21; Don Wallance, *Shaping America's Products* (New York, 1956), pp. 99–101.

Paula Trock
Danish, 1889–1979

Trained in Denmark, Sweden, and Finland, Trock received many important commissions for handweaving (including curtains for the United Nations building in New York), and was awarded gold medals at the Milan Triennale in 1954, 1957, and 1960. In 1928 she founded a weaving school and workshop in Askov, Denmark (transferred to Sønderborg in 1934), directing it until interrupted by the war in 1942. In 1948 she established the Spindegarden at Askov, a new workshop where lighter and more texturally varied yarns for handweaving were produced. She also experimented there with other fibers and methods in her own weaving, among them plastic threads and open weaves, and about 1950 began to make her designs available for commercial furnishing fabrics (VII-61), mainly for Unika-Vaev.

References: Bent Salicath and Arne Karlsen, eds., *Modern Danish Textiles* (Copenhagen, 1959), p. 18; Arne Karlsen, *Made in Denmark* (New York, 1960), pp. 160–61.

Earl Tupper
American, lives in Costa Rica, born c. 1908

Inventor of a method to mold polyethylene plastic and to make it pliable without cracking, and of a seal to keep containers airtight and waterproof, Tupper founded the Tupper corporation in the early 1940s. Heralded for their modern, new material and for their economy, his cool, pastel-colored containers (VI-19, 20) and other products were first sold in stores, but his great success came after 1951, when he began to market his products directly to consumers in "Tupperware home parties." Tupper sold his firm in 1958.

References: "Tupperware," *Time,* Sept. 8, 1947, p. 90; Elizabeth Gordon, "Fine Art for 39¢," *House Beautiful,* vol. 89 (Oct. 1947), pp. 130–31.

Utility Furniture Design Panel
British, 1943–1952

As the war effort got underway in Britain in 1939, it became increasingly evident that materials for home industries would be in short supply and that machinery would be needed to regulate their distribution. Strict quotas and rationing led the Board of Trade in 1942 to establish an Advisory Panel on Utility Furniture "to produce specifications for furniture of good, sound construction in simple but agreeable designs for sale at reasonable prices, and ensuring the maximum economy of raw materials and labor." The result of their efforts was a line of very simple, well-crafted pieces of oak or mahogany satisfying all home requirements, introduced in 1943, which became the standard range produced by all manufacturers. One panel member, the Cotswold furniture designer and manufacturer Gordon Russell, saw beyond the wartime supply scheme, envisioning a greater social good for the future "to raise the whole standard of furniture for the mass of the people." His ideas were received with enthusiasm, and in 1943 he was made chairman of a separate Design Panel. At war's end, with the prospect of continued restricted supplies, three new standard lines for all furniture makers were introduced by the Design Panel: "Chiltern," mainly a continuation of the stolid 1943 designs; "Cotswold" (III-86), more expensive veneered and paneled furniture in a broader range; and "Cockaigne" (later "Cheviot"), machine-made furniture, which never went into production. Various designers, including Edwin Clinch and H. T. Cutler, who had designed the 1943 line, worked with the panel on the "Cotswold" designs, with Russell having the final say on all proposals. Russell remained on the panel until 1947, when he left to become director of the Council of Industrial Design, while the Utility Furniture Design Panel itself survived until 1952, when Britain's recovery was at last assured.

Monograph: London, Geffrye Museum, *CC 41: Utility Furniture and Fashion, 1941–1951* (Sept. 24– Dec. 29, 1974).

Reference: "Utility CC 41," *Design,* no. 309 (Sept. 1974), pp. 62–71.

Gino Valle
Italian, born 1923

As an architect and urban planner, Valle (with a number of collaborators) has been responsible for industrial and commercial constructions in north Italy, particularly in the region of his native city, Udine. His design work has focused principally on devising mechanical systems for indicating transportation schedules, and time, for the firm of Solari. His direct-reading indicator boards, found in air and rail terminals throughout the world, use the same modular flap units as his domestic table clocks (I-48), and his achievement in both areas was recognized with a Compasso d'Oro in 1956 for his "Cifra 5" clock and one in 1963 for his indicator board. A graduate in architecture from the university of Venice (1948), Valle studied at the Harvard Graduate School of Design in Cambridge, Massachusetts, in 1951.

Monograph: Milan, Padiglione d'Arte Contemporanea di Milano, *Gino Valle: Architetto 1950–1978* (1979) (biblio.).

References: "Fewer Queues, Fewer Questions," *Design,* no. 215 (Nov. 1966), p. 66; Jocelyn de Noblet, *Design* (Paris, 1974), p. 347, nos. 291–93; Vittorio Gregotti, *Il disegno del prodotto industriale* (Milan, 1982), pp. 342–43.

Van Keppel-Green
American, established Los Angeles, 1938–1972

In 1938 Hendrik Van Keppel (American, born 1914) and Taylor Green (American, born 1914) established their first interior design office in Los Angeles, opening a custom retail shop the following year to sell furniture of their own design. The firm developed an immediate reputation for its clean-lined, functional modern furniture for outdoor use and in particular for its metal-framed seating strung with yacht cord. After a brief existence, the shop was closed during the war, and when it reopened the partners for the first time began to produce their furniture on a commercial basis with industrial materials. The cotton-cord furniture, originally made with gas pipe, was revised and produced in enameled steel (III-87). The firm's production expanded in 1948; during the 1950s Van Keppel and Green designed furniture not only for their own shop but also for Balboa Chrome, Brown-Saltman, and Mueller, and in the 1960s, for Brown Jordan.

Reference: James J. Cowen, "Van Keppel-Green . . . Design Team," *Furniture Field* (1951).

Gertrud Vasegaard
Danish, born 1913

One of Denmark's most admired potters, Vasegaard was born into a family of potters on the island of Bornholm, where she returned to work after studying at the School of Arts and Crafts (Kunsthandvaer-kerskolen) in Copenhagen from 1930 to 1932. She opened a studio, first with her sister (1933–35) and then alone (1936–48), building a reputation for the demanding standards she applied to the production and decoration of her handmade stoneware. From 1945 to 1959 she also designed production pieces for Bing & Grøndahl, most notably her decorated bowls and vases and her subtly glazed porcelain tea service (1957; II-66) clearly influenced by Chinese ceramics. Vasegaard later designed several table services for Royal Copenhagen, and since 1959 has maintained a studio in Copenhagen with her daughter Myre Vasegaard. Her work was awarded a gold medal at the Milan Triennale in 1957.

References: Erik Zahle, ed., *A Treasury of Scandinavian Design* (New York, 1961), p. 294, nos. 262, 321; University Park, Pa., The Pennsylvania State University, *Danish Ceramic Design* (Oct. 18, 1981–Jan. 24, 1982), n.p.

Kristian Vedel
Danish, born 1923

Apprenticed as a cabinetmaker, Vedel was trained as a furniture designer at the Royal Danish Academy of Fine Arts (Kongelige Danske Kunstakademi) in Copenhagen (1945) under Kaare Klint and participated in the furniture exhibitions of the Copenhagen Cabinetmakers' Guild. Applying Klint's standards of economy, simplicity, and function, Vedel created two innovative works for Torben Ørskov soon after opening an independent design office in Copenhagen in 1955: a child's chair formed as a curved plywood shell fitted with slots at various heights for the seat (III-88) that won him a silver medal at the Milan Triennale of 1957, and a series of containers in melamine (VI-21). In 1963 Vedel designed the successful "Modus" furniture series for Søren Willadsens. He was awarded the Lunning Prize

for his work in 1962.

References: "Thirtyfour Lunning Prize-Winners," *Mobilia* (special issue), no. 146 (Sept. 1967), n.p.; Vienna, Österreichisches Museum für Angewandte Kunst, *Sitzen 69* (Jan.–Mar. 1969), no. 10.

Paolo Venini
Italian, 1895–1959

Although trained as a lawyer, Venini established the most progressive glass factory in Italy, first in partnership with Giacomo Cappellin, Andrea Rioda, and Vittorio Zecchin (1921), and then, independently, from 1925. His clear and transparent, lightly tinted glasses in simple, traditional, utilitarian forms were heralded as examples of a new functionalist style at the Monza Biennale in 1923, and were shown subsequently at the Triennale in Milan from 1933. During the 1930s Venini began to develop effects of color and texture in his glasswares by reviving traditional Venetian decorative techniques and inventing new ones. By 1945 he had become the leading manufacturer of colored glasswares, and his simple shapes enriched by a great variety of decorative processes were widely imitated and favorably compared to the clear white crystal being produced in Scandinavia. Among the techniques invented by Venini in collaboration with Fulvio Bianconi, who joined the firm in 1948, were *vetro pezzato* (1950), which has a patchwork effect of squares in different colors, and varieties of *zanfirico*, which is based on the traditional process of embedding threads of opaque-white or colored glass within a clear glass matrix (II-67, 68). Although principal designer of the firm, Venini made it a practice to collaborate with outside artists and designers, including GIO PONTI (from 1927), Carlo Scarpa (from 1932), Eugene Berman (1951), Ken Scott (1951), FRANCO ALBINI (1954), and MASSIMO VIGNELLI (1956). After his death the factory was taken over by his widow, Ginette, and his son-in-law, LUDOVICO DE SANTILLANA, who have maintained the high standards set by Venini and encouraged new designs by such artists as TOBIA SCARPA (II-55) and TAPIO WIRKKALA (II-73, 74).

References: Ada Polak, *Modern Glass* (London, 1962), pp. 55–56, 66–67, pls. 50A, 51A,B, 52, 64A,B, 65A,B; Washington, D.C., Smithsonian Institution, *Venini Glass* (1981), *passim*.

Kurt Versen
American, born Sweden, 1901

A consultant, designer, and manufacturer who after studying in Germany and coming to America (1930) was determined "to bring the importance of lighting and its economics into proper perspective," Versen worked on lighting for numerous stores, office buildings, and public structures, including the Philadelphia Saving Fund Society building (an early use of indirect lighting, 1931) and the New York World's Fair (1939). His wide range of lamps and fixtures, developed at the urging of architects who were seeking more flexible light sources in keeping with the contemporary look of their interiors, was manufactured by his own firm and received much attention in the 1940s and 1950s. His floor lamp from about 1946 (IV-36) incorporated a wrist-action swivel that allowed the lamp to be used for direct or indirect illumination. His lamps were included in the "Good Design" exhibition at the Museum of Modern Art in New York in 1951.

References: Buffalo, Buffalo Fine Arts Academy, Albright Art Gallery, *Good Design is Your Business* (1947), figs. 33–37; Eliot Noyes, "The Shape of Things: Lamps," *Consumer Reports* (Nov. 1948), pp. 506–8; Edgar Kaufmann, Jr., *What Is Modern Design?* (New York, 1950), fig. 59; Jay Doblin, *One Hundred Great Product Designs* (New York, 1970), no. 25.

Vittoriano Viganò
Italian, born 1919

A graduate in architecture from the Politecnico in Milan (1944), Viganò first worked in the studio of GIO PONTI and then independently as an architect, a leading exponent of the Brutalist school; urban planner; and industrial and exhibition designer. His early furniture in molded plywood (for Rima), glass, and steel, and his many lamps for Arteluce, including his tri-directional lamp (IV-37), were completely independent of the rationalist Milanese style. By the early 1960s Viganò had devoted himself primarily to teaching, on the faculty of architecture at the Milan Politecnico.

References: "Nuovo disegno per due lampade," *Domus*, no. 389 (Apr. 1962), p. 49; Andrea Branzi and Michele De Lucchi, eds., *Il design italiano degli anni '50* (Milan,

1981), pp. 45, 54, 132–33, 144, 153, 159, 205.

Lella Vignelli
Italian, born 1930s
Massimo Vignelli
Italian, born 1931

Designers of graphics, tablewares, furniture, exhibitions, and interiors, the Vignellis have developed a stylistic language of clean, oversimplified, often oversized, forms that has made theirs one of the most influential design offices in the United States since the 1970s. Their more familiar work includes logos for American Airlines, Lancia, and Ford; logos and package designs for Bloomingdale's, Barney's, and Saks Fifth Avenue; plastic tablewares for Heller (VI-22); glass for Venini; metalwork for San Lorenzo (V-46); furniture for Knoll and Sunar; and showrooms for Hauserman and Artemide. Raised in Italy and trained at the school of architecture at the university of Venice, with a year of work and teaching in Chicago (1958–59), the Vignellis opened their first design studio in Milan in 1960. In 1964 Massimo cofounded Unimark in Chicago for the design of corporate identity programs, and in 1971 they established their present independent consulting firm. Elegant, assured, and lucid, the Vignellis' superfunctional style flourishes in the post-modern 1980s. "Simplicity, which was such a big thing throughout the whole modern movement, began to be eroded by complexity in the seventies. . . . Of course, everybody has his own personal language. That's why we'll always be sort of minimal even though we don't like being characterized that way" (1983).

Monograph: *Design: Vignelli* (New York, 1981).

References: Stephen Kliment, "The Vignellis—Profile of a Design Team," in *Designer's Choice* (New York, 1981), pp. 6–12; Barbaralee Diamonstein, *Interior Design: The New Freedom* (New York, 1982), pp. 176–91; Stan Pinkwas, "King and Queen of Cups," *Metropolis* (Jan.–Feb. 1983), pp. 12–17.

Villeroy & Boch
German, established Mettlach, 1836

A large German ceramic- and glassmaking firm that in 1836 united the factories founded separately in the eighteenth century by François Boch and by members of the Villeroy family, Villeroy & Boch now specializes in ceramic tiles as well as in ceramic and glass tablewares and sanitary fittings. Although known for their well-executed wares in traditional styles, the firm also produced objects from the late 1960s that shared the bright colors and stacking features of Italian and other services of the same period. In the early 1970s Helen von Boch (German, born 1938), an eighth-generation member of the Boch family, collaborated with Federigo Fabbrini (Italian, born 1930s) in the design of the "Sphere" and "Bomba" (VI-3) services, tour-de-force essays (of stoneware and plastic, respectively) in the technique of fitting a variety of table pieces together into one portable unit.

References: "Design in Action: Inner Beauty," *Industrial Design*, vol. 18 (May 1971), p. 34; Sylvia Katz, *Plastics: Designs and Materials* (London, 1978), pp. 71–72.

Jean-Pierre Vitrac
French, born 1944

"Design," according to Vitrac, must be directed to the "conception of radically new products," as his inventive, variable lamp for Verre Lumière (IV-38) demonstrates. His industrial design firm, established in Paris in 1974, has begun to position itself internationally with an office in Milan and representation in New York and Tokyo, competing for packaging, interior, and product design commissions from major corporate clients. His products encompass furniture, lighting, tableware, plastics (VI-23), sports equipment, and technical instruments.

František Vízner
Czechoslovakian, born 1936

Vízner attended the schools of glassmaking in Nový Bor (1951–53) and Železný Brod (1953–56) and then the Academy of Applied Arts in Prague (1956–62). From 1962 to 1967 he designed decorative objects in pressed glass for the Dubí glassworks, and from 1967 to 1977 worked in free-blown forms at the Škrdlovice glassworks, as well as on monumental glass decoration. Since 1977 he has concentrated on colored glass, heavy in form and with crisp, cut edges and matte, etched, and sandblasted surfaces (II-69).

Monographs: Prague, *František Vízner—Sklo 1961–1971* (1971); *František Vízner: Sklo* (Prague, 1982).

Reference: Corning, N.Y., The Corning Museum of Glass, *Czechoslovakian Glass: 1350–1980* (May 2–Nov. 1, 1981), nos. 132–33.

Stanislav V'Soske
American, 1900–1983

A designer and manufacturer, V'Soske produced the first hand-tufted carpets in America in 1924, in the factory he opened with his brothers in Grand Rapids, Michigan (expanded in the late 1930s to include factories in Puerto Rico). The fine quality, handcrafted wool carpets that he designed, as well as those of other artists and designers ranging from Stuart Davis and GEORGE NELSON to MICHAEL GRAVES that he manufactured, brought V'Soske carpets a prestigious name and commissions from influential clients among corporations, museums, private individuals, and the government (the carpet for the Green Room in the White House in the 1950s). V'Soske developed the sculptured, or molded, carpet, using several pile heights and densities of wool and contrasting cut-and-looped piles to vary the texture of the surface and create a sense of depth through shadows. His own designs in vibrant colors encompassed figurative subjects ("Riders in the Spring"), lyrical abstractions, and variations on traditional patterns ("Romanesque," VII-62).

References: "V'Soske 1959 Exhibition of Rugs," *Interiors*, vol. 118 (Apr. 1959), pp. 134–35; "The V'Soske Rugmakers," *American Fabrics*, no. 51 (Fall 1960), pp. 83–86.

Wilhelm Wagenfeld
German, born 1900

One of this century's great industrial designers, Wagenfeld began his career in the mid-1920s at the Bauhaus, as a pupil and teacher in the metal workshop, then directed by László Moholy-Nagy. His most notable product of that period was a glass and chromium-plated-metal table lamp composed in clear geometric shapes (designed with J. K. Jucker), which has been recently reproduced by Tecnolumen. On leaving the Bauhaus in 1929 to work independently, Wagenfeld abandoned the rigid formalism of that institution in favor of a more pragmatic attitude toward the nature of materials and technical processes involved in designing high quality, inexpensive items for industry. During the 1930s Wagenfeld worked in porcelain (for Rosenthal and Fürstenburg) and in glass for the Vereinigte Lausitzer glassworks and the Jenaer glassworks, where he created a tea service in heat-resistant glass that is still in production today. He taught industrial design at the Berlin Hochschule für Bildende Künste and in 1954 established his own workshop in Stuttgart. In the postwar period Wagenfeld has continued to design elegant, unadorned, clean-lined products for industry that have been widely imitated: glass and metalwork for the Württembergische Metallwarenfabrik (II-70, 71; V-47, 48), appliances for Braun, and light fittings for Peill and Putzler, which were awarded a gold medal at the Milan Triennale of 1954. In 1957 Wagenfeld received a grand prize at the Triennale for his entire production.

Monographs: Zurich, Kunstgewerbemuseum, *Industrieware von Wilhelm Wagenfeld* (Oct. 7–Nov. 13, 1960); Cologne, Kunstgewerbemuseum, *Wilhelm Wagenfeld: 50 Jahre Mitarbeit in Fabriken* (Oct.–Dec. 1973) (biblio.); Stuttgart, Württembergisches Landesmuseum, *Wilhelm Wagenfeld: Schöne Form, Gute Ware* (Apr. 4–June 8, 1980).

Katsuji Wakisaka
Japanese, born 1944

Trained in textile design in Kyoto (1960–63), Wakisaka worked consecutively for Itoh in Osaka (1963–65), Samejima in Kyoto (1965–68), and Marimekko in Helsinki (1968–76) as a designer of printed fabrics. Since 1976 Wakisaka has designed both printed and woven fabrics for Larsen in New York and Wacoal (VII-63) in Tokyo—his work for

Wacoal being chosen by the Japan Design Committee for special exhibition in 1980.

Reference: "Bright Spell Forecast," *Design*, no. 298 (Oct. 1973), pp. 58–61.

Don Wallance
American, born 1909

A metalwork and furniture designer, Wallance chronicled the industrial process through case studies of well-designed and well-produced objects in his book *Shaping America's Products* (1956). Included was his own "Design 1," a brushed stainless-steel cutlery service with a distinctive ladlelike soup spoon (V-49), created for Lauffer in 1954, and manufactured by Pott. The success of this American design in direct competition with Scandinavian services led to Wallance's series of highly sculptural flatwares for Lauffer, the latest, "Design 10," created in 1978–79 in plastic. His best-known furniture is his seating for Philharmonic Hall in New York's Lincoln Center (1964).

Writings: Donald A. Wallance, "Design in Plastics," *Everyday Art Quarterly*, vol. 6 (1947), pp. 3–4, 15; Don Wallance, *Shaping America's Products* (New York, 1956).

Reference: Ada Louise Huxtable, "Stainless Comes to Dinner," *Industrial Design*, vol. 1 (Aug. 1954), pp. 30–38.

Gilbert Watrous
American, born 1919

A graduate in industrial design from the Illinois Institute of Technology in Chicago, Watrous won a special prize in the international competition for floor lamp design at the Museum of Modern Art in New York for his tripod lamp with a fully adjustable arm on a magnetic swivel (IV-39). From 1957 to about 1962 he was a partner in Visual and Industrial Design in San Diego, working on product design (for Stromberg-Carlson, Convair) and exhibition installations.

Reference: W.J. Hennessey, *Modern Furnishings for the Home*, vol. 1 (New York, 1952), p. 245.

Hans Wegner
Danish, born 1914

One of the great mid-century furniture designers, Wegner has created new forms out of the techniques and materials of traditional cabinetmaking. Apprenticed to a cabinetmaker in his native town of Tønder in Jutland, Wegner studied furniture design at the School of Arts and Crafts (Kunsthandvaerkerskolen) in Copenhagen before opening his own office in Gentofte in 1943. He was associated from 1940 with Johannes Hansen, who produced his first design in 1941, with others following during the 1940s as war production would allow. In 1947 Wegner exhibited his now-famous "Peacock" chair (III-89) at the Copenhagen Cabinetmakers' Guild exhibition and achieved international recognition at the Guild exhibition of 1949 with his classic round (III-90) and folding (III-91) chairs. Although Wegner later designed excellent tubular-steel furniture and leather-upholstered pieces such as the "Bull" chair and ottoman (1960), he has remained best known for the early, elegant wooden chairs that have stayed in continuous production. "A lot of my stuff never sees the light of day. . . . Many of them are attempts to break new ground. But I'm not allowed to. Wegner has to look like Wegner" (1979).

Monographs: Johan Møller-Nielsen, *Wegner: En dansk Møbelkunstner* (Copenhagen, 1965); Henrik Sten Møller, *Tema med Variationer: Hans J. Wegner's Møbler* (Tønder, 1979).

References: Arne Karlsen, *Made in Denmark* (New York, 1960), pp. 56–63; Irving Sloane, "Hans Wegner: A Modern Master of Furniture Design," *Fine Woodworking*, no. 20 (Jan.–Feb. 1980), pp. 36–42.

Daniel Weil
Argentine, lives in England, born 1953

In trying to establish a "new imagery for electronics to escape from the mechanical imagery of the box," Weil has since 1981 devised a series of digital clocks, radios, and lights for Parenthesis that are encased in soft plastic envelopes (I-49). Screen-printed in colorful flat patterns and revealing their wiring and

electronic parts, the appliances are both art and objects, and have been sold as production pieces at reasonable cost and in special limited editions at galleries. Weil, who was trained in architecture in Buenos Aires (graduated 1977) and in industrial design at the Royal College of Art, London (1978–81), believes that design should be more than just technical or stylistic solutions, and that it should be also concerned with ideas and the intellect, melding the vocabulary of twentieth-century art with the objects of everyday life.

Reference: Terry Ilott, "Martian Crafts," *Crafts*, no. 62 (May–June 1983), pp. 30–33.

Reinhold Weiss
German, lives in the United States, born 1934

Educated at the Hochschule für Gestaltung in Ulm, West Germany (1959), where he worked with HANS GUGELOT, Weiss joined Braun in 1959 as associate director of the product design department and executive designer of the appliance division. His award-winning table fan (I-50) was considered a model of the austere design and scientific method advocated by both Ulm and Braun, a product that lent itself to systematic mathematical analysis, an ordered assemblage of interrelated component parts. In 1967 Weiss immigrated to the United States, where in Chicago he joined Unimark, the firm co-founded by MASSIMO VIGNELLI, and in 1970, established an independent design office there. Weiss has since received international recognition for graphic and product design, ranging from the American Institute of Graphic Arts award for package design (1972) to a gold medal at the Industry Fair, Brnö, Czechoslovakia (1982).

Reference: Tomás Maldonado and Gui Bonsiepe, "Science and Design," *Ulm*, vols. 10–11 (May 1964), pp. 16–18.

Robert Welch
British, born 1929

With a background in silversmithy at the Royal College of Art, London, but specializing in stainless steel, Welch has pursued both paths, opening a silver studio-workshop in Chipping Campden in the Cotswolds in 1955 and becoming designer-consultant to Old Hall. Like his colleague DAVID MELLOR, he brought the concerns for time-honored craftsmanship and form seen in his unique silver pieces to his design for industry, including several lines of stainless-steel flatware and hollow ware for Old Hall (V-50), cast-iron and enamel cookware for Prinz (1966) and Lauffer (1970), stoneware for Brixham Pottery (1970), clocks for Westclox, and lamps for Lumitron. He has held the distinction of Royal Designer for Industry since 1965.

Monograph: Colin Forbes, ed., *Robert Welch: Design in a Cotswold Workshop* (London, 1973).

References: Graham Hughes, *Modern Silver throughout the World* (New York, 1967), nos. 144, 146–49, 389–91, 393; Fiona MacCarthy, *British Design since 1880* (London, 1982), figs. 151, 155–56, 187, 190, 200, 217.

W. Archibald Welden
American, born 1900s

Head of design for Revere Copper and Brass, Welden created the "Revere Ware" line of copper-bottom stainless-steel cookware in 1939, based on extensive research into ease of use and cleaning, heating efficiency, tooling and manufacturing, and consumer preferences. In the 1950s he augmented Revere's range with a series with heat-resistant metal (V-51), rather than molded-plastic, handles, directed toward the institutional market. Self-taught, Welden was a designer-craftsman of architectural ornaments and decorative metalwork. After closing his studio (by 1933), he became an independent designer for Revere, working closely with the company's technicians to adapt his designs for mass-production techniques, and conversely, to adjust production methods to the particular needs of his high-quality cookware.

Reference: Don Wallance, *Shaping America's Products* (New York, 1956), pp. 41–45.

Don Wight
American, born 1924

An artist, photographer, and designer of textiles, Wight studied at Alfred University, New York (1942–43), and at Black Mountain College, North Carolina (1945–47), under Josef and ANNI ALBERS. In 1947 he served as an apprentice weaver and textile designer in the studio of DOROTHY LIEBES in San Francisco. In New York from 1948 to 1966, and

abroad until 1977, Wight supplied textile print designs for numerous firms, including those of Liebes, JACK LENOR LARSEN (VII-64), Brunschwig, Bates, and Schumacher. His printed fabric "Garden of Glass" was shown at the "Good Design" exhibition at the Museum of Modern Art in New York in 1951 (and again in 1954), and he received A.I.D. Design Awards in 1954 and 1958.

Tapio Wirkkala
Finnish, born 1915

Craftsman and designer of glass, ceramics, metal, wooden objects, lighting, furniture, appliances, graphics, and exhibitions, Wirkkala has been the most versatile and internationally celebrated of Finnish designers since the war, with outstanding powers of formal innovation, rooted in the materials and processes of handicraft. Educated at the Institute of Industrial Arts (Taideteollisuuskeskuskoulu), Helsinki (1936), where he was later art director (1951–54), Wirkkala became glass designer for Iittala in 1947 after sharing first prize with KAJ FRANCK in a competition organized by the glassworks. He achieved international recognition in the late 1940s and 1950s with his "Kanttarelli" glassware (II-72) and laminated wood dishes (VIII-10), which evoked forms, patterns, and textures found in nature. In addition to designs for such Finnish firms as Airam and Hackman (V-53), Wirkkala has worked abroad for RAYMOND LOEWY (1955–56), Rosenthal (since 1959; V-52), and Venini (since 1965; II-73, 74). His creations for these firms have made him the most premiated of all modern designers, with seven grand prizes in Milan in three Triennale exhibitions between 1951 and 1964.

Monographs: Washington, D.C., Smithsonian Institution, *Rut Bryk-Tapio Wirkkala* (1956–59); Helsinki, The Finnish Society of Crafts and Design, *Tapio Wirkkala* (1981).

References: "Interview with Tapio Wirkkala," *Domus*, no. 619 (July–Aug. 1981), pp. 6–7; Pekka Suhonen, "Counterpoints in Tapio Wirkkala's Output," *Form Function Finland*, no. 2 (1981), pp. 38–43.

Edward Wormley
American, born 1907

As designer for Dunbar (since the 1930s), Wormley worked in forms inspired by historical styles as well as in a modern vocabulary, consistently refining the company's production of wood and upholstered furniture meant to appeal to vastly divergent tastes. His postwar "contemporary" models, reflecting influences from Scan-

dinavia and Italy and featuring the versatility of function thought necessary for "modern living," were well respected, so much so that in both 1951 and 1952, six of his designs were included in the "Good Design" exhibitions at the Museum of Modern Art in New York. A student at the Art Institute of Chicago (1926–27), Wormley worked in the design studio of Marshall Field's in Chicago (1928–30) and for Dunbar from 1931 to 1941. From 1945 he had his own design firm in New York, but continued to provide furniture designs for Dunbar (III-92), carpets for Alexander Smith, and textiles.

References: George Nelson, ed., *Chairs* (New York, 1953), pp. 41, 62–63, 73, 93, 158, 161; W. J. Hennessey and E. D. Hennessey, *Modern Furnishings for the Home*, vol. 2 (New York, 1956), *passim*; Edgar Kaufmann, Jr., "Edward Wormley: 30 Years of Design," *Interior Design*, vol. 32 (Mar. 1961), p. 190.

Russel Wright
American, 1904–1976

A versatile designer of home furnishings and interiors, Wright is credited with popularizing modern design in America in the late 1930s. His "American Modern" group—bleached maple ("blonde") streamlined furniture (1935) and lamps, spun-aluminum tableware, and primarily his ceramic dinnerware (1937)—brought his name and his conviction that "good design is for everyone" to all Americans. His 1946 Iroquois "Casual China" (II-75), a rethinking of his earlier dinnerware in seven compatible colors, was simple in form, with depressed handles and grips that allowed for easy stacking, and had a highly fired porcelain body so resistant to chipping and breakage that it was sold with a one-year guarantee. Wright continued to design tablewares—"Highlight" glass and pottery (1951) and "Flair" glassware (II-76); furniture—the fifty-piece "Easier Living" line for Stratton (1950) and a well-known folding plywood chair for Samsonite (1950); and plastics—Melmac dinnerware for Northern Industrial Chemical. His work as a consultant for the State Department in developing cottage industries in Southeast Asia, beginning in 1956, brought him to the attention of Japanese authorities, for whom he

designed in 1965 over one hundred products for Japanese manufacturers. Giving up most design work, he became a consultant for planning and programming for the National Park Service in 1967.

Writings: Russel and Mary Wright, *A Guide to Easier Living* (New York, 1951).

Monograph: William J. Hennessey, *Russel Wright: American Designer* (Cambridge, Mass., 1983).

References: *Current Biography* (1950), *s.v.*; Diane Cochrane, "Designer for All Seasons," *Industrial Design*, vol. 23 (Mar.–Apr. 1976), pp. 46–51.

Sori Yanagi
Japanese, born 1915

One of Japan's leading industrial designers (he was the first-prize winner of the inaugural Japanese Competition for Industrial Design, 1951), Yanagi is fully cognizant of Western ideas, technology, and methods, although he retains in his work as much as possible of the sensibility, materials, and forms revered by generations of Japanese craftsmen. He is very much involved in solving the problems of daily life, carefully working out his designs so that a porcelain sauceboat will not drip or a metal pot boil over. He is also concerned with the logic and structure of his products and with the process of molding successfully the organic curves of his wooden furniture (III-93) or his ceramics. Yanagi studied painting and architecture in Tokyo and worked in the office of the French designer Charlotte Perriand, who was in Japan in the 1940s as an advisor on product design.

References: "Produzione recente di Sori Yanagi," *Stile Industria*, no. 28 (Aug. 1960), pp. 42–45; Bruno Munari, "Design According to Yanagi," *Domus*, no. 609 (Sept. 1980), pp. 40–41; Tokyo, Crafts Gallery, The National Museum of Modern Art, *Contemporary Vessels: How to Pour* (Feb. 10–Mar. 22, 1982), nos. 192–99.

Marco Zanini
Italian, born 1954

A graduate of the university of Florence, Zanini and several other young architects in 1980 became associates of ETTORE SOTTSASS, JR., in Sottsass Associati, an industrial design firm in Milan with work that includes graphics, industrial machinery, and modular furniture. Zanini has also focused on the design of furniture and glass for

Memphis, giving monumental, ceremonial forms to otherwise simple objects—glasses, cocktail pitchers, and flower vases (II-77).

Writings: Marco Zanini, "A Well Travelled Man," in *Design ist unsichtbar* (Vienna, 1981), pp. 464–74.

References: Barbara Radice, ed., *Memphis: The New International Style* (Milan, 1981), pp. 65–66; Christine Colin, "Memphis a encore frappé," *Décoration Internationale*, no. 51 (Dec. 1982–Jan. 1983), pp. 54–57, 206.

Marco Zanuso
Italian, born 1916

Architect, planner, and industrial designer, Zanuso has led rationalist postwar Italian design through the body of his widely premiated work, through his teaching at the Milan Politecnico (from 1949), and through his position as an editor of *Casabella* (from 1947). Trained as an architect at the Politecnico (1939), Zanuso established an independent office in Milan in 1945. In the 1948 low-cost furniture design competition at the Museum of Modern Art in New York, Zanuso submitted a chair design, which included a new mechanical joining device for the tubular-steel frame from which the fabric seat was suspended. This concern for structure and the nature of materials has continued to characterize Zanuso's product work, including the "Lady" armchair (1951; III-94), an innovative application of foam rubber upholstery; the "Lambda" chair (1962; III-95), an entirely sheet-metal construction; and the child's stacking chair (1964; III-96), the first structural use of polyethylene in furniture. Collaborating with RICHARD SAPPER from 1958 to 1977, Zanuso designed a number of electronic products, including the "Grillo" telephone (1965; I-53), and the "Doney" (1962; I-51) and "Black" (1969; I-54) televisions, which provide visually elegant solutions to miniaturized functions. Zanuso has at the same time designed plants for Olivetti.

Monograph: Gillo Dorfles, *Marco Zanuso: Designer* (Rome, 1971).

References: Paolo Fossati, *Il design in Italia* (Turin, 1972), pp. 107–13, 207–19, pls. 177–235 (biblio.); Andrea Branzi and Michele De Lucchi, eds., *Il design italiano degli anni '50* (Milan, 1981), pp. 303–4.

Otto Zapf
German, born 1931

A designer of furniture for Knoll since 1973, Zapf has conceived component office systems as well as the recent (1981) "Heli" series of upholstered chairs and sofas. The head of his own firm, Zapf has also designed lighting, notably his "Light Column" of 1972 (IV-41), which was awarded a Bundespreis "Gute Form" in the same year.

Reference: Darmstadt, Rat für Formgebung, *Bundespreis Gute Form '72* (from Jan. 23, 1972), p. 6.

the Musée des Arts Décoratifs in Montreal in 1984.

References: "In the Showrooms: Furniture," *Interiors,* vol. 109 (Mar. 1950), p. 122; "Merchandise Cues," *Interiors,* vol. 111 (Feb. 1952), p. 114; Jay Doblin, *One Hundred Great Product Designs* (New York, 1970), p. 62.

Eva Zeisel
American, born Hungary, 1906

In April 1946, following its exhibition of furniture by CHARLES EAMES, the Museum of Modern Art in New York held a second solo exhibition—"Modern China by Eva Zeisel"—to present the porcelain table service that the Museum and Castleton china had commissioned from the Hungarian-born potter. "Museum" china (II-78) was intended to express the modern functional style in ceramics, which major factories in Europe (particularly Arzberg and Berlin in Germany) had already begun to produce before the war, a style of simple, undecorated shapes and often, like the "Museum" china, sold in plain white. The sculptural forms of this service were developed by Zeisel in a softer, even more expressive, style during the 1950s, in a tubular metal knock-down chair with a plastic, zippered cover for Richards-Morgenthau in 1950, wooden objects for Salisbury Artisans from 1951, and dinnerware for Hall china in 1952. Trained as a painter at the Royal Academy in Budapest, Zeisel worked first in the Kispester earthenware factory in Budapest and at various ceramic factories in Germany (1927–32). From 1932 to 1937 she worked at the Lomanossova factory in Leningrad and at the factory in Dulewo, and finally as art director in the Central Administration of the Glass and China Industry of the U.S.S.R., in Moscow. In 1937 Zeisel came to the United States, teaching at the Pratt Institute of Arts in New York (1939–53) and at the Rhode Island School of Design in Providence (1959–60), while also designing for industry. In 1983 she was awarded a Senior Fellowship by the National Endowment for the Arts, and her work will be the subject of a retrospective exhibition at

Selected Bibliography

Appliances

Beeching, Wilfred A. *Century of the Typewriter.* New York, 1974.

Braun, Ernest, and MacDonald, Stuart. *Revolution in Miniature: The History and Impact of Semiconductor Electronics.* Cambridge, 1978.

Casimir, H.B.G., and Gradstein, S., eds. *An Anthology of Philips Research 1891–1966.* Eindhoven, 1966.

Los Angeles, University of California, Frederick S. Wight Art Gallery. *Design Process Olivetti 1908–1978.* Mar. 27–May 6, 1979.

Mayall, W. H. *The Challenge of the Chip.* London, 1980.

Stockholm, Nationalmuseum. *Telefonen 100 ar: Design och kommunikation.* May 5–June 27, 1976.

Zurich, Kunstgewerbemuseum. *Stile Olivetti: Geschichte und Formen einer italienischen Industrie.* Apr. 8–May 20, 1961.

Ceramics and Glass

Arnö-Berg, Inga. *Serviser fran Gustavsberg.* Örebro, 1971.

Beard, Geoffrey. *International Modern Glass.* London, 1976.

Beard, Geoffrey. *Modern Glass.* New York, 1968.

Blair, Dorothy. *A History of Glass in Japan.* New York, 1973.

Buchwald, Gunnar, and Schlüter, Mogens, eds. *Kastrup and Holmegaard's Glassworks, Denmark, 1825–1975.* Copenhagen, 1975.

Copenhagen, Kastrup & Holmegaard Glassworks. *150 Years of Danish Glass.* N.d.

Corning, N.Y., The Corning Museum of Glass. *Czechoslovakian Glass: 1350–1980.* May 2–Nov. 1, 1981.

Corning, N.Y., The Corning Museum of Glass. *Glass 1959: A Special Exhibition of International Contemporary Glass.* Summer 1959.

Corning, N.Y., The Corning Museum of Glass. *New Glass: A Worldwide Survey.* Apr. 26–Oct. 1, 1979.

Düsseldorf, Kunstmuseum. *Fins Glas.* Jan. 12–Feb. 25, 1973.

Düsseldorf, Kunstmuseum. *Leerdam Unica: 50 Jahre modernes niederländisches Glas.* May 13–June 26, 1977.

Fauster, Carl U. *Libbey Glass since 1818: Pictorial History & Collector's Guide.* Toledo, 1979.

Frankfort, Museum für Kunsthandwerk. *Modernes Glas aus Amerika, Europa, und Japan.* May 15–June 27, 1976.

Glass Is Our Material. Oslo, 1961.

Hanover, Kestner-Museum. *Rosenthal: Hundert Jahre Porzellan.* Apr. 29–June 13, 1982.

Hanover, Kestner-Museum. *Venini—Orrefors Glass.* Apr. 27–July 30, 1957.

Hiort, Esbjørn. *Modern Danish Ceramics.* New York, 1955.

Hokkaido, Hokkaido Museum of Modern Art. *World Glass Now '82.* July 17–Aug. 29, 1982.

Jevnaker, Hadeland Glassworks. *Hadeland Glassworks.* Mar. 13–Apr. 4, 1980.

Lagercrantz, Bo. *Modern Swedish Ceramics.* Stockholm, 1950.

Lassen, Erik, and Schlüter, Mogens. *Dansk glas: 1925–1975.* Copenhagen, 1975.

Lewenstein, Eileen, and Cooper, Emmanuel, eds. *New Ceramics.* New York, 1974.

Liège, Musée Curtius. *Aspects de la verrerie contemporaine.* 1958.

London, Victoria and Albert Museum. *Three Centuries of Swedish Pottery: Rörstrand 1726–1959, and Marieberg, 1758–1788.* Apr. 16–May 31, 1959.

New York, Museum of Contemporary Crafts. *Glass: Czechoslovakia and Italy.* N.d.

Niilonen, Kerttu. *Finnish Glass.* Helsinki, 1966.

Paris, Musée des Arts Décoratifs. *Céramique française contemporaine.* Oct. 16, 1981—Jan. 4, 1982.

Paris, Musée des Arts Décoratifs. *Verriers français contemporains: Art et industrie.* Apr. 2–July 5, 1982.

Polak, Ada. *Modern Glass.* London, 1962.

Rotterdam, Museum Boymans-van Beuningen. *Acht Deense Ceramisten.* Dec. 16, 1976—Jan. 30, 1977.

Schlüter, Mogens. *Glashandvaerk i Danmark.* Copenhagen, 1973.

Steenberg, Elisa. *Swedish Glass.* New York, 1950.

Stennett-Willson, Ronald. *The Beauty of Modern Glass.* London, 1958.

Stennett-Willson, Ronald. *Modern Glass.* New York, 1975.

Stockholm, Nationalmuseum. *Gustavsberg 150 ar.* Oct. 7, 1975—Jan. 25, 1976.

Stockholm, Nationalmuseum. *Svenskt glas 1954.* Stockholm, 1954.

Tokyo, The National Museum of Modern Art, Crafts Gallery. *Contemporary Vessels: How to Pour.* Feb. 10–Mar. 22, 1982.

University Park, Pa., The Pennsylvania State University, Museum of Art. *Danish Ceramic Design.* Oct. 18, 1981—Jan. 24, 1982.

Washington, D.C., Smithsonian Institution Traveling Exhibition Service. *Venini Glass.* 1981.

Furniture

Aloi, Roberto. *Esempi di arredamento moderno di tutto il mondo.* 6 vols. Milan, 1950–53.

Aloi, Roberto. *Mobili tipo.* Milan, 1956.

Artaria, Paul, ed. *Schwedische Möbel.* Basel, 1954.

Bergen, Vestlandske Kunstindustrimuseum. *Norske møbler i fortid og natid.* May–June 1967.

Bermpohl, Richard, and Winkelman, H. *Das Möbelbuch; ein Nachschlagewerk über Möbel.* Gütersloh, 1958.

Buttrey, D. N., ed. *Plastics in Furniture.* London, 1976.

Cambridge, Mass., Massachusetts Institute of Technology, Hayden Gallery. *Furniture by Architects: Contemporary Chairs, Tables and Lamps.* May 16–June 28, 1981.

Campbell-Cole, Barbie, and Benton, Tim, eds. *Tubular Steel Furniture.* London, 1979.

Caplan, Ralph. *The Design of Herman Miller.* New York, 1976.

Cincinnati, Cincinnati Art Museum. *Change of Pace: Contemporary Furniture 1925–1975.* Oct. 4, 1975—Jan. 4, 1976.

Cologne, Kölnisches Stadtmuseum. *Möbel italienisches Design: Kultur und Technologie im italienischen Möbel 1950–1980.* Nov. 29, 1980—Jan. 25, 1981.

Copenhagen, Den Permanente. *Fritz Hansen, 1872–1972.* 1972.

Ditzel, Nanna, and Ditzel, Jørgen, eds. *Danish Chairs.* Copenhagen, 1954.

Dunnett, H. McG. "Furniture since the War." *Architectural Review,* vol. 109 (Mar. 1951), pp. 151–66.

Frey, Gilbert. *The Modern Chair: 1850 to Today.* New York, 1970.

Hiort, Esbjørn. *Moderne dänische Möbelkunst.* Stuttgart, 1956.

Joel, David. *The Adventure of British Furniture 1851–1951.* London, 1953.

Joel, David. *Furniture Design Set Free: The British Furniture Revolution from 1851 to the Present Day.* London, 1969.

Kaufmann, Edgar, Jr. *Prize Designs for Modern Furniture from the International Competition for Low-cost Furniture Design.* New York, 1950.

Kettiger, Ernst, and Vetter, Franz. *Furniture and Interiors.* Zurich, 1957.

La Jolla, La Jolla Museum of Contemporary Art. *The Modern Chair: Its Origins and Evolution.* Mar. 25–May 15, 1977.

Larrabee, Eric, and Vignelli, Massimo. *Knoll Design.* New York, 1981.

London, Whitechapel Art Gallery. *Modern Chairs: 1918–1970.* July 22–Aug. 30, 1970.

Lyall, Sutherland. *Hille: 75 Years of British Furniture.* London, 1981.

Mang, Karl. *History of Modern Furniture.* New York, 1979.

Meadmore, Clement. *The Modern Chair: Classics in Proportion.* New York, 1975.

Milan, Centrokappa. *Plastic Chair International Exhibition.* Sept. 10–Oct. 30, 1975.

Nelson/Eames/Girard/Propst: The Design Process at Herman Miller. Design Quarterly (special issue), nos. 98–99 (1975).

Nelson, George. *Storage.* New York, 1954.

Nelson, George, ed. *Chairs.* New York, 1953.

New York, The American Federation of Arts. *Please Be Seated: The Evolution of the Chair, 2000 BC–2000 AD.* 1968.

New York, Cooper-Hewitt Museum. *Innovative Furniture in America.* Fall 1981.

Page, Marian. *Furniture by Architects.* New York, 1980.

Paris, Musée d'Art Moderne de la Ville de Paris. *Structures gonflables.* Mar. 1968.

Paris, Musée des Arts Décoratifs. *Les Assises du siège contemporain.* May 3–July 29, 1968.

Paris, Musée des Arts Décoratifs. *Knoll au Louvre.* Jan. 12–Mar. 12, 1972.

Pfannschmidt, Ernst Erik. *Metallmöbel.* Stuttgart, 1962.

Pile, John F. *Modern Furniture.* New York, 1979.

Prete, Barbara, ed. *Chair.* New York, 1978.

Ritter, Enrichetta. *Design italiano mobili: Furniture, meubles, möbel.* Milan, 1968.

Russell, Gordon. *Looking at Furniture.* London, 1964.

Saint Louis, City Art Museum of Saint Louis. *Product Environment: Exhibition of New Furniture.* Apr. 24–June 7, 1970.

Santini, Pier Carlo. *Facendo mobili con.* Florence, 1977.

Vienna, Österreichisches Museum für Angewandte Kunst. *Sitzen 69: Moderne Tischlersessel und ihre Werkzeichnungen.* Jan. 24–Mar. 16, 1969.

Young, Dennis, and Young, Barbara. *Furniture in Britain Today.* New York, 1964.

Zurich, Kunstgewerbemuseum. *Gute Möbel.* Nov. 11, 1961–Jan. 7, 1962.

Lighting

Baroni, Daniele, *L'Oggetto lampada.* Milan, 1981.

Hopkinson, Ralph G., and Collins, J. B. *The Ergonomics of Lighting.* London, 1970.

Larson, Leslie. *Lighting and Its Design.* New York, 1964.

Phillips, Derek. *Lighting.* London, 1966.

Metalwork

Berlin, Internationales Design Zentrum. *Essen und Ritual.* Berlin, 1981.

Cologne, Arbeitsgemeinschaft des Deutschen Kunsthandwerks. *Metal: Germany.* Jan. 20–Mar. 5, 1967.

Hiort, Esbjørn. *Moderne dänische Silberkunst.* Stuttgart, 1955.

Hughes, Graham. *Modern Jewelry: An International Survey 1890–1963.* New York, 1963.

Hughes, Graham. *Modern Silver throughout the World: 1880–1967.* New York, 1967.

Mendini, Alessandro. *Paesaggio Casalingo: La produzione alessi nell'industria dei casalinghi dal 1921 al 1980.* Milan, 1979.

Minneapolis, Walker Art Center. *Knife, Fork, Spoon.* 1951.

New York, Museum of Contemporary Crafts. *Designed for Silver.* Sept. 23–Dec. 4, 1960.

Nuremberg, Gewerbemuseum. *Gold & Silber, Schmuck & Gerät von Albrecht Dürer bis zur Gegenwart.* Mar. 19–Aug. 22, 1971.

Persson, Sigurd. *Modern Swedish Silver.* Stockholm, 1951.

Stewart, Richard. *Modern Design in Metal.* London, 1979.

Stockholm, Nationalmuseum. *Danskt silver, 1900–1950.* Feb. 14–Mar. 12, 1950.

Stockholm, Nationalmuseum. *Ungt svenskt silver.* Sept.–Oct. 1965.

Washington, D.C., Smithsonian Institution, Renwick Gallery of the National Collection of Fine Arts. *Georg Jensen—Silversmithy: 77 Artists 75 Years.* Feb. 29–July 6, 1980.

Plastics

Beck, Ronald D. *Plastic Product Design.* New York, 1980.

DuBois, John Harry. *Plastics History U.S.A.* Boston, 1972.

Gloag, John. *Plastics and Industrial Design.* London, 1945.

Katz, Sylvia. *Plastics: Designs and Materials.* London, 1978.

Millett, R. *Design and Technology: Plastics.* Exeter, 1977.

New York, Museum of Contemporary Crafts. *Plastic as Plastic.* Nov. 23, 1968—Jan. 12, 1969.

Prague, The Museum of Decorative Arts. *Design and Plastics.* Oct.–Dec. 1972.

Rotterdam, Museum Boymans-van Beuningen. *Bakeliet: techniek/vormgeving/gebruik.* May 23–July 20, 1981.

Washington, D.C., Smithsonian Institution Traveling Exhibition Service. *400 Examples of American Plastics.* 1956.

Textiles

Colchester, The Minories. *A Choice of Design, 1850–1980: Fabrics by Warner & Sons Limited.* Sept. 19–Oct. 25, 1981.

Constantine, Mildred, and Larsen, Jack Lenor. *Beyond Craft: The Art Fabric.* New York, 1973.

Johnston, Meda Hunter. *Design on Fabrics.* New York, 1967.

Larsen, Jack Lenor, and Weeks, Jeanne. *Fabrics for Interiors: A Guide for Architects, Designers and Consumers.* New York, 1975.

Sampe, Astrid. *Swedish Textile.* Stockholm, 1981.

Talley, Charles S. *Contemporary Textile Art: Scandinavia.* Stockholm, 1982.

Troupp, Lotte. *Modern Finnish Textiles.* Helsinki, 1962.

Washington, D.C., Smithsonian Institution Traveling Exhibition Service. *Ryijy: Rugs from Finland. 200 Years of a Textile Art.* 1979–81.

General

L'Agence Européenne de Productivité de l'Organisation Européenne de Coopération Économique. *L'Esthétique industrielle aux États-Unis.* Paris, 1959.

Akron, Akron Art Institute. *Off the Production Line: An Invitational Exhibition of Products Designed for Industry.* Feb. 11–Mar. 27, 1956.

Akron, Akron Art Institute. *The Product as an Object, Ohio.* May 20–July 15, 1973.

Akron, Akron Art Institute. *Useful Objects for the Home.* Nov. 2–Dec. 2, 1947.

Algard, Göran, and Romell, Roland. *Sweden Today.* Stockholm, 1970.

Amsterdam, Visual Arts Office for Abroad. *Design from the Netherlands.* 1981.

Arrhenius, Lilly. *Swedish Design.* Stockholm, 1957.

Banham, Mary, and Hillier, Bevis, eds. *A Tonic to the Nation: The Festival of Britain 1951.* London, 1976.

Banham, Reyner. "*Design by Choice.*" New York, 1981.

Banham, Reyner. "Epitaph: Machine Esthetic." *Industrial Design* (Mar. 1960), pp. 45–47.

Banham, Reyner. "The History of the Immediate Future." *RIBA Journal,* vol. 68 (May 1961), pp. 252–57.

Banham, Reyner. "Industrial design e arte populare." *Civiltà delle macchine* (Nov.–Dec. 1955), pp. 12–15.

Banham, Reyner. "Neoliberty." *Architectural Review,* vol. 125 (Apr. 1959), pp. 231–35.

Banham, Reyner. *Theory and Design in the First Machine Age.* New York, 1960.

Banham, Reyner. "Where Are You, Universal Man, Now That We Need You?" *RIBA Journal,* vol. 84 (July 1976), p. 295.

Banham, Reyner, ed. *The Aspen Papers: Twenty Years of Design Theory from the International Design Conference in Aspen.* New York, 1974.

Banham, Reyner, ed. "1960 Series." *Architectural Review,* vol. 127 (Feb.–June 1960), pp. 93–100, 183–90, 253–60, 325–32, 381–88.

Bayley, Stephen. *In Good Shape: Style in Industrial Products 1900 to 1960.* London, 1979.

Baynes, Ken. *Industrial Design and the Community.* London, 1967.

Beer, Eileene Harrison. *Scandinavian Design: Objects of a Life Style.* New York, 1975.

Belvin, Marjorie Elliott. *Design through Discovery.* New York, 1980.

Berlin, Internationales Design Zentrum. *Design als Postulat am Beispiel italien.* Sept. 6–Oct. 14, 1973.

Bernadotte, Sigvard, ed. *Moderne dansk boligkunst.* 2 vols. Odense, 1946.

Bernsen, Jens. *Design: The Problem Comes First.* Copenhagen, 1982.

Best, Alastair. "Transparently Beautiful." *Design,* no. 239 (Nov. 1968), pp. 26–31.

Best, Alastair, and Brutton, Mark. "Utility." *Design,* no. 309 (Sept. 1974), pp. 63–71.

Bestetti, Carlo, ed. *New Forms in Italy.* Milan, 1962.

Bicknell, Julian, and McQuiston, Liz, eds. *Design for Need: The Social Contribution of Design.* Oxford, 1977.

Bill, Max. "The Bauhaus Idea: From Weimar to Ulm." In *The Architects' Year Book,* vol. 5 (1953), pp. 29–32.

Bill, Max. *Form—A Balance Sheet of Mid-Twentieth Century Trends in Design.* Basel, 1952.

Bishop, Terry, ed. *Design History: Fad or Function?* London, 1978.

Blake, John, and Blake, Avril. *The Practical Idealists: Twenty-Five Years of Designing for Industry.* London, 1969.

Bonsiepe, Gui. *Diseño industrial: Artefacto y proyecto.* Milan, 1975.

Bonsiepe, Gui, and Kietzmann, Renate. "Finale." *Ulm,* vol. 21 (1968).

Borngräber, Christian. *Stil Novo: Design in den 50er Jahren—Phantasie und Phantastik.* Frankfort, 1979.

Branzi, Andrea, and De Lucchi, Michele, eds. *Il design italiano degli anni '50.* Milan, 1981.

Braun-Feldweg, Wilhelm. *Industrial Design heute: Umwelt aus der Fabrik.* Reinbek bei Hamburg, 1966.

Braun-Feldweg, Wilhelm. *Normen und Formen industrieller Produktion.* Ravensburg, 1954.

Budapest, Magyar Nemzeti Galéria. *Forma és Struktúra.* June 24–Aug. 31, 1980.

Buffalo, Buffalo Fine Arts Academy, Albright Art Gallery. *Good Design Is Your Business.* 1947.

Buffalo, Buffalo Fine Arts Academy, Albright Art Gallery. *20th Century Design: U.S.A.* May 3–June 14, 1959.

Caplan, Ralph. *By Design: Why There Are No Locks on the Bathroom Doors in the Hotel Louis XIV and Other Object Lessons.* New York, 1982.

Caplan, Ralph, ed. *Design in America: Selected Work by Members of the Industrial Designers Society of America.* New York, 1969.

Champaign, University of Illinois, Krannert Art Museum. *For Your Home.* Apr. 17–May 15, 1966.

Christoffersen, Agner. *Applied Arts in Denmark.* Copenhagen, 1948.

Cologne, Kunstgewerbemuseum. *Sehen und Hören: Design & Kommunikation.* Mar. 8–June 3, 1974.

Copenhagen, Danish Design Council. *Danish Design 1980.* Copenhagen, 1980.

Copenhagen, Danish Society of Arts and Crafts and Industrial Design. *D B & D.* Copenhagen, 1972.

Cornford, Christopher. *The Kinship of Art and Technology.* London, 1966.

Coulson, Anthony J. *A Bibliography of Design in Britain 1851–1970.* London, 1979.

Darmstadt, Deutscher Werkbund. *Made in Germany. Produktform. Industrial Design. Forme industrielle.* Munich, 1966.

Darmstadt, Rat für Formgebung. *Bundespreis "Gute Form."* Annual exhibition, from 1969.

Darmstadt, Rat für Formgebung. *Verband deutscher industrie Designer.* 1964.

Design ist unsichtbar. Vienna, 1981.

Detroit, The Detroit Institute of Arts. *An Exhibition for Modern Living.* Sept. 11–Nov. 20, 1949.

Diffrient, Niels; Tilley, Alvin R.; and Bardagly, Joan C. *Humanscale 1-2-3.* Cambridge, Mass., 1974.

Diffrient, Niels; Tilley, Alvin R.; and Harman, David. *Humanscale 4-5-6.* Cambridge, Mass., 1981.

Diffrient, Niels; Tilley, Alvin R.; and Harman, David. *Humanscale 7-8-9.* Cambridge, Mass., 1981.

Doblin, Jay. *One Hundred Great Product Designs.* New York, 1970.

Dorfles, Gillo. *Il disegno industriale e la sua estetica.* Bologna, 1963.

Drexler, Arthur, and Daniel, Greta. *Introduction to 20th Century Design from the Collection of The Museum of Modern Art.* New York, 1959.

Dreyfuss, Henry. *Designing for People.* New York, 1955.

Edinburgh, Royal Scottish Museum. *Enterprise Scotland 1947.* 1947.

Egbert, Donald Drew. *Social Radicalism and the Arts, Western Europe: A Cultural History from the French Revolution to 1968.* New York, 1970.

Farr, Michael. *Design in British Industry: A Mid-Century Survey.* Cambridge, 1955.

Faulkner, Thomas, ed. *Design 1900–1960: Studies in Design and Popular Culture of the 20th Century.* Newcastle upon Tyne, 1976.

Fossati, Paolo. *Il design in Italia: 1945–1972.* Turin, 1972.

Frampton, Kenneth. "Apropos Ulm: Curriculum and Critical Theory." *Oppositions,* vol. 3 (May 1974), pp. 17–36.

Gandelsonas, Mario. "Neo-Functionalism." *Oppositions*, no. 5 (Summer 1976).

Garner, Philippe. *Contemporary Decorative Arts*. New York, 1980.

Giedion, Siegfried. *Mechanization Takes Command: A Contribution to Anonymous History*. New York, 1948.

Good, Elizabeth. *Tableware*. London, 1969.

Grassi, Alfonso, and Pansera, Anty. *Atlante del design italiano: 1940–1980*. Milan, 1980.

Grillo, Paul Jacques. *Form, Function, and Design*. New York, 1975.

Hald, Arthur. *Swedish Design*. Stockholm, 1958.

Hald, Arthur, and Skawonius, Sven Erik. *Contemporary Swedish Design: A Survey in Pictures*. Stockholm, 1951.

Hamburg, Museum für Kunst und Gewerbe. *Angewandte Kunst in Europa nach 1945*. June 29–Aug. 21, 1963.

Hamburg, Museum für Kunst und Gewerbe. *Finnland gestaltet 1982*. Jan. 21–Mar. 7, 1982.

Hamilton, Richard. "Ulm." *Design*, vol. 126 (June 1959), pp. 53–57.

Hammond, John. *Understanding Human Engineering*. Surrey, 1978.

Hård af Segerstad, Ulf. *Modern Finnish Design*. New York, 1969.

Hård af Segerstad, Ulf. *Scandinavian Design*. Stockholm, 1961.

Hatje, Gerd, and Hatje, Ursula. *Design for Modern Living: A Practical Guide to Home Furnishings and Interior Decoration*. New York, 1962.

Height, Frank. "Design in the Soviet Union." *Design*, no. 228 (Dec. 1967), pp. 28–32.

Helsinki, Finnish Society of Crafts and Design. *Finland: Nature, Design, Architecture*. 1980–81.

Hennessey, William J. *Modern Furnishings for the Home*. Vol. 1. New York, 1952.

Hennessey, William J., and Hennessey, E. D. *Modern Furnishings for the Home*. Vol. 2. New York, 1956.

Heskett, John. *Industrial Design*. New York, 1980.

Hillier, Bevis. *The Decorative Arts of the Forties and Fifties*. New York, 1975.

Hirzel, Stephan. *Kunsthandwerk und Manufaktur in Deutschland seit 1945*. Berlin, 1953.

Holland, Laurence B., ed. *Who Designs America?* Garden City, N.Y., 1966.

Huldt, Åke H., and Benedicks, Eva, eds. *Design in Sweden Today*. Stockholm, 1948.

Jensen, Robert, and Conway, Patricia. *Ornamentalism: The New Decorativeness in Architecture and Design*. New York, 1983.

Johnson, Philip. *Writings*. New York, 1979.

Karlsen, Arne; Salicath, Bent; and Utzon-Frank, Mogens, eds. *Contemporary Danish Design*. Copenhagen, 1960.

Karlsen, Arne (and Tiedemann, Anker). *Made in Denmark*. New York, 1960.

Kettiger, Ernst, and Vetter, Franz. *Furniture and Interiors*. Stuttgart, 1957.

Klöcker, Johann, ed. *Zeitgemasse Form: Industrial Design International*. Munich, 1967.

König, Heinrich, et al., eds. *Gestaltete Industrieform in Deutschland*. Düsseldorf, 1954.

Kron, Joan, and Slesin, Suzanne. *High Tech: The Industrial Style and Source Book for the Home*. New York, 1978.

La Jolla, Calif., La Jolla Museum of Contemporary Art. *Italian Re Evolution: Design in Italian Society in the Eighties*. Sept. 10–Oct. 31, 1982.

Lindkvist, Lennart, ed. *Design in Sweden*. Stockholm, 1972.

Ljubljana. *Biennial of Industrial Design*. Bio 1 (1964), Bio 2 (1966), Bio 3 (1968), Bio 4 (1971), Bio 5 (1973), Bio 6 (1975), Bio 7 (1977), Bio 8 (1979), Bio 9 (1981).

London, Council of Industrial Design. *Britain Can Make It*. Sept. 1946.

London, Council of Industrial Design. *Design in the Festival*. London, 1951.

London, Council of Industrial Design. *Designs of the Year 1959, Selected from the Design Centre and Including the Duke of Edinburgh's Prize for Elegant Design*. May 15–June 13, 1959.

London, Council of Industrial Design. *Enterprise Scotland*. 1945.

London, Geffrye Museum. *CC 41: Utility Furniture and Fashion, 1941–1951*. Sept. 24–Dec. 29, 1974.

London, Heal & Son Limited. *Classics: An Exhibition at Heal's*. Spring 1981.

London, Victoria and Albert Museum. *Britain Can Make It*. 1946.

London, Victoria and Albert Museum. *Two Centuries of Danish Design*. Apr. 18–June 3, 1968.

London, Victoria and Albert Museum. *The Way We Live Now*. Nov. 7, 1978—Mar. 4, 1979.

London, Victoria and Albert Museum, Boilerhouse Project. *Art & Industry*. Jan. 18–Mar. 2, 1982.

London, Whitechapel Art Gallery. *This Is Tomorrow*. 1956.

Long Beach, Calif., Long Beach Museum of Art. *Seven Decades of Design*. 1967–68.

Lyons, Musée des Beaux-Arts. *Formes danoises: L'Art de l'intérieur au Danemark*. 1964.

MacCarthy, Fiona. *British Design since 1880: A Visual History*. London, 1982.

MacCarthy, Fiona. *A History of British Design, 1830–1970*. London, 1979.

Mäki, Oili, ed. *Finnish Designers of Today*. Helsinki, 1954.

Maldonado, Tomás. "Comments: Design-Objects and Art-Objects." *Ulm*, vol. 7 (Jan. 1963), pp. 18–23.

Maldonado, Tomás. *Design, Nature and Revolution: Toward a Critical Ecology*. New York, 1972.

Maldonado, Tomás. "Nuova funzione dell'industrial design." *Casabella* (Mar. 1966), pp. 8–9.

Maldonado, Tomás. "Three Ways of Seeing a Profession." *Industrial Design*, no. 9 (Feb. 1962).

Maldonado, Tomás. "Verso un nuovo design." *Casabella* (June 1966), pp. 14–15.

Maldonado, Tomás, and Bonsiepe, Gui. "Science and Design." *Ulm*, vols. 10–11 (May 1964), pp. 8–29.

Malmö, Malmö Museum. *Form 1960*. Sept. 3–Oct. 2, 1960.

Massobrio, G. *Album degli anni cinquanta*. Rome, 1977.

Milan, Museo Poldi Pezzoli. *Milano 70/70: Un secolo d'arte*. Vol. 3, *Dal 1946 al 1970*. From May 30, 1972.

Milan, Palazzo delle Stelline. *Design & design*. May 29–July 31, 1979.

Milan, La Rinascente Compasso d'Oro. *Premio Compasso d'Oro*. Annual exhibition, 1954–58. In cooperation with the Associazione per il Disegno Industriale, 1959–65 (annually to 1962). Organized by the Associazione per il Disegno Industriale from 1967.

Milan, Triennale. *Esposizione internazionale delle arti decorative e industriali moderne e dell'architettura moderna*. IX Triennale (1951), X Triennale (1954), XI Triennale (1957), XII Triennale (1960), XIII Triennale (1964), XIV Triennale (1968), XV Triennale (1973), XVI Triennale (1979).

Moles, Abraham A. "Functionalism in Crisis." *Ulm*, vols. 19–20 (Aug. 1967), pp. 24–25.

Møller, Viggo Sten. *Dansk Kunstindustri*. Copenhagen, 1970.

Mumford, Lewis. *Art and Technics*. New York, 1952.

Munich, Deutsches Museum. *5 Jahre Bundespreis "Gute Form."* July 20–Sept. 22, 1974.

Munich, Modern Art Museum. *Kunst und Industrie*. Jan. 1970.

Munich, Münchener Stadtmuseum. *Beispiele: Möbel und Geräte der Wohnung unserer Zeit*. Oct. 25, 1968—Jan. 12, 1969.

Munich, Die Neue Sammlung. *Gute Form aus der Schweiz*. July 16–Sept. 8, 1957.

Munich, Die Neue Sammlung. *Die Gute Industrieform*. July–Aug. 1955.

Munich, Die Neue Sammlung. *Textilien, Silbergeräte, Bücher: Eine Auswahl aus den verborgenen Depots*. July–Sept. 1980.

Nelson, George. *George Nelson on Design*. New York, 1979.

Nelson, George. *How to See: Visual Adventures in a World God Never Made*. Boston, 1977.

Nelson, George. *Problems of Design*. New York, 1957.

Nelson, George, ed. *Living Spaces*. New York, 1952.

New York, American Craft Museum. *For the Tabletop*. Oct. 11–Dec. 28, 1980.

New York, American Craft Museum. *Pattern: An Exhibition of the Decorated Surface*. Oct. 15, 1982—Jan. 28, 1983.

New York, Cooper-Hewitt Museum. *MAN transFORMS*. Oct. 1976.

New York, Cooper-Hewitt Museum. *Place, Product, Packaging*. Jan. 20–Mar. 19, 1978.

New York, Cooper-Hewitt Museum. *Scandinavian Modern Design: 1880–1980*. Sept. 14, 1982—Jan. 2, 1983.

New York, Industrial Designers Society of America. *Industrial Design—U.S.A.* Jan. 1967.

New York, The Metropolitan Museum of Art. *The Arts of Denmark*. Oct. 15–Jan. 8,.1960.

New York, Museum of Contemporary Crafts. *Objects for Preparing Food.* Sept. 22, 1972 —Jan. 1, 1973.

New York, Museum of Contemporary Crafts. *Portable World.* Oct. 5, 1973 —Jan. 1, 1974.

New York, The Museum of Modern Art. *The Design Collection: Selected Objects.* New York, 1970.

New York, The Museum of Modern Art. *Good Design.* Biannual exhibition, 1950–55. Shown also at Chicago, The Merchandise Mart.

New York, The Museum of Modern Art. *Italy: The New Domestic Landscape.* May 26–Sept. 11, 1972.

New York, The Museum of Modern Art. *Modern Art in Your Life.* New York, 1949.

New York, Society of Industrial Designers. *Industrial Design in America, 1954.* New York, 1954.

Noblet, Jocelyn de. *Design: Introduction à l'histoire de l'évolution des formes industrielles de 1820 à aujourd'hui.* Paris, 1974.

Nordness, Lee. *Objects: U.S.A.* New York, 1970.

Noyes, Eliot F. *Organic Design in Home Furnishings.* New York, 1941.

Ohl, Herbert. "Planning the Pattern of Living." *Ulm,* vol. 21 (1968), pp. 17–23.

Oslo, Kunstindustrimuseet. *Norsk/ Norwegian Industrial Design.* Oslo, 1963.

Papanek, Victor. *Design for the Real World.* New York, 1974.

Paris, Centre de Création Industrielle. *Design français.* Oct. 22–Dec. 21, 1971.

Paris, Centre de Création Industrielle. *Qu'est-ce que le design?* Oct. 24–Dec. 31, 1969.

Paris, Centre de Création Industrielle. *Le Rangement.* 1974.

Paris, Musée des Arts Décoratifs. *Domus: 45 Ans d'architecture, design, art.* May 31–Sept. 23, 1973.

Paris, Musée des Arts Décoratifs. *Formes scandinaves.* Nov. 7, 1958—Jan. 31, 1959.

Paris, Musée des Arts Décoratifs. *Les Métiers de l'art.* From Nov. 27, 1980.

Pasadena, Pasadena Art Museum. *California Design.* 5 (1959), 8 (1962), 9 (1965), 10 (1968), 11 (1971), '76 (1976).

Pevsner, Nikolaus. *Visual Pleasures from Everyday Things. An Attempt to Establish Criteria by Which the Aesthetic Qualities of Design Can Be Judged.* London, 1946.

Pica, Agnoldomenico. *Storia della Triennale di Milano, 1918–1957.* Milan, 1957.

Plath, Iona. *The Decorative Arts of Sweden.* New York, 1966.

Pye, David. *The Nature of Design.* New York, 1964.

Rabi, Isidor I., et al. "Technology: A Boon and a Danger." *American Institute of Architects Journal,* vol. 46 (Sept. 1966), pp. 64–66.

Radice, Barbara, ed. *Memphis: The New International Style.* Milan, 1981.

Reilly, Paul. "The Challenge of Pop." *Architectural Review,* vol. 142 (Oct. 1967), pp. 255–57.

Rogers, Meyric C. *Italy at Work: Her Renaissance in Design Today.* Rome, 1950.

Saarikivi, Sakari; Niilonen, Kerttu; and Ekelund, Hilding. *Art in Finland.* Helsinki, 1952.

Salicath, Bent, ed. *The Lunning Prize Designers' Exhibition.* Copenhagen, 1957.

Schmittel, Wolfgang. *Design Concept Realisation.* Zurich, 1975.

Singer, Charles, et al., eds. *A History of Technology.* Vols. 6–7, *The Twentieth Century,* ed. Trevor I. Williams. New York, 1978.

Skien, Ibsenhuset. *Aktuell Svensk Form.* Oct. 3–21, 1982.

Spielmann, Heinz, comp. *Moderne deutsche Industrieform.* Hamburg, 1962.

Stavenow, Åke, and Huldt, Åke H. *Design in Sweden.* Stockholm, 1964.

Stockholm, Nationalmuseum. *Danskt 50 Tal: Scandinavian Design.* Oct. 7–Nov. 29, 1981.

Stockholm, Nationalmuseum. *Industridesign under 200 ar.* Feb. 15–Apr. 16, 1978.

Streichler, Jerry. "The Consultant Industrial Designer in American Industry from 1927 to 1960." Ph.D. dissertation, New York University, 1962.

Stuttgart, Landesgewerbeamt. *Wie Wohnen: Bautechnik, Möbel, Hausrat.* 1949–50.

"Thirtyfour Lunning Prize-Winners." *Mobilia* (special edition), no. 146 (Sept. 1967).

Venturi, Robert. *Complexity and Contradiction in Architecture.* New York, 1966.

Venturi, Robert, et al. *Learning from Las Vegas.* Cambridge, Mass., 1972.

Vienna, Museum des 20. Jahrhunderts. *Industrial Design aus italien.* Mar. 2–Apr. 30, 1972.

Walker, John A. *Glossary of Art, Architecture and Design.* London, 1973.

Wallance, Don. *Shaping America's Products.* New York, 1956.

Washington, D.C., Corcoran Gallery of Art. *Living Today: An Exhibition of Contemporary Architecture, Furniture, Interior Decoration.* Apr. 19–June 22, 1958.

Washington, D.C., Smithsonian Institution, National Collection of Fine Arts. *Finnish Arts and Crafts.* June 5–26, 1952.

Washington, D.C., Smithsonian Institution Traveling Exhibition Service. *Design in Germany Today.* 1960–61.

Wichmann, Hans. *Aufbruch zum neuen wohnen.* Basel, 1978.

Wichmann, Hans. *Kultur ist unteilbar: Schriften und Vorträge zu Umwelt—Mensch—Gestaltung.* Starnberg, 1973.

Ympärillämme, Esineitä. *The Things Around Us.* Helsinki, 1981.

Zahle, Erik. *Scandinavian Domestic Design.* London, 1963.

Zentralstelle zur Förderung Deutscher Wertarbeit. *Gestaltende Industrieform in Deutschland.* Düsseldorf, 1954.

Zilliacus, Benedict. *Decorative Arts in Finland.* Helsinki, 1963.

Zilliacus, Benedict. *Finnish Designers.* Helsinki, 1954.

Zurich, Kunstgewerbemuseum. *Angewandte Kunst aus Dänemark.* Oct. 11–Dec. 7, 1952.

Zurich, Kunstgewerbemuseum. *Ausstellung Finnisches Kunstgewerbe veranstaltet vom Finnischen Kunstgewerbeverband Ornamo.* Mar. 11–Apr. 15, 1951.

Zurich, Kunstgewerbemuseum. *Dänisches Silber und Handwerk.* Jan. 26–Feb. 25, 1962.

Zurich, Kunstgewerbemuseum. *Design—Formgebung für Jedermann: Typen und Prototypen.* June 16–Sept. 18, 1983.

Zurich, Kunstgewerbemuseum. *Finlandia.* Feb. 3–Mar. 5, 1961.

Zurich, Kunstgewerbemuseum. *Die Gute Form SWB.* Aug. 21–Oct. 3, 1954.

Zurich, Kunstgewerbemuseum. *Kunsthandwerk aus Österreich.* Nov. 8–Dec. 21, 1958.

Zurich, Schweizerischer Werkbund. *Good Design in Switzerland.* Spring 1957. Also circulated by Washington, D.C., Smithsonian Institution Traveling Exhibition Service, 1957–58.

Acknowledgments

This project is intended to provide a record of the recent history of consumer design. Spanning international boundaries and unprecedented in many of its aspects, it owes much to the generous assistance of the designers and manufacturers who helped shape this history. We would particularly like to thank the contributing authors who served as an informal advisory committee for the selection of objects in the exhibition and publication. In addition, the following have offered valuable suggestions and thoughtful advice concerning the material herewith included: Marianne Aav, Harriet Andersson, Florence Knoll Bassett, George Beylerian, Yvonne Brunhammer, Giuseppe Chigiotti, Jay Doblin, John Fleming, Dagmar Hejdová, Richard Latham, Jesse Marsh, Jarno Peltonen, Tapio Periäinen, Lisa Licitra Ponti, Astrid Sampe, George Tanier, Peter Thornton, Gino Valle, and Hans Wichmann.

For their able translations of the essays we would like to thank Edward A. Cooperrider, Ulrich W. Hiesinger, Jesse Marsh, and John Shepley, as well as the authors who provided translations.

In the preparation of the biographies of designers whose work is represented in the exhibition we are profoundly indebted to Carol Hogben, who read the manuscript in an earlier version. His distinguished catalogue of the 1970 Whitechapel Art Gallery exhibition "Modern Chairs" has been a model in the field of contemporary design. Many others have answered questions and pursued elusive information. In this regard we would particularly like to thank: Roxanne Dacy, Nancy Reedy, the Austrian Consulate General, the British Trade Development Office, the Commercial Consular to the French Embassy, the Commercial Office of Spain, the Consulate General of Denmark, the Consulate General of Finland, the Consulate General of the Socialist Federal Republic of Yugoslavia, the Design Council (Bridget Kinally), the Finnish Society of Crafts and Design, the German American Chamber of Commerce, the Italian Trade Commission, the Japan Trade Center, the Netherlands Chamber of Commerce, Inc., the Swedish Trade Office, and the Trade Commission of Norway.

We would like to thank colleagues in other institutions who kindly made their collections available for study: Sidney Goldstein, Stewart Johnson, Gillian Moss, Allan Needell, Patricia O'Donnell, Penelope Hunter Stiebel, Doris Stowens, Christa Mayer Thurman, and William Warmus. For generously providing us with valuable research materials we would profoundly like to thank: Marco Cavallotti and Lenka Bajželj. We are also indebted generally in our research to: Philip Cutler, Richard A. Fees, Edward J. Gately, Ulrich W. Hiesinger, Christopher Wilk, and members of the Collab Committee.

The realization of so large and complex a project has depended on the enormous efforts of the Museum staff. We would particularly like to thank Carol Homan for energetically compiling a design library by loan as well as Barbara Sevy for her purchases. We would also like to thank Anne Schuster for her work on the bibliography; Will Brown and Eric Mitchell for special photography; Tara Robinson and Larry Snyder, who worked closely with George Nelson and his assistant Dan Lewis in realizing the installation; as well as the Registrar's office.

Of our departmental staffs who worked tirelessly and enthusiastically on all phases of the exhibition our warmest thanks in the Department of European Decorative Arts after 1700 are owed particularly to Donna Corbin as well as to Nancy D. Baxter, Melanie Ingalls, Jude Jansen, Barbara Pflaumer Jordan, Kathryn Plummer, Suzanne F. Wells, and volunteers Barbara Brooks, Barbara Hornoff, Phebe O'Neill, Judy Scarlet, and Pamela Wagner. Members of the Department of Publications who patiently and inventively produced the book under pressure are: Sherry Babbitt, Melanie Bartlett, Susan Channing, Bernice Connolly, Leslie March, Susan Moerder, Susan Soltys, Phillip Unetic, Jane Watkins, and Orly Zeewy, who laid out this book under the direction of Laurence Channing.

Index

Index of Manufacturers

Orrefors
(AB Orrefors Glasbruk, Orrefors, Sweden), II-14, 30, 45, 46

Parenthesis
(Parenthesis, Milan), I-49

Philco
(Philco Corporation, Philadelphia), I-31

Poligalant
(Poligalant, Volčja draga, Yugoslovia), VI-9

Poltronova
(Poltronova S.p.A., Pistoia, Italy), III-6, 21

Portescap
(Portescap, La Chaux-de-Fonds, Switzerland), I-22

Pott
(C. Hugo Pott GmbH & Co. KG, Solingen, Germany), V-31, 32, 49

Poulsen
(Louis Poulsen & Co. A/S, Copenhagen), IV-18, 19, 21

Prestini
(James Prestini, Chicago), VIII-6, 7

Printex
(Printex Oy, Helsinki), VII-13, 25, 26, 51

Prolon
(Prolon Manufacturing Co., Florence, Massachusetts), VI-16

Race
(Ernest Race Ltd., London), III-70, 71

Rainbow
(Rainbow, Milan), VII-12

R.E.M. di Rossetti Enrico
(R.E.M. di Rossetti Enrico, Milan), I-7

Renata Bonfanti
(Renata Bonfanti, Musselente, Italy), VII-4

Revere
(Revere Copper and Brass, Inc., Rome, New York), V-51

Revox
(Studer Revox AG, Regensdorf, Switzerland), I-23

RFSU Rehab
(RFSU Rehab, Stockholm), V-11; VI-8

Riihimäen Lasi
(Riihimäen Lasi Oy, Riihimäki, Finland), II-63

Rohi
(Rohi Stoffe GmbH, Geretsried, Germany), VII-19

Rörstrand
(Rörstrand AB, Lidköping, Sweden), II-47

Rosenlew
(Oy W. Rosenlew Ab, Pori, Finland), V-40

Rosenthal
(Rosenthal AG, Selb, West Germany), II-9, 12, 16, 31, 49, 58; V-52

Rosti
(Rosti A/S, Ballerup, Denmark), VI-2

Royal Copenhagen
(The Royal Copenhagen Porcelain Manufactory A/S, Copenhagen), II-42, 62

Sabattini
(Sabattini Argenteria S.p.A., Bregnano, Italy), V-36

Salviati
(Salviati & C., Venice), II-4

Sambonet
(Sambonet S.p.A., Vercelli, Italy), V-37, 38

Sangetsu
(Sangetsu Co., Ltd., Japan), VII-28

San Lorenzo
(San Lorenzo srl, Milan), V-46

Saporiti
(Saporiti Italia, Besnate, Italy), III-32, 75

Schott
(Jenaer Glaswerk Schott & Genossen, Mainz, West Germany), II-35

Scot Simon
(Scot Simon, New York), VII-55

Seguso
(Seguso Vetri d'Arte, Murano, Italy), II-48

Silver & Stal
(AB Silver & Stal, Vingaker, Sweden), V-28

Sinclair Radionics
(Sinclair Radionics Ltd., London), I-40, 41

Sitterle Ceramics
(Sitterle Ceramics, Croton Falls, New York), II-60, 61

Skrdlovice
(Center of Arts and Crafts, Skrdlovice Glassworks, Prague), II-69

Söderström
(G. Söderström, Helsinki), III-60

Soinne
(Soinne & Kni, Finland), VIII-10

Solari
(Solari & C/Udine S.p.A., Udine, Italy), I-48

Sony
(The Sony Corporation, Tokyo), I-43–46

Sormani
(Sormani S.p.A., Arosio, Italy), III-17

Spindegarden
(Spindegarden, Aabenraa, Denmark), VII-61

Stelton
(A/S Stelton, Copenhagen), V-18, 26

Steuben
(Steuben Glass, New York), II-24

Stilnovo
(Stilnovo S.p.A., Milan), IV-3

Stockmann
(Oy Stockmann AB Orno Kerava, Sweden), IV-22, 31

Stuttgarter
(Stuttgarter Gardinenfabrik GmbH, Herrenberg, West Germany), VII-11, 20

Sunar
(Sunar, Norwalk, Connecticut), III-29

Süssmuth
(Glashütte Süssmuth GmbH, Immenhausen, West Germany), II-64

Tampella
(Tampella Ltd., Tampere, Finland), VII-27, 54

Tecmo
(Tecmo, Barcelona), III-73

Tendo
(Tendo Co., Ltd., Tokyo), III-93

Terraillon
(Terraillon, Annemasse Cedex, France), I-55

Teuco-Guzzini
(Teuco-Guzzini srl, Recanati, Italy), I-19

Thema
(Thema S.p.A., Limena, Italy), III-74

Thomas
(Thomas Der Rosenthal AG, Selb, West Germany), II-53

Thonet
(Thonet, York, Pennsylvania), III-77

Tiroler
(Tiroler Glashütte KG, Kufstein, Austria), II-52

Torben Ørskov
(Torben Ørskov & Co. A/S, Copenhagen), III-88; V-24; VI-21

Toso
(Toso Vetri d'Arte, Murano, Italy), II-77

Towle
(Towle Manufacturing Co., Newburyport, Massachusetts), V-20

Tupper
(Tupper Corporation, Orlando, Florida), VI-19, 20

Ums-Pastoe
(Ums-Pastoe bv, Utrecht, The Netherlands), III-59

Unika-Vaev
(Unika-Vaev A/S, Copenhagen), VII-47, 48

Utility
(Utility Furniture Design Panel), III-86

Van Besouw
(Van Besouw NV, Goirle, The Netherlands), VII-50

Van Kempen & Begeer
(Van Kempen & Begeer, Zeist, The Netherlands), V-5

Van Keppel-Green
(Van Keppel-Green, Beverly Hills, California), III-87

Venini
(Venini S.p.A., Murano, Italy), II-55, 67, 68, 73, 74

Verre Lumière
(Verre Lumière S.A., Puteaux, France), IV-38

Versen
(Kurt Versen Co., Englewood, New Jersey), IV-36

Viking
(Viking Glass Co., New Martinsville, West Virginia), II-43

Villeroy & Boch
(Villeroy & Boch, Mettlach, Germany), VI-3

Vitsoe
(Vitsoe, Frankfurt, West Germany), III-72

Vodder
(Niels Vodder, Allerød, Denmark), III-36

Vortice
(Vortice Elettrosociali S.p.A., Zoate, Italy), I-56

V'Soske
(V'Soske, New York), VII-62

Wacoal
(Wacoal Interior Fabrics, Tokyo), VII-63

Warner
(Warner & Sons, Ltd., London), VII-56

Wengler
(R. Wengler, Copenhagen), III-23

Western Electric
(Western Electric Co., Inc., New York), I-10

Winchendon
(Winchendon Furniture Co., Winchendon, Massachusetts), III-51

WMF
(Württembergische Metall-warenfabrik AG, Geislingen, West Germany), II-70, 71; V-47, 48

Yamaha
(Nippon Gakki Co., Ltd., Hamamatsu, Japan), I-3

Zanotta
(Zanotta S.p.A., Nova Milanese, Italy), III-13, 14, 20, 22, 27, 97

Zapf
(Zapf Möbel In-Design, Königstein, West Germany), IV-41

Zerowatt
(Zerowatt S.p.A., Nese/Bergamo, Italy), I-32

Photographic credits

Photographs have been supplied by the designers, manufacturers, or owners, as well as:

Essays: p. xii nose: courtesy Eleutherian Mills-Hagley Foundation Inc., panel: courtesy The Design Council, London; p. xiii courtesy Museum of Modern Art, New York; p. xv transistors: courtesy Bell Laboratories, Triennale: courtesy Finnish Society of Crafts and Design; p. xx Rodolfo Facchini, courtesy Ignazia Favata; p. xxii Atelje Pavšlč; p. xxiv Aldo Ballo; p. 8 Philadelphia Museum of Art, bequest of C. Otto von Kienbusch; p. 9 courtesy Computervision; p. 10 Chrysler: courtesy Chrysler Historical Collection, orchids: courtesy Longwood Gardens; p. 14 chip: Rex Lowden; p. 18 Farabola; p. 19 "Lambda": Ugo Mulas and Fototecnica Fortunati, child's chair: Aldo Ballo, sewing machine: Fotogramma; p. 20 Aldo Ballo; p. 24 "Visiona": François Puyplat; pp. 28–30 courtesy Rosenthal AG; p. 34 courtesy Alderman Company; p. 35 Stan Ries; p. 39 room: courtesy The Design Council/F.O.B., London, restaurant: courtesy The Design Research Unit, London, Design Centre and *Design:* courtesy The Design Council, London; pp. 40–41 courtesy The Design Council, London; p. 98 Thun: courtesy Furniture of the Twentieth Century, Inc., Leach: Philadelphia Museum of Art, gift of the American Institute of Interior Designers, Hamada: Philadelphia Museum of Art, gift of Mrs. Albert M. Greenfield; p. 99 Rie: Philadelphia Museum of Art, gift of the American Institute of Interior Designers, Voulkos: Philadelphia Museum of Art, gift of Paul M. Ingersoll, Arneson: Philadelphia Museum of Art, purchased, Baugh-Barber Fund, Gropius and Moore: courtesy Rosenthal AG; p. 100 Gate and Hald: Philadelphia Museum of Art, gift of Fisher, Bruce and Company; p. 101 Labino: Philadelphia Museum of Art, gift of Mr. and Mrs. Stanley Bernstein; p. 118 courtesy Museum of Modern Art, New York.

Plates: 2 Will Brown, 3 Louis Schnakenburg, 4 Strüwing Reklamefoto, 7 Will Brown, 8 Eric Mitchell, 9–11, 14, 16–18, 20 Will Brown, 23 Strüwing Reklamefoto, 28 Will Brown, 30 courtesy Ignazia Favata, 32 Will Brown, 38 Serge Libiszewski, 39–40 Will Brown, 41 Toni Nicolini, 44 Aldo Ballo, 45 Eric Mitchell, 49, 52–54, 60 Will Brown.

Appliances: I-1 Aldo Ballo, I-2 Color Industriale, I-3 Eric Mitchell, I-9 Aldo Ballo, I-11 Fotografiska AUD, I-23 Daniel S. Roher, I-25 Will Brown, I-26–27 Aldo Ballo, I-28 Ezio Frea, I-31 Joseph Szaszfai, I-33, 38–39 Will Brown, I-40, 42 Eric Mitchell, I-48 Foto Seguini, I-49 Will Brown, I-51–52 Aldo Ballo, I-53 Eric Mitchell, I-56 Will Brown.

Ceramics and Glass: II-4 Will Brown, II-8 Eric Mitchell, II-11 Will Brown, II-15 Eric Mitchell, II-18, 22–23 Will Brown, II-24 Eric Mitchell, II-30, 34 Will Brown, II-37 A. J. Wyatt, II-41 Eric Mitchell, II-42 Will Brown, II-44 James Welling, II-45 Eric Mitchell, II-56 Studio Osmo Thiel, II-59, 65 Will Brown, II-66 Ole Woldbye, II-70–72, 75 Will Brown, II-76–77 Eric Mitchell, II-78 Walter Civardi, Pratt Institute.

Furniture: III-9 Eric Mitchell, III-10 Rodolfo Facchini, III-13 Masera, III-17 courtesy Ignazia Favata, III-18 Will Brown, III-20, 22 Masera, III-23 K. Helmer-Petersen, III-28 Will Brown, III-31 Ole Woldbye, III-32 Will Brown, III-34 Eric Mitchell, III-35–37 Will Brown, III-40 Strüwing Reklamefoto, III-45 Aldo Ballo, III-46 Will Brown, III-47 Eric Mitchell, III-50–51 Will Brown, III-52 Strüwing Reklamefoto, III-57, 59 Will Brown, III-60 PF-Studio, III-67 Will Brown, III-68 Aldo Ballo, III-69 L. Sully-Jaulmes, III-71 Eric Mitchell, III-75–76, 79, 81, 83 Will Brown, III-85 Robert David, III-86 courtesy The Design Council, London, III-88 Will Brown, III-89–91 Louis Schnakenburg, III-93 Will Brown, III-97 Aldo Ballo.

Lighting: IV-2 Eric Mitchell, IV-4 Aldo Ballo, IV-10 Eric Mitchell, IV-14 Aldo Ballo, IV-18–19 Fotografi Bessing A.V. Produkton, IV-20–21 Eric Mitchell, IV-22 Aimo Hyvärinen, IV-23 Poul Christiansen, IV-24 Will Brown, IV-26 Jacqueline Vodoz, IV-27–29 Will Brown, IV-32 Aldo Ballo, IV-35 Will Brown, IV-40 Eric Mitchell.

Metalwork: V-1 Mimosa Kiel, V-2 Eric Mitchell, V-3 James Welling, V-4 Eric Mitchell, V-5 Keltum B.V., V-6–7 Eric Mitchell, V-9–11 Will Brown, V-18–19 Eric Mitchell, V-20, 24–25 Will Brown, V-26–28 Eric Mitchell, V-29, 31–33 Will Brown, V-34 Pietinen, V-35 Studio Kollar, V-37 Serge Libiszewski, V-38 Lucis Aetei, V-39 Aldo Ballo, V-41 Eric Mitchell, V-44–45 Will Brown, V-46 Aldo Ballo, V-47–52 Will Brown, V-53 Eric Mitchell.

Plastics: VI-2 Will Brown, VI-3 Eric Mitchell, VI-8 Will Brown, VI-9–10 Eric Mitchell, VI-11 Aldo Ballo, VI-12 Toni Nicolini, VI-13–14 Aldo Ballo, VI-18 Eric Mitchell, VI-19 Will Brown, VI-20 Eric Mitchell, VI-21–23 Will Brown, VI-24 Eric Mitchell.

Textiles: VII-1, 7–8, 10, 12, 14–15, 20–24, 27–31, 34, 37 Will Brown, VII-38 Eric Mitchell, VII-39–43 Will Brown, VII-45 Eric Mitchell, VII-46–50, 52 Will Brown, VII-53, 55 Eric Mitchell, VII-56–57, 59–61, 63 Will Brown.

Wood: VIII-1–3 Eric Mitchell, VIII-4 Will Brown, VIII-5–7, 9 Eric Mitchell.